SOUND AND MUSIC

Musica and her Attendant Musicians. This XIVth century miniature comes from M. Severinus Boethius, De Musica. *Paying homage to the enthroned figure of Music playing the portative organ are musicians playing the principle instruments of the Middle Ages. Above her King David plucks the psaltery. Beside him are lira da braccio and lute. Percussions are beside her, tambourine and clappers, and below her, nakers. The winds below her include bagpipes, shawm and trumpets. Both* haut *and* bas *instruments are illustrated. They were never played together. A surprising omission is the harp. Biblioteca Nazionale, Naples.*

SOUND AND MUSIC

FOR THE PLEASURE OF THE BRAIN

JACK ORBACH
Queens College
City University of New York

UNIVERSITY PRESS OF AMERICA, INC.
LANHAM - NEW YORK - OXFORD

Copyright © 1999 by
University Press of America,® Inc.
4720 Boston Way
Lanham, Maryland 20706

12 Hid's Copse Rd.
Cumnor Hill, Oxford OX2 9JJ

All rights reserved
Printed in the United States of America
British Library Cataloging in Publication Information Available

Library of Congress Cataloging-in-Publication Data

Orbach, Jack.
Sound and music : for the pleasure of the brain / Jack Orbach.
p. cm.
Includes bibliographical references and indexes.
Contents: Historical perspectives—Dimensions of auditory
perception—The psychology of music.
1. Music—Psychological aspects. 2. Music—Acoustics and
physics. I. Title.
ML3830.O73 1999 781'.11—dc21   99—10086 CIP

ISBN 0-7618-1376-4 (pbk: alk. ppr.)

♾™ The paper used in this publication meets the minimum
requirements of American National Standard for Information
Sciences—Permanence of Paper for Printed Library Materials,
ANSI Z39.48—1984

To Music

Thou cherished art, in how many grey hours,
When life's wild cycle encompassed me,
Hast thou kindled my heart to love's warmth,
Hast thou transported me to a better world!

Oft, a sigh flowing from thy harp,
A sweet, divine chord of thine
Disclosed to me a heaven of better times.
Thou cherished art, for that I thank thee!

                     Franz von Schober

An die Musik

Franz Schubert

Op. 88, No. 4

CONTENTS

Figure Credits   xiii

Prologue: A Psychologist's View of the Musical Enterprise   xvii

PART A. HISTORICAL PERSPECTIVES

1. The Origins of Western Music   3
   Reason and Emotion
   The Musical World of Antiquity
      The Biblical Hebrews
      Greek Myths

2. Traditions of Western Music   21
   Music in Greek Chronicles
   Music in Imperial Rome
   The Judeo-Christian Musical Tradition
      In the Synagogue
      In the Christian Church
      The Rise of Hasidism
   Early Music Notation

3. The Secular Movement and Religious Accompaniments   47
   The Development of Polyphony
   The Madrigal
   Lassus and Palestrina

The Beginnings of Baroque
Stringed Instruments
Opera and Oratorio

4. Science and Music   69
Classicism and Romanticism

5. The Evolutionary Significance of Music   73

PART B. DIMENSIONS OF AUDITORY PERCEPTION

6. Sound Waves   81
Vibration
Musical Intervals and the Ratio of Small Whole Numbers
Comparisons of Sound and Light
  Physical and Perceptual Dimensions
  Hue and Tonal Mixtures Compared
  Dimensions of Time and Space
The Acoustic Medium
Velocity of Sound

7. Perception of Pitch   105
Pitch and Frequency
Equivalence of Intervals
Absolute and Relative Pitch
Range of Audibility of Pitch
Pitch Discrimination as a Function of Intensity
Pitch Sensitivity

8. Intensity & the Perception of Loudness   131
Intensity
Specification of Loudness
Loudness Sensitivity

9. Perception of Timbre   139
Introduction
Resonance and Harmonics
Fourier Analysis
Tonal Fusion
Consonance and Dissonance
  The Pythagorean Intervals
  Beats

10. Perspectives on Tonal Color   157
    Critical Bandwidth
    Past Experience and Context
    Noise
    Combination Tones
    Tonal Color
        Vowels and Consonants
        Synthesis of Complex Waves
        The Vibrato
        Computer Music
        Pitch of Musical Instruments

11. The Development of Musical Scale   189
    The Greek Tetrachord
    The Harmonic Series
    Pythagorean Intonation
    Just Intonation
    Ecclesiastical Modes
    Mean-tone Temperament
    Equal Temperament
    The Indian SA-grama Scale:an Eastern example

12. Perspectives on the Significance of Musical Scales   221
    Circle of Fifths
    Cross-cultural Comparison of Scales
    Tonality and Modulation
    Tonal Expectations
    Are Scales Really Necessary?

PART C. THE PSYCHOLOGY OF MUSIC

13. How We Hear and Why We Don't   237
    The Quality of Sensation
    Auditory Mechanisms
    Sound Localization and Stereo
    Hearing Impairment
    Tune Deafness or Melody Apraxia

14. Active Listening   265
    Attention and Habituation
    Auditory Masking
    Attending to a Melody
    Organizing Principles
    Rhythm

15. Some Performing Skills 289
    Transcription
    Sight-reading
    Improvisation
    Musical Expression
    Rhythm
    On Musical Notation
        Words and Symbols in Musical Notation
        Pitch Notation and the Great Staff

16. Musical Training 305
    The Importance of Early Training
    Learning Solfège in Childhood
    Dalcroze and Eurhythmic
    Kodaly and Musical Literacy
    Orff's Instruments and Method of Instruction
    Suzuki's Method of Early Violin Playing
    Some Principles of Learning to Play a Musical Instrument
    Teaching Machines

17. Musical Aptitude and Achievement 331

18. Musical Enjoyment and the Meaning of Music 347
    The Musical Setting
    The Meaning in Music
    The Earthling as Listener
    Development of Musical Taste
    Musical Syntax
    Subjective Organization

19. Music and the Brain 361
    Cerebral Organization
    Brain Damage and 'Amusia'
    Hemispheric Specialization

20. Music Therapy 379
    The Ancient Theory of Excesses and Imbalances
    Modern Conceptions

Epilogue: Music Criticism – Who Sets the Standards? 391

References 399

Name Index 403

Subject Index 405

FIGURE CREDITS

Frontispiece. Musica and Musicians. Miniature by M. Severinus Boethius, '*De Musica.*' Biblioteca Nazionale, Naples. With permission of The Ministry of Cultural Affairs, Italy.

Fig.1.1. A paleolithic scene from a cave of the Trois-Frère (Ariège).   5

Fig. 1.2. *The Worship of the Egyptian Bull God*, by Follower of Philippino Lippi. © The National Gallery, London.   9

Fig. 1.3. (Left) A detail from a fresco of an Etruscan Aulos Player. The Leopardi Tomb at Corneto Torquinia. (Right) Apollo Bowing the Lira da Braccia. A detail from Apollo on Mont Parnassus by Petrus Tritonius (c.1507).   12

Fig, 1.4. *Marc'antonio Pasqualini Crowned by Apollo*, by Andrea Sacchi. Courtesy of The Metropolitan Museum of Art, Purchase, Enid A. Haupt Gift and Gwynne Andrews Fund, 1981. (1981.317).   14

Fig. 1.5. Contest Between Apollo and Pan. Woodcut from *Ovidio Metamorphoseos Volgare* (c.1501).   15

Fig.1.6. *Apollo and the Muses*, by Martin de Vos. Courtesy of Musée Royaux des Beaux-Arts de Belgique, Brussels.   17

Fig.1.7. A detail from Orpheus and Euridice by Nicolas Poussin (c.1640). Courtesy of Musée de Louvre, Paris.   19

Fig, 2.1 Comedy scene in an ancient Greek play. Roman relief, Naples.   23

Fig. 2.2. The universe as a stringed instrument.   26

Fig. 2.3. Pythagoras, Philolaus and Jubal. XVth century woodcut From *Theoretica Musica* by Franchino Gaffurio.   28

xiv   Figure Credits

Fig. 2.4.	*Saint Cecelia* by Domenico Zampieri (c. 1820). Courtesy of Musée de Louvre, Paris.	31
Fig. 2.5.	Photograph of a Jew blowing a shofar.	37
Fig. 2.6.	A Gregorian chant of the tenth century.	39
Fig. 2.7.	Cantillations for reading the Torah.	43
Fig. 2.8.	Guido of Arezzo notating music.	44
Fig. 2.9.	Guido's hand.	46
Fig. 2.10.	Jongleurs.	46
Fig. 3.1.	*Lutanist* by Ludwig Businck. Courtesy Rijksmuseum, Amsterdam. *The Bagpiper* by Albrecht Dürer (1514). Print from the collection of the New York Public Library.*	49
Fig. 3.2.	The wind bands of European cities. *The musicians gallery at Whiehall* by Hans Holbein. Courtesy of the British Museum, London.	50
Fig. 3.3.	Miniature of Jan von Ockeghem among his singers. (c.1527). Cliché Bibliotèque nationale de France.	52
Fig. 3.4.	*Madonna with Child and Angels*, by Giovanni Boccati Da Camerino (c. 1460).	53
Fig. 3.5.	*A Musical Bath*, by a miniaturist of the Lombardy school (XVth century). Courtesy of Estense Library, Modena.	54
Fig. 3.6.	*Lutanist and violist*. Cliché Bibliotèque Nationale de France.	55
Fig. 3.7.	*The Enraged Musician* by Hogarth. Engraving of 1741. Print from the collection of the New York Public Library.*	56
Fig. 3.8.	The troubador. Woodcut by San Pedro (c. 1547).	57
Fig. 3.9.	Palestrina presenting his music to the Pope.	59
Fig. 3.10.	A chorus of the baroque.	60
Fig. 3.11.	A baroque scene, by Pieter Lastmann (c. 1618).	61
Fig. 3.12.	A scene from Jean-Baptiste Lully's *Alceste*. Engraving by Jean Le Pautre.	66
Fig. 4.1.	Etienne Delaune's *Seven Liberal Arts and Sciences* (1569). Print fron the collection of the New York Public Library.*	70
Fig. 4.2.	Daumier's lithograph, *The Orchestra during the Performance of a Tragedy* (1852). Print from the collection of the New York Public Library.*	72
Fig, 6.1.	Expanding concentric waves caused by dropping a stone into a pool of mercury.	82
Fig. 6.2.	Longitudinal waves.	83
Fig. 6.3.	A vibrating metal strip creating air waves.	85
Fig. 6.4.	A vibrating tuning fork writing on moving sheet	87
Fig. 6.5.	Effects on pitch of stopping the G string of a violin.	90
Fig. 6.6.	The mechanism of a siren.	91
Fig. 6.7.	The multiple vibrations of a stretched string.	93
Fig. 6.8.	Vibrations in an open organ pipe.	95
Fig. 6.9.	Vibrations in a closed organ pipe.	96
Fig. 6.10.	Bell suspended in bell jar.	102
Fig. 7.1.	The missing fundamental.	108

Figure Credits

Fig. 7.2.	Pitch consisting of chroma and height. Adapted from Shepard, 1965.	113
Fig. 7.3.	The double helix of chroma and fifths. Adapted from Shepard, 1982.	114
Fig. 7.4.	Notation of the endless rise in chroma. From Godel, Escher, Bach: An eternal braid by D. Hofstadter. Copyright ©1979 by Basic Books, Inc. Reprinted by permission of Basic Books, a member of Perseus Books, L.L.C.	115
Fig. 7.5.	The endless staircase of Penrose and Penrose, 1958.	117
Fig. 7.6	Curves of equal loudness. Adapted from Fletcher and Munson, 1922.	125
Fig. 7.7.	Pitch varies with the intensity as well as with the frequency of sound waves.	127
Fig. 9.1.	Glass goblet vibrating.	142
Fig, 9.2.	Composition of frequency components required to perceive the pitch of the fundamental frequency. Adapted from Rasch, R, A. and Plomp, R. 1982.	145
Fig. 9.3.	Fourier analysis of a complex waveform.	147
Fig. 9.4.	Phase relations.	154
Fig. 9.5.	Generation of beats.	155
Fig. 10.1.	Critical bandwidth. Adapted from Rasch, R. A. and Plomp, R. 1982.	158
Fig. 10.2.	Consonance as a function of bandwidth. Adapted from Plomp, R. and Levelt, J. M. Tonal consonance and critical bandwidth, *J. Acoust. Soc. Amer.*, 1965, 38, 548-560. Copyright, © 1965. Printed with permission of the Acoustical Society of America.	159
Fig. 10.3.	Two complex tones a fifth apart.	160
Fig. 10.4.	Vocal tract configurations for several vowel sounds. With permission from Encyclopaedia Britannica Inc., ©1974.	169
Fig. 10.5.	Sawtooth waves synthesized.	174
Fig. 10.6.	Square waves synthesized.	175
Fig. 10.7.	Triangular waves synthesized.	176
Fig. 10.8.	Synthesized waveforms. A summary.	177
Fig. 10.9.	The effect of phase in synthesizing waveforms.	178
Fig. 10.10.	Scaling of timbre. Adapted from Grey, J. M. Scaling the musical timbre, *J. Acoust. Soc. Amer.*, 1977. 61, 1270-1277. Copyright, © 1977. Printed with permission of the Acoustical Society of America.	183
Fig. 10.11.	The range of musical instruments.	188
Fig. 11.1.	One octave of the piano keyboard.	190
Fig. 11.2.	An attempt to notate the harmonic series.	198
Fig. 11.3.	The Pythagorean ascent in 12 successive fifths.	202
Fig. 11.4.	Frère Jacques played enharmonically.	219
Fig. 12.1.	Circle of fifths.	225
Fig. 13.1.	The outer ear leading to the cochlea.	241
Fig. 13.2.	The middle ear ossicles.	242
Fig. 13.3.	Schematic cross-section through the cochlea.	244

Figure Credits

Fig. 13.4. One cross-section through the cochlea magnified. 245
Fig. 13.5. Cross-section through the organ of corti magnified. 245
Fig. 13.6. A diagram of the cochlea unrolled. 246
Fig. 13.7. Travelling waves and their envelopes. Adapted from Békésy, 1960. 248
Fig. 13.8. Basilar membrane deformed by sound. Adapted from Tonnedorf, 1960. 249
Fig. 13.9. Auditory pathways in the brain. 251
Fig. 13.10. Audiograms. 259
Fig. 14.1. Masking curves. Adapted from Wegel and Lane, 1924. 270
Fig. 14.2. Sound power of orchestra and tenor. From Sundburg, 1977. 272
Fig. 14.3. Deutsch's scale illusion. Adapted from Deutsch, D. Two-channel listening to musical scales. *J. Acoust. Soc. Amer.*, 1975, 57, 1156-1160. Copyright, © 1975. Printed with permission of the Acoustical Society of America. 278
Fig. 15.1. *America* or *My Country 'tis of Thee*. The musical notation. Music by Henry Carey. Lyrics by Samuel Francis Smith. 299
Fig. 15.2. Seven musical clefs. 301
Fig. 15.3. The evolution of the clefs. According to Vincent D'Indy. 302
Fig. 16.1. Sol-fa hand signs. 317
Fig. 17.1. Inheritance of musical aptitude. Bach's genealogy. 332
Fig. 17.2. Davies' test of the appreciation of melodic contour. 339
Fig. 17.3. Davies' sweep-frequency. 340
Fig. 20.1. David playing the harp before King Saul, engraving by Van Leyden (c. 1530). Print from the collection of the New York Public Library.* 382
Fig. 20.2. Concert for banishing a nobleman's melancholia. Miniature of the XVth century. Bibliotèque Nationale, Paris. 384

*Figs. 3.1, 3.7, 4.1, 4.2 and 20.1 are reproduced courtesy of the Print Collection, Miriam and Ira D. Wallach Division of Art, Prints and Photographs, The New York Public Library. Astor, Lenox and Tilden Foundations.

Prologue

A PSYCHOLOGIST'S VIEW OF THE MUSICAL ENTERPRISE

The views presented here are not those of a musician or of a music critic, but those of a psychologist who considers music as a science as well as an art.

Considering music as an art, the psychologist studies several classes of people:

- *The listener* leads the psychologist to focus on esthetics, taste, enjoyment, mood and feeling in listening, on the role of biological and experiential factors, on attention and personality.
- *The performer* leads the psychologist to focus on musical aptitude and its assessment, and the role of biological and experiential factors in the determination of musical talent. Methods of training for the development of performance skills are evaluated. Both sensory and motor skills are examined as well as style and interpretation. An important subject is social context and the problem of motivating the student of a musical instrument to practice the instrument.

- *The composer* leads the psychologist toward the study of musical creativity that is influenced by both biological and experiential factors.
- *The technologist.* Of interest here are the skills of those who make the musical enterprise possible, the instrument maker, the recording engineer, the acoustician, the architect, the musical therapist and the music teacher.

For the pleasure of the brain means that music has an appeal as a science to reason. The view expressed here is that the more you know about music the more you will enjoy it. In this book, I will examine what is known about the musical enterprise in all its facets. I will also review the functioning of the brain in the process of hearing, as well as feeling in the gut in the process of enjoying musical compositions.

Considering music as a science, many subdisciplines are involved:

- *The physics of music.* What is sound and how is it produced? How does the sound of music differ from the sound of noise? The physical attributes of individual sound waves are examined: frequency, amplitude, complexity, and the phase of waves sounded together. Complex wave forms are shown to be analyzable into component sine waves by Fourier analysis. This leads to an analysis of musical tones and their harmonics, as well as the musical interval between notes. Finally, the various scale temperaments and tunings are derived, including harmonic, Pythagorean, just, mean-tone, and equal.
- *The phenomenology and psychophysics of music.* Here, the question changes to "What do you hear?" - pitch, loudness, timbre, duration, rhythm, consonance, dissonance, beats, auditory illusions, the missing fundamental, sound localization, the masking of sound, etc. Thresholds and just noticeable differences (JNDs) are determined and the psychophysical laws of Weber, Fechner, and Stevens are evaluated. Methodology in psychoacoustics and the scaling of loudness are reviewed. The *Gestalt* laws of perceptual organization are considered in understanding what makes a melody, as well as the phenomenon of transposition.
- *The theory of music.* Topics included are the various diatonic scales, major and minor, the circle of fifths, intervals, tuning and

beats, and the construction of melody, harmony, counterpoint and rhythm.
- *The psychophysiology of hearing.* Here the focus is on the receptive ear, conduction of sound waves, neural transduction, and projection mechanisms in the central nervous system, leading to the cerebral cortex and hemispheric specialization. Dichotic listening experiments are discussed, and the sodium amytal test for hemispheric specialization is described. The causes, measurement, and treatment of conduction and nerve deafness are reviewed.
- *Assessment of musical aptitude and talent.* Problems of measurement are presented. Topics include auditory discrimination and memory; motor coordination and proprioception; the skills of absolute and relative pitch; and talent and intelligence. Seashore, Wing, and Davies tests of musical aptitude.
- *Musicianship training.* Case histories of eminent musicians are given. Topics include methods of training, role of motivation, style and interpretation.
- *Musical therapy.* The ancient theory of the balance of humors is cited, and modern practice is indicated.
- *Cross-cultural comparisons.* Musical practices in various parts of the world are suggested.
- *The history of musical practice.* The earliest known reference to the musical enterprise is inscribed by ancient peoples on a stone wall in a cave in France that is about 40,000 years old. The ancient Greek myths and the Hebrew Bible reveal much regarding musical activities before the beginning of the Christian era.

As you can see, the musical enterprise is a multifaceted thing. Recently a college in the New York area distributed the following ad in a flyer describing their music program: "Attend a four-year college that takes music as seriously as you do. Whether your interest is in music performance, music business, music education, audio recording or video music. . . (we) offer the specialized training you need. Our internship program will also help place you in a world-class studio, record company, multimedia organization or any number of music industry firms. . . Make music your life."

Acknowledgements

This book is directed to the educated layperson who is interested in music and psychology. Though it is meant to be a scholarly work, I have tried to avoid academic jargon. There are no scholarly notes and very few citations that tend to break the continuity of the narrative. Original data are sometimes cited but only when absolutely necessary. Deutch's edited book, *The Psychology of Music* (1982), was indispensable in this endeavor.

Early versions of the chapters on scales, how we hear and why we don't, and active listening were originally published in the high-end audio magazine *The Absolute Sound*. I thank the editor, Sallie Reynolds, for her insights on the craft of writing and for her helpful editorial assistance.

The Reverend Alexander Harper, one of my early-music performance colleagues, helped me with my depiction of the role of the church in the development of early music.

My wife, Hilary Ryglewicz, a published author, provided me with invaluable editorial assistance. I can see her wise counsel in every chapter of this book. Of course, I am ultimately responsible for content, expression and format.

This book is dedicated to my four children, Shelley, Betty Ann, Judy, and Karen. Without being aware of it, they have all contributed to the writing of this book. I have learned a lot from each of them. My son, Shelley, is today a folk guitarist, composer of folk-style songs and cantorial soloist. Before her untimely death, Betty Ann was an amateur flautist, and I had great fun playing flute and recorder duets with her. She is greatly missed. Karen is today a talented amateur poet. Judy studied opera singing for a number of years. Her story is worth recounting:

All my children started piano lessons when they were just learning to read. I explained to each of them that music was a universal language that all children should be exposed to, and learn some aspect of the musical enterprise to a satisfactory level of competence, like the learning of one's native tongue, English in our case. Piano was the initial musical vehicle that I provided but, if the piano did not furnish sufficient pleasure, each child could switch to a musical instrument of his or her own choosing after a year or so of piano or after the basics of the musical language had been acquired. (I would have preferred that they begin with solfège or 'ear training,' as it is called, but the instruction was not available in our community when they were growing up.) After a year or two of piano instruction, Judy came to me and asked if she could switch to another instrument.

"What instrument would you like to study?" I asked.

"I'd like to try the oboe," she said with some trepidation.

I was taken aback by her request. "You know Judy," I said. "Playing the oboe involves a craft, the making of double reeds. I wonder whether you want to get involved in such a time-consuming enterprise. Why don't you consider another woodwind like the single reed clarinet? The reed for the clarinet can be purchased commercially in any music shop."

Judy accepted my suggestion. She was obviously game.

After consulting a clarinet teacher, I took Judy to a local music shop where she selected a clarinet from a list recommended by the music teacher. And she was on her way with an enthusiasm that I admired. But it didn't take long and she was back asking for a change.

"It's really not the clarinet that interests me, Dad, but rather the oboe," she said.

"Well as you already know, Judy, that is quite another kettle of fish," I reminded her. "You're choosing an instrument that requires the skill of a craftsperson," I said. "You will probably have to make your own reeds and that's quite a time-consuming enterprise."

But, this time, Judy was not dissuaded. And again, after consulting an oboe teacher in New York, we bought an oboe of her choosing. I watched Judy as she acquired the skill to make her own reeds and our home was filled with the reedy sound of Judy practicing. Judy had now begun junior high school, and her mother and I found ourselves quite frequently invited to hear the school choir in which Judy sang. It was a great pleasure because Judy had a very pleasant voice, and she was sometimes selected to sing a solo with choir accompaniment. As we were returning home, I remarked to my wife that we might yet have a professional musician in the family. But, while still in high school, Judy appeared once again with the complaint that the oboe was really not her instrument.

"What would you like instead?" I asked once again.

"You know, Dad, I'd like to try the cello."

Having learned my lesson twice over, I now sought to rent a cello. There wasn't much time left before Judy would enroll in college and leave home. And I guessed right this time. When Judy left for college, she gave up the cello. But she did join the choir in college and seemed to have a great time singing. At a college performance, I remember hearing a performance of Boris Godounov with Judy in the chorus.

Some years later, when I began to write the chapter on musical training in this book, I gave Judy a draft of the chapter to review. As readers will see, this chapter emphasizes the use of the voice in early solfège training. Several weeks later, Judy handed the draft of the chapter back to me. Before she could utter a single comment, she burst into tears.

"What's the matter?" I asked. Between sobs, Judy blurted out, "How come you never gave me voice lessons?"

"But, Judy," I said, "you had the choice of any instrument. How come you never asked for voice lessons?"

"How was I to know?" Judy responded, "I was never told that voice training was an option. I never thought of the voice as a musical instrument."

Looking back, I must admit that Judy's natural propensity for the voice should have been perfectly obvious to me but as parent, I simply overlooked the cues.

Determined to overcome lost opportunities, Judy began voice lessons on her own. With great pleasure, I watched her as she honed that personal instrument of hers and we heard her sing in a number of amateur operatic productions. Today, Judy is successfully pursuing another career but I believe that she continues to be disappointed that she missed the opportunity to study voice at an earlier age and obtain the boost that, I believe, early voice training might have provided in fostering a successful singing career. I hope that one day she will resume participating in musical activities as an *amateur* (the French word *amateur* literally means 'lover.') To my great pleasure, Judy has recently expressed her desire to return to singing when her current schooling is completed.

NOTE ON AUDITORY ILLUSTRATIONS

A number of auditory illustrations are cited in the text. A recording of many of these illustrations can be found on an LP disc attached to a special issue of *the Journal of the Audio Engineering Society* devoted to auditory illusions, Sept., 1983, volume 31 number 9. This fascinating journal issue can be ordered from the Society by phoning 212 661 2355. There is a small charge. You will need stereo headphones to perceive the binaural auditory illusions.

PART A.
HISTORICAL PERSPECTIVES

Chapter 1

THE ORIGINS OF WESTERN MUSIC

REASON AND EMOTION

Thinking and feeling: they are so inextricably bound together in the experience and pursuit of music. In the realm of emotion, there are the feelings of pleasure and aesthetic appreciation that are elicited by music. There is also the gamut of feelings that include excitement and calm, frenzy and fear, satisfaction and disappointment, esteem and frustration, hilarity and sadness, curiosity and boredom, not just in listening to music but also in performing and composing music.

In the realm of reason, there are the facts and figures associated with music, the ever-growing body of knowledge and understanding that can contribute to the musical experience. If we look back in time to the period of the ancient Greeks, we see that music had already become a scientific endeavor dealing with numbers and consonances. To Pythagoras, there was something special, even mystical, about simple mathematical ratios, such as 2/1 and 3/2, that he discovered in the sound of music. When he plucked a stretched string and then shortened it to two-thirds its normal length, he discovered that he could produce the pleasant-sounding interval of the perfect fifth. Pythagoras derived a musical scale of seven different notes from this interval of the perfect fifth, 3/2 (see Chapter 11). Since then, over a period of two and a half millenia, the musical enterprise has penetrated into the burgeoning sciences, and has become a science in its own right. In our age, the study of music includes subject matter as diverse as sound and vibrations, intervals and scales, musical instruments and timbre, acoustics and architecture, hearing and personality, learning and memory, neuronal and glandular discharge, brain function and psychopathology, history and biography, and emotional and esthetic experience. The musical enterprise is no longer merely an art of listening, performing, and composing music. Its practitioners delve into the physical, biological, and behavioral sciences in their quest for musical understanding.

In short, music has become an elaborate and intricate endeavor involving reason as well as emotion. A deeper appreciation of music seems to emerge when understanding joins emotion in the pursuit of esthetic musical experience. In this book, we will focus our attention on music as a science, in the belief that understanding enhances enjoyment.

To begin with, consider the experience of music from a physiological point of view. The activities of sense organs, brain, and glands, are inextricably interwoven in the fabric of experience. Through the door of the ears, the sounds of music can rouse the organism into all manner of involuntary as well as voluntary responses. The glands and autonomic nervous system are set in motion during musical activity. Heart rate and respiration are apt to change. Depending, of course, on the type of music, the balance of nervous discharge in the sympathetic and parasympathetic systems is affected. The person may sweat or shiver. The blood vessels of the face and other parts of the body may dilate or constrict. Tears may be shed. Adrenaline may be discharged into the bloodstream; so may the sex hormones, testosterone and estrogen. This very blood, with its chemical constituents, is pumped to the brain and bathes it. Countless neurons respond by altering their pattern of discharge. The rhythm of brain waves may shift from alpha to beta and back to alpha. Thoughts are set off "Did I hear an oboe in that passage" the listener might ask himself. "I recognize that piece. It sounds like Beethoven. I thoroughly enjoyed it."

Now consider the experience of music from a psychological point of view. Like all other modalities of esthetic experience, musical taste develops with exposure and sophistication. The listener who is naive is less likely to derive pleasure from Stravinsky or even Mozart, compared to the experienced listener. What is found early in life to be strange-sounding and unorganized can turn into a favorite piece of music later on. Part of the explanation for the development of musical taste has to do with physical maturation. Another part has to do with sheer familiarity with the music and its associations. But there is still another part that has to do with the acquisition of a body of information and understanding: the historical context of the piece, the life of the composer and his intentions, the ethnic background, the instruments involved, the skills of the performer and his interpretation and style, the expectations of the listener, all contribute to the experience and the development of musical taste.

The duality of reason and emotion can be observed in every age as the history of music unfolds. We will see it again and again as we follow the beginnings of musical endeavor.

Fig. 1.1. A paleolithic scene from the cave of the Trois-Frères (Ariège) going back some 40,000 years. A man wearing a mask and wrapped in the fur of an animal is playing a musical bow and dancing behind a troop of reindeer. Charming the reindeer seems to be the object of the impersonation and the dance.

The earliest evidence of musical activity among humans is found on the stone walls of ancient caves. One scene shows a man wearing an animal mask and skin, playing what looks to be a musical bow, and dancing as he follows a troop of reindeer. Perhaps he is singing as well. Archeologists found this painting on the wall of a cave in the Ariège and have dated it back some 40,000 years! This means that music has been evolving as a human pursuit for at least 40,000 years to become what it is today, an art and a science. The musical instrument pictured in the cave, the bow or something like it, is still played by certain African tribes, and the sounds tribe members produce today cannot be too dissimilar from those our ancestors of the paleolithic age must have heard in their day. Even the masquerade, the animal mask, the dance as well as the music, can still be experienced in Africa and on islands in the South Pacific. These observations lead us to suspect that the man pictured in the cave was attempting to charm the reindeer while masquerading as an animal, or cast a spell over them with music and dance. In its remote past, music must have been regarded not so much as an art to be enjoyed but as a powerful force and magical tool.

The ancient Greek myths include similar musical and magical scenes, but they go back just 3,000 years. To judge from cave paintings, music has a very long past; unfortunately it has but a relatively short recorded history. And, of course, none of the sounds dating before recorded history have been preserved.

Here is an early scenario. Picture to yourself an era long ago when primitive humans lived on mounds and in caves in order to protect themselves from the elements and from the wild predators roaming the area around them. People understood little about natural phenomena, the cycles of light and darkness, the rising and setting of the sun, the lushness of summer and the barrenness of winter, the renewal of spring and the decline of fall, the lightning and thunder of the storm, and the rainbow that appears with the sunshine. Their belief was that the gods controlled all these events, the refreshing rain that makes things grow, the prized health and fertility of people, the uncontrollable fire that consumes one's possessions, the frightening animals who fight and kill, and the mysterious events of birth, puberty, marriage, and death. In order to placate the gods, people made sacrifices to them, exalted them, and exhorted them to forgive their human transgressions. As the people prayed, they danced and sang, and acted out the things they wanted to have happen. When a man wanted sun or wind or rain, he called his people together to dance a sun-dance, or a wind-dance, or a rain-dance. When he wanted food, he acted out the hunt in a bear-dance. When a woman wanted a baby, she displayed herself in a fertility dance, and when she wanted to put her children to sleep, she crooned a lullaby to charm them to drowsiness.

These activities slowly evolved over the ages into rites, ceremonies, festivals and celebrations. Along with their elaborate incantations, early men and women made music by hand-clapping and foot-stamping, by humming and swaying, by shouting and shrieking, by ululating and sobbing, by grunting and speaking words over and over again. These movements and sounds were the roots from which music and dance grew. If grunts and yells are singing, then those men and women of many ages ago must have sung even before they learned how to speak rationally. In these cries can be heard joy and sorrow, pain and rage, fear and revenge, in short, man's earliest expressions of his innermost emotions. To this day, we still look upon music as a satisfying way to show our feelings. By means of rhythm and melody especially, humans have learned that they can express their most diverse and complex feelings.

According to anthropologists, the first step toward a musical instrument was the striking together of two stones to produce repeated beats. In these efforts, thought, reason, and problem solving were important elements. The next step came with the stretching of the skin of an animal over a hollowed tree-trunk, or some other natural container, to produce a drum. Still another early rhythm-maker was the gourd filled with pebbles, which was shaken like a rattle. Later humans learned to produce varying pitches by plucking stretched strings and blowing into pipes. With these instruments, and with their voices, humans could imitate the sounds of nature, the songs of birds, the barks of animals, the blowing of the winds, the roar of the waves, the beating of the rain, and the crashing of thunder. Those who were more gifted must have been honored for their skill. Some of the native men of Australia still imitate the leaps and cries of the kangaroo in their dances and with their voices. The women accompany these dances by singing a tune of four notes over and over, knocking two pieces of wood together to keep time.

Eventually the musical enterprise became more than an artless toil. Music evolved over the ages into an art for the sake of self-expression, deep feeling, and esthetic delight. We can conclude that music became an art in its own right when singers chanted to entertain themselves and their fellow creatures.

THE MUSICAL WORLD OF ANTIQUITY

The poets were the first historians of music. Every civilization seems to possess some poetic legend describing the origin and creation of music. In nearly every such legend, it is the gods who discover music and pass it on to humans. The Hebrews seem to be alone among the people of antiquity who ascribed to music an historical rather than a supernatural origin. A seventh generation descendant of the biblical Cain, a man named *Yuval* (Jubal), was credited with the introduction of musical instruments (Genesis 4, 21). In later chronicles, he was said to have invented a flute and a little three-cornered harp called the '*kinnor*.' *Yuval* is shown in medieval painting and sculpture surrounded by musical instruments (see Fig. 2.3). From a book found in a Mexican monastery in the eighteenth century comes the story that *Yuval* was listening to the strokes on the anvil of a forge and noticed the difference in pitch of the sounds: some tones were high, some low. The similarity to the human voice struck him and he tried to imitate these various sounds. With these attempts, *Yuval* became the first singer of the Hebrews.

The Biblical Hebrews. Music played a prominent role in biblical times. In the *Five Books of Moses*, in *Judges, 2 Samuel*, in *1 Chronicles*, and other books of the Bible, men and women sang and played the lyre and pipe, the horn and percussion, at celebrations. The lyre seems to have occupied a special place among the Hebrews as it did among the ancient Greeks. It belonged to the class of instruments called harps, having seven strings, and was used to accompany the chanter or reciter of poetry. It could be played by plucking the strings with the fingers or with a *plectrum*.

After leading the children of Israel out of Egypt and after the Red Sea had parted to let them pass, Moses sang a great song of triumph. And his sister Miriam took a *timbrel* in her hand and led all the women in music and in dance. While the children of Israel were still in the Wilderness, the Lord commanded Moses:

> Make thee two trumpets of silver...that thou mayest
> use them for the calling of the assembly and for the
> journeyings of the camp.

Numbers 10, 2

Fig. 1.2. *The Adoration of the Golden Calf* by Filippino Lippi (c. 1500). Here we see passion triumphing over reason. National Gallery, London.

Then followed an explanation of the meaning of the trumpet calls. One trumpet alone summoned the princes; two summoned the entire tribe; an 'alarm' gave the signal to go forward. The trumpets also called the people to ceremonies: a fanfare accompanied the crowning of a king, and announced festivals, wars, and the anger of God. In short, the ancient Hebrews used the trumpet in their day much as we might use the bugle today.

Samuel, the last of the judges, established a school of prophesy and music. It was here that the young shepherd boy, David, hid himself to escape the wrath of the troubled King Saul. David was the great musician of his day. His legacy to mankind is the *Psalms*. Unfortunately we do not know the music that David sang to accompany these sublime verses, but composers in every age have been inspired to set them to music, and we have these settings as a musical homage to David.

It is a great pity that David's music did not survive, as his poetry did, for he practiced a form of musical therapy. When King Saul was agitated or depressed, David came to play the lyre and sing to him. There is no doubt that David succeeded in comforting the troubled king, for he was summoned repeatedly. We can only guess at the sounds that David had available on the lyre, and at the melodies that he drew from the instrument.

After David became king, he had the Ark of the Lord brought up to Jerusalem. On the occasion of its arrival, David, girt in a linen apron, came dancing before the Lord with all his might. He and all the Israelites shouted with joy to the sounds of the *shofar*. The tumult brought Saul's daughter, Michal, to the window and she saw King David leaping and dancing in an unseemly fashion before the Ark of the Lord. The sight angered her and she despised David; the leader of the Israelites, chosen by God, should not debase himself in the view of the slave girls as a commoner might, she said. But David replied:

> I was dancing before God. . .
> Not only will I make merry
>   before the Lord, but I will demean myself even more.
> I will be lowly in your esteem, but in the esteem of slave
>   girls. . . I will be honored.

2 Samuel 6, 14-22

Here was Israel's king, beloved for his courage and admired for his reason, overcome with wild abandon and unable to contain himself. David's behavior reflects this duality of reason and emotion, as do his *Psalms*.

David's son Solomon used music as a sacred and profane art. We have his musical-poetic compositions in the *Song of Songs*, in *Proverbs* and, some say, in the *Book of Ecclesiastes*. If we accept the *Song of Songs* literally, we must conclude that music could be used in biblical times for purposes other than religious ceremonies. The Jewish historian, Josephus, tells us that Solomon had 200,000 singers, 40,000 harpists, 40,000 *sistrum* players (the *sistrum* was a metal rattle), and 200,000 trumpeters. This must be an outrageous hyperbole, but remember that the king's resources were unrestricted in those days.

During the reigns of David and Solomon, the Levites, descendants of the tribe of *Levi*, were selected as cult musicians to dedicate their energy to performing music in religious rituals. The servants of the sanctuary and the guardians of the tabernacle, they bore the sacred vessels and the ark itself. They were charged with preparing the animals for sacrifice. The Levites preserved, transcribed and interpreted the Law and read it every seventh year at the *Feast of Tabernacles*. When the first Temple was completed, around 950 B.C., it included a special school for music students, divided into many classes, and taught by the elders. Thus was born the profession of musical education.

After the death of Solomon, the music of the Temple in Jerusalem seems to have lost some of its splendor. And when Nebuchadnezzar destroyed the Temple in 586 B.C., the Hebrews were exiled out of the Promised Land. On the shores of the rivers of Babylon they mourned and wept as they remembered Zion. They hung their lyres on willow trees and refused to heed their conquerors who exhorted them to sing (Psalm 137; see below).

Greek Myths. The ancient Greeks were prominent practitioners of the art of music. In their myths, the very earliest musicians were the gods themselves. Hermes, the messenger of the gods, made the lyre out of the hollow shell of a tortoise on which he strung some dried cowgut and gave it to Apollo, who drew the most melodious sound from it. Hermes also made the shepherd pipe for himself, and he played it enchantingly. Though not distinguished as a musician, Zeus's daughter Athena invented the double flute, called the *aulos*. Seeing herself one day reflected in a pool of water playing on the flute, Athena threw it away, displeased because her puffed cheeks disfigured her countenance. She pronounced the severest maledictions against any one who should play the flute again. But the satyr Marsyas accidentally found this very instrument, and he soon acquired a remarkable skill playing it.

Fig. 1.3. On the left, a detail from a fresco of a Etruscan aulos player (c.480 B.C.). A reed instrument not unlike two oboes, the aulos, emitted a shrill, penetrating sound. The aulos belonged to the followers of Dionysus and was played at Dionysian rites, consisting of wild dances, and dramatic orgies. The Leopardi Tomb at Corneto Tarquinia.

On the right, a detail from Parnassus *by Raphael (c.1510) showing Apollo bowing the lira da braccia. The nine strings remind us that Apollo was the leader of the nine muses. As the protector of poetry, light, and health, Apollo wrought many charms with music. He represents the civilizing influence of music. One of the great advantages of a stringed instrument like the lira da braccia is that each string can be stopped against the fingerboard to produce tones higher than those produced by the open string. In Greek antiquity, the finger-board did not yet exist. Vatican, Rome.*

Apollo is a beautiful figure in Greek poetry. Shining and bright, he was the master musician who delighted Olympus with his playing of the golden lyre. As the divine artist who taught mortals the art of healing, Apollo represented reason. In the festivals of the gods and of men, Apollo sang and played while the muses danced around him. His musical prowess was legendary. But he was not always pre-eminent. In one story, a jury of *Phrygians* preferred the passionate music of their compatriot Marsyas to that of Apollo. Still animated by the magic sparkle of Athena, their inventor, the pipes, in Marsyas's hands, played the divine music as though by themselves. Hearing this, Apollo insisted upon a contest, this time with the muses as jury. Marsyas agreed and even accepted Apollo's condition that the winner of the contest could do as he pleased with the loser. All this seemed fair enough. But when the muses too seemed to favor Marsyas's music, Apollo began to resort to wile in order to win the contest. He played his lyre upside down and challenged Marsyas to do the same, knowing full well that the pipes could be blown from one end only. He also sang while he accompanied himself on the lyre, and again Marsyas could not match this feat with his pipes. Finally, Apollo sang the praises of Olympus, and to this the muses could not fail to respond. Marsyas was vanquished. Apollo directed that he be bound to a tree and flayed alive. In this way was Athena's curse fulfilled and, in the end, reason triumphed over passion.

In Ovid's version of the myth, a river was formed out of the tears of the satyrs, nymphs, shepherds, and gods of Olympus, all mourning Marsyas. Through the Middle Ages, the story of Marsyas's defeat remained familiar principally as an allegory of temerity punished. But Dante interpreted the flaying as a purification of the soul, to unite it with God.

In yet another musical contest, involving Apollo, we see once again the conflict between reason and emotion. This time it is Pan, the god of passionate nature, playing his pipes, who triumphed over Apollo. But even in defeat Apollo prevailed. It was the music critic, King Midas, who judged against him, whereupon Apollo transformed his insensitive ears into those of an ass.

14   Sound and Music

Fig. 1.4. Marc'Antonio Pasqualini crowned by Apollo (c.1640), by the Italian baroque classicist, Andrea Sacchi. Apollo has won the musical contest with the satyr, Marsyas, who lies bound and defeated with his bagpipes broken on the ground. The naked Apollo is portrayed as rational, pure, and bright. His instrument is the lyre, which symbolizes reason, in contrast to the satyr's passionate pipes. The defeat of the passions is also symbolized in the figure of the nymph Daphne, which decorates the upright harpsichord. Daphne has turned herself into a laurel tree in order to escape the amorous intentions of Apollo. Pasqualini, a famous seventeenth century Roman singer, is portrayed as the peerless musician, playing the upright harpsichord, which, here, lacks a conventional sounding board. Metropolitan Museum of Art, N. Y.

In these myths, Pan was the pastoral god of the forests, fields, flocks and fertility. Half man, he is pictured as goat from the waist down, with goat legs and also with goat ears and horns. Pan is reputed to have led the satyrs in their orgiastic revels, and to have caused 'panic' in the Persian army at the Battle of Marathon in 490 B.C.

In still another myth, Pan pursued the nymph, *Syrinx*, and when she fled into the river, he changed her into a bed of reeds. Pan made his pipes, or *syrinx*, from a series of these stopped reeds which he is often pictured as playing. Ranging in length from long to short to produce a musical scale, Pan's pipes 'sang as sweetly as the nightingale in the Spring.' Claude Debussy's *Syrinx* for unaccompanied flute of 1912 harks back to this myth.

Pan is also said to have pursued another nymph, *Echo*, and, when she denied him, had his shepherds destroy all but her voice.

Fig. 1.5. The musical contest between Apollo and Pan is portrayed in two tableaux. On the left, Pan is playing his pipes. A lowly deity, he was confined to the wind instruments, symbolic of passion and abandon. On the right, Apollo is playing the lira da braccia. King Midas is the judge in the contest. Woodcut from Ovidio metamorphoseos volgare *(c.1501).*

In these ancient tales of musical contests, the lyre represented the higher side of Greek character: moderation, balance, control, intelligence, and taste. In contrast, the pipes were associated with the rites of Dionysus and represented the baser side of Greek character: the drunken side, wild and orgiastic.

Amongst the ancient Greeks, music became an art and a science that combined singing, declaiming, playing a musical instrument and dancing with mathematics and astronomy. Music took its name from the nine muses who presided over some aspect of literature, the arts, and the sciences. They were thought to be the daughters of Zeus and *Mnemosyne* (Memory). Pictured as nymphs, their customary occupation was singing and dancing. The great lyric poet Pindar called the lyre theirs (as well as Apollo's), but it is their voices that were said to be lovely beyond compare. In contests with the *Sirens* who bewitched Greek heroes with their song, the muses came out victorious (see Fig. 1.6).

The most distinguished of the muses was *Calliope*, the muse of epic poetry. Shown holding a roll of parchment or a trumpet, she was the protector of kings, whom she endowed with the eloquence of song. *Clio* was the muse of history; she is pictured holding a half-open scroll. *Euterpe*, with her double flute, was the muse of lyric poetry and music. *Thalia*, holding a comic mask in one hand and a crooked staff in the other, was the muse of comedy. *Melopomene*, leaning on a club and holding a tragic mask, was the muse of tragedy. *Urania*, holding the globe and tracing mathematical figures with a wand, was the muse of astronomy. *Erato*, playing a nine-stringed lyre, was the muse of lyric and erotic poetry. *Polyhymnia*, shown holding her forefinger to her lips or carrying a scroll, was the muse of the sublime hymn. Finally, *Terpsichore*, shown dancing with a seven-stringed lyre, was the muse of the dance. Adorned with wreaths of palm leaves, laurel, roses, and the feathers of the vanquished Sirens, the muses were pictured as beautiful maidens dancing in a circle around their leader, Apollo. Worshipped in Greece and Rome, the muses had dedicated to them a temple and a grove. The swan, nightingale, and grasshopper were sacred to them.

The muses got their name from a root that indicates eloquence or ardor or desire, the tension of anger that sometimes leaps out in impatience, the sort of tension that aches to know and to act. The muses animate, stir up, excite and arouse. The multiplicity of muses implies that there is a multiplicity of different arts.

Fig. 1.6. Apollo and the Muses by Martin de Vos (c. 1590). In the center is Apollo playing his lyre. The muses were nine beautiful maidens who personified music including poetry, theatre and dance as well as history and astronomy. Musee Royaux des Beaux-Arts de Belgique, Brussels.

Continuing the myths: after the muses came a few mortals so excellent in their art that they almost equalled the divine musicians. Of these, the greatest was the legendary Orpheus. His mother was a muse who gave him the gift of music. His father was a Thracian prince and he grew up in Thrace where a most musical culture fostered his art. Apollo presented him with his lyre and the muses taught him to play it, and soon there was no limit to his power when he played and sang. Orpheus had no rival save the gods themselves. His music moved not only the beasts of the forest, but also the rocks on the hillside, and he turned the course of the rivers with his playing. In Orpheus, the duality of reason and emotion is evident. When his wife, Euridice, died from the bite of a serpent, Orpheus was inconsolable. Placing himself in great danger, he descended into the underworld to try to get Euridice back. The charms of his lyre so moved the infernal deities, Hades and Persephone, that they consented to Euridice's return to earth. Only one condition was set. Orpheus, who was to lead her up, was enjoined not to look back upon her till they reached the upper world. Forgetting his promise, the impatient Orpheus looked back and lost Euridice forever. There are a number of parallel stories, biblical and secular, but it is this one in particular that has inspired a number of poets and composers, most notably, Gluck, whose operatic version, *Orpheus and Euridice*, is perhaps the most memorable.

In the Greek myths, the *Sirens* appear again and again. They were sea nymphs, living on an island in the Aegean, who bewitched passing sailors by the irresistible spell of their singing and lured them to destruction. Sailors leapt from their vessels or crashed them against the formidable rocks of the turbulent Aegean in pursuit of the Sirens. No one knew what they looked like, for no one who saw them ever lived to return. Nevertheless, they were frequently depicted as part woman, part bird.

Origins of Music

Fig. 1.7. Orpheus and Euridice by Nicholas Poussin (c.1640). With his lyre, Orpheus charmed the animals, birds, trees and rocks. The tragic story of his love for Euridice, and how she was lost to him forever, was used as the subject for many pieces of music. Courtesy of the Musée de Louvre, Paris.

One version of the death of the Sirens is told in connection with the Argonauts, who made a hazardous voyage to Colchis under the leadership of the Greek hero, Jason, in quest of the Golden Fleece. Orpheus was also on board the Argo and, when the Argonauts wearied, Orpheus would strike the lyre and they would be roused to fresh zeal and their oars would smite the sea in rhythm with the melody. If a quarrel threatened, Orpheus would play so tenderly and soothingly that the fiercest spirits would grow calm and forget their anger.

The argonauts endured many perils before they succeeded in their quest. On their way lay the dreaded *Symplegades*, the rocks that closed together and dashed in pieces the vessel passing through them, and beyond this peril lay the island of the Sirens. To protect themselves, the Argonauts had a dove fly through before them, and followed rowing with all their strength. At this point, it was Orpheus who saved the Argonauts from the spell of the Sirens. When the Argonauts heard singing so enchantingly sweet that it drove out all other thoughts except a desperate longing to hear more, and they turned the Argo to the shore where the Sirens sat, Orpheus snatched up his lyre and played a melody so clear and ringing that it drowned out the sound of those fatal voices. The rocks stood firm, the vessel was put back on her course, and the winds sped her away from that dangerous place. If Orpheus had not been there, the Argonauts would have left their bones on the island of the Sirens. Instead, it was the Sirens who perished for to fail meant their own destruction.

Another version of the death of the Sirens was told in connection with the voyage home of Odysseus and the Greek heroes after their victory against Troy. During this voyage, Odysseus faced the mortal danger of the Sirens by having himself bound to the mast of his vessel so that he could hear their seductive sounds and still escape. He stuffed his companions' ears with wax so that they would not be bewitched. Though the song of the Sirens rang out in beautiful cadences, and Odysseus's heart ached with longing, the ropes held and the danger was safely passed. Doomed to die if anyone could withstand the spell of their singing, the Sirens threw themselves into the sea and perished.

Chapter 2

TRADITIONS OF WESTERN MUSIC

MUSIC IN GREEK CHRONICLES

The pinnacle of Greek culture was attained during the time of Plato and Aristotle, around 500 B.C. The lyric poem had already been perfected, as had the Greek drama. In these works of art, we see the expression of powerful emotion. At the same time, the musical scale and the lyre and pipes were undergoing further development, and the musical endeavor was moving toward reason and understanding. The chronicles of the day bear this out.

In Plato's *Republic*, music occupied a leading position among the arts. Plato drew an analogy between the movement of the soul and musical progressions. Therefore the aim of music cannot be mere 'amusement,' but rather a harmonic education, perfection of the soul and quieting of the passions. The primary role of music is pedagogical, which means the building of character, morals, and reason. Every melody, every rhythm, and every instrument has its own special effect on the nature of man. In short, there is a correspondence between tonal harmonies and cosmic cycles such as the seasons of the year, the parts of the day, birth and death, man and woman, the sun and the moon, the oscillations of weather, and the processes of growth, healing and reincarnation.

At the height of Athenian culture, Solon was the champion of music. As Athens' chief lawgiver, he laid down the rules as to how music was to be performed and applied to the common good. He felt that music promoted moral sturdiness and responsible citizenship, and he advocated that musical training be given to Athenian youth. The practice of music by slaves was prohibited, as music was considered the mark of nobility. Musical education was reserved for free Athenians, and a man's knowledge of music ranked him as a cultured man.

This high esteem of music extended to the musicians themselves. The Greeks held musical competitions not unlike the Olympiads, in which the winner was accorded the status of a hero. Thus the pipe virtuoso, Midas of Agrigendum, was praised by Pindar as a conquering hero, and the trumpet player, Herodorus of Megara, became a national figure by winning the competition ten times.

Poetry seems to have arisen from the emotions that are expressed verbally during singing and dancing. Even as the classical period of Greek literature approached in the fifth century, the close connection between the three rhythmic arts was still evident. The lyrical odes of Pindar and the dramatic odes of Aeschylus and Sophocles were written for musical performance that included processional or dances movements of the singers. The lyric poem as a *genre* in its own right was about to emerge.

The poet-singers of the day were called lyric poets because they declaimed to the accompaniment of the lyre. Though Terpander of Lesbos was said to be the originator of lyric poetry, the reputation of Sappho, his pupil, surpassed his own.

Sappho of Lesbos was one of the most celebrated poets of the ancient world. She is known to have flourished in the sixth century B.C. and to have established a school for girls. Little else is known about her save for some facts gleaned from her poetry: that she was married, had a child, and loved women. But even those facts are disputed. She was the author of cultist hymns, odes, elegies and epigrams, of which only two pieces, the odes, *To Aphrodite* and *To a Maiden*, have survived in complete form. But there are many additional fragments. These poems display strong feeling and a glowing imagination. Sappho is said to have invented several meters. As a lyricist, she was unparalleled. Unfortunately the melody of her verse, partly the secret of her eloquence, is lost in translation.

Sappho is pictured in Renaissance art with a six-stringed cithara. In 1819, Franz Grillparzer fashioned a stirring poetic drama, *Sappho*, out of the legend that tells how she threw herself from the high Leucadian cliffs into the sea when she found that her love for the youth Phaon was unrequited, and that her own handmaiden was preferred.

Fig. 2.1. Comedy scene in an ancient Greek play. The aulos was used as an accompaniment and this added to the dramatic effect. Roman relief, Naples

The close association of music and poetry with dance can be seen in our museum-libraries, in many pictures of ancient dancing figures, on tablets, monuments and urns. Egyptian artifacts that predate the Greek period reveal that the Egyptians danced and sang in religious ceremonies as well as in secular entertainments. Prehistoric art the world over treats dancing and music-making along with hunting and fighting as the essential activities of humans. Earlier, we saw intimations of this in a cave painting dated 40,000 years ago.

As an expression of the cult of Dionysus, the art of dancing found its way into the ancient Greek drama. According to a number of chronicles, the actor made his first appearance before a Greek audience in the sixth century B.C. By that time, the familiar recitation of odes was supplemented with dramatic action. The producer-manager-actor Thespis became the symbol of the new theater. As an actor, Thespis assumed successive diguises by donning a number of masks. His counterpart was played by the chorus, a declaiming, singing, and dancing body of men who were charged with a variety of functions in the drama. The chorus served as counselor to the protagonist, or as a divine voice, or human conscience, contributing incidental music and filling intermissions with song. While singing its *strophes*, the chorus of the drama executed dances that were not merely rhythmic gestures but also expressions, in mime, of the ideas in the dramatic poem. In addition, the chorus prefaced many scenes with expressions of feeling, often accompanying them on the *aulos*. But above all, the chorus assumed the role of the narrator, telling of events preceding the drama and explaining details that could not be revealed by the actor. The modern playwright still uses the device of the narrator, on occasion.

The ancient Greeks seem to have had no harmony except the singing together of voices in octaves, as in the chorus of the drama. But they did have groups of singers answering each other in what is called antiphony, a style later developed within the Judeo-Christian tradition. We will return to this style of chanting later.

Many ancient peoples sang in a scale of five notes, the pentatonic scale. The five notes might be related to each other in a variety of ways, like the five black keys of the piano, for example. This scale is found in countries throughout the world, in the Orient, Arabia, South America, Africa and among the American Indians. The ancient Greeks, too, developed a number of musical scales that were based on a pentatonic progression. These scales will be encountered again a millenium later, for they were elaborated and transformed into the ecclesiastical modes. Each of the Greek modes was thought to create its own mood. To Plato, for example, the *Lydian* mode was wailing; the *Ionian*, mellow and sensuous, suitable for drinking bouts; the *Doric*, militant; and the *Phrygian*, peaceful. Secular music required one mode, sacred music another. The cult of one god required one particular mode for worship together with its instrument, different from that required by the cult of another god.

The interval of the semitone appeared in the musical scale as the lyre and pipes developed. We know that it was already present in the musical scales of antiquity because an ancient flute, found in Egypt, was tuned to play this interval.

The first cithara, a form of lyre, was supposed to have been an instrument of four strings that could be tuned in one of the four primary tetrachords, *Dorian, Phrygian, Lydian, and Ionian*, each having one half-step and two whole steps as intervals. If two *citharas* were tuned in different registers, but had one note in common, together they could form a scale. It did not take long before such a seven-note scale could be played on single seven-stringed instruments.

In the sixth century B.C., Terpander of Lesbos perfected these tetrachords. His melodies, called nomes, were supposed to have had moral effects on the Spartan youth, giving them spirit and courage. As in Athens, each mode was thought to have its own special effect on conduct and character.

After the Messenian war, Sparta was in such a terrible state of upheaval that the Delphic Oracle was consulted.

> When Terpander's cither shall sound
> Contention in Sparta shall cease.

So the Spartans called upon Terpander of Lesbos to help them, and through the power of his song, peace was restored. Terpander's collection of melodies from all parts of the known world was unfortunately lost, but his seven-stringed *kithara* survives. It was he who increased the number of strings from four to seven, and seven strings became the official number in Sparta. When the attempt was made to increase the number of strings to eight in order to encompass the octave, a protest was lodged. This was a curious matter, as we shall see later.

The almost legendary Pythagoras is responsible for the discovery of the relationship between musical sounds and numbers. This has proved to be the cornerstone of modern theories of pitch. A mathematician and philosopher who lived in the fifth century B.C., Pythagoras made an enormous impression on the imagination of the ancient Greeks. Fabulous stories were told about him during his lifetime, and these were embellished during the many centuries thereafter.

He was said to have possessed a golden hip, to have lectured in two different places at the same time, and to have remembered his previous lives.

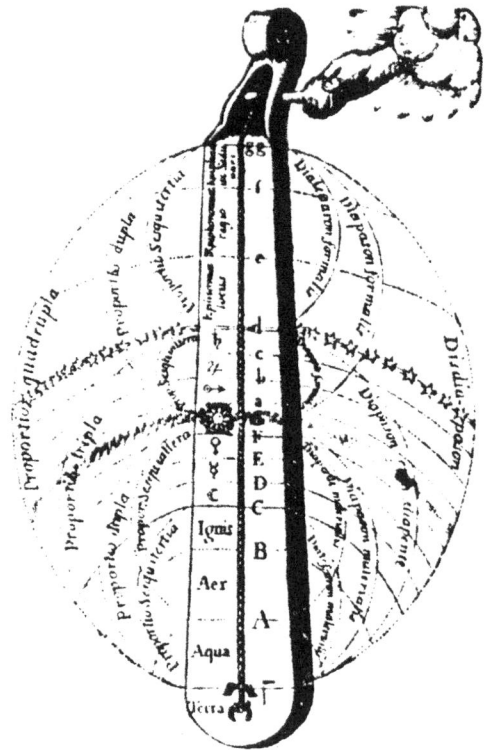

Fig. 2.2. The universe is shown in the shape of a stringed instrument. This illustrates the Pythagorean dictum that man's soul must be attuned to the harmony of the spheres in order to maintain health.

He claimed that he could hear the beautiful harmony produced by the motion of celestial bodies. Such extravagant claims have led modern critics to wonder whether this person was anything more than a myth.

The story is told about a courtesan who was shut up in the house of a rival. Angered by the incarceration, she tried to set fire to the building. The remonstrances of her friends were to no avail, so

Pythagoras was consulted. Though engaged in observing the stars at the time, Pythagoras quickly realized what was happening and concluded that the woman must have been excited by some music played in the *Phrygian* mode. Pythagoras sent for a musician and ordered him to play something in a calmer mode, whereupon the woman's anger left her and she desisted.

Pythagoras preached the sanctity of all life and the abstention from meat and fish because he believed that each soul wanders through the bodies of many living things. His critics ridiculed some of his doctrines, such as transmigration of souls, the harmony of the spheres, and the spherical shape of the earth, but his admirers and adherents accepted it all very seriously.

Pythagoras gained considerable political influence through a semi-religious order that he organized among the elite of his followers. Members of this order adopted the most ascetic discipline and developed an hierarchical social system, which was antithetical to the then-current way of life in the city-states. Pythagoras quickly incurred the enmity of the forces of the budding Greek political democracy of the day.

As a mathematician, Pythagoras is said to have drawn in the sand a square on each of the three sides of a right-angle triangle and to have shown that the square on the hypotenuse is equal to the sum of the squares on the other two sides. Though enunciated long before Pythagoras, this theorem is ascribed to him and is known by his name. It is one of the Pythagorean *universals*; another is the ratio of the circumference to the diameter of a circle, called π. This ratio, 22/7, applies to every circle, no matter what its size.

The slogan that 'all things are number' is based on the many observations Pythagoras made of regularities in nature, such as the fact that the lengths of two stretched strings that sound consonant when plucked are in the ratio of small whole numbers. For example, if a stretched string is shortened to one-half its normal length, an octave is produced. Other examples of the regularities in nature and numerical universals are found in the dimensions of geometrical figures and in the gyrations of heavenly bodies. On observations such as these is based the modern scientific dictum that all natural phenomena can be described and understood in mathematical terms.

Fig. 2.3. Pythagoras, Philolaus and Jubal. A XVth century woodcut depicts the ascertaining of pitch, from Theoretica Musica *by Franchino Gaffurio, Milan. In quaint medieval garb, Pythagoras is shown, above right, experimenting with pitches produced by striking glasses partly filled with water and by striking different-sized bells. Below, he is shown establishing the numerical relationship between pitch, and the length of a vibrating string (left) and, along with Philolaus, a blown pipe (right). The biblical inventor of musical instruments, Jubal, is shown (upper left) listening to the pounding of an anvil.*

In Pythagoras we have a quantum leap forward in the understanding of music from a physical point of view, and in the recognition of the duality of reason and emotion in human pursuits. Pythagoras taught the ancient Greeks that music and the other arts are part of the harmony of the spheres. This was expressed by the Pythagoreans emphasis on simple numerical ratios. Recent studies have suggested a close connection between the disposition of columns in Greek temples and these simple numerical ratios, such as the interval of the fifth, 3/2. While the Pythagoreans frequently drifted into a mysticism of numbers, their musical theory laid the foundation for modern psychoacoustics.

MUSIC IN IMPERIAL ROME

Slowly the Hellenic world declined. The onslaught of imperial Rome was too much for cultured Hellas to withstand. But it was not the conquerors who forced their culture on the vanquished, but rather the defeated who gave their culture to the victors. Unfortunately, the materialistic Romans could not really appreciate the culture they inherited from a civilization that was alien to their own. The lofty spiritual flights of the Greeks sank to the level of trivialities, and sublime thoughts degenerated into mere entertainment. The contemplative chants intoned by the Greek crowds assembled at spots hallowed by the Oracles became sensuous fanfares introducing bloody spectacles at the *Circus Maximus*, fanfares designed to drown out the agonized cries of the tortured. Hundreds of thousands attended these spectacles, as well as the gladiatorial contests and the chariot races. And all these events were accompanied by music. The victorious legions marched to the very ends of the known world, to the roll of drums and the blast of trumpets.

The Romans were not musical innovators. They invented no new musical instruments of any note. Whatever they had was imported from the vanquished territories. The flute, for one, was played at solemn services and at the *Bacchanalia*. It is true that Rome developed a theater of its own, but it was devoted mainly to the performance of satirical pieces, which pandered to the popular taste. Even as the empire began its decline, music continued to accompany sensual feasts and cruel spectacles. No wonder the Hebrews and early Christians of that era abhorred this use of music, considering it a human degradation.

The Romans wrote treatises on the Greek modes. To each of the seven tones within the octave, they gave the name of a heavenly body and to every fourth tone they gave the name of a day of the week. These tones were arranged in ascending order and in overlapping tetrachords.

B	C	D	E
Saturn	Jupiter	Mars	Sun
Saturday			
E	F	G	A
Sun	Venus	Mercury	Moon
Sunday			
A	B	C	D
Moon	Saturn	Jupiter	Mars
Monday			
(*Lundi*)			
D	E	F	G
Mars	Sun	Venus	Mercury
Tuesday			
(*Mardi*)			
G	A	B	C
Mercury	Moon	Saturn	Jupiter
Wednesday			
(*Mercredi*)			
C	D	E	F
Jupiter	Mars	Sun	Venus
Thursday			
(*Jeudi*)			
F	G	A	B
Venus	Mercury	Moon	Saturn
Friday			
(*Vendredi*)			

Though the English names of the days of the week are sometimes taken from the Norse gods (*Wotan, Thor*, and *Freya*), the names of the Roman gods are retained in French.

It is interesting to speculate why our week has seven days and why there are four weeks in a lunar month. There seems to be no astronomical reason. Clearly, this decision antedated the biblical story of creation. Our week might have had four days (derived from the

Greek tetrachord) and there might have been seven weeks in the lunar month. Imagine a day of rest coming one in four. Humans might never have been created!

Fig. 2.4. Saint Cecelia by Domenico Zampieri (c.1620). Cecelia is seen singing and playing the seven-stringed bass viola da gamba. Pathos and contemplation are fused in this portrait. A living music stand (cupid) holds Cecelia's music. Courtesy of Musée de Louvre, Paris.

One Roman figures prominently in the legends associated with of music. She is honored as its patron saint. During the pontificate of Urban I around the year 230, this woman of noble birth, named Cecelia, became a Christian in childhood. Still at an early age, the story goes, Cecelia vowed to remain a virgin, but her parents gave her in marriage to a young Roman nobleman. Distraught, Cecelia persuaded her husband to respect her vow and also to become a Christian himself. Shortly thereafter, he suffered martyrdom and, in anticipation of the same fate, Cecelia distributed her possessions among the poor. When this became known, the prefect of Rome ordered Cecelia to be taken to her own home and there to be burned in her bath. But the virgin, though exposed to the boiling water for a whole day, was unhurt. Even the axe of the executioner failed to sever her head after three strokes. In the end, however, she did win the double wreath of martyrdom and virginity, and everlasting respect. To this day, the Church of Saint Cecelia is one of the most notable in Rome. As a woman of great musical accomplishment, and as the alleged inventor of the organ, Cecelia became the patron saint of music and musicians, and musical societies are frequently called by her name. The day of her death, November 22, is celebrated in many countries as Music Day. John Dryden's memorable ode, *Alexander's Feast: A Song for Saint Cecelia's Day*, stands as a monument to her legend. Geoffrey Chaucer and Alexander Pope have also celebrated her in literature, and she has been the subject of many paintings. An example is shown in Fig. 2.4.

The music of the ancient world is practically lost. Only the cantillations of the eastern synagogues and churches provide us with an inkling of the religious music of antiquity. The modern folksong in Asia and northern Africa probably has not changed much in two thousand years and more, and we have that material to help reconstruct the secular music of antiquity. For the rest, we can do little more than rely on instruments dug from ancient tombs, on reliefs and paintings of musical scenes found on urns and other artifacts, and on allusions in the texts of antiquity. It is true that we have the Pythagorean scale, which indicates the pool of notes that the ancient Greek composers could draw from (see Chapter 11). The contour of the melody might have been indicated by signs for the rise and fall of pitch. And the vowels in the lyrics might have suggested pitch from their formants (see Chapter 10). Finally, the lyrics might have suggested the rhythm of the composition.

For example, the syllables 'totē tatote' might be syllables traditionally used in the playing technique of lip-activated instruments: the 't' representing the articulation, and the vowels representing the relative pitches. Or they could be solmization syllables. A system of syllables (ta, to, tē, te) might represent the four notes of the tetrachord. Attempts have recently been made to reconstruct the sounds of antiquity but these are largely based on conjecture. Musicologist, Eric Werner, has painted a portrait of the origins of the Judeo-Christian world of music as revealed in text and artifact. We will now turn to this era.

THE JUDEO-CHRISTIAN MUSICAL TRADITION

We have seen how reason and emotion blended in the music of antiquity. This blend has varied from time to time, sometimes favoring reason, sometimes emotion, but never has one dominated completely. Music is a multi-tiered structure with the blend of reason and emotion at the very foundation of its structure. In Western music, melody occupies a central position, and it was the early Jews and Christians who were responsible for the shaping of the melodic line into an artistic creation. Again the story begins in the biblical past.

The ancient Hebrews must have enjoyed a considerable reputation as a people of song. This is known not only from Hebrew sources but also from the chronicles of their hostile neighbors. An Assyrian document tells us that King Sennacherib received as tribute from King Hezekiah many Hebrew musicians, both male and female. We are told in the Bible that, during the Exile, the Babylonians demanded of their Hebrew captives to entertain them with the music which they brought from the Promised Land, but the Hebrews demurred:

> By the rivers of Babylon
>   we sat and wept
>   when we remembered Zion.
> On the aspens of that Land
>   we hung up our harps,
> Though there our captors asked of us
>   the lyrics of our songs,
>   and our despoilers urged us to be joyous:
> "Sing us one of the songs of Zion!"

> How can we sing a song of the Lord
> in a foreign land?
> If I forget you, Jerusalem,
> may my right hand be forgotten!
> May my tongue cleave to my palate
> If I remember you not,
> If I place not Jerusalem ahead of my joy.

Psalm 137, 1-6.

For conquerors to show such an interest in the music of a vanquished enemy can only mean that the enemy had a reputation for its music and it suggests the esteem in which the Hebrews were held.

Before the Exile, the beloved King David had become the patron of Hebrew music. Considering the numerous *Psalms* attributed to him, David towers above the ancient poets, with the notable exception of Homer. A great king, a brilliant soldier, and a gifted poet and musician, David organized the cult music of the *Levites*. Many centuries later, Byzantine Christianity identified David with Jesus, the Faithful Shepherd, and with Orpheus, the divinely talented singer.

Musical services are described in *I Chronicles*, verses 15, 16, and 25. In one passage:

> David commanded the chiefs of the Levites to appoint their brethren
> as chanters, to play on musical instruments, harps, lyres and
> cymbals, to make a loud sound of rejoicing.

I Chronicles, 15.

These services were later cited as the model for all sacred worship. But a more modest service had to develop first.

Early Christianity was a movement of the poor and the meek. It opposed the elaborate service and the hierarchy of the established temple religion, which was headed by a priestly aristocracy. The early Christians focused on the ideology of the Kingdom of Heaven and did not recognize the rule of priestly dynasties. While the Hebrew Temple employed an instrumental ensemble and a choir, the later synagogue had but a lay cantor and no musical accompaniment save for the congregational responses. It was the more modest synagogue worship that served as the model for early Christian liturgy.

The Hebrews, who were responsible for the rise of early Christianity, were not positively disposed toward the arts because they saw in music, painting and sculpture the continuation of idolatry, pagan rites and worship. The Epicurean philosophy and Dionysian rites emphasized earthly pleasure, and their followers were led to the sensual experiences of music. The early Christians followed their Hebrew forbears. They, too, could not abide the sensuality of the Epicureans and the Dionysians, and at the beginning of the patristic period music was ignored if not suppressed. During its first eight centuries, the Christian church was hostile to instrumental music.

Still, music continued to be heard all around the organizers of the church and eventually they had to pay attention to it. Properly guided, they must have come to believe that music could very well develop within the framework of Christian doctrine, and could become the handmaiden of the church.

Even before the beginning of the Christian era, many musical forms were created. But for the ancient Hebrews, the principal form was the psalm, and the principal institution in which to perform it was the Temple in Jerusalem, where services were conducted with musical accompaniment.

In the Synagogue. Musical liturgy took four forms of worship in the synagogue, and these became the model for Christian ecclesiastical service.

1. Simple solo *psalmody* was chanted by the cantor, and the congregation was not required to participate in any active way.

2. For the response *psalm*, the verses were divided in halves. The first part was chanted by the cantor, and the congregation responded with the second part:

Cantor: Blessed be the name of the Lord;
Congregation: Blessed be his name forever and ever.

3. For the *antiphon*, not only were the verses divided, but the chanters, too, were divided into two groups and chanted in alternation:

First Group: O give thanks unto the Lord for He is good;
Second Group: For His mercy endureth forever.

4. For the refrain *psalm*, the cantor chanted a short series of stanzas, and the congregation interjected a refrain verse between stanzas:

> Cantor: Give us thy protection,
> Deliver us from danger;
> Grant us joy and honor as the closing hour draws nigh.
> Congregation: O Lord, we stand in awe before thy deeds.
> Cantor: All their sins forgiving,
> Show favor to thy chosen as the closing hour draws nigh.
> Congregation: O Lord, we stand in awe before thy deeds.

The acclamations, such as *hallelujah, amen,* and *selah,* have themselves become texts of innumerable musical compositions. These were chanted at the end of various prayers or calls, such as *Sing unto the Lord a new song.*

The psalms could be sung to many melodies but particular melodies became attached to particular psalms. How was a specific melody chosen? One way was by adopting *contrafacts*, a practice that is still common today. A *contrafact* is a familiar melody that is borrowed for a new text. The anthem, *My Country, tis of Thee*, is a contrafact of the older, *God Save the King*; the hymn, *Rock of Ages*, is a contrafact of the older Hebrew, *Ma'oz Tzur*. In liturgy, this practice has a long history. The Catholic Church based many of its hymns on *contrafacts*. Martin Luther made it a practice to take the songs of the street and use them in the church with sacred texts. "Why should the devil have all the fine tunes?" he is said to have asked. The first recorded use of *contrafacts* is in the *Book of Psalms,* in which, now and then, an individual *psalm* bears a superscription that seems totally unrelated to the content of the *psalm* below. For example, *Psalm* 56 begins, "To the leader upon 'Mute dove far away' by David." This direction includes the first line of a folk song familiar to the psalmist, thus identifying for him the tune to which the verses should be sung.

Eventually, psalms were sung by all strata of society, by the laity as well as by the clergy, even by children. In the early church, there must have developed a high regard for musical ability and skill, for those who possessed good voices, though they might be simple people, were frequently made deacons.

Two musical instruments were prominent in temple service. A primitive organ having ten pipes, called *magrepha* in the *Talmud*, was played regularly during the period of the second Temple. Its sound was said to be loud enough to be heard outside Jerusalem proper. What powered this organ is not clear. The Greek water organ, the *hydraulis*, is also mentioned in the *Talmud*, but its use was prohibited in the Temple.

The *shofar* or ram's horn has been sounded in the course of Hebrew worship, certainly since the time of Moses. The ram was one of the animals of sacrifice, and the Hebrews used its horns as sacred instruments. Today, the *shofar* can still be heard on the Jewish New Year and on the Day of Atonement in every Jewish community the world over, in memory of the wanderings of the Children of Israel.

Fig. 2.5. A Jew wrapped in a tallith ushering in a Jewish festival with the remarkable sounds of the shofar.

The second Temple was destroyed in 70 A.D., but the great migration of Jews westward from the Middle East did not gain momentum until about the year 900. In the meantime Christianity severed its connection with its mother-religion, Judaism, at the Council of Nicea in 325.

We saw earlier that very little is known of the ancient Hebrew songs except what we read in biblical texts, such as David's *Psalms* and Solomon's *Song of Songs*. We do know that a new musical tradition evolved once early Christianity came in contact with Greek and Roman civilization.

In the Christian Church. In the transition from the music of Greek antiquity to that of the Christian church, the music of Byzantium played an important role. After its establishment as capital of the Roman Empire, Constantinople became the center of a civilization based on many traditions, both Occidental and Oriental. The tie to the ancient Greek and Hebrew traditions was loosening. Byzantine music slowly became church music and followed the destiny of the church. But the historical roots of church music are very clear.

In early Christian liturgy, the central elements were the *Psalms*, the *Doxology*, the *Thrice Holy*, and the *Lord's Prayer*. They all originated among the Hebrews and, except for the *Lord's Prayer*, they still form the core of synagogue liturgy to the present day. In addition, the early church adopted various hymns, songs of praise and thanksgiving, to express Christian devoutness, and these items served as the musical mediation between man and God. Though the church Fathers approved liturgical singing, they continued to voice opposition to the playing of musical instruments, whose tones were considered sensuous and profane. These restrictions were formalized when Gregory the Great ascended the papal throne in 590. Gregory excluded worldly matters from spiritual education. Recognized as belonging to a human activity that was essentially profane, musical education was thus limited. Music could be accepted only as it related to the liturgy.

Gregory was the first of the popes to organize and codify the many chants that were sung in the church and to establish rules for their composition. Known as Gregorian chant, or plainsong, these chants consisted of a single melodic line, which was nothing more than a succession of notes spanning an octave or less. Of course, they can be ornamented and made to soar.

In the last analysis, it was through the church that early Judaism made its lasting musical contribution. It has been estimated that about 60 percent of Gregorian chants can be traced to Hebrew

Alleluia: Angelus Domini

Fig. 2.6. A Gregorian chant of the tenth century.

sources. The church itself has always maintained that both its liturgy and its music are of Hebrew origin. In the Lamentations, which are chanted during Holy Week, Catholics have preserved the ancient Hebrew structure. The numbers of the verses are sung in Hebrew and the verse is cantillated in a melody derived from synagogue tradition.

For centuries, Gregorian chants were the only music officially sanctioned by the church. These chants were carried from Rome all over the Christian world. As they spread, Gregorian music served to unify peoples, for it brought them together, in the service of divine worship, to chant the melodies they held in common. Gregorian music was a powerful expression of Romanesque art, which was marked by solemnity and piety.

Gregory's music took a firm hold all over Italy. This was a distinct advantage for the church Fathers, who sought to perpetuate this musical tradition but, at the same time, it retarded the creation of new musical idioms. One of the few musicians in Italy who was genuinely innovative during this period was Guido of Arezzo. We will encounter him later, for it was he who initiated the tradition of musical notation that is with us to this day.

A remnant of temple music that was retained after the Temple's destruction was the melismatic element. This was the melodic adornment or ornament sung on a single syllable of the psalm. The melism seems to have been a special feature of temple worship and it has never ceased to be used in synagogue chant. It was adopted by the church and became a principal feature in the chanting of Christian hymns, adorning the syllables of acclamations such as *hallelujah,* and reaching a pinnacle of grandeur many centuries later, in the music of Handel, Bach, and Mendelssohn. But it was in Hebrew worship that the practice seems to have begun. To this day, cantorial prayers are adorned with these melismatic forms evoking piety and religious ecstasy.

Sequences of melisms slowly evolved into rather impressive technical coloraturas. These were retained as musical motifs or melodies. It is clear that melody is a very effective carrier of information, in that it retains its identity in the face of numerous variations in register and timbre. When asked to reproduce a melody, a person will vary the register of it from occasion to occasion without recognizing any change. Most people remember melodies not in terms of absolute pitches but in terms of patterns and relationships between tones. The Hebrews seem to have discovered this fact, that melodies can be transposed without losing their identity, thus making them ideal as mnemonic devices. The ancient Greeks and Egyptians also knew these techniques and practiced them, but it was probably the Hebrews who introduced them in the Middle East.

Frequent repetition of motifs led to the establishment of melodic modes, which are patterns of tones consisting of two or three motifs chained together. Traditional synagogue music is based upon the various modes of the ancient period, and many Jewish melodies are derived from these same modes. This system of musical modality, together with that of the ancient Greeks, was bequeathed to the early church and formed the basis for the development of the ecclesiastical modes and the later scales of tonal music.

By the fifth century, St. Augustine had already written a work entitled *De Musica*, about what we would now call poetry and music. In it, he considered the *Hallelujah* chant the pinnacle of church music. As such, it was frequently sung without uttering the word itself. First the consonants were omitted and later even its vowels, *A, E, U, I, A*, were replaced. Called the *Jubilus*, this became a wordless hymn having mystic and ecstatic overtones. Thus was the Divinity glorified, with pure melody.

As time passed, the 'song without words' became a new musical art form. No longer bound to the church, it could be used to express any human sentiments, sacred and profane. It began to flourish when the choirs of musical instruments arrived on the musical scene, around the time of the Crusades. It provides one of the most profound of human experiences in the world today.

The Rise of Hasidism. There is evidence that the wordless hymn goes back to ancient Hebrew practice. The *Talmud* speaks of the wordless chanting of the *Hallel*, and numerous passages refer to the wordless hymn as an ancient practice. But then, during the Middle Ages, a number of Rabbis warned against wordless chanting, a practice they called *Cabalistic*. With the rise of *Hasidism*, however, the wordless hymn re-emerged as an ecstatic form of worship.

Hasidism originated among Polish Jews around the middle of the eighteenth century. As a movement, it emphasized piety, worship, and contemplation rather than learning, dogma, and ritual. The *Baal Shem Tov* (Master of the Good Name) was its early inspirational leader. With the reputation of a gentle teacher and a healer of spiritual wounds, and with nature as his guide, the *Baal Shem Tov* found joy and holiness everywhere. He beheld God in everything and everything in God. Filled with mystical ecstasy, he improvised stirring prayers utterly unlike the melancholy ones of his youth. Through stories and parables, he taught his disciples not to despair even if they were not learned, that a warm and joyful heart is more acceptable to God than a head crammed with esoteric knowledge. He dwelt on the affirmation of life, on chant, love, compassion and the brotherhood of man. The masses learned to love their master, and a new optimism and enthusiasm pervaded the community. Lives that had been austere became inspired. Prayers once recited mechanically were now uttered with fervor. Great significance was attached to the movements of the torso and the hands, to clapping and finger snapping, leading to group dancing and singing. *Hasidic* ceremonies such as the wedding became fervent celebrations of dance and song. The Christian slogan, 'when you sing as you pray, you pray twice,' seems to apply to the Hassidim.

In the opinion of the early *Hasidim*, music and singing were ranked higher than explicit prayer. Instead of rendering the text, the *Hasidim* rendered the melody and thought the words. The *Hasidic niggun* evolved as a song without words, sung spontaneously and with a joyful heart. Though sung without words, most *niggunim* still carried syllables such as *ah, ay, oy, hey, bam*, and *ya-ba-bam*, and were always sung with enthsiasm, fervor, and joy. With the development of the *Hasidic niggun*, the pendulum swung away from the intellect in the direction of the emotions. It was sung (and danced) in order to attain the highest transport of the soul, disembodiment. By interceding with music, fallen souls were purified, sick souls were healed, and the frenzied were soothed and led back to sanity.

The structural organization of artistic creation, such as binary and ternary form, can also be traced back to Judeo-Christian sources. It was Rabbi Yehudai Gaon, living in Babylonia in the eighth century, who seems to have introduced ternary form into religious music. He suggested that the opening prayer (the *bracha*) and the closing prayer (the *chatima*) be chanted in the same mode, and the prayer between them in a contrasting mode (ABA). This form became part of musical tradition and flourished from the late Middle Ages, through the time of Bach and the classical period, to the present day. In literature, it is clearly evident by the twelfth century in the *ballades* of the French *trouvères*. Rabbi Yehudai's endorsement of ternary form may have been the first expression of a rational structural organization in Western music.

EARLY MUSICAL NOTATION

Up to the eighth century or so, secular music still had no institutional patron or guardian, and instrumental music was still regarded as profane and therefore forbidden. Those who valued the music needed to record it for the benefit of future generations. This was as much a problem for religious as it was for secular music. The problem was first tackled by the synagogue and solved later by the church.

What had to be retained in memory, and it was by then a considerable tradition, was the cantillation of scriptural lessons and the various musical modes. The words could be written down, but what about the melodies? There was a system of unwritten cantillations, and it had worked well as long as oral tradition and personal teaching flourished. But by this time the cantors must have felt the urgent need to record the many cantillations for posterity, to insure the preservation of the tradition. For this they invented a system of written mnemonic signs. Called accents, or *ta'amim* in the scriptures, these musical mnemonic signs specified not single tones but rather whole musical phrases or melisms. This was a rather primitive kind of musical notation, to be sure, but it was considered satisfactory until Guido of Arezzo introduced his notation in the the eleventh century. Finally, in the early sixteenth century, the system of scriptural *ta'amim* was transcribed into Guido's notation of single tones.

Fig. 2.7. Cantillation for reading the Torah. Ta'amim or accents are shown above their Hebrew names and are illustrated in modern notation.

Guido of Arezzo was a monastic music teacher and an innovator of great talent. As an educator, his aim was to simplify the process of learning to read music. To make it easier for his singers to remember the relative pitch of notes, Guido hit upon the idea of having them attach a different syllable to each of the sounds of the then current six-tone diatonic scale. He was aware that every singer of sacred music knew the *Hymn to St. John the Baptist*, the phrases of which rise one step on each succeeding line. The Latin words and melody can be found below on p. 45.

Fig. 2.8 Guido of Arezzo notating music.

Each of the musical intervals between the successive syllables consists of a whole tone, except between mi and fa, which is a semitone. When first introduced, this system must have been difficult to learn. We know that Guido used his hand as a mnemonic to guide his singers. Each joint represented a different syllable and tone, and a new scale started on every fourth tone. This is the basis of Guidonian solmization. Not until the thirteenth century, however, 150 years after the death of Guido, was the system actually recorded.

```
c  d  f  d e d
Ut queant la-xis           That servants we
d   d  c d e e
Re-sonare fibris           With loosened voice
efg  e  d   c  d
Mi--ra gestorum            Miracles and power
f  g  a gf d  d
Fa-muli tu--orum           Of thy deed may praise
gag  e f  g d
Sol-ve polluti             Take heavy guilt
a   g a f  g a  a
La-bi-i re--a-tum          From defiled tongues
gf   d c   e d
Sancte Iohannes            Saint John.
```

Guido's pupils learned to associate the initial syllables of each line with the corresponding sounds of the Hymn:

```
c    d   e   f   g   a
Ut   Re  Mi  Fa  Sol La
```

At the beginning of the seventeenth century, when the ecclesiastical modes were being superseded by the modern major and minor scales, the seventh syllable, '*Si,*' was added (probably an acronym of *Sancte Iohannes*). And the more euphonious '*Do*' was substituted for '*Ut.*' This '*sol fa*' system is used to this day in a method of music training called *solfège*. Its introduction by Zoltan Kodaly in Hungary, in the early twentieth century as an aid in musical instruction, is noteworthy. Many Western children learn some system of *sol fa* in school today.

Gradually Gregorian chant, psalmody, and other forms of musical worship came into conflict with the local secular life and the folk music of the indigenous population. And eventually the church had to relax its strictures in order to permit congregants to borrow its music for secular purposes. The medieval man sang his psalms and canticles in church, and then carried the melodies home with him, transforming them into profane songs that expressed love of women, wine, and adventure.

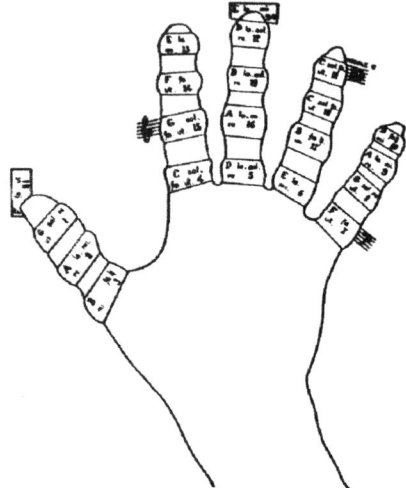

Fig. 2.9. 'Guido's hand' was an aid to sightsinging. Guido of Arezzo divided the octave into six tones, ut, re, mi, fa, sol, la, and the leader of the choir used his fingers, subdivided as in the illustration to cue the choir boys.

Fig. 2.10. The jongleurs accompanied their songs with dances and plays, recited legends, acrobatic stunts and magic tricks.

Chapter 3

THE SECULAR MOVEMENT AND RELIGIOUS ACCOMPANIMENTS

People have always sung as they worked in the field, as they marched to war, and as they gathered to celebrate together in the home or outdoors, and mothers have always crooned their children to sleep with lullabies. Early people fashioned crude musical instruments to amuse themselves as they wandered with their flocks or as they danced on the green. It is here that the roots of secular music can be found. But in the Europe of the early Middle Ages, the flowering of secular music had to await the Crusades when the culture of western Europe made contact with the Middle East, and there began a flow of fresh ideas westward. New musical instruments were introduced. An impetus was given by the growth of chivalry, a movement that profoundly affected the manners of the Western world, especially in relation to women. The life of the knight brought honor to his lady, and his adventures were recounted and celebrated in verse and music. With the development of the vernacular languages, much of the literature took the form of songs sung by the *troubador*, the *minstrel*, and the *minnesinger*.

At first, these songs consisted merely of a succession of individual tones that formed a melody. We have seen how melodies were shaped and refined in Europe during the Middle Ages as Gregorian chants evolved. But the sounds of nature are much richer than individual melodies, because many sounds are heard at the same time: the songs of birds, the rustling of leaves, and the rush of water, all occurring together to form a chorus of sounds. The makers of music must have always recognized the potentialities of a music in which tones sounding together enrich the musical texture. This brings us to the next tier in the musical structure, a tier which is occupied by counterpoint and harmony. In the late Middle Ages, counterpoint evolved from the simultaneous singing of two or more singers, each singing his own melodic line. Harmony evolved from the musical accompaniment that singers provided themselves as they sang, when they played a musical instrument such as the lute.

At this point in the history of music, the professional musician appeared, usually as a bard, sometimes blind, who sang at courtly banquets about the deeds of Gods and kings. This was the *troubador*. Later, he appeared as a trained member of a group of singers or players attached to court or temple. Still later, he appeared as a wandering *troubador* or *minstrel*. The craft was handed down from father to son, and musical dynasties were formed. Conservatories took charge of systematic musical education.

The art of the troubadors derived from liturgical chant, preserving in the transformation the scales that defined the pool of tones that could be used for musical composition. As they traveled through France, England, Germany and Italy, the minstrels sang of heroic and amorous adventures. Courtly love dominated the age and imposed its rules on the lives of people, and on the expression of those lives in music.

In short, poetry and music were fused in the love songs of the Middle Ages. The lance-carrying knights, themselves, were often poets and musicians as well. They were soon to take over the new style of music, which appeared around the tenth century in the church, and spread it all over Europe.

Troubador art is said to have originated in Provence and spread from France to Germany, Italy, and Spain. The troubador himself was a poet and he often left the actual singing and playing of his songs to paid servants. These singers and players were the *jongleurs* who wandered from court to court. They sang their masters' music and often added dance and a lively dialogue to their plays. Meanwhile the Germans developed their own brand of lyricism. The *minnesingers* created poems expressing the homage rendered by the knight to his lady. Compared with the spirited, sensuous and graceful love lyrics of the French poets, the Germans' art sometimes seems stolid and heavy.

The voice was the earliest instrument, but attempts to mimic and supplement it grew during the latter Middle Ages. These efforts led to the development of our modern string, wind and percussion

Fig. 3.1. Renaissance instruments were considered noble or plebian. Refined people cultivated stringed instruments like the lute on the left, by Ludwig Businck, 1630. Rijksmuseum, Amsterdam. The passionate bagpipes on the right is by Albrecht Dürer, 1514. The bagpipes was the instrument of the peasants. They were not considered suitable for noblemen This print is from the collection of the New York Public Library, New York.

instruments. The church was the primary setting for this development. But, as noted earlier, both secular and sacred music developed in parallel as the Renaissance approached.

Fig. 3.2. Wind band in a procession. The musical bands of European cities enlivened Renaissance festivals with their brassy and reedy playing.

There is a debate regarding the place of origin of polyphony. Some anthropologists believe that it was the pygmies in Africa who invented the strict form of counterpoint we call the *canon*, in which the leader and members of the chorus enter singing, one after the other, with exactly the same melody, before the singer ahead has finished. It seems not at all unlikely that the African canon anticipated the appearance of polyphony in Europe.

THE DEVELOPMENT OF POLYPHONY

Early Christian music was monophonic. An example is the Gregorian chant, consisting of a single melodic line, which was basically nothing more than a succession of tones. When many voices joined together, they sang in unison or, more accurately, in octaves, since the range of voices varied. But the beauty and expressive quality of many voices singing together led singers to try singing parallel melodic lines separated by consonant intervals other than the octave. This slowly evolved into a new category of music, which had a vertical or harmonic component added to the established horizontal melodic line, and the music of the Western world changed in a fundamental way.

Secular and Religious Accompaniments 51

Multivoiced music, called *organum*, began in the ninth century. *Organum* centered on a fixed melody of sustained tones, the *cantus firmus*, usually a Gregorian chant. This chant was accompanied by another melodic line which paralleled the first at the interval of a fourth or fifth. Eventually this second melody changed its shape by ceasing to parallel the first at all times, and became a new melody in its own right. When sung together, the two melodies might sometimes parallel each other, to be sure, but they might also move in opposite directions, cross, and continue for a while obliquely, and then move in parallel again.

The individual melodic lines of this free organum, as it came to be called, became increasingly independent of each other. More melodic lines were added, and each carried its own text. The principal voice, called the 'tenor' part in those days, might preserve the liturgical word (the *mot*) along with the sustained tones of the cantus firmus, while the upper parts might declaim a variation, might paraphrase, or might even offer a commentary on the principal voice. These multi-voiced songs, expressing both the original text and commentaries, became *motets*. Of liturgical origin, the motet soon found its way into secular music. It was picked up by troubadors who used popular melodies in filling out its polyphonic structure. The result was an animated art form, rich and expressive. The age of polyphony or counterpoint was born.

Instruments came to substitute for the voice in the performance of many of these compositions. If a singer was not available an instrumentalist might play his part. In this way the Western ear became accustomed to a new non-vocal and non-verbal sound. Gradually, it became the acknowledged practice to perform the vocal literature of the fourteenth and fifteenth centuries on instruments. Guillaume de Machaut, a leading French musician-poet of the fourteenth century, permitted the playing of his ballades on the organ, bagpipes and other instruments, and he made this choice the performer's right. The musicians of our day who play Renaissance instruments in a mixed consort exercise that same right when they decide, as performers, which instruments are to play what parts.

Paintings and literary documents of the day, as well as descriptions of marriage ceremonies and religious solemnities, attest to the variety of musical instruments in use by the fourteenth century. *Viols, harps, psalteries, lutes, hurdy-gurdies, trumpets, drums, chimes, cymbals, bagpipes, horns, flutes, shawms, crumhorns, nakers,* and *tabors* were some of the more popular instruments. Some are said to have originated in the Orient. These instruments had a limited capacity to vary in loudness, and they were ordinarily played with limited dynamic variation.

By the fifteenth century, music had moved into the royal court. An extraordinary enthusiasm for music developed among the European nobility, including kings, princes, and princesses. Every nobleman showed his breeding by engaging in music, and many were actually capable players, singers, and composers. Courting a lady frequently involved singing and playing the clavichord or lute. Some musicians were formally attached to the court and they became an essential part of the king's retinue. They followed their king everywhere, even to war. Other musicians worked under the patronage of the local nobleman.

Fig. 3.3. Miniature of Jan von Ockeghem among his singers. A master of Flemish music of the XVIth century, von Ockeghem spent his energies on technical mastery of polyphony rather than on artistic realization. Many of his compositions are problems that he seems to have set himself in order that he might add, through their solution, to the technique of composition. Perhaps the boldest piece of the polyphonic style is von Ockeghem's canon for 36 voices, Deo Gratias. We see in von Ockeghem the preeminence of reason over emotion. Bibliotèque Nationale, Paris.

Fig. 3.4. Madonna with Child and Angels by Giovanni Boccati da Camerino (c. 1460). This is an example of the many representations of angelic concerts in Renaissance art. Here the enthroned Madonna is surrounded by an ensemble of angel musicians. The Renaissance instruments, depicted realistically, were characterized as haut *(loud) and* bas *(soft). In this angelic ensemble, the lute, timbrel and cymbals are seen in upper left; rebec, bagpipes and harp in upper right; portable organ and dulcimer at bottom. The* bas *and* haut *instruments were rarely played together. If this were an actual concert, the* haut *instruments would have drowned out the* bas *instruments. Rather than reflecting sixteenth century musical practice, this painting portrays a celestial glorification of the Virgin and Child. Such an ensemble could only be found in heaven.*

Fig. 3.5. A musical bath in the north of Italy in the fifteenth century. Here are depicted the charms of bathing in one of the gardens of Northern Italy. One could eat and drink and be amorous while musicians played and sang. To the right are the wind and the tabor players. To the left, three singers are evidently performing a French chanson. A Lombardy School miniature. Estense Library, Modena.

But the vogue for music was not confined to aristocratic circles. Every person of culture was expected to take part in improvised musicales. Otherwise, he or she was considered uncouth and wanting in social grace. In many places in Europe, even peasants who lacked breeding could be seen, singing with lutes, and dancing with pipes.

Fig. 3.6. Lutes and viols were the most popular instruments for social music making in the fifteenth and sixteenth centuries. Lutes were even made available in barbershops for the waiting gallant. Here we have depicted the two patrician instruments of the late Renaissance (c. 1670). Cabinet des Estampes, Bibliotèque Nationale, Paris.

With the development of polyphony, the art of building a musical structure flowered. Many styles were attempted. One style that deserves mention consisted in writing a single melodic line and deriving, from it alone, a whole polyphonic web by reading it not only forward, but also backward, or upside down, or in different rhythms and tempos. This was not merely unimaginative artifice. It represented the Gothic principle of building a whole cathedral out of small structural and ornamental nuclei in order to achieve an organic unity and, at the same time, enjoy the craftsman's feat in doing so.

Late Gothic polyphony reigned in Germany, shaped by Luther's Reformation. With the Protestant aim, to make the congregation as well as choir sing, the composer strove for simplicity by adapting Gregorian hymns and secular folk music. Luther had no reservations regarding the street song; he simply expunged the bawdy lyrics.

Fig. 3.7. The Enraged Musician. An engraving by Hogarth, 1741. A study in cacaphony. Print in the collection of the New York Public Library, New York

THE MADRIGAL

The madrigal was a short lyric poem of amatory and pastoral character set to music. It flourished during the sixteenth century and became the most popular musical art form of the secular Renaissance. The first madrigals were Italian, and they became so popular that serious church musicians could not avoid writing them. Among these musicians was the great composer Palestrina.

One of his madrigals, set to the words of Petrarch, began as follows:

> Nor did Diana ever please her lover
> So much as when through good fortune he saw her naked
> In the midst of cool waters.

As one can see from this fragment, the mood could be light-hearted. Often the poems described fantastic images of animals and birds: lamb, leopard, lizard, snake, falcon, peacock and swan, all symbols of men and women in pursuit of love. The music for these texts was usually in two or three voices. The style was ornamental and foreshadowed the Italian baroque of the seventeenth century. A French influence was evident in the polyrhythmic textures and in the simultaneous singing of different texts after the fashion of motets. Sometimes, the two or three stanzas of the poem would be sung by the different voices at the same time, giving a richer meaning to the piece. The texts were carefully declaimed, and the meaning was reflected in the music itself. The contrapuntal parts moved in a free and unrestricted way.

Fig. 3.8. The troubador. Woodcut entitled 'Carcel de Amor' by San Pedro (c. 1547).

Nowhere did the madrigal flourish as in Elizabethan England. The English had imported it from Italy, but soon an avalanche of delightful madrigals fell on English ears, all composed by the great English musicians of the day, among them Morley, Byrd and Gibbons. Morley in particular represents the pinnacle of madrigal art. His melodies were light, graceful and merry.

LASSUS AND PALESTRINA

In the madrigal, the Renaissance composers fused Flemish polyphony with Italian poetry and French chansons. This genre was ingenious in its construction, its mood was frequently joyful, and its ideas were worldly. However, as the sixteenth century advanced, the European composers were affected by the upheaval in the Catholic Church in the Netherlands, France and Italy, an upheaval called the Counter Reformation that lasted a century. Once again, the secular song encountered opposition. Two great musical figures contributed to the return from the earthly to the devout, from the lighthearted and amorous to the sombre and spiritual.

A Netherlander, Orlandus Lassus, wrote innumerable erotic chansons before he mended his ways and turned to the sentiments of the church. His output of some two hundred known compositions embraced every musical form of the century. The lovesick complaint of the Italian madrigal, the subtle delicacy of the French chanson, the robust sounds of the German part-song seemed to emerge from the heart of the genuine Italian, Frenchman and German. Lassus rose to majestic heights in his Psalms. He conveyed serenity and devotion in his Masses. He spoke with the voice of a mystic in his motets and madrigals. There is no one style in his music, as few pieces resemble each other. Nevertheless, they all reflect a mastery of the techniques of musical composition from the simple song form to the complicated polyphonic mass. In short, Lassus, the Dutchman, synthesized two hundred years of European musical history and culture.

The other great composer of the day was Palestrina. He served the church of the Counter Reformation. His patron was no less than the Pope, Julius III, to whom Palestrina dedicated a volume of masses and a collection of madrigals. When he died, in 1594, he was mourned in Rome as the Prince of Music. His became the model for church polyphony. With the possible exception of his collection of madrigals, Palestrina's whole output was sacred music. But even the madrigals had a spiritual tone. Meditation, awe, devoutness and elation permeated his works.

Fig. 3.9. Giovanni Pierluigi da Palestrina presenting his music to his patron, Pope Julius III.

THE BEGINNINGS OF BAROQUE

As the Renaissance faded, Italy reflected the changing times. Though the Counter Reformation stifled the secular substance of music, the form and splendor of its art continued to evolve. The faithful were lifted from quiet devotion into the world of the triumphant and opulent church. God was praised by a richly decked clergy surrounded by statues and paintings under the vaults of a mighty cathedral, before altars ornamented with gold and silver. The religious celebrations were accompanied by the resonant music of multiple choirs, orchestras and mighty organs. The ardor of religious struggle and fanaticism were mirrored in the baroque art and music of the day. In short, the baroque style has been likened to a mighty shout in praise of God.

The baroque artist frowned on the strict forms and the harmony of proportions because they were narrow, restrictive and coercive. The new and unfamiliar attracted him. The more astonishing and the more contrary to the accepted rules of art, the more he welcomed it. The early seventeenth century composer tried his chords and modulations on his keyboard instrument and shaped the most unfamiliar and even bizarre sounds.

Fig. 3.10. A chorus of the baroque.

The dramatic and monumental world of the early baroque is reflected in the tonal color of Gabrieli's multiple choirs, and in the large number of instruments in his orchestras. The emotional power and glow of this Venetian's music overshadowed even Palestrina's art

Secular and Religious Accompaniments 61

and influence. In his choral and instrumental writing, Gabrieli laid the foundation for the modern orchestra.

Fig. 3.11. A baroque scene, by Pieter Lastmann (c 1618). Music of warm sonority lifted the faithful into the world of the triumphant church.

STRINGED INSTRUMENTS

The early European multi-stringed instruments looked something like the ancient Greek lyre. Paintings of these instruments show a resonating soundbox that must have been added as a frame by early peoples to enhance its dynamic range. It was played by plucking the strings with the fingers or with a plectrum. Instruments of similar design can be seen in Egyptian wall paintings dating from 1500 B.C. The lyre evolved into the *rote* (or *rotta*) in Europe during the Middle Ages, and people began to play it with a bow. Once a fingerboard was added, so that the strings could be shortened or 'stopped' by pressing a finger on a string, the lute and bowed vielle began to emerge. The forerunner of the modern stringed instruments, the lute sported a long neck, and this became a distinguishing feature of the instrument. Some believe that a lute-like instrument first appeared much earlier together with the lyre, about 4000 years ago, and that one did not evolve from the other.

Whenever and however it originated, the lute was brought to Europe from the Middle East in the thirteenth century by the crusaders, and it flourished during the next three centuries. The Arab style of plucking with a plectrum was abandoned in favor of the fingers. The neck had fitted on it seven to ten gut frets to show the player where to stop the strings.

In India, the lute developed the broad-necked form seen on the modern sitar and its variants. Like the sitar, the Western viola d'amore has a series of stretched wires that vibrate in sympathy with those plucked. These wires lie under the fingerboard, which has no frets. The pegs to tighten these wires are generally above those of the bowed or plucked strings. The sound of the sympathetic strings lends a delicate silvery echo to the music. The viola d'amore is played by supporting it on the shoulder.

In the Renaissance and baroque periods, the *viola* was the generic Italian name for all stringed instruments that were bowed. There were two main classes: *viola da gamba*, held between the knees, and *viola da braccio*, played at the shoulder. These latter instruments are the prominent forerunners of the modern violin, viola, cello and bass.

These two new families of stringed instruments began to appear around 1530 in Italy. We can see them in the paintings of Ferrari of the 1530's. By 1556, Philibert Jambe de Fer was publishing quaint descriptions of the new instrument: the violin is very different from the (more familiar) treble viol. The body is smaller and flatter, and it sounds harsher (ruder). It was not played by gentleman merchants and other virtuous people, as was the viol. It was rather commonly used for dancing. On the other hand, the violin had positive features as well: it was easier to tune and was possible to hold while leading wedding processions or mummeries.

During the second half of the sixteenth century, the violin became a professional instrument and its principal repertoire was dance music, but little survives that was meant specifically for the violin. The earliest dances written for the instrument were performed at the French court around 1581. It is notable that the violin is sometimes mentioned as an alternative to the viol, as in Holborne, Morley, and Dowland. But it is a substantially different instrument: it has four strings tuned in fifths (rather than six strings, tuned in fourths and a third, like the modern guitar); it has a narrower, unfretted fingerboard, a more rounded back and shoulders, and f-shaped rather than c-shaped holes. Its pegbox is surmounted by a simple scroll instead of a carved gargoyle head. Bows are not simply accessories to the *da gamba* and *da braccio* instruments. Each bow served its own instrument and schools of bow-making slowly emerged. The violin bow is longer and lighter, and is held overhand. The sound of the violin is loud and shrill compared to the treble viol.

In Italy, the violin slowly made its way into more elevated company. We find it played at the Florentine court in 1589 to celebrate the wedding of Ferdinand de Medici to Christine of Lorraine. A *symfonia* by Marenzio, played at the wedding, included a *violino* along with lute, harp, and other strings. The Italians hastened to furnish the violin with an honorable pedigree. According to Bernardi (1581), it was invented by Orpheus and the muse, *Calliope*. Sappho of Lesbos designed the bow, which she fitted with horsehair, and she was the first to hold the violin on the upper arm (*da braccio*).

The true pedigree of the baroque violin shows a three-way fusion of the exalted *lira da braccio* with the renaissance fiddle (both having bodies with a 'waist') and the *rebec* (having a pear-shaped body that was held on the upper arm). It derives its strength and richness from its triple parentage. This baroque instrument is remarkably expressive, agile and sonorous, compared to the treble viol cousin.

By the seventeenth century, the violin had overcome all the doubts and prejudices against it, and it invaded every area of musical performance, church, chamber, and opera house. By Paganini's day, the solo repertoire had become prodigiously difficult, and the members of the violin family began to eclipse all other stringed instruments. The violin became the principal instrument of the symphony orchestra and the principal violinist became the concertmaster.

None of this would have been possible without the craftsmanship and artistry of the early violinmakers. Within a period of less than a hundred years, they brought this instrument to the peak of perfection, as we know it today. There were two great schools of violin makers, both in Italy: at Brescia, Gasparo de Salo and Paolo Maggini; at Cremona, Andrea Amati and his grandson Nicola, who died in 1684. Shortly thereafter, the greatest of all violinmakers flourished in Cremona, Antonio Stradivari. His craftsmanship became the model for all future violin making.

A member of another Cremona family of great violin makers was Giuseppe Antonio Guarneri (del Gesù). He was a peer of Stradivari and his violins are greatly prized today and frequently outsell Stradivari's.

The prominence in Western music of the modern string quartet rests on its special qualities, among them an expressiveness ranging from restrained lyricism to dramatic excitement, a rich timbre and resonance, a dynamic range from a crescendo unequalled in earlier stringed instruments to a whisper, and opportunity for varying performance with bow (ricochet to bouncing to *legato*), single and double stops, *pizzicato* and harmonics. The dynamic range and timbre can be broadened still further by fitting a mute on the bridge of the instrument. Tuning can be finely adjusted, the sound-post can be re-positioned for optimal sound, and the body of the instrument can be supported comfortably under the chin or resting on the floor. The hand-held end of the modern bow (derived from 'bow and arrow') has a screw arrangement to permit the performer to change the tension of the horsehair for optimal performance, and rosin is used to rub on the horsehair in order to increase the friction and provide a grip on the strings.

OPERA AND ORATORIO

As pointed out earlier, classical tragedy originated in the cult of Dionysus. When the sixteenth century humanists re-read the ancient authors, they re-discovered the theatre of antiquity. The musical element prominent in the Greek chorus was imitated: singers and accompanists were introduced into a new kind of drama. During the early baroque period, a musical recitative style developed that was capable of conveying delicate shades of feeling and deep emotion in the text. Poets and musicians began to collaborate on this new expressive style, and together they built it into a unified art form. This art form is called opera.

The first opera known to us in its entirety is *Euridice*. Written by Rinuccini for the marriage of Henry IV of France, with a musical setting by Peri and Caccini, it was the product of just such a collaboration between poet and musician. *Euridice* was first performed at the Pitti Palace in Florence in 1600. This and other early operas were well received, assuring a bright future for this new genre.

At first, the play was the thing; the music was secondary. Italian opera had to await a composer who would elevate melody and song to their proper place in the drama. Claudio Monteverdi was that composer. In his opera, *Orfeo*, the orchestral music was part of the action and helped to establish the mood on the stage. Monteverdi's last operas were musical and dramatic portrayals of profound and moving human emotions.

As the baroque age continued into the late seventeenth century, the musical stage grew in a remarkable way. There were 60 theaters in Bologna alone, not counting those in convents and colleges. In one year, in Venice, 350 different operas were performed in 16 theaters. The proportions of this operatic craze can be judged by the fact that all of Venice had a population of 150,000 in those days.

After Monteverdi, Allesandro Scarlatti became a leading spirit of early opera. At least one new opera by Scarlatti appeared every year. In his hands, the opera became more ample, the recitative was used to widen the field of action, the aria became a focal point in the drama, and the orchestral curtain raiser developed into the overture.

In seventeenth century France, opera flourished under the powerful and sinister court musician, Jean-Baptiste Lully. Of Florentine birth, he had the reputation as a master of intrigue in court. Though a schemer, a real estate dealer who amassed a fortune, and a Don Juan, he was a supreme musician and artist. Lully's operas, really lyric tragedies, differed from the Italian model in that they included ballet and choir, and prominent rhythmic elements frequently outweighed the melody. When they were prominent, Lully's melodic lines reflected the sound of the French language. Lully brought French opera to the height of a great art.

In England, opera flourished under Henry Purcell. He was really a church composer, though his dramatic gifts led him to the stage. He collaborated with Dryden on 'arrangements' of Shakespearean plays. In Purcell, however, the music is ornamental and incidental to the drama. Only one true opera was composed by Purcell,

Dido and Aeneas, a work in which the music dramatizes the action and creates a deep emotional atmosphere to the love story.

Fig. 3.12. A scene from Jean-Baptiste Lully's Alceste *performed in the Cour de Marbre at Versailles in 1674. Engraving by Jean Le Pautre.*

It is to Germany that we must turn for the beginnings of oratorio. In Germany at that time there was deep distress as a result of the Thirty Years War and its aftermath, and the people turned to religious music. The Protestant Reformation shaped this music. The congregations sang their chorales, which formed the basis for a new art. An example is *A mighty fortress is our God*. The music embellished the words of the Bible and the essence of Protestant thought. While opera flourished elsewhere, the cantata and oratorio became the great treasures of Protestant art.

For the German Protestants, the church was an asylum within which they found protection and solace. The solemn music gave them the hope of an existence in the hereafter. And when the music was not solemn, it was certainly imposing, as for example Handel's *Hallelujah Chorus*. In the small churches, amateur musicians were recruited from the congregation. Being faithful Lutherans, these people served not only because of their love of music but also because they believed that music served the glory of God and the benefit of the congregation.

In short, the religion of the German baroque found an outlet in the cantata and oratorio. As spiritual 'operas,' the texts dealt with religious themes. They were drawn from the *Passion of the Lord* and the *New Testament*. Heinrich Schutz was an early exponent of this genre. After studying with Gabrieli in Venice, Schutz returned to Germany to translate the Italian style into his native idiom. Though the spell of Italian music can be felt in his work, the roots of his music are in the German soil. At an advanced age, Schutz composed four settings of the *Passion* using the texts of the four Gospels. No instruments were used. Schutz renounced all the trappings of the ornamented Italian style. Even the recitatives were sung in the old unaccompanied way.

As opera and oratorio were developing as musical art forms, scientific pursuits were beginning to burgeon: in astronomy, physics, chemistry and medicine. Scientific discoveries in acoustics were beginning to affect the pursuit of music, and this will be the subject of our next inquiry.

Chapter 4

SCIENCE AND MUSIC

The age of baroque opera and oratorio was also the age of the great rationalists, the philosophers, astronomers, and physicians of the day. Among them were Descartes, Locke, Kepler, Newton, and Harvey. The duality of reason and emotion is reflected in many debates that took place during the seventeenth century. Some composers defended their compositions by scholarly argument and dissertation. However inspired their art, they felt that it would gain stature and acceptance if it could be explained and analyzed on a rational basis. The child of Pythagorean number, music must have struggled for equality with the newly emerging sciences, for to be classified as a science was to be accorded an intellectual rank, not just an emotional one.

At the same time, the scholars of the day became interested in the physical nature of music. Somewhat earlier, in the sixteenth century, Agrippa von Nettesheim had attempted to relate four-part vocal harmony to other quaternities of antiquity such as earth, air, fire, and water. Leibniz, one of the great philosopher-mathematicians of the period called music 'the unconscious arithmetic of the soul.' Kepler wrote about the 'harmony of the heavens.' Because of their differing velocities, Kepler believed that planets produce different sounds that combine into a celestial symphony.

70   *Sound and Music*

Other scholars tried to establish a rational basis for the musical scale and for harmony. Analogizing to the seven colors of the rainbow: red, orange, yellow, green. blue, indigo, and violet, Newton proposed seven primary tones in the musical scale. Borrowing from Pythagoras, Galileo showed how simple fractions of a stretched string produce different frequencies of sound and different intervals between tones. These examples illustrate the importance of number in the development of music.

Fig. 4.1 The seven liberal arts and sciences, recognized in the medieval system of education, have traditionally been represented allegorically by musical instruments. Here is an engraving of two, by Etienne Delaune, 1569. Arithmetic on the left and music on the right are depicted as young maidens surrounded by appropriate symbolic objects. Arithmetic plays the triangle amidst her writing table, rule, hourglass and tomes. Music plays the cymbals as accompaniment to her song and dance, with lutes and a flute, representing harmony and melody, lying about. The five other arts and sciences are grammar (trumpet), logic (cornett), rhetoric (tenor viol), geometry (mandora), astronomy (the bass shawm). These seven subjects, together with philosophy and metaphysics, comprised the 'gateway to wisdom.' Print from the collection of the New York Public Library, NY.

A music museum was established in Rome by Michel Todini, an early experimenter in acoustics and a builder of musical machines. The modern period of music, as a science as well as an art, had begun.

With the development of the new scientific tools of investigation, together with the logic of induction, the physical nature of sound could be studied in the laboratory. There was a new emphasis on observation and experimentation and this led to the replacement of traditional concepts, such as phlogiston and ether with oxygen and air particles. When this occurred, an understanding of the nature of sound and its transmission emerged. It is to these new concepts that we will soon turn our attention.

CLASSICISM AND ROMANTICISM

In our review of music in the Western world, we have noted a recurring shift between the spirit of reason and emotion. After the baroque period and to the present day, composers have alternated between periods of traditionalism and experimentation. The more traditional period is governed by reason and is characterized by stability, objectivity and balance. The experimental period is characterized by unrest, exaggeration, subjectivity, and by a flouting of the rules of musical structure.

A new age of reason, called Classicism, developed in the latter part of the eighteenth century. Its adherents derived their principles from the tradition of early Greek and Roman literature. The art of this era embodied formal elegance, simplicity, dignity, and correctness of order and style. In music, the rules of construction (the grammar) were set forth during the early baroque period by composers like Frescobaldi. Later, Handel and Bach elaborated these rules, and composers thereafter found themselves constrained to follow the rules slavishly. The age of classicism in music is considered to have reached its zenith when Haydn, Mozart, and especially Beethoven, of the Viennese School, perfected the musical forms of their day and invented new ways to exploit the rules.

Just as this new age of reason was flourishing in Austria, the anti-intellectual movement known as Romanticism began to appear in the literature of Rousseau and others. Its adherents reacted against the formalistic strictures of Classicism. They demanded a return to simplicity and naturalness, to primitive human instincts and powerful feelings. In music, Romanticism is characterized by greater freedom of form and style, by greater subjectivity and emotional appeal. Romantic music, however, is never formless; new forms appeared, of which the art song, the symphonic poem, and the music drama are examples. Composers of Romantic music contributed principally to the development of secular melodic line, lush harmony and orchestral color. Early Romanticists include Weber and Schubert, while Berlioz, Schumann, Mendelssohn, Brahms, Chopin, Wagner and Tchaikovsky are among those who represent the golden age of the Romantic movement. Late Romanticists include Mahler, Sibelius and Strauss.

Critics of romantic music focus on its tendency toward maudlin sentimentality, the 'saccharin' and the '*schmaltz.*' A reaction against these excesses of the Romantic movement gained impetus around the beginning of the twentieth century, particularly with the development of impressionism in the music of Debussy, and atonality in the music of Schoenberg. Much of the serious music of the twentieth century is neo-classical in spirit and represents a return to the age of reason. But the music of passionate Romanticism and stark Classicism seem to coexist at the present time.

Fig. 4.2 Daumier's lithograph, The Orchestra during the Performance of a Tragedy. One musician cannot help showing his sleepiness. The others around him seem to have already fallen asleep. After all, what else can they do as they wait for their cue to begin to play? Boredom in the Pit seems a more apt title for this caricature of foibles in the musical profession. I hope, dear reader, that your reading of this book does not elicit such a reaction. Print from the collection of the New York Public Library, New York.

Chapter 5

THE EVOLUTIONARY SIGNIFICANCE OF MUSIC

Most people find music emotionally appealing. These emotions range from joy to sorrow, from elation to despair, and from excitement to boredom. Whatever the emotion, there is an aesthetic pleasure in listening, in performing, and in composing music. A significant amount of time is spent by most members of our society listening to music, singing, and/or playing a musical instrument. The question is, why? What is the origin of these musical activities, and what do people derive from them?

Let us begin with the proposition that music has evolutionary significance in the life of the human. Darwin proposed that musical activity evolved from the vocalizations of monkeys and apes, which served as emotional signals between members of the group. These vocal-emotional signals have survival value to these animals. By applying the principle of the evolutionary continuity of species, Darwin concluded that musical-emotional signals must have survival value to the human species.

But Darwin's proposal can be challenged, primarily on the grounds that the sounds apes make have none of the properties of human music. The vocalizations of apes are principally hooting, barking and lip-smacking. They are emitted in relation to feeding, courtship and mating, danger, satisfaction, and excitement in general. They seem to be involuntary or semi-voluntary patterns of behavior, for the most part like human laughing, crying, screaming, gasping, coughing, sneezing and exclaiming. The natural, unlearned calls of the chimpanzee express feelings more than they convey information. Though not in the service of the intellect, ape vocalizations have survival value. They alert members of the group to danger, and frighten the predator. They invite interaction with others. They call attention to themselves and to members of the opposite sex and same sex. So far we are with Darwin.

But ape vocalizations are not based on a pool of defined pitches or on the rhythmic patterns that are so characteristic of human music. There is no sequencing of intervals as in a melodic line. There is no sustained rhythm. And the vocalizations are largely unplanned and unshaped by past experience, as far as we can tell. Apes have never been observed to play with sounds as human babies do when they babble. Occasionally you do hear the chimpanzee beat out a tattoo with his knuckles, and he may even move his head back and forth during the tattoo, but no regular rhythm can be identified. Nor will the chimpanzee respond to the strains of human music. Harlow and other primatologists have observed rhesus monkeys rock rhythmically, but these are frequently abnormal responses of fear and pain of monkeys deprived of mother and peers.

So how do we derive human music from ape vocalizations? Since the natural vocal communications between higher primates seem to be so primitive, attempts have been made to teach apes to speak in some human fashion. All these efforts have ended in failure. The ape cannot acquire any reasonable repertoire of vocal sounds upon which a vocal language must be based. Nor does the ape possess a brain that is able to elaborate its inputs into the complexities and subtleties of a vocal language. Though it is now clear that chimpanzees and gorillas are capable of acquiring the elements of a manual sign language, the essence of music (the variations of pitch and a sustained rhythm) is missing from such a language. At best, the ape can learn to sign the names of objects and verb commands such as 'open' by widening the distance between the hands. Furthermore, apes have never been observed to develop any kind of language spontaneously, without special tutoring by humans, just by hearing or seeing instances of it. Unlike the remarkable facility shown by human children of barely two and three years of age in acquiring speech, apes of comparable age seem to be disappointingly dense, and require laborious tutoring to achieve the basic elements of language. Whatever the final verdict on ape manual communication, the basis for any kind of musical activity seems to be lacking in these animals.

Perhaps man's earliest music was in the nature of love songs, songs that evolved from the sounds made by apes during courtship. But no ape has ever been observed to serenade his prospective mate vocally with anything more than a hoot and a bark, and perhaps lip-smacking. Nothing the ape utters in his serenade to the opposite sex has the temporal and hierarchical organization, the sequencing and patterning, of human song. The human has a propensity to create organized vocal patterns, and this has overshadowed and outstripped every type of vocalization the human might have inherited from his non-human ancestors.

Evolutionary theory implies a continuity from some proto-typic ape to man. But there seems to be a clearcut discontinuity between the highest vocal and manual achievements of present-day apes and what every normal human being can do as a matter of routine. It is true that modern apes and humans might have had a common ancestor, now extinct, who might have engaged in primitive musical activities that were dropped by the ape-like descendants like the chimpanzee but retained by *Homo sapiens*. But that seems unlikely. Many of us now believe that Darwin's guess that human music evolved from the vocalizations of apes is wrong. A limited number of mutations can hardly transform an ape-like creature with not a single song in its heart into a human being possessing a vocal repertoire of sounds that is bursting to be heard.

To judge from the songs of the Aborigines, fertility is celebrated in song and dance, not as the expression of individuals but as members of a group. Many other calls are used by members of the group, to locate one another, to indicate emotional and motivational states, and to excite the group members to attack. Man's earliest vocalizations must have served practical purposes and were not emitted for the sheer pleasure of it. It is the evolution of human behavior to engage in musical activity for the sheer pleasure of it that is so intriguing.

Though ape vocalizations might have evolved into human language over eons, the human propensity to engage in musical activities cannot be so derived. We are still left with the question: in what way is man better able to adapt to his environment with the aid of music and increase his chances for survival? And, why would any set of mutations favoring musical activity be selected for transmission to human offspring? Language is a practical skill. Its survival value is obvious. But what about music?

Does the human need music, to listen to it and perform it, any more than he needs painting or sculpture? If he does, then deprivation should harm him in some way. We know, for instance, that light is essential for the normal development of the visual system. Light deprivation causes physical degeneration in the retina and psychological ill effects. On this score, musical stimulation is obviously very different from light stimulation. It seems not at all unlikely that people could go without listening to music for unlimited periods without any apparent ill effects. Should we then conclude that humans have no biological need for music? Consider an analogy: people can go without sex for unlimited periods without suffering obvious personal harm. Yet we would not conclude that humans have no need for sex. Musical activity may be like sexual activity in this respect, essential for the survival of the species but unnecessary for the survival of the individual.

Nevertheless, it is difficult to imagine why a culture such as ours could not survive without music. Though a lack of music might not be harmful to us today, it might have been harmful among primitive people. Perhaps modern societies have outgrown the biological need for music.

For non-literate people, music might have had distinct survival value. Before the development of writing, music provided a mnemonic framework for the storage of knowledge, information, and events. With the aid of songs and poems, rhythmic gesture and dance, non-literate people might have been able to form a repository of knowledge. The epics, myths and tales of the ancient world were thus codified in an oral tradition. Such ritualized sequences of behavior are easier to remember than those now recorded in books. Perhaps these primitive mnemonic devices evolved into song and dance, as we know them today.

When, in the course of evolution, humans lost the claws that grasp and teeth that tear prey, they also lost their ability to protect themselves against predators. Now vulnerable physically to the vagaries of the environment, the individual had to seek protection by using his wits and by cooperating with his neighbor. Any activity that fostered group cohesiveness was likely to have survival value. Humans hunted together, ate and drank together, fought together, loved together, prayed together and, above all, spoke to each other of their common experiences. The women who bore the children were periodically helpless and could not easily survive as individuals without mutual support. Their men-folk assisted and protected them from danger, and they made themselves attractive for them. Music and dance may have accompanied the rites of childbirth. Humans drank together, became intoxicated, and were lifted to a trance-like state. These Dionysian rites were celebrated in song and dance. All of these activities fostered the binding of individuals into a cohesive group.

Any time teamwork was required, music swept men into cooperative action. Voices were raised together. The Roman oarsmen of the ancient world chanted in rhythm to synchronize their movements. Battle cries and marches synchronized the behavior of the tribe in their struggle to survive. Voices were raised together in supplication, to appease the Gods or to praise or otherwise worship the one God of Abraham. David celebrated music:

> Sing joyfully to the Lord, all you lands;
>   break into song; sing praise
> Sing praise to the Lord with the harp,
>   with the harp and melodious song.
> With trumpets and the sound of the horn
>   sing joyfully before the king, the Lord.
>
> Let the sea and what fills it resound,
>   the world and those who dwell in it;
> Let the rivers clap their hands,
>   the mountains shout with them for joy
> Before the Lord, for he comes,
>   for he comes to rule the earth;
> He will rule the world with justice
>   and the peoples with equity.
>
> *Psalm 98, 4-9*

A common history developed. It was recited and cherished as a common heritage that united the group. But without the written word, how would this heritage be preserved and passed on from generation to generation? The primitive human needed a medium through which to store this common heritage. Language served as the medium, but the details of events could easily be forgotten. How could the ancestral tales be best preserved? Primitive people used rhythm and rhyme, pitch and prosody as mnemonic devices to retain what they might otherwise forget. Blind Homer sang his poems and a great civilization developed around his epic tales of Gods and heroes. The lines of the great Greek tragedies were sung and the chorus chanted and mimed the action in dance. So was group cohesiveness fostered.

With the development of the written word, the mnemonic trappings that were so effective in preserving the history of the group were no longer required. Books would now serve to preserve the common heritage. Music, that supreme mnemonic, might have faded away were it not for the fact that the evolutionary adaptations around group cohesiveness had taken hold. Musical activity developed into an experience in its own right, functionally autonomous from its earlier associations, with its own rules and prescriptions, serving both the individual and the group in the pursuit of everyday affairs. Music as we know it slowly evolved. The modulation of timing in the movement of bodies and vocal chords created sustained rhythm and the modulation of the pitch of vocalizations created the melodic line.

Physical survival is one thing. But there is also the need for psychological well being--tranquillity, stirred emotion, self-fulfillment, self-esteem, enjoyment and pleasure. Anything that promotes these feelings is likely to have survival value. In the course of history, music became the great pastime for enjoyment. It aroused the emotions and calmed the troubled spirit.

The sounds of nature were preserved through song. The storm, the brook, the animal and the bird, all were mimicked in the sounds of the voice, the lyre and the pipe. Performers were honored and talents were fostered. No longer required for intellectual discourse, music serves as an outlet for emotional expression.

Perhaps in the future, the individual rhythms exemplified by heart rate and respiration rate will be supplemented by cooperative or complementary rhythms without which we will not survive in a world of instant death. All peoples, singers, players, dancers, will have to work together for the common good of humanity, toward a common rhythm and melody. What if the political leaders of the world were required to perform a Beethoven quartet before a summit meeting could take place?

PART B.
THE DIMENSIONS OF AUDITORY PERCEPTION

Chapter 6

SOUND WAVES

We learn a great deal about our environment by listening to the sounds around us. Many objects emit sounds. Out in the country, there are the sounds of nature, the rustling of leaves, the rippling of water in the brook, the howling of the wind, the roar of the surf, the chirping of birds, the galloping of horses, etc. In the city, there are the sounds of industry and household, the din of traffic in the street, the rumble of the subway below, the roar of jet engines overhead, the drone of the power mower, the drip of the water faucet, the music on the radio, the snore of our neighbor, etc. Above all, there are the sounds of speech, made by the human voice, that enable us to communicate with one another when we are face-to-face or on the telephone. What do all of these sounds have in common?

    All sources of sound vibrate. This vibratory motion causes the air particles that surround the sound source to vibrate, and those air vibrations that reach our ears impart vibratory motion to our eardrums. Finally, this vibratory motion is transmitted to the auditory mechanism in the peripheral organ of hearing, the cochlea, which activates the acoustic nerves and brain to give us the experience of hearing. It is the

82   *Sound and Music*

physical basis of sound that concerns us here, the vibratory activity and its transmission to our ears.

VIBRATION

Sound is generated by causing an elastic body to vibrate. The vibrating body may be solid like a stretched violin string or a tuning fork, or it may be gaseous like a column of air in an organ pipe. The only requirement is that the body be elastic, so that it continue its back and forth movement after it has been set in motion. Because of their differences in elasticity, a block of concrete is harder to set in vibratory motion compared to the prongs of a tuning fork.

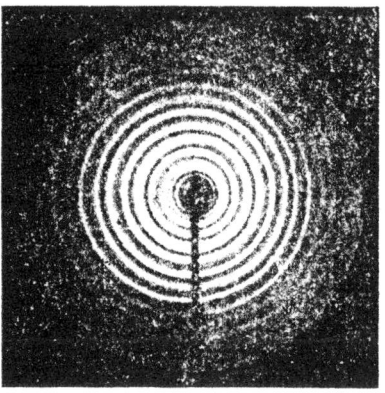

Figure 6.1. Expanding concentric waves. A pebble dropped into a pool of mercury creates a disturbance of ripples that moves in expanding concentric circles. These ripples travel along the surface and look like sine waves in cross-section. However, the mercury particles themselves move up and down, at right angles to the direction of propagation of the ripples.

Consider the ripples that move in ever-expanding concentric circles when a pebble is dropped into a pool of still water. Like the pebble, a sound source creates a disturbance of ripples in the air, which travels outwards. But unlike the waves of water, which travel only on the surface, sound waves travel in all directions at once. Also, unlike the pebble-in-water analogy, air particles move back and forth, and not as water molecules flow in one direction in a stream. If tagged (or colored with a dye) so that they can be observed, air particles at the sound source are seen to impart motion to nearby air particles, and these, in turn, are seen to impart motion to those near them, and so on. Nearly everyone has seen a long line of closely spaced dominoes standing on end collapse, one after the other, when the first domino is made to fall against the second. This disturbance does not result in any substantial displacement of dominoes from their original position. A similar motion occurs when a person at the end of a line of tightly packed people gives the person next to him a shove and this person is pushed into the person next to him down the line, and so on. Imagine this motion travelling from person to person to the head of the line without anyone actually taking a single step. When sound is transmitted through air, the movement of air molecules creates a local disturbance. This disturbance, best described as a wave of compressions and rarefactions of air molecules, is transmitted away from the sound source in all directions.

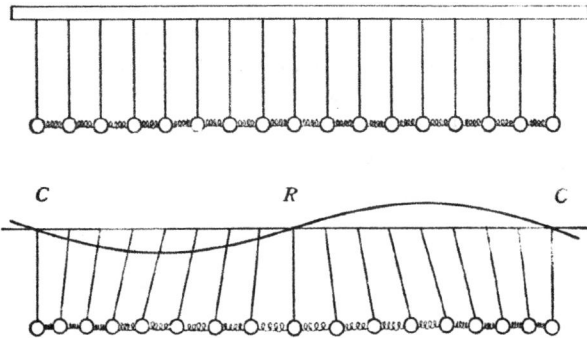

Fig. 6.2. Longitudinal waves. The arrangement of heavy balls, connected linearly by springs, illustrates longitudinal waves, which consist of to-and-fro displacements. If we strike the first ball, the remaining balls will alternately bunch together and spread apart, producing regions of compressions (C) and rarefactions (R). Air particles vibrate in this manner. If we plot the degree of displacement of each ball along the ordinate (plotting each displacement to the left in the downward direction, and each displacement to the right in the upward direction), we end up with a curve of sine wave motion. In the case of air particles, the disturbance created by sound travels, not just in one direction, but in all directions at the same time.

Vibrations of a solid body like a stretched string involve repetitive movements of the body from its resting position to displacements on either side. Its momentum would keep it moving back and forth indefinitely, were it not for friction, which progressively dampens the successive displacements so that they finally die out. The very same events take place in a gas, like a column of air in a pipe, when it is set in vibratory motion.

Once they have been generated, sound waves travel from the vibrating body to the ears of the listener. The eardrum, too, is an elastic body and it can be set in motion by the vibrations of the acoustic medium which, in our case, is usually air. Since we are land dwellers, our ears are bombarded with fluctuations in air pressure produced by vibrating bodies. If these fluctuations are periodic or regular in some way, we perceive musical sounds including speech; if aperiodic or irregular, we tend to perceive noises.

A comparison of the two sine waves, shown below in Fig. 6.3, reveals that the upper one has a longer wavelength, and a larger amplitude, than the lower one.

We can make a metal strip, fastened at one end, to vibrate by plucking it at the free end. This is how a Jew's harp is played. The motion of the metal strip, back and forth, is responsible for the twang that we hear.

With the metal strip as our model, we can consider wave motion more closely. Each train of regular waves has two attributes, frequency and amplitude. Let us begin with one position of the vibrating metal strip, say the original position of rest; one back-and-forth-movement and back to the original position, is called a cycle. It is important to note that each cycle consists of a double vibration: a displacement to one side of the resting position and back, followed by a displacement to the other side of the resting position and back. The length of the cycle is its wavelength (measured in feet or meters), and the number of these cycles, executed in one second, is the frequency. For example, 200 cycles per second (cps), also referred to as 200 *Hertz* (*Hz*), means that 200 double vibrations can be counted in each second. The maximum extent of displacement from the position of rest is called the amplitude (usually measured in millimeters).

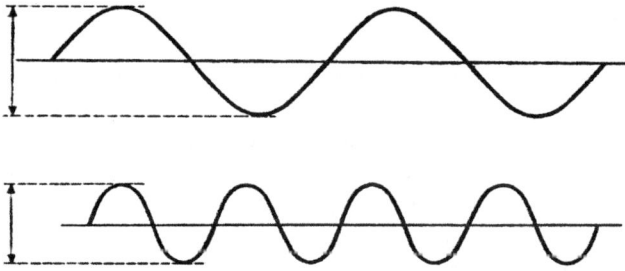

Fig. 6.3. When one end of a metal strip is held in a vise and the projecting end is made to vibrate, the strip will produce a tone of a certain frequency. The pitch of the tone will vary with the length of the metal strip: the longer it is, the lower will be its frequency (upper wave), and vice versa (lower wave). Its loudness will vary with the force applied and the amplitude of its vibrations. Like a vibrating column of air in an organ pipe closed at one end, the vibrations will include the odd multiples of the fundamental frequency. Such metal strips of varying length and thickness are used to produce tones in instruments like the harmonica and the Jew's harp.

The velocity of sound in air (1128 feet per second, on the average) is equal to the product of wavelength and frequency. This means that there is an inverse relationship between frequency and wavelength: the greater the frequency, the shorter the wavelength, and vice versa. If we assume that the range of audible frequencies is 20 to 20,000 *Hz*, a calculation reveals that the wavelengths of audible sound in air vary from about 15 to 0.015 meters. These wavelengths are extremely long compared to the wavelengths of light that range up to no more than 750 billionths of a meter. Because the wavelengths of low tones are so long, many components of musical sound can travel around corners, whereas light waves cannot.

Instead of a metal strip, suppose that we use a tuning fork that vibrates at a particular frequency when struck. If we attach a stylus to the end of one prong, and position the vibrating tuning fork so that the point of the stylus touches a moving sheet of paper, the stylus would trace a s mooth and regular wave pattern on the paper. This waveform is called a sine wave, and it is the simplest form of sound wave. It has all its energy concentrated at just one frequency. Sinusoidal vibrations can be produced by simple mechanical systems and they are perceived as pure tones.

Fig. 6.4 shows a vibrating body producing compressions and rarefactions of air particles. This can be represented as a sine wave. Also shown is what happens to the sine wave when the vibrating body is struck harder (the amplitude increases) and when it is shortened (the wavelength decreases and the frequency increases).

This figure illustrates a waveform, as the stylus might trace it, after the prongs of the tuning fork are struck with a moderate degree of force. Note the amplitude of the waveform, which is the maximum displacement from a resting position (or the maximum pressure produced by displacement of air particles). If struck with a greater degree of force, the extent of displacement of the free end of the prong would increase and the waveform traced on the moving paper would have greater amplitude. Under these circumstances, we would say that the intensity of the sound increased, not its frequency. In general, the greater the amplitude of vibration, the louder the sound appears to be. Conversely, as the amplitude diminishes, the softer the sound becomes. It is customary to treat amplitude as a physical dimension of the sound stimulus, and loudness as its perceptual counterpart. The relationship between amplitude (or intensity) and loudness is discussed in Chapter 8.

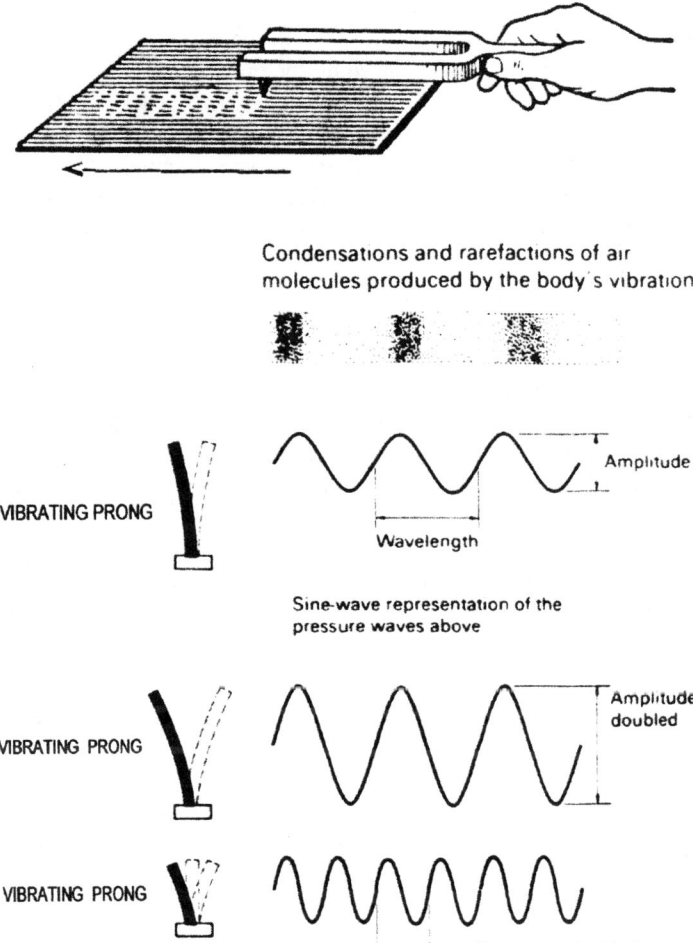

Fig. 6.4. *A tuning fork is similar to a vibrating metal strip, except that it has two prongs and is made with precision. When adjusting the pitch of the tuning fork, the effective length of the prongs may be increased by filing the yoke between the prongs or by changing the mass of the prongs. If provided with a stylus on one prong and the tuning fork is struck, the stylus will trace the sine wave motion of the prong on a moving sheet of paper.*

If the prong of the tuning fork were shortened and then struck with the same force, the vibrations would be more rapid; that is, more waves per second would be traced on the moving paper, and we would say that the frequency of the sound increased (not its amplitude). In general, the greater the frequency of vibration, the higher the perceived pitch of the sound. It is customary to treat frequency as another physical dimension of the stimulus and pitch as its perceptual counterpart. The relationship between frequency (or wavelength) and pitch is discussed in Chapter 7.

It is important to note that the pitch is generally unaltered by changing the force with which the prongs of the tuning fork are set in motion. The pianist expects to produce a tone of a particular pitch by depressing a particular key regardless of whether he plays pianissimo or fortissimo. Moreover, he expects that the pitch of the piano tone will not drop as the music fades away. Later on we will re-examine these simple relationships, between amplitude and loudness on the one hand, and between frequency and pitch on the other. For the fact is that amplitude does affect pitch to a limited degree, and frequency does affect loudness. Unfortunately, this complicates the relationships between physical and perceptual dimensions that were formerly thought to be one-to-one.

MUSICAL INTERVALS AND THE RATIO OF SMALL WHOLE NUMBERS

Given two tones with frequencies f_1 and f_2, their ratio, f_1/f_2, defines the distance between them, or the musical interval. For example, if the two frequencies are 300 *Hz* and 200 *Hz*, their ratio, 3/2, defines their musical interval. Whenever the ratio of frequencies is 3/2, the musical interval is a 'fifth,' as we shall see.

Let us begin our discussion of musical intervals with the stretched string. Here is an interesting example of an elastic body that vibrates to produce a musical sound. If the middle of a violin string is plucked (or bowed), each point along the string will make a back-and-forth movement with maximum displacement around the middle. If a tiny stylus is attached to the middle of the string, its point touching a moving sheet of paper, a waveform would be traced that is more jagged than that traced by the tuning fork. This is because the string vibrates not only as a whole, but also in parts (see Fig. 6.7). The resulting pitch is richer or more colorful than that produced by the tuning fork. We refer to this difference as one of timbre or tonal quality.

The specific pitch produced by the vibrating string depends on three variables: its mass, tension and length. Since the mass is fixed by its diameter and cannot be varied, and the tension remains constant once the string is tuned, it is only by varying the length of the string that the performer can vary the pitch of the tones sounded during actual performance. By pressing the string with the fingers of the left hand, he effectively shortens it.

Thus the frequency of vibration of a stretched string, and hence the pitch, is inversely proportional to the vibrating length. If L is the length of a string, and its frequency is f, shortening the string to 1/2L doubles the frequency to 2f and raises the pitch one octave (e.g. C to c; 262/524); shortening the string to 2/3L increases the frequency to 3/2f and raises the pitch the interval of a fifth (e.g. C to g; 262/393); and shortening the string to 3/4L increases the frequency to 4/3f and raises the pitch the interval of a fourth (e.g. C to f; 262/349). Notice that the ratios that produce the intervals of octave, fifth, and fourth consist of small whole numbers, 2/1, 3/2, 4/3, etc. These intervals are called the Pythagorean consonances: pleasant-sounding when the two pitches are sounded together.

Length of String in inches	Frequency in Hz	Pitch Name
13	200	G_1
1/2(13)= 6.5	2(200)=400	G
2/3(13)= 8.7	3/2(200)=300	D
3/4(13)= 9.8	4/3(200)=267	C
4/5(13)=10.4	5/4(200)=250	B
5/6(13)=10.8	6/5(200)=240	Bb

90 Sound and Music

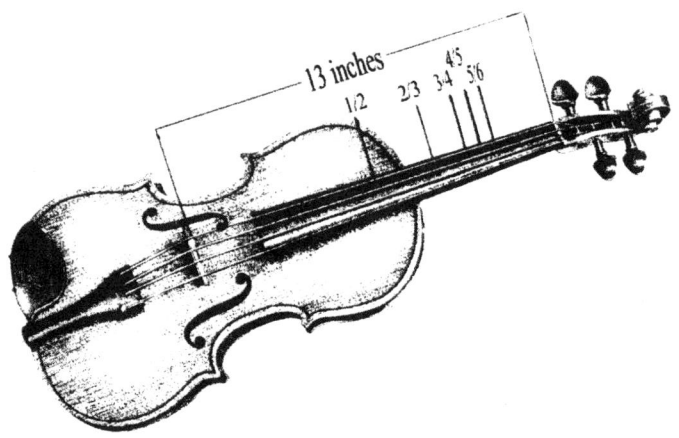

Fig. 6.5. Effects on pitch of stopping a string of the violin. The lowest string, the G string, is tuned to vibrate with a frequency of about 200 Hz. To raise the pitch of this string, the violinist presses on it with a finger of his left hand, thus reducing its vibrating length. Shortening the string to a fraction of its normal length, which is about 13 inches, raises the frequency by the inverse of that fraction. For example, halving the length of the string doubles the frequency, and the resulting tone sounds an octave higher. Shown in the figure are reductions to 1/2, 2/3, 3/4, 4/5, and 5/6 of 13 inches, resulting in pitches of G, D, C, B, and Bb. See the table above.

The same principles apply to the sounds of a siren. Let us direct a stream of air at an obstructing disk that has a series of holes all around its peripheral edge through which the air can blow. Suppose the disk has 11 equidistant holes, and we rotate the disk 40 times per second. This produces 440 air puffs per second (or a frequency of 440 Hz), and the listener hears the tone A above middle-C. Doubling the rotation rate to 80 rps doubles the frequency of air puffs to 880 and produces an A tone one octave higher. Increasing the rotation rate by one-half, to 60 rps, increases the frequency by one-half (660 *Hz*) and a fifth higher is heard (660/440 = 3/2, E above A). Similarly, increasing the rotation rate by one-third, to 53.3 rps, increases the frequency by one-third (586.7 *Hz*) and a fourth higher is heard (586.7/440 = 4/3, D above A).

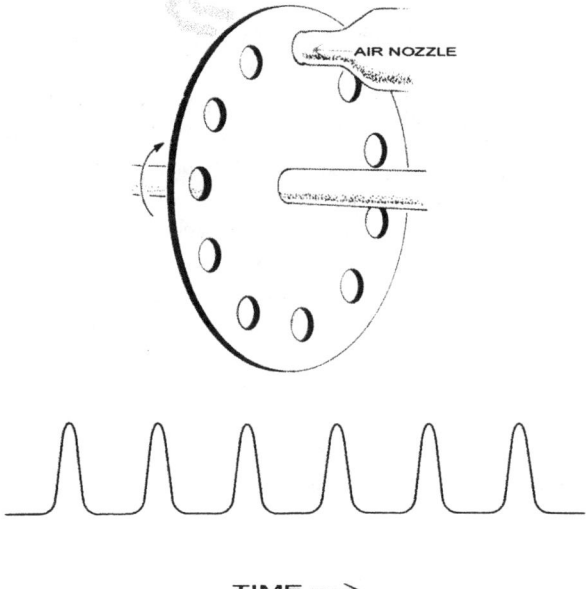

Fig. 6.6. The mechanism of a simple siren. A stream of air from a nozzle is directed toward the rotating disk and puffs of air pass through the successive holes. These puffs actually constitute periodic vibrations of the air, and the number of puffs per second determines the pitch of the siren. This disk has 11 holes. If it revolves 40 times per second, it will produce 440 puffs per second, and this is responsible for a pitch of the A above middle C. The waves produced by the periodic puffs are shown below.

We have already seen that the vibrating prongs of a tuning fork trace a smooth and regular waveform called a *sine wave*. A taut string or air column in a pipe made to vibrate is sometimes also described as producing a sine wave. But this is inaccurate. The truth is that no acoustic instrument of any sort (with the possible exception of the tuning fork) produces a tone consisting of just *one* frequency. All musical instruments produce complex tones consisting of many constituent sine waves or pure tones, called harmonics. The composition of a violin tone is examined in Fig. 6.7 below. The lowest frequency of a complex tone is called the *fundamental* tone, or first harmonic. It is the fundamental that determines the name of the tone because it is usually more intense than the other harmonics and is clearly heard. The frequencies of the upper harmonics are exact multiples of the frequency of the fundamental. Thus, if the frequency of the fundamental is f, the upper harmonics have frequencies of 2f, 3f, 4f, and so on. The number and relative intensity of these harmonics determine the timbre or tonal quality of each tone. It is true that a tuning fork, when properly bowed, vibrates with simple harmonic motion and produces a pure tone. But if the tuning fork is struck a blow with a hammer, the result is no longer a pure tone, but rather a clang which has a complex waveform. Those harmonics that are audible greatly affect the timbre or tonal quality of the sound. Musical instruments that generate a larger number of audible harmonics generally produce sounds that are richer and more complex. For this reason, the tone of a violin sounds richer than the same tone produced by a tuning fork.

A word on terminology: the harmonics above the fundamental are also called *overtones*. The first overtone is the second harmonic, the second overtone is the third harmonic, etc. Another term for harmonics that you may encounter is *partials*. However, partials also include non-harmonic overtones (overtones that are not related to each other in the ratio of small whole numbers) like those that occur in the sound of gongs and in other complex and non-periodic sounds called noises.

The physical basis of harmonics is that a vibrating body, such as a string or column of air, vibrates simultaneously as a whole and in sections of 1/2, 1/3, 1/4, etc. of its length. These secondary vibrations usually have a smaller amplitude, and the tones they produce are correspondingly less loud. The upper harmonics fuse so well with the fundamental tone as to produce the impression of a single tone. Nevertheless, it is the presence and pattern of harmonics that determines the timbre, or color, of this tone. Though they produce tones that match in frequency and amplitude, the violin's tone sounds different from the oboe's because their harmonic structures are different.

Sound Waves 93

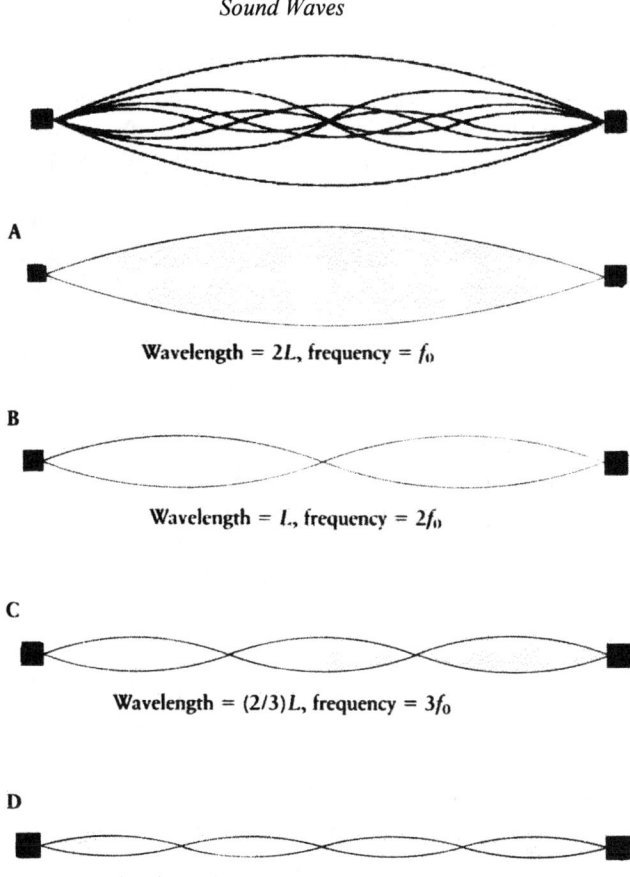

Fig. 6.7. The multiple vibrations of a stretched string. If L is the length of a stretched string, then its wavelength is 2L, and its fundamental frequency is proportional to the inverse of the wavelength. However, plucking a stretched string causes it also to vibrate in a number of frequency multiples, called harmonics. This composite vibratory pattern is shown at the top. A, B, C and D are derived from the top vibratory pattern. A illustrates the fundamental wave. B, C, and D, illustrate the second, third, and fourth harmonics, having frequencies two, three, and four times the fundamental frequency. These are the first four harmonics of the string.

Now, let us turn our attention to the musical pipe. Anyone who has ever blown across the top of a soda bottle knows that it is possible to excite the air enclosed in the bottle so that it will vibrate and emit a particular pitch. If you have done this, you know that the bottle stops sounding the moment you stop blowing, in contrast to the string whose vibrations decay slowly. Also, you know that the larger the bottle, the lower the pitch of the sound. A series of bottles, selected for their size, can actually sound all the notes of the scale.

In organ pipes and other wind instruments, an enclosed air column is made to vibrate in a direction parallel to the length of the pipe. The density of air particles in a vibrating column of air varies from compressions to rarefactions. This was illustrated in Fig. 6.4. The frequency of vibration of the air column is determined by the time it takes a sound wave to travel from one end of the pipe to the other. Thus, varying the length of the pipe will vary the frequency of vibration of the air column. The longer the pipe, the lower the frequency, and vice versa. Like a stretched string, an air column in a pipe vibrates not only as a whole but also in parts, thus producing harmonics. This requires some explanation.

There are two types of organ pipes, those open at the top and those that have the top closed. The bottom end of the pipe is always open. The lowest note, which corresponds to the longest wavelength that the pipe is capable of producing, is the fundamental.

In a pipe open at both ends, the region of greatest concentration of air particles, called a node (N), is at the middle. The region of greatest rarefaction is at the two loops (L), one at each end. In Fig. 6.8(a), you can see that the open pipe encompasses just one-half of the wavelength of its fundamental tone (one-half of a double vibration). This means that the wavelength of the fundamental tone is twice the length of the pipe. In addition to the fundamental, the air column may break into waves having two nodes between the loops at the two ends. This is clearly the second harmonic because its frequency is twice that of the fundamental (Fig. 6.8(b)). Similarly, the same pipe may generate a frequency that is three times the fundamental, making it the third harmonic (Fig. 6.8(c)). In general, open pipes can generate all the harmonics, those that are even, as well as those that are odd, all multiples of the fundamental (twice the fundamental, three times the fundamental, four times the fundamental, etc.).

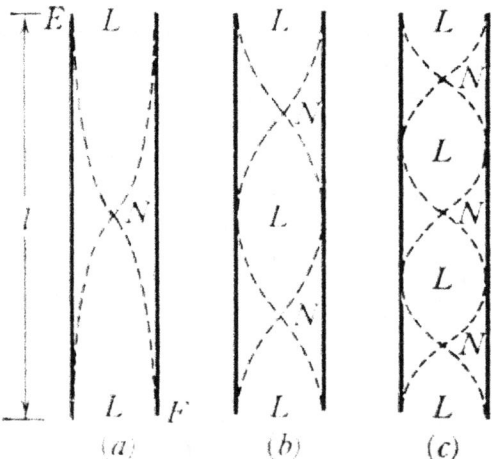

Fig. 6.8. In an open organ pipe (a), there is always a loop (L) at each end and a node (N) in the middle. The wavelength of the fundamental frequency is thus twice the length of the pipe (2l), and the fundamental frequency is proportional to the inverse of the wavelength. Even as this is going on, the air column also breaks into upper harmonics that have extra nodes. Shown in (b) and (c) are the second and third harmonics that have two and three nodes, respectively, and emit frequencies two and three times that of the fundamental frequency. Compared to the organ pipe closed at one end, shown in Fig. 6.9, the even as well as the odd harmonics are present.

In a pipe closed at one end, such as the flute in its lowest register, the region of greatest compression of air particles (the node, N,) is at the closed end, while the region of greatest rarefaction (the loop, L) is at the opposite or open end. The wavelength of the fundamental of such a pipe is four times its length, as you can see in Fig. 6.9(a). Thus, the fundamental frequency of a pipe closed at one end is always one-half that of the pipe of the same length open at both ends. The air column in a closed pipe can also vibrate in parts. In Fig. 6.9(b), you see pictured the next harmonic. In this case, the pipe contains three-quarters of the wavelength of this harmonic. Its frequency is three times the fundamental, which makes it the third harmonic. In Fig. 6.9(c), you see pictured the harmonic after that.

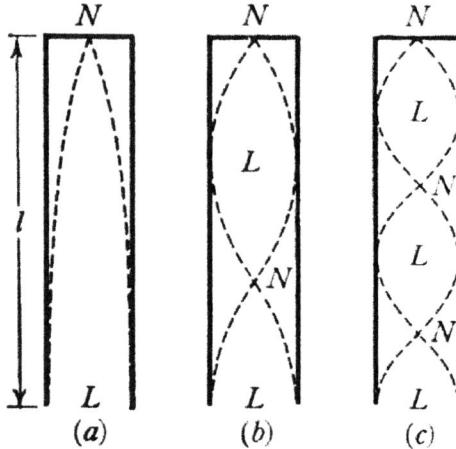

Fig. 6.9. In an organ pipe closed at one end (a), there is always a node (N) at the closed end and a loop (L) at the open end. Hence, the wavelength of the fundamental will be four times the length of the pipe (4l), and the fundamental frequency will be proportional to the inverse of the wavelength. The air column will also vibrate with extra nodes. Shown in (b) and (c) are the third and the fifth harmonics that have two and three nodes, respectively, and emit frequencies three and five times the fundamental. Since there is always a node at the closed end, this organ pipe can only produce odd-numbered harmonics. In each of the cases illustrated, there is an integral number of quarter wavelengths, but only the odd numbers of quarter wavelengths, 1, 3, 5, etc., are possible.

Here, the pipe contains *five* quarters of the wavelength of this harmonic. Its frequency is five times the fundamental, which makes it the fifth harmonic. Notice that the second and fourth harmonics are missing. This should convince you that, while the pipe open at both ends emits both odd and even harmonics, the pipe closed at one end emits only the odd harmonics. Since there is always a node at one end of this pipe and a loop at the other end, only the odd harmonics are possible.

The selection of particular pipes for the organ depends on the fact that the frequency of the fundamental of the closed organ pipe is always one-half that of the open one of the same length. An open eight-foot organ pipe has a frequency of about 70 *Hz*, roughly two octaves below middle C. A sixteen-foot open pipe, or an eight-foot pipe closed at one end, sounds one octave lower. In actual organs, pipes of different lengths, some open and some closed, are used to produce the required frequencies and tonal qualities. Closed organ pipes have a more hollow sound because only odd harmonics are present. Open organ pipes have a fuller sound because they include both even and odd harmonics. Any musical instruments that have vibrating bodies attached at one end, or consist of a pipe closed at one end, cannot generate the even harmonics, and this has audible effects on their tonal qualities.

COMPARISONS OF SOUND AND LIGHT

Physical and Perceptual Dimensions. From the time of Helmholtz until recently, the relationships between the physical dimensions of sound and light, on the one hand, and their perceptual counterparts, on the other, have been summarized as follows:

Tone Perception	Physical Dimensions of Sound or Light Waves	Color Perception
Pitch	Frequency or Wavelength	Hue
Loudness	Amplitude (Intensity)	Brightness
Timbre	Complexity	Saturation

In this table, the perceptual attributes of pitch, loudness and timbre (as well as hue, brightness and saturation) are unidimensional variables, each related to one, and only one, physical dimension. According to this conception, musical experiences are based on the sensations of pitch, loudness, and timbre, not on the physical dimensions of frequency, intensity, and complexity. Physicists measure the frequency, but the listener perceives pitch. Physicists measure intensity, but the listener perceives loudness. Physicists analyze the complex tone into its harmonic components, but the listener perceives the timbre or tonal quality.

We know today that the relationships between the three perceptual attributes and the physical dimensions of the stimulus are more complicated. For example, pitch and loudness are each joint functions of frequency *and* intensity; and timbre is a function not only of complexity of the sound waves but also of the envelope of the tone (slope of the 'attack' and 'decay' functions), context, and vibrato. These modern developments will be discussed later.

Of course, a complete account of musical experiences does not begin and end with the perceptual attributes of pitch, loudness, and timbre. Music consists not only of isolated complex tones that have a certain pitch and loudness. Music also consists of rhythmic patterns of tones and a volume of tones that are extended not only in time but also in space. To the bare bones of sound, the listener adds organization and meaning, transforming the sound into music. Like a recited narrative, music derives its meaning from the context and from the past experiences of the listener.

Hue and Tonal Mixtures Compared. In our systems of color and tone, hue is a continuous dimension while pitch is discontinuous. By mixing limited numbers of hues, three or four 'primary colors,' it is possible to produce all the intermediate hues that are visible to the human observer. But pitches, unlike hues, cannot be mixed to produce intermediate pitches. For example, mixing a C and a G a fifth apart will not yield an intermediate E, as orange can be obtained by mixing a red with a yellow. The two component tones do not disappear in the resultant. As a matter of fact, it makes no sense to speak of a resultant for there are no such laws of tonal mixture, as there are for color. In fact, there are no primary pitches like the three or four primary colors (see Tonal Fusion in Chapter 9).

Though there are continua of sound as there are continua of color, traditional Western music does not permit every possible sound to be used in musical compositions. The scales of Western music define a permissible pool of tones, that is to say, a limited number of fixed, discrete pitches, five to twelve in the octave, which are then built into musical instruments, making these particular tones available to musicians.

The octave interval is frequently regarded as primary and native. When singing together, voices in different registers tend to fall into octave separations. Is there something about the auditory system that yields perceptual similarities when the frequency ratio is just 2/1? Alternatively, does the similarity come about because the harmonics of the octave above a particular tone are also the upper harmonics of that tone?

The octave seems never to have entered the music of antiquity, perhaps because it is too large an interval for music that has a limited range. Later we shall see that early Greek music was not, at first, based on the interval of the octave. Pythagorian tuning (c.530 B.C.) is based on the interval of the fifth, 3/2, not the octave. In this ancient Greek system, the octave is not exactly 2/1. Finally, it should be noted that there tends to be a perceptual 'stretching' and 'compression' of the octave at the extremes of the audible spectrum.

Dimensions of Time and Space. Another comparison of hearing and seeing reveals that they are both distance modalities: sample molecules at the source of stimulation do not have to enter the sense organs, as is required for taste and smell. But, while vision is primarily a spatial modality, hearing is primarily a temporal modality. The visual scene is extended in three dimensions: left-right, up-down, and near-far. It can be frozen in time, as is the scene in a snap-shot or painting. Beside hue, brightness, and saturation, the principal attributes of vision include pattern in space, and duration. The temporal dimension is added in the visual art of cinematography and the result is apparent motion.

Now, consider the auditory pattern. In the case of music, the medium is time. Music cannot be frozen in time as is a visual scene. A melody is recognizable only if presented over a period of time. You cannot stop the music after a fraction of a second and expect to obtain a delightful moment of musical experience. We have just seen that the principal attributes of tones are pitch, loudness, timbre, and rhythm. But what about the dimension of space in music?

Most sounds have a perceived place of origin and a perceived location. They can be left or right, up or down, and near or far. The sounds of an orchestra are spread out in space just as the musicians are seen to be distributed on the stage. Despite this, the location of musical sounds is rarely treated as a musical attribute. It is true that good quality stereo equipment is designed to reproduce the location of the various voices of the orchestra, band, and choir, but most listeners do not yet pay much attention to instrumental location, nor have composers routinely specified the spatial location of the various sounds in their score. It seems strange that composers in the past would have neglected such a potential musical attribute. Imagine what a piece of music would sound like if the spatial attribute of music were utilized in the concert hall. The composer would specify in his score how the various instruments should be distributed on stage, or in the concert hall as a whole: cellos on the left, for example, woodwinds on the right, and percussion along the back of the hall, <u>behind</u> the audience. Such notations in the score have been tried in the past with notable effect. For example, Beethoven specified a trumpet call off-stage in his opera, *Fidelio*, and in the *Leonora Overtures* that are played at symphony concerts. A more dramatic example is found in Act 1 of Mozart's *Don Giovanni*. At one point, Mozart put two bands on either side of the stage and gave them each, along with the orchestra in the pit, a different dance to play together in counterpoint, a waltz, a country dance, and a minuet! How can the listener keep track of the separate melodies? The timbre and rhythmic differences, together with the spatial separation of ensembles, make this a memorable experience.

But consider Giovanni Gabrielli's sonic feasts in Venice around the beginning of the seventeenth century. St. Mark's cathedral has two organs, one at each side. Gabrielli took advantage of the spatial separation of organs. He placed a choir and orchestra near each organ and had them play and sing antiphonally, back and forth, in alternation. The effect was stunning. But consider the problems encountered in rehearsal by the performers who were so far apart from each other. Sound travels slowly, as we shall see and there is a significant delay between the two sets of voices. If choir 2 depended on choir 1 for their cue, they would be late in starting and they would not be properly synchronized with their colleagues. Choir 1 would hear them lagging. Even if the conductor stood between to cue them, each choir would still hear the other lagging and they would have to resist the impulse to slow down. Only the conductor in the middle would hear the two choirs synchronized. Luckily, the reverberations of the cathedral help to blend the sound for the audience and the disparate beginnings and endings become blurred. Today, with stereo equipment, we can capture the spatial dimension on tape and appreciate Gabrielli's sonic effects in our living rooms.

In recent years, composers like Luciano Berio have begun to pay much more attention to the spatial distribution of sounds on the stage. And since the advent of stereo, listeners have become more attuned to the spatial dimension in music.

Sound and light waves share another property: that of diffraction but there is an interesting difference between them in this regard. The degree to which waves bend around obstacles and turn corners depends on the wavelength of the waves and the dimension of the obstacle. The greater the wavelength and the smaller the obstacle, the greater the degree of bending. The tone, middle C, has a wavelength of roughly 1.3 meters, while the color, red, has a wavelength of roughly 0.0000006 meters. Light waves are actually two million times shorter than sound waves. As a matter of fact, light waves are so short that they will not visibly bend around obstacles or turn corners. You simply cannot see around an obstacle; but you can hear around it. Sound waves are long enough to bend around obstacles and turn corners. The person looming in front of you in a concert hall can be a formidable obstacle; he can prevent you from seeing the musicians on the stage. But he cannot prevent you from hearing the music.

THE ACOUSTIC MEDIUM

For the human land dweller, sound travels through air. Among the ancient Greeks, it was Aristotle who suggested that air itself serves as the conductor of sound. A sounding body displaces the adjacent air which, in turn, displaces the air particles next to it and so on, until the ear drum is itself displaced by the compressions and rarefactions of air particles. The common medical stethoscope, used for hundreds of years to listen to the heart and lungs of patients, operates on this principle. When it is placed on the chest, the diaphragm is set in motion by the beating heart, and the vibrations of two columns of air particles are transmitted to the physician's ears.

If air is the medium through which sound is conducted, then there should be no sound in a vacuum. This was shown experimentally by Guericke in 1657. He evacuated the air in a glass jar containing a ringing bell. As he pumped the air out of the jar, the sound of the bell became fainter and fainter until it ceased, though the hammer could still be seen to vibrate and strike the bell. The sound became audible again as the air was allowed to return. This result was verified in 1660 by the renowned chemist, Robert Boyle. The experiment is shown in Fig. 6.10. Thereafter, it was shown that water, and gases other than air, will conduct sound. Even solids like the wood body of a violin, or the sounding board of the piano, will conduct sound and amplify it. This phenomenon is frequently called resonance.

The fact that sound travels readily through water is utilized in underwater signalling between submarines (and, of course, between marine creatures like whales). And, since solids too transmit sounds, you can hear the approach of the distant train before it is in sight, and before you can otherwise hear it, by placing an ear to the iron rail.

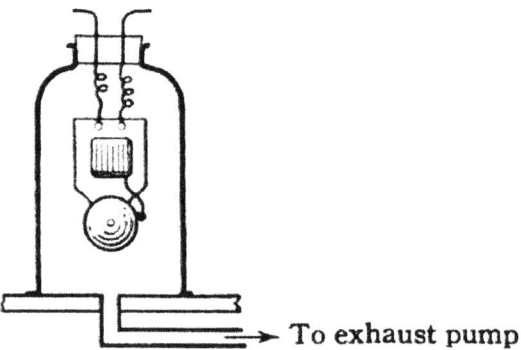

Fig. 6.10. Bell in glass jar. Sound is transmitted through a medium such as air. To prove this, an electric bell is suspended in a glass jar, which is properly insulated against air leaks. The sound of ringing is clearly heard but, as the air is evacuated by means of an exhaust pump, the sound of ringing becomes weaker and weaker until it finally ceases. The motion of the hammer shows that the bell is still ringing. When the air is permitted to return, the bell is heard once again.

VELOCITY OF SOUND

It is well known that sound takes an appreciable time to travel from one point to another. In comparison, light seems to travel with incredible swiftness. Many determinations of the velocity of sound were made in the seventeenth and eighteenth centuries, but they were discrepant because nobody realized how many variables needed to be controlled to obtain a consistent result. A gun was fired some miles from an observer, who saw the flash of the gun almost instantaneously but heard the report only after an appreciable interval of time. The distance to the gun divided by the time interval yielded the velocity of sound in air. This determination, however, depends upon the direction and velocity of the wind, the temperature and humidity of the air, and the reaction time of the observer. Consider the variable of temperature, for example. Sound velocities determined during the summer and then during the winter, when a difference in temperature of 36° centigrade was recorded, yielded a difference in velocity of 42 feet per second.

Sound is now known to travel at about 1,128 feet per second in dry air at 20° centigrade. In the fresh waters of Lake Geneva, on the other hand, the velocity of sound turned out to be about four times faster and, in salt water, faster yet. These differences in the velocity of sound in air, fresh water, and salt water are accounted for by the differences in the density of these media.

Light, travelling at the much greater velocity of 186,000 miles per second, reaches the distant observer much earlier than sound originating at the same place. Thus, the flash of the firing cannon at a distance is seen before its boom is heard and, of course, the lightning flash invariably precedes the peal of thunder. It is very disconcerting to watch the conductor of the orchestra from a distance, for he seems to be waving his baton at a bunch of laggard musicians who respond only after an appreciable delay.

Nerve impulses travel through the nervous system at a much slower velocity than sound travels in air. Even the fastest transmitters of nerve impulses, the large diameter neurons, are limited in their repetition rate by the absolute refractory period of about 0.5 milliseconds, the period after the firing of the neuron during which the fiber is exhausted and must replenish itself before it can fire again. This is an important observation, for it means that the rate of neural firings can only reach up to a maximum of perhaps several hundred impulses per second, no more. As a consequence, audible sound frequencies beyond that range, up to 20,000 *Hz*, cannot be matched by the rate of neural firing. Those theorists of pitch perception who believe that pitch can be encoded in the rate of transmission of nerve impulses have had to contend with this limitation in neural firing rate. The volley theory of pitch perception, which we will review later, was designed to overcome this limitation.

Chapter 7

PERCEPTION OF PITCH

The tones that make up a musical piece vary principally in pitch, loudness, timbre and duration. Pitch is the quality of sound that we refer to as 'high' or 'low': usually, women's voices are high and men's voices are low; the piccolo produces a high pitch and the double bass a low pitch. ('High' and 'low' are to be distinguished from 'loud' and 'soft' which refer to the quality of loudness.)

In Western music, it is pitch that has been considered the most salient characteristic of tones. This is because melody occupies a central position in this music. We ordinarily think of melodies as consisting of a series of tones varying primarily in pitch. Some melodies move up and down within a narrow range of pitch steps. An illustration is the anthem, *America* or *My Country 'Tis Of Thee* (see Fig. 15.1). Other melodies move within a broader range of pitches, such as *The Star-Spangled Banner*. Our musical scales (major and minor, for example) are actually elaborate and intricate pitch alphabets, providing the composer with a pool of notes from which to draw for the composition of melodies.

Musically untrained listeners are generally unable to recognize the absolute pitch of musical tones. Informing the listener that a certain tone is F#, for example, will not etch this fact in his long-term memory. The F# can be repeated over and over again and the listener will forget what it sounds like after an interval as short as a minute or two. This is particularly true if he is played a host of other unnamed tones during that interval. In this way, he can be distracted from rehearsing, and he will neither recall nor recognize the F#. It is true that a small number of people seem to be endowed with the ability to recognize the absolute pitch of different tones (as most of us identify different colors, such as crimson and royal blue, without the need to make comparisons). But, the best most musically untrained listeners can do is characterize tones as high, or low, or intermediate. With musical training, however, most listeners can become sensitive to the more precise relationships between tones. Translated into the realm of the physical stimulus, this means that listeners become sensitive to the ratio of frequencies of tones. In the terminology of perception, this means that it is the musical interval to which listeners learn to recognize.

PITCH AND FREQUENCY

Suppose we play the following sequence of frequencies to a group of Americans, all frequencies equal in intensity and duration, and ask them to identify the tune: 260, 260, 290, 330, 260, 330, 290 *Hz*. Some musically untrained Americans would recognize the tune without being able to identify it, but most would name the tune, 'Yankee Doodle,' and sing the words along with the melody, if asked. Some more musically tutored individuals might be able to transform the sequence of frequencies into its solfège equivalent, and sing it in a convenient register: do, do, re, mi, do, mi, re. Trained musicians are able to do all this and more; they should recognize that the successive intervals are, 'unison, ascending major second, another ascending major second, descending major third, ascending major third, and descending major second.' This demonstrates that musicians possess good 'relative pitch,' an ability to recognize the relations between tones. These people behave as though they have developed an internal representation of pitch relationships among notes permanently etched in the brain. Nearly everyone can acquire this ability to discriminate intervals. Occasionally, a listener is found who will identify each note perfectly, 'middle C, C, D, E, C, E, D,' and might even point out that each note is slightly flat (middle C is usually tuned to 262 *Hz*, not 260). This individual has perfect or absolute pitch. There is a controversy as to whether the ability to acquire absolute pitch is given genetically, or whether special tutoring can confer this ability on almost anyone.

(A limited number of listeners might fail to recognize the tune altogether. If they had been exposed to American tunes all their lives, we might wonder whether this failure is the result of some kind of 'tune deafness,' or a more global amusia. We will examine these conditions in Chapter 19. They are relatively rare and are not well understood.)

This little musical exercise illustrates why the pitch of a tone has been equated with a particular frequency of vibrations. The truth is that pitch has been thought traditionally to be a one-dimensional attribute of tones, related to frequency in a one-to-one fashion. For example, the A above middle C, to which the modern orchestra is tuned, is identified with 440 *Hz*.

It was Galileo who proposed this relationship between pitch and frequency. Two millenia earlier, Pythagoras had worked out the dependence of pitch upon the length of taut strings. He knew that decreasing the length of the string to one-half raises the pitch one octave. He also worked out the corresponding simple ratios for the intervals of the fourth and the fifth (3/4 and 2/3). But he had no quantitative knowledge of the relation of pitch to frequency. This was Galileo's contribution. In 1681, the experimental evidence of Robert Hooke clinched the matter. Hooke rotated a wheel that had brass teeth along its edge, and allowed an object to strike the moving teeth. Rapid rotation produced a sound having an identifiable pitch. Doubling the speed of rotation raised the pitch exactly one octave; increasing it by one-third raised the pitch the interval of a fourth, and increasing it by one-half raised the pitch the interval of a fifth. In Chapter 6, we saw that this is how the siren works.

If the waveform is sinusoidal and a pure tone is heard, Galileo's law holds: pitch varies as a simple function of frequency. But the tones used in music are invariably complex; they consist not only of a fundamental frequency which gives the tone its name, but also include a number of overtones or harmonics which give the tone its characteristic tonal color or timbre. The untutored listener is unaware of the individual overtones in a complex tone because the overtones fuse with the fundamental to make a single rich tone, much as the component hues in a mixture of pigments fuse to produce a rich color. Though unaware of the component pitches, the listener is nevertheless conscious of the rich quality of the resultant tone.

The law that pitch varies as a simple function of frequency was finally challenged in the 1920s. If a listener attempts to adjust the frequency of a pure tone to match that of a complex tone, his matches sometimes deviate from the expected. These deviations are minor in the mid-range of pitches, but the sources of error reveal that frequency is not the only determinant of pitch. We will discuss two sources of error here: the missing fundamental and the influence of intensity on pitch. We will conclude that pitch is not the unidimensional attribute of sound, implied in Galileo's law.

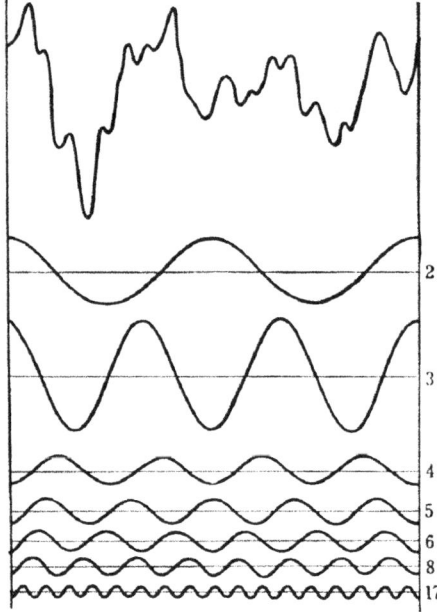

Fig. 7. 1. The missing fundamental. When a complex wave is subjected to a Fourier analysis, its constituent frequencies and their relative amplitudes may be found. Shown at the top is the waveform produced by the open G-string of a violin. The relative amplitudes of the second, third, fourth, fifth, sixth, eighth, and seventeenth harmonics are shown below. Note that the fundamental frequency is absent. Apparently the body of the violin will not resonate to G=196 Hz. The listener supplies the fundamental, perhaps as the repeated difference tone of the upper harmonics (588-392=196; 784-588=196; etc.).

Perception of Pitch

The lowest of the violin strings is the G string. When we pluck this string to make it vibrate, its fundamental frequency should be 196 *Hz*, for we hear the G below middle C, corresponding to 196 *Hz*. If the jagged waveform of this G is displayed on the oscilloscope screen and is subjected to harmonic analysis in order to reveal the harmonic structure, we will see on the screen the many constituent sine wave-forms, all integer multiples of the fundamental. But the fundamental frequency of 196 *Hz* itself is missing!

This phenomenon is known as the 'missing fundamental.' The physical explanation is that the body of the violin cannot resonate to a frequency as low as 196 *Hz* and it is simply not present as a component in the sound. Nevertheless, the auditory mechanism in the brain supplies the fundamental frequency for we hear it clearly, and identify it as the fundamental of a complex tone. Here is an exception to the rule that the pitch of a tone is determined by the strength of its fundamental frequency. In this case, the fundamental frequency is simply not present, and the pitch of a complex tone must be determined by something else.

In the past, the harmonics were thought to influence the *timbre* of the tone but not its apparent pitch because they are not sufficiently intense. But how can the fundamental be heard when it is not present in the sound? The explanation offered by some psychologists is that the fundamental frequency is generated in the brain by the harmonics as a result of the summation of difference tones. Consider, for example, the overtone series of 400, 600, 800, and 1000 *Hz*, similar to that produced by the G string of the violin. The successive difference tones are 600-400 *Hz*; 800-600 *Hz*; and 1000-800 *Hz*. These overtone differences, all 200 *Hz*, might each be too weak to be audible. But together they would sum to yield an audible fundamental of 200 *Hz*. Many psychologists do not accept this explanation; for, if a noise is added to the tone of the G-string which masks the region of 200 *Hz*, the perception of the fundamental ought to be affected, but it is not (Licklider, 1954). A more satisfactory explanation for the missing fundamental has not yet been found.

In music, complex tones with weak or absent fundamentals are common. And, despite the masking of a fundamental by other tones in the musical complex, the fundamental is often heard. The truth is that listeners hear more than the sum total of all frequencies actually present in the sound stimulus (and frequently they hear a lot less because one tone masks another, as we will discover in Chapter 14).

The alleged one-to-one relationship between pitch and frequency can be questioned on other grounds. In the early 1920s, Harvey Fletcher began a series of celebrated studies that led to the development of the audiometer, an instrument designed to vary the intensity of each of a large number of different frequencies, from inaudibility up to intensities so great that they elicited tactile sensations, including pain. While varying their intensity, it became clear that the apparent pitch of these tones varied, demonstrating that pitch depends not simply on the frequency of the tones but also on their intensity. For a particular frequency beyond the midrange of audibility, the lower the intensity, the lower the apparent pitch and, conversely, the higher the intensity the higher the apparent pitch (see Fig. 7.7). Since the perceived pitch of a tone has turned out to be a joint function of frequency and intensity, pitch and loudness can no longer be viewed as independent attributes of tone perception as implied by the Galilean law of pitch as a function of frequency alone.

There is still another reason to question the alleged one-to-one relationship between pitch and frequency. From the standpoint of frequency, all twelve tones within the octave are reduplicated seven and one-third times on the piano. This means that the interval of a perfect fifth somewhere near the bottom of the piano keyboard is equivalent in frequency ratio (3/2) to the same interval in any register, including the very highest register. (It also means that a melody remains unaltered in pitch and completely recognizable though all the notes are changed, provided that the successive intervals in the melody are retained. This is known as musical transposition.) However, the listener is less sensitive to the difference between pitches at the low end of the keyboard as compared to the same difference of pitches higher on the keyboard. Listen to successive octaves as you move from one end of the keyboard to the other. Though they are equal in frequency ratios compared to octaves at the high end, the low octaves sound more and more compressed. Here, again, we have to raise the question regarding the alleged one-to-one correspondence between pitch and frequency. Each musical interval is unique in its frequency-ratio, but the corresponding subjective scale of pitch varies according to the position on the continuum of audible frequencies.

We must conclude that pitch cannot be specified by the frequency of vibrations alone. Quite apart from this, there is a fundamental problem in treating pitch as though it were a linear dimension. The arrangement of keys on the piano in a linear sequence from low to high, though it facilitates performance is conceptually misleading. This arrangement does not reflect the unique significance of the octave interval. Most listeners hear the two notes of the octave as more similar than the two notes of any other interval. On the piano keyboard, however, the two keys of the octave stand further apart than the two keys of any other interval in the octave.

The idea that musical tones separated by an octave have more in common than tones more closely spaced goes back to antiquity. Pythagoras noted that the consonance of two pitches is related to the simplicity of the numerical ratio of the two frequencies. The octave is first in consonance with a ratio of 2/1, followed by the perfect fifth, 3/2, the perfect fourth, 4/3, etc. It is clear, however, that small deviations from the simple ratio are tolerated by the modern listener and even preferred. For most listeners, the best octave is not the interval that is precisely 2/1, but one slightly larger and, hence, more complex numerically (2.02/1). The pitches produced by eminent performers of stringed instruments and preferred by the audience often fail to conform to the predicted simple ratios. In our musical age, the major and minor thirds (5/4 and 6/5) are preferred over the numerically simpler perfect fifth and fourth (3/2 and 4/3). Remember too that the Western scales to which the keyboard and wind instruments have been tuned for the last 150 years are equal-tempered. This means that all the musical intervals within the octave deviate from the simple Pythagorean ratios to an audible degree. The fifth is $\sqrt[7]{2}/1$, or 1.498/1, not 1.5/1, and the fourth is $\sqrt[5]{2}/1$, or 1.335/1, not 1.333/1. Though beats are produced by playing together any two tones of the equal-tempered scale, the experience of roughness or throbbing does not seem to reduce the musical qualities of the piece. For most listeners, the presence of beats actually enhances musical enjoyment! (See Chapter 9 for an extended discussion of beats.)

We have seen that the psychophysical scale for pitch is based on the tradition that pitch varies as a simple function of frequency. But today, most authorities are convinced that pitch, as a perceptual experience is not a unidimensional variable. The musician identifies a series of adjacent notes within the octave (C, D, E, etc.) as belonging to one dimension of pitch, called chroma. He also recognizes which octave he is in (below middle C, above middle C. etc.) as a second dimension of pitch, called height. In this sense, the linear arrangement of keys on the piano is misleading. It places two successive Cs far apart, though they have the same chroma and sound very much alike.

At the same time, it places the C and D next to it close together, though they differ in chroma and sound very different. There should be a way to represent chroma and height in a more rational manner.

Roger Shepard suggested as early as 1962 that the distribution of pitches be pictured on a helix or spiral that ascends the shell of an invisible cylinder. Tones varying in chroma (e.g., C, C#, D, D#, etc.) are found around the circumference of the helix, and tones varying in height (e.g., C, C', C"; or, D, D', D", etc.) are found along the axis of the helix. No where does the physical dimension of frequency appear. Here was an early attempt to represent the multi-dimensionality of pitch. The advantage of the helical representation of pitch over the linear or piano-like representation is that the distance between points corresponding to the two tones of each octave has been greatly reduced in order to picture properly the special status of the octave.

A psychophysical relationship implies a relationship of two ordered variables, in this case, the psychological scale of pitch with the physical scale of frequency. In a psychophysical experiment, the judgments of listeners are 'greater' or 'lesser,' 'higher' or 'lower,' etc. In contrast, a multidimensional cognitive structure implies similarity and differences of tones. Using a multidimensional scaling technique, listeners are asked to judge the degree of similarity of pairs of tones in order to reveal a cognitive structure for pitch. In such a structure, the more similar pitches lie closer together and the less similar pitches lie further apart. Will a cognitive structure for pitch, derived from a multidimensional scaling technique, resemble Shepard's pitch spiral?

Krumhansl and Shepard (1979) asked listeners to judge the relatedness of tones belonging to the chromatic scale. This experiment was conducted in a musical context by first establishing a tonicity in the minds of the listeners. To accomplish this, the listeners were presented with a major scale which ended, not with the tonic, but with one or another pitch above the tonic. The listeners were required to judge how good the last pitch was as a completion of the scale. Many listeners were clearly influenced in their judgments by both chroma and height, but the musically sophisticated were more influenced by chroma. From these data, Shepard (1982) derived a multidimensional scaling solution, which occupied a three-dimensional space. He viewed this structure from two directions. In one direction, he saw the tones arranged chromatically around a circle, with a gap in it to represent the shift in octave. In another direction, he saw the tones arrange in a circle of fifths, with the octave notes occupying the same position in the circle. By cutting through the circle of fifths with a straight line, the seven pitches belonging to a particular major scale were separated from the rest.

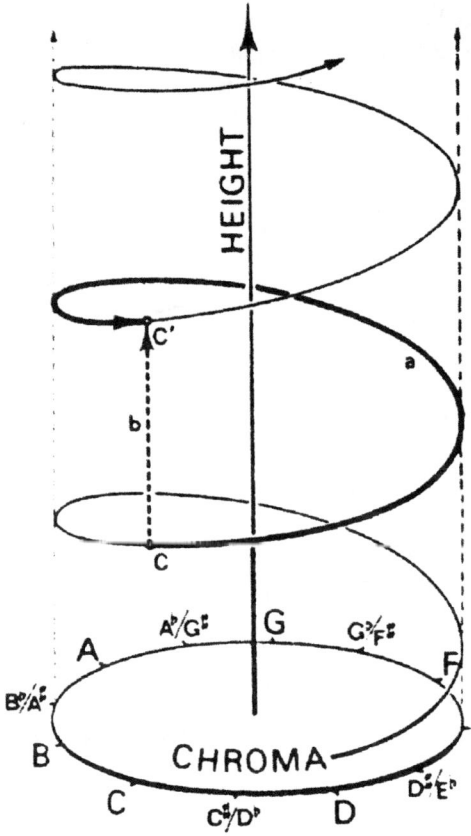

Fig. 7.2. Pitch consisting of chroma and height. In 1965, Roger Shepard proposed that pitch, traditionally regarded as a unidimensional variable, is really bidimensional. Around the circumference of a spiral is the variable he called 'chroma.' The tones of the chromatic octave are represented around one turn of the spiral, and this is repeated over and over again on successive turns of the spiral. Movement from one turn to the next produces a variation in 'height.' Adapted from Shepard, 1965.

Based on this analysis, Shepard constructed a model of the cognitive structure of pitch, which consisted of two intertwining spirals. One spiral has represented on it all pitches separated by whole tones, C, D, E, F#, G#, A#, C; the other by whole tones, C#, D#, F, G, A, B, C#. Links between the two spirals represent semitones, and the vertical dimension represents height. If the intertwining spirals are viewed from above, a circle of fifths is seen, and again, a straight line through the circle separates the seven tones of the major scale from the rest (see Fig. 7.3).

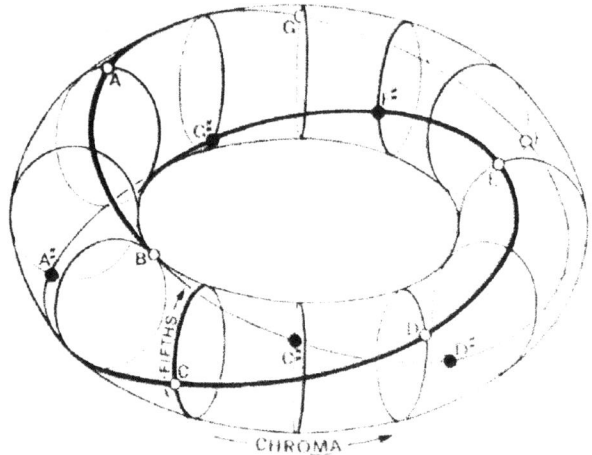

Fig. 7.3. The double helix of chroma and fifths. Geometric representation of tones varying in chroma and fifths as a double helix wound around a torus in four-dimentional space Adapted from Shepard, 1982.

In short, the value of Shepard's double spiral model lies in its success in capturing a number of important facts about pitch discrimination. Among these facts are the psychological significance of the octave, the circle of fifths, and the major scale.

Is pitch really multidimensional? Here is what Shepard had to say on the question: "...The fact that individual listeners can be shown to differ...implies that pitch must be multidimensional. If pitch were only a matter of separation of pitch height or log frequency, listeners would be expected to differ only in their fineness of discrimination of pitches that are more or less close to each other in log frequency. In fact, they differ markedly in the extent to which they are sensitive to special musical relations such as the octave and the perfect fifth" (Shepard, 1982, p. 370).

Shepard has presented some fascinating illusions that are based on this helical conception of pitch. If you have available the recording of illusions recommended in the Prologue of this book, listen to the endlessly ascending scale before you continue this discussion. The following score shows how the auditory 'barber pole effect' is produced. In this example, chroma is varied while height remains constant: two successive ascending octaves of the C major scale are played, but the second octave sounds like a duplicate of the first.

Fig. 7.4. Notation of the endless rise in chroma. It is possible to vary chroma while holding height constant. Here is the score for the endless rise in chroma, but not in height. The intensity of each tone is indicated in the score by the size of the corresponding note. Whenever middle C is played, it is always the most intense note; the B and D on either side of it are less intense; the A and E on either side of B and D are less intense again, etc. Follow the progress of the chromatic scale in the first measure, and then in the second which is identical to the first. You will see that two consecutive ascending octaves have indeed been played, but the scale ends exactly where it began, on middle C. Adapted from Hofstadter, 1979.

In a series of demonstrations, Shepard has shown that pitch-height and pitch-chroma can be varied independently of each other. First, height can be varied while holding chroma constant. For one demonstration, white noise is passed through a filter with a bandwidth of one octave. This sound has no identifiable pitch-chroma because all chromas (C, C#, D, D#, etc.) are equally represented. When the center frequency of the octave-filter is moved up continuously over the audible range, a rushing sound is heard, changing from a deep rumble at the low end to a fine hiss at the high end. This is the variation in pitch-height that Shepard refers to. There is no concomitant variation in pitch-chroma, for the listener is unable to identify any specific tones.

Returning to Fig. 7.4, pitch-chroma is varied while height is held constant. Starting in a low register, the chromatic scale is played ascending through middle C and beyond. The intensity of each note is increased from inaudibility, progressively, to a maximum at middle C, and then decreased, progressively, beyond middle C, to inaudibility. As this voice-line ascends toward middle C, a second chromatic scale is added exactly one octave below, and the same intensity changes are made, i.e., the intensity is increased pro-gressively, from inaudibility as middle C is approached, and then decreased above middle C. As this second chromatic line ascends toward middle C, a third is added, again one octave below, waxing and waning in the same way, then a fourth and a fifth, and so on repetitively.

Thus, at any point in time, there is always a chromatic line, waxing as it approaches middle C. The resulting percept is fascinating. The listener hears an endlessly ascending chromatic scale which seems to approach middle C without ever getting there, that is, without any ascent in height from octave to octave. The effect is reminiscent of the rotating barber pole on which a spiral seems to ascend continuously, but never gets anywhere. This illusion illustrates the fact that pitch-chroma can be varied without a concomitant variation in pitch-height. The composer, Jean-Claude Risset, used this type of illusion with great effect in incidental music for the play, *Little Boy*, by Pierre Halet. The theme of the play is a repetition of the bombing of Hiroshima in the nightmare of a pilot. The bomb falls endlessly in a tonal cascade of ever-descending pitches.

These demonstrations by Shepard provide further evidence that the auditory system processes stimulus frequency in ways more complicated than those implied by the traditional correspondence between pitch and frequency.

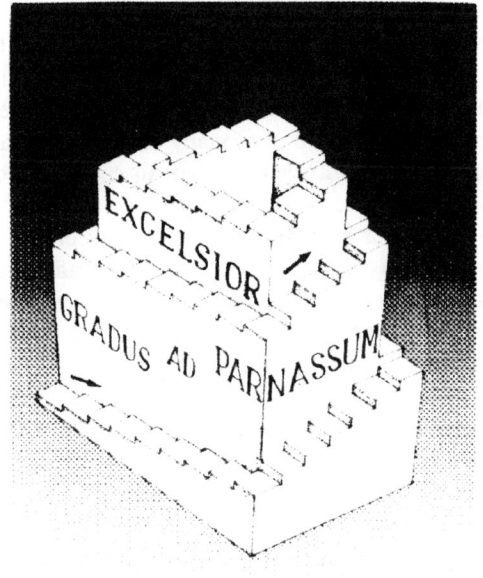

Fig. 7.5 The endless staircase of Penrose and Penrose (1958). A visual analogy to Shepard's endlessly ascending scale.

EQUIVALENCE OF INTERVALS

The ability to remember the *absolute* pitch of a melody is very rare. Unless the absolute pitch registers in the first place, there is no possibility of remembering it as such. Most people remember a particular pitch by abstracting it from the patterned musical signal, and by coding it, first, as a note belonging to a specific octave and, second, as forming a specific interval with the notes adjacent to it. Both of these interval discriminations are very imperfect.

1. Two pitches having frequencies in the ratio 2/1 are an octave apart, and are frequently reported to be perceptually equivalent. All musicians, and some musically untutored individuals, are aware of the equivalence of octaves. As a matter of fact, it has been shown in conditioning experiments that humans and animals both generalize

their acquired responses to notes an octave apart. Furthermore, if a person having absolute pitch makes an error in identifying a note, it is frequently to place the note in the wrong octave, again attesting to the equivalence of octave notes. In Western music, all the different notes of the diatonic scale are contained within the range of one octave. The scale can then be reduplicated in as many octaves as the audible range permits. These octave equivalences seem to cut across cultures, and may be regarded as universal and unlearned.

However, octave equivalence sometimes breaks down. If we assume that notes an octave apart are indeed equivalent, it follows that melodies should be recognized even after their constituent notes are shifted from one octave to another. To test this prediction, Deutsch (1972) played the tune Yankee Doodle, varying the octave register of each of the constituent notes. All subjects recognized the tune when all constituent notes were played in one register, high, medium, or low. However, when each note of the tune was played in one of the three registers, with no two successive notes drawn from the same octave, not a single subject recognized the tune. You can try this little demonstration on your friends. But keep them ignorant of the name of the tune. Once they know it, they will probably recognize the tune. For this reason, the demonstration will probably not work on you.

2. Pairs of notes separated by the same frequency ratios, regardless of their absolute frequencies, produce the same intervals. For example, two frequencies in the ratio 3/2 are perceived a fifth apart regardless of their absolute pitch level. In the equal-tempered scale, the smallest interval has been given the ratio $^{12}\sqrt{2}/1$. It is heard as a semitone regardless of register. Similarly, all intervals of three semitones, $(^{12}\sqrt{2})^3/1$, are heard as minor thirds, whether they are low or high or intermediate in the audible range. Attneave and Olson (1971) demonstrated that subjects transpose familiar melodies by preserving the ratios between successive notes. Again, this type of transposition is not unique to Western music (Nettl, 1956). Chords, too, are given the same name if their component tones stand in the same relationship. For example, 4/5/6 represents the frequency relationship of all justly tuned major triads, and 10/12/15 represents the frequency relationship of all justly tuned minor triads. This is elaborated in Chapter 11.

All intervals can be transformed in certain ways without any substantial change in their perceptual qualities. One example is the inversion: an interval of N semitones is frequently judged to be similar to another of 12–N semitones. In musical terms, this means that thirds and sixths, fourths and fifths, seconds and sevenths, are all inversions of each other. Plomp et al (1973) provided experimental evidence for the perceptual similarity of inverted intervals. They found that confusion of identity occurred when judgments were made of intervals that were inversions of each other, intervals such as fifths and fourths. Chords are subject to the same confusion: two chords remain harmonically equivalent even when their component notes are moved to adjacent octaves.

We recognize transposed melodies not only because specific intervals have been retained in the transposed version, but more specifically because the direction of pitch changes has been retained. Werner (1925) created a scale of micro-intervals and showed that melodies were still recognized after they were transposed to his scale, where the intervals between constituent notes were grossly diminished. That the direction of pitch change is the critical factor is revealed by White's (1960) demonstration that melodies could still be recognized after all intervals, large and small, were changed to one semitone, leaving unchanged only the directions of pitch change.

Another kind of transposition retains the notes of the scale but changes the starting note. Compare *Frère Jacques* starting on the tonic of the major scale (say C), with *Frère Jacques* starting on D of the same scale (as Mahler wrote it in his First Symphony), or starting on E, or F, etc. Though the names of the notes are unchanged in the transposed versions (for there are no accidentals), the sequence of intervals is changed. Each of these versions of Frère Jacques is said to be in a different mode (Dorian, Phrygian, and Lydian -- see Chapter 11 on scales). A melody transposed to these different modes, though intriguingly different in quality, is still easy to recognize, thus attesting to the perceptual equivalence of modal transposition.

To account for the equivalence of intervals and their inversions has not been easy. Those interested in a proposed neural mechanism should consult Deutsch (1969).

Absolute and Relative Pitch

The traditional test of pitch discrimination involves a comparison of two notes played on a musical instrument such as a piano. Typically, the subject is presented with a pair of tones, sounded consecutively, and is asked to make judgments about sameness and difference or higher and lower. If the subject is a child, the instructions may be misunderstood ('higher' or 'lower' may be taken, erroneously, to mean 'louder' or 'softer'), and this may be the very simple explanation for the apparent failure to discriminate. Because this is a trivial case, we will ignore it.

Some people can retain an internal pitch standard and can use it when a judgment of pitch is required. If the traditional pitch test imposes a delay before the second tone is presented, then it is necessary for the subject to retain a tonal image of the first in order to make a successful judgment of the second. To the degree that a tone can be stored, it can be used as an internal standard. Choir members learn to hold a tonal image for a brief period and can sing it, or a related tone, on command.

The possession of an internal standard is more dramatically illustrated by the person with absolute or perfect pitch. This person carries around with him some sort of internal representation of tones such that, at any time, in any place, he can reproduce or recognize them. This capacity is fairly rare. Most musicians possess relative pitch, which means that they are able to reproduce or recognize tones, but only after they have been given a named tone as a standard for comparison.

The difference between absolute and relative pitch is illustrated as follows: the person possessing absolute pitch can recognize a note anywhere, any time, produced by any tone generator: early in the morning, coming in from a noisy street, played by an oboe or piano, or any other instrument. In contrast, the person possessing relative pitch cannot do any of this. He must be provided with a named tone before he can identify or sing any other named tone.

In its extreme form, absolute pitch can be so startling as to appear incredible. Some people can name any note instantly, suggesting that a judgment of comparison with just *one* internalized standard is not likely to be the explanation. These persons actually recognize each note very accurately and may make a wry face if the note is slightly flat or sharp. The sense of absolute pitch is sometimes so strong that a piece played in a key different from the original sounds quite wrong. For most of us who do not possess absolute pitch, such transpositions go absolutely unnoticed.

Is absolute pitch an ability to be regarded with reverence? Certainly good musicianship does not require absolute pitch. It should be treated as a curiosity that confers little or no obvious advantage to its possessor. As a matter of fact, it can confer a distinct disadvantage to both the performer and listener. The person with absolute pitch may feel genuinely uncomfortable under a number of circumstances: when the music is transposed from the familiar key, when the orchestra is tuned to an unfamiliar standard, when the phonograph turntable is rotating at a rate slightly off the correct one, and when the live performer is slightly off pitch.

Some years ago, a debate waged between Bachem (1948) and Neu (1947, 1948) about absolute pitch. The argument centered on whether absolute pitch could be learned (or was learned) or whether it was a native endowment.

There is strong evidence that learning plays some part in the development of absolute pitch. Certainly, before anyone can demonstrate the possession of absolute pitch, he must learn the names of the notes. But, as Chomsky has argued about the acquisition of speech, the competence may be built in. Sergeant (1967) showed that early training has a considerable bearing on the development of absolute pitch. Perhaps there is a critical period during which early experiences are effective. Before or after this critical period, training is less effective or is quite ineffective. As with all nature-nurture debates, it is impossible to tease out the contributions of each independent of the other.

Ward (1963) has given some unusual accounts of absolute pitch in animals including rats and dogs. There is the case of a parrot that always whistled the first four bars of Beethoven's *Fifth Symphony* in the correct key (C minor). It is interesting to speculate whether songbirds maintain the same key in their song or whether they sing equivalently in different keys on different occasions. If they do maintain their song in a specific key, can they be taught to change key?

Is absolute pitch quite distinct from relative pitch or is the difference simply one of degree? Ward (1970) attempted to demystify absolute pitch by pointing out that absolute judgments in other sensory modalities pass without comment. We recognize the color red, the taste of salt or the smell of camphor without the need to compare with some anchor point. Viewed in this way, it is surprising that so few of us possess absolute pitch, not that so many of us do not possess it.

Perhaps most of us did possess the competence for absolute pitch in childhood but have lost it as a result of certain early musical experiences. In school, we hear tunes played in varying keys. When we are taught to sing a tune, rarely are we made to sing it in the same key on every occasion. Thus, we learn to sing each tune in many different keys. Without absolute pitch themselves, teachers and parents will unwittingly transpose the tune to a new key whenever they sing it. The end result is that most of us learn to attend merely to the relationships of tones and not to their absolute pitch values. The song becomes the same song in any pitch. If our elders possessed absolute pitch and sang always in one key, we too might exhibit absolute pitch.

This argument is persuasive and may prove to be correct. However, its cogency is vitiated by the fact that judgments in the non-auditory sense modalities are often relative, not absolute. Consider the following examples: visual judgments in a two-choice situation are usually relative, not absolute - bigger than or smaller than, brighter than or dimmer than, nearer than or farther than, etc. The color of an object depends upon the color and brightness of the background, that is, the judgment is relative to the visual surround. Similarly, the flavor of a food depends upon what you just tasted a moment ago.

In short, it is still not clear whether absolute pitch is a separate ability or the extreme end of a continuous variable. The truth is that relative choice seems to be quite common in all mammalian species studied thus far, including humans, and absolute pitch seems special because of its rarity. Although intense training and perseverance at maturity can result in improvement in absolute pitch judgments, success tends to be of short duration. On the other hand, training during early childhood might produce absolute pitch, though how this takes place has never been determined.

It does seem clear that absolute pitch will not guarantee successful musicianship. If the person with absolute pitch is forced to transpose and he wavers (because it makes him feel uncomfortable), he might even be judged unmusical!

Perhaps the distinction between absolute and relative pitch is not as hard and fast as it might seem. A possessor of absolute pitch carries around his internal standards all the time, while the person with relative pitch carries a standard for shorter periods and needs to renew it from time to time because he loses it or it wanes.

Of course, even those with unassailable absolute pitch occasionally commit errors. To understand this ability better, it is important to determine under what conditions possessors of absolute pitch do, in fact, make errors. For example, does the ability deteriorate in the face of changes in timbre?

In an experiment by Lockhead and Byrd (1981), possessors of absolute pitch were able to identify the pitch of tones with 99% accuracy when piano tones were played, but with just 58% accuracy when pure tones were played. It was already well known that octave errors are the most common, but when these were excluded, accuracy was still below 70%. Lockhead and Byrd concluded that timbre serves as an important clue in identifying the absolute pitch of a sound.

Belzano (1984) repeated this experiment on subjects who could identify piano tones perfectly. The stimuli were pure tones covering almost three octaves, from A=110 *Hz* to Ab=831 *Hz*. After each trial, during which the note was named (and the octave specified), a two-second glissando was played, sweeping upward from 0 to about 5,000 *Hz*. The glissando was meant to erase any tonal standard retained from the previous trial. No feedback on accuracy was provided. In the analysis, octave errors were excluded. Using Shepard's pitch dichotomy, this means that the identification of chroma was tested, not height. The results showed that the chroma of pure tones was correctly identified an average of 88% of the time. Most errors were in the lowest octave, where the pitch was judged slightly higher than it actually was. Errors were seldom greater than one semitone. When the range of pure tone stimuli was extended upward two octaves, the few errors committed were a semitone flat. This led Balzano to conclude that the subjective scale for pitch at the upper and lower extremes is stretched.

Though there does appear to be a reduction in accuracy when pure tones are used as stimuli, the drop is small, perhaps up to 15%, and the errors are mainly restricted to the low octave.

Balzano conceded that some possessors of absolute pitch can demonstrate their ability only when piano tones are used as stimuli. For them, timbre seems to furnish an important clue. If used in such an experiment, these people would not be expected to perform as accurately. However, most possessors of absolute pitch do not require the cue of timbre to identify tones in absolute terms.

Since interval recognition is slow and more prone to error than chroma recognition, Balzano concluded that absolute pitch involves the direct recognition of chroma and is not based on the interval perception on which relative pitch is based.

RANGE OF AUDIBILITY OF PITCH

Though the number of individual frequencies in the frequency spectrum is indefinitely large, pitch perception is finite in that there is both a low and a high end. When Galileo established the relation between pitch and frequency, he raised the problem of determining the lowest and highest audible frequencies.

During the nineteenth century, there were many determinations ranging as low as 8 Hz and as high as 55,000 *Hz*. The yield, in octaves, was between 10 and 20. Based on modern determinations, the rule of thumb is 20-20,000 *Hz* (as every audio equipment buff knows) or something less than 10 octaves. Why was there so much variability in the early work?

1. It is difficult to judge where hearing leaves off and other sensations begin, or vice-versa. Ascending in frequency at the low end of the spectrum, when do successive throbs or tactile vibrations become a continuous low tone? Using a dog whistle to produce sounds at the high end of the spectrum, when does the tiny hiss of the highest tone fade into a breath sound or swish?

2. The determination of the limits of hearing was complicated by the absence of the fundamental (the so-called missing fundamental) or the presence of certain harmonics. For example, one might hear an instrument calibrated for 8 *Hz* only because the third harmonic (24 *Hz*) was audible and concludes erroneously that 8 Hz is audible. At the upper limit, the presence of harmonics, though inaudible, might contribute to difference tones. A signal might contain 40,000 *Hz* but a lower harmonic, say 20,000 *Hz,* might actually be heard but, being more intense, might lead to the erroneous impression that 40,000 *Hz* was heard.

3. Age is known to be a factor in the audibility of sound, particularly high-frequency sound. By the time a person reaches the fifties, the upper limit of hearing is more likely near 15,000 *Hz*. This is not just the effect of the aging process. It is known that exposure to prolonged high-intensity sound will damage the Organ of Corti, the sound-sensitive receptor surface in the cochlea, leading to a loss of

Perception of Pitch 125

hearing, and there is no known treatment to reverse the process of destruction or to produce regeneration of the delicate receptive hair cells.

4. Error in the determination of the limits of hearing is introduced when intensity is not accurately controlled. It is clear that the range of audibility increases with increasing intensity. A range of 30-15,000 Hz might be increased to 20-20,000 by increasing the intensity of the tones at the two extreme ends of the sound spectrum. This matter is treated later.

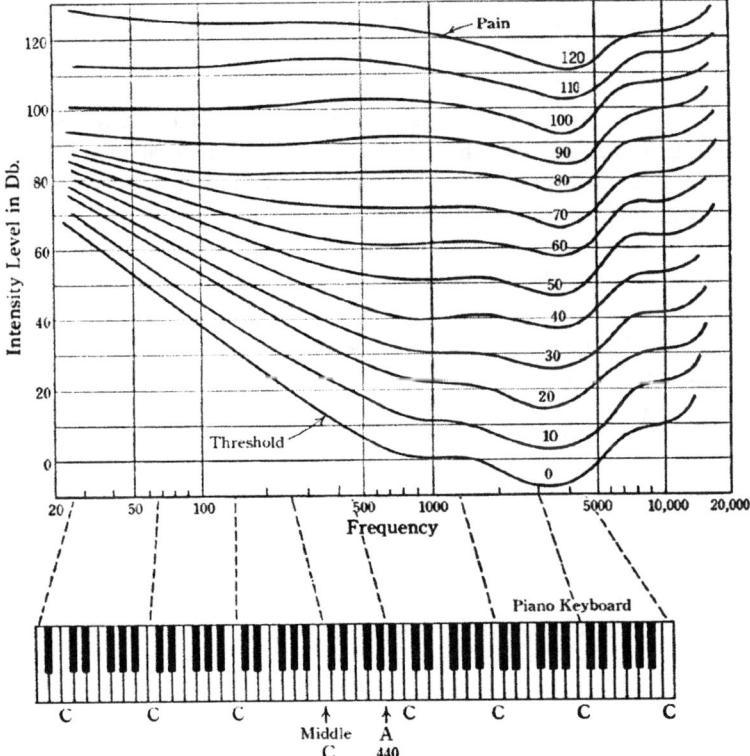

Fig. 7.6. Curves of equal loudness for persons of acute hearing. For each loudness level (0, 10, 20, 120 dB), intensity is plotted as a function of frequency. All frequencies that fall on a single curve are judged to be equally loud. It is clear that the ear is most sensitive to differences in intensity in the region of 2,000 to 5,000 Hz. Sounds above 120 dB are frequently reported to be painfully loud. Adapted from Fletcher and Munson, 1922.

Pitch Discrimination as a Function of Intensity

In 1922, Harvey Fletcher at the Bell Laboratories developed the modern audiometer, designed so that intensity of each of a large number of different frequencies could be varied from inaudibility up to the production of unpleasant tactile sensations. There is a lower limit for 'just barely hearing' and a threshold for 'feeling' or 'hurting.' Fletcher's equal loudness contours are illustrated above in Fig. 7.6. The subject varies the intensity of a series of different pitches until they all sound equally loud. The greatest sensitivity is found between 500 and 4,000 *Hz*. Sound below 500 and above 4,000 *Hz* require greater intensity to make them appear as loud as those between 500 and 4000 *Hz*.

Fletcher and Munson also found that high-pitched sounds appear higher in pitch than they really are, as they are made more intense, and low-pitched sounds appear lower than they really are, as they too are made more intense.

The highest and lowest curves might be extended so that they appear to cross at each end, enclosing an area in which lie all the audible sounds of a person with normal hearing. Beneath the lowest curve the sounds are inaudible, and above the highest curve the sounds are uncomfortable or even painful. Auditory defects in pitch perception can be judged by determining how much of this enclosed area is reduced or is missing. This is how the modern audiogram was designed to be read.

As a byproduct of the creation of the audiogram, the problem of the limits of hearing received a new solution. For example, the absolute thresholds for high and low tones vary with intensity. Reading the lower curve horizontally, it is clear that a greater intensity is required at the two ends to achieve audibility. Note that the higher curves become flatter so that, at these higher levels, pitch is less a function of intensity and more closely related to frequency alone.

Perception of Pitch

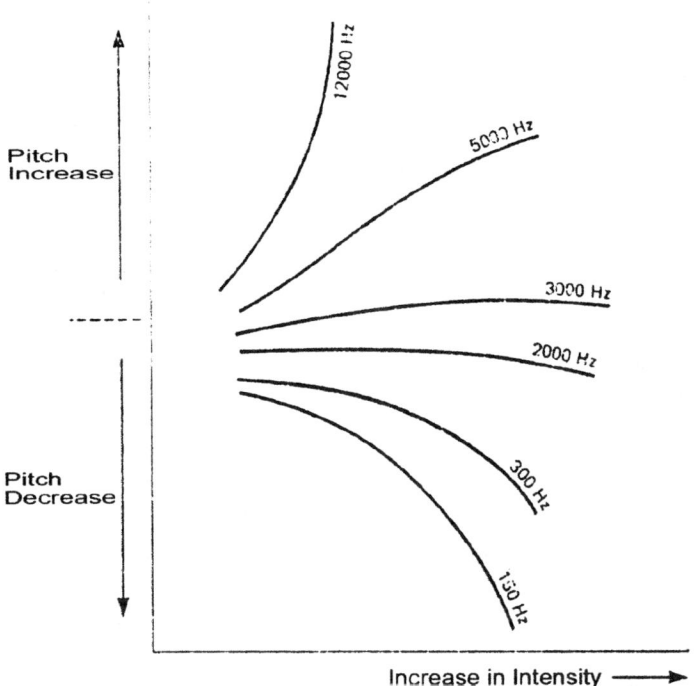

Fig. 7.7. The traditional view is that pitch varies with the frequency of the sound. But this figure suggests that pitch varies also with the intensity of the sound. As the intensity is increased, the higher-frequency tones appear higher and higher in pitch, while the low-frequency tones appear lower and lower in pitch. In the middle of the frequency band, 2,000 to 3,000 Hz, there is little effect on pitch as a result of an increase in intensity.

Here are some examples of frequencies emitted by various species in the course of their everyday living:

Species	Type of Sound	Frequencies (Hz)
Human	Conversation	200-800
Dog	Growling	450
	Barking	450-900
Cat	Meowing	760-1500
	Purring	200-400
Elephant	Trumpeting	640
Whale	Communicating	256,000
Dolphin	Communicating	100,000

PITCH SENSITIVITY

How many differences in pitch are discriminable within the audible range? Can the major and minor tones of Didymos, 9/8 and 10/9, be discriminated? These questions seemed important when equal temperament was considered as the standard (see Chapter 11). In 1827, Delezenne studied pitch sensitivity by using a movable bridge near the middle of a taut string. He noted that the just noticeable difference (JND) is equivalent to about half a comma (the difference between major and minor tones). Hence, he concluded that these two basic intervals of just temperament are discriminable.

For a time, it was generally believed that the difference limen for pitch is less than 0.5 Hz, at least in the middle of the musical range. However, twentieth century researchers have determined that the difference limens are larger than originally thought. The determinations of Shower and Biddulph (1931) have become the standard:

Frequency (Hz)	62	125	250	500	1,000	2,000
Difference Limen (Hz)	2.64	3.10	2.64	2.60	3.60	3.80

For pitch, Weber's Law, that $\Delta I/I$ is constant, does not appear to hold. Instead, ΔI is more or less constant between 62 and 2,000 Hz.

Above 5000 Hz, frequency discrimination deteriorates 10 to 20 times, probably because the frequency principle in the cochlea drops out of commission and 'place' on the basilar membrane becomes the only mechanism of pitch discrimination (see Chapter 13).

We are now ready to move on to the second attribute of the musical tone, loudness.

Chapter 8

INTENSITY & THE PERCEPTION OF LOUDNESS

INTENSITY

Sounds can be very intense. The *Concorde* produces supersonic booms that can shake a house and shatter glass. They can even shake the listener. But such intense sounds do not have to sound especially loud. It depends on who is listening. Even the most powerful sound will not cause a person who is hard of hearing to hear. Ultimately, it is the auditory mechanism, the ear and the brain, that determines how loud a sound appears to be, not just its intensity. So we must distinguish between intensity and loudness.

Earlier, we described musical sounds as waves initiated by a vibrating source that sets air particles in periodic motion. Up to now, we have focused on the frequency of motion of these sound waves. Now, let us turn to their amplitude, or degree of displacement.

In the language of the physical sciences, a vibrating musical source transfers *energy* to air particles, making them move in waves of contractions and rarefactions that spread out in all directions. The *rate* at which acoustic energy is radiated from a musical instrument is called the *power* output of that instrument.

Power is an important concept in engineering. Our ears are sensitive to acoustic power, that is, to the rate at which acoustic energy is transmitted to the eardrum. The unit of power is the watt. To illustrate, the power amplifier of an audio system might deliver 30 watts to the loudspeaker, while a 60 watt amplifier will deliver twice as much power in the same amount of time. A 150 watt lightbulb consumes energy at twice the rate of a 75 watt lightbulb.

The *power density* of a sound is determined by the acoustic power (energy/time) transmitted through a specified surface oriented in a direction perpendicular to that of the propagated wave. Expressed in watts per square meter, the power density can be thought of as the *intensity* of the sound. As you move away from a sound source, the power density decreases. Doubling your distance from the sound source decreases the power density by a factor of four. Tripling your distance decreases the power density by a factor of nine, and so on.

Instead of specifying the power density itself, however, it is customary to specify how many times the power density is greater than the power of a reference sound. This reference sound has the power of one-trillionth of a watt per square meter ($P_r = 10^{-12}$ watt/meter^2). It was selected as a reference level because it is near the absolute threshold of human subjects (near the weakest sound that humans can hear). The intensity of a sound is thus a ratio of two power densities and it is measured in decibels (dB), after Alexander Graham Bell, the inventor of the telephone and the phonograph, and the founder of the I.T.T. Corporation.

Mathematically, I_s (intensity in dB) = $10 \log_{10} P_s/P_r$

where P_s = power density of the sound source in watts/meter^2

and P_r = power density of the reference level in watts/meter^2

For convenience, the dB scale is a logarithmic one. This means that a power ratio of 100 corresponds to 20 dB, a power ratio of 1000 corresponds to 30 dB, a power ratio of 10,000 corresponds to 40 dB, and a power ratio of 100,000 corresponds to 50 dB. As you can see, the number of dB equals 10 times the number of zeros in the power ratio greater than 10. Since the human ear is sensitive to intensities of up to 120 dB or so, musical sounds can have power densities that are billions of times above the reference level (the power density at the threshold of hearing). As a matter of fact, an intensity of 120 dB is painfully loud to most people.

Since $10 \log_{10} 2/1 = 3$, a doubling of the power of the signal increases the intensity about 3 dB. For example, if 1 watt of power produces 60 dB of sound intensity through a loudspeaker, then 2 watts produces 63 dB, 4 watts produces 66 dB, and 8 watts produces 69 dB. If the speaker is driven with 100 watts, it will produce 80 dB of sound intensity. However, many speakers would be destroyed by so much power.

Atmospheric pressure is about $10^6 dynes/cm^2$. A quick calculation reveals that the human can detect variations in sound pressure of two parts per ten billion. Like the eye, the ear is a remarkably sensitive sense organ. At a frequency of roughly 3,600 Hz, where sensitivity seems greatest, a tone can be heard when the ear drum moves 4.5 billionth of a millimeter (4.5 x 10^{-10} cm.). That amplitude is less than 2% of the diameter of the hydrogen molecule!

Theoretically, we should just be able to hear a 1-watt, 3,500 Hz test signal at a distance of 564 kilometers, but, of course, there is no way of checking this out because there is always noise interference in the environment masking the test signal. Threshold determinations are similarly affected: we cannot hear sounds whose intensities are near reference level because the ambient noise level is high. Today, we have to look far and wide to find a quiet place. Even when we are alone indoors, we are surrounded by the racket of heating or air conditioning and the appliances of modern living. The average sound level in a concert hall well packed with attentive listeners approaches 40 dB! In order to reduce the ambient noise to a minimum, thresholds are determined in an anechoic chamber. But, even there, the sounds of the heart, of respiration and of digestion are not negligible, and will interfere with threshold determinations.

An orchestra produces a wide range of sound levels in a concert hall, from about 40 to 100 dB (varying by a factor of one million). A rock band might reach 130 dB, ten billion times more intense than the threshold level. Here are some additional average intensities. The sound level of conversational speech ranges from 40 to 70 dB (varying by a factor of one thousand). At 3 meters, in open air, the clarinet may reach 86 dB, the piano 94 dB, and the bass drum 113 dB. Every time we double the distance, the intensity drops 6 dB, or so.

As you can see, the auditory system has a very wide dynamic range, far wider than any audio system can reproduce. The smallest increment of sound intensity that can be appreciated as a just noticeable increase in loudness is in the neighborhood of 0.1-1.0 dB.

Power Density (P) (Watts/Meter^2)	Sound Source Example	Intensity (dB) $10 \operatorname{Log}(P/10^{-12})$	Loudness Designation
10^2		130	(Pain)
1	Live rock concert	120	Triple forte
10^{-3}	Subway train	90	Fortissimo
10^{-4}	Noisy traffic	80	Fortissimo
10^{-5}	Busy street	70	Forte
10^{-6}	Loud conversation	60	Mezzo-forte
10^{-7}	Soft conversation	50	Mezzo-piano
10^{-8}	Hushed concert hall	40	Piano
10^{-9}	Whisper	30	Pianissimo
10^{-10}	Bedroom at night	20	Triple piano
10^{-12}		0	Threshold

While intensity is a physical measurement, loudness is subjective. How loud a sound is depends on who is listening, where the sound is generated and transmitted, and under what conditions. A sound that is just audible to one person with normal hearing may be 15 dB or more above threshold for another.

Loudness varies not only as a function of intensity but also as a function of frequency. This can be seen in the audiogram that is discussed in Chapter 13. (In the audio industry, the intensity level control is often labeled 'volume.' However, psychologists appropriated this term in the 1930s to describe an alleged fifth quality in music which listeners seemed to be able to judge with some consistency. Experiments have shown that the quality of 'volume' in music is a joint function of frequency and intensity: sounds lower in pitch and louder have a greater 'volume' than sounds higher and softer. Furthermore, a high and loud sound might have the same 'volume' as a lower and softer sound. Considering this history of the term 'volume,' it is misleading for manufacturers of audio equipment to use that label for a control that varies intensity alone. It is especially misleading because switching on the traditional 'loudness control' on a preamplifier *reduces* the bass response as 'volume' is increased.

Manufacturers should drop the term 'volume' for the knob that controls intensity and replace it with 'intensity level' or some equivalent.)

SPECIFICATION OF LOUDNESS

The role of intensity in determining the dynamics of music must be addressed. Since loudness is subjective, it is not identical to sound pressure level, or the physical dimension of intensity. On the input side, there are two aspects of musical dynamics. One is the sensitivity of the listener to hear weak sounds. The second is the capacity of the listener to hear small differences in intensity. On the output or performance side, there are also two aspects of musical dynamics. One is the ability of the performer to control the intensity of the produced sound. The other is the ability of the performer to vary intensity in subtle and musically significant ways.

Several loudness scales have been proposed in recent years, but none of them match the usefulness and precision of the pitch and tempo scales that are used in music. An example of a loudness scale is the sone scale, which was derived in a purely psychophysical way (Stevens, 1936). The loudness of a sine wave of 1000 Hz, played with a sound pressure level of 40 dB, is assigned a loudness value of 1 sone. A tone judged to be twice as loud is assigned the loudness of 2 sones, and one twice as loud again is assigned a loudness of 4 sones, and so on. In general, a sound of N(L) sones is N times louder than a sound of L sones. Unfortunately, this scale is not a very reliable one, because subjects are uncertain in their judgments when setting a sound twice as loud as another.

If the sound energy is limited to one critical band, the loudness, L, in sones, increases monotonically with intensity, I. Stevens' power law is usually written in the form:

$L = kI^n$

where k and n are empirically chosen constants.

With the exponent n = 0.33, for example, an increase of 9 dB doubles the loudness. Thus, the judged loudness of a sound rises slowly at low intensities, but faster and faster as the intensity increases progressively from low to high. The relation embodied in Stevens' power law can be interpreted to mean that equal intensity ratios result in equal loudness ratios.

In musical notation, the specification of loudness is much less precise than the specification of pitch or of tempo. For example, if we want to specify the dynamic modulation in a passage, that is the periodic variations in intensity, we speak of a crescendo or diminuendo, of an attack or a release, etc. But these are specifications of relative loudness only, nothing more.

The number of assignable degrees of loudness is certainly less than 10. There are six standard markings of dynamics in musical notation: pianissimo, piano, mezzo-piano, mezzo-forte, forte, and fortissimo. It is impossible to assign numbers to these degrees of loudness, illustrating how imprecise these markings are. Perhaps this is good, for it permits a wide range of interpretation. But, compared with tempo markings, such as *adagio* or *allegro* that can be specified precisely by the number of metronome beats per minute dynamics markings are primitive indeed.

The fact is that the physical intensity underlying loudness is hard to control. This is because the acoustic conditions, such as the absorption and reflection of sound, the presence or absence of an audience, the relative position of sound source and listener, and disturbing noises, all vary from time to time. If we attempted to specify loudness by citing the intensity of the sound alone, we would lose the influences of all these factors. Add to this list the fact that listeners differ in their ability to hear sound, and we must conclude that loudness is extremely variable, starting with sound production at one extreme, all the way to sound perception, at the other. In comparison, the scales of frequency and tempo are fixed and specifiable in precise terms.

In the audio business, the volume of a sound refers to its loudness. However, as already pointed out, volume is not equivalent to loudness. The volume of a piece of music is affected by varying not only the intensity of the sound but also its pitch and timbre.

LOUDNESS SENSITIVITY

In the midrange of intensities, Weber's Law for loudness seems to hold quite well. The Weber fraction, or just noticeable difference (JND), $\Delta I/I$, turns out to be something in the order of 0.1 between 30 and 100 dB. With 325 discriminably different loudnesses at 1,000 *Hz*, and about 1,500 discriminably different pitches, Stevens calculated a total of about 340,000 discriminably different tones. This number had a bearing on Helmholtz's resonance theory of hearing, for it suggested how many resonators were required to mediate this degree of discriminability. With just 20,000 hair cells per cochlea according to Corti and assuming that each mediates just one JND, the problem seemed formidable.

Following the development of the concept of sensory quanta, Stevens, Morgan and Volkman (1941) have argued that difference limens are never found when the difference between tones is less than one quantum. On the other hand, a tonal increment of two quanta is always discriminable. Just how many hair cells are necessary to mediate the gamut of JNDs is no longer an issue, with the adoption of von Bekesy's wave theory of pitch perception.

So ends our review of the second perceptual attribute of the musical tone, loudness. We are now ready to tackle the third, timbre.

Chapter 9

PERCEPTION OF TIMBRE

INTRODUCTION

Let us start with the traditional view. Together with pitch and loudness, timbre is a principal attribute of musical tones. Timbre permits us to judge whether two tones having the same pitch, loudness, and duration are played by two different musical instruments or not. Most of us can distinguish the tones of violin and clarinet because they differ in timbre. Some of us can even distinguish two different violins playing the same tone because they too differ in timbre. This attribute is often described as tonal quality, tonal color, texture and complexity.

    The attribute of timbre applies to more than just musical instruments. We speak of the timbre of the human voice, the birdcall, and the chirp of the cricket; of siren, bell and gong; and even of thunder, surf and patter of rain. We also speak of timbre as the perceptual counterpart of the complexity of waveform or spectral composition of sounds. From a physical standpoint, the spectral composition refers to the relative amplitudes of the various harmonic constituents of a complex tone. We will see later that this traditional view of timbre has been revised and expanded as a result of a new understanding derived from sound synthesizer technology.

Like all other attributes of music, timbre obeys the law of perceptual constancy. This means that a sound source can be reliably identified by its timbre over a wide range of perceptual conditions. A bassoon, for example, is readily identified regardless of the pitch or loudness of the note it plays. Furthermore, the bassoon remains identifiable even when it is surrounded by the sounds of other instruments, such as the flute, oboe and clarinet, or even when it is heard on a pocket-sized transistor radio, despite the fact that its sound is badly distorted.

Variety adds a layer of richness to music. In traditional orchestral music, the timbre of a theme is frequently varied by moving it from one instrument or set of instruments to another. Listen to the last movement of Beethoven's Ninth *(Chorale)* Symphony, the movement containing Schiller's *Ode to Joy*, with this in mind. After a tentative four-bar fragment in the woodwinds, the familiar folk melody (occupying sixteen bars with an additional eight-bar reprise) is introduced by the cellos and bass, *sotto voce*. This melody is repeated several times, rising progressively in volume and tension as it moves from one choir of instruments to another: starting with violas and cellos, it moves to violins and to brass and woodwinds in a remarkable swell of tone. With a leap into an uncharted symphonic sea of sound, Beethoven then transforms this simple folk melody into a lofty hymn to joy with words by Schiller. The first stanzas are sung by baritone solo with chorus on the reprise. The remaining seven stanzas are sung by the vocal quartet in successive variations and with mounting tension, each time with chorus on the reprise. Singing the first two stanzas once again, the chorus brings this section to a close in a mightly crescendo. The movement continues in a more restrained manner but with ever-mounting tension, again using the original folk melody in endless variations, and concludes with breathless excitement.

Leaving aside the melodic variations, the ornamentations and the lyrics, notice how Beethoven modulates the timbre by moving the folk melody from one choir of instruments to another, and back and forth between vocal soloists and chorus. This happens to be a remarkable display of tonal color, but it is not unique. Such displays flourished in the romantic period: for example, in the orchestral compositions of Berlioz, Wagner and Mahler who used masses of sounds to display the timbre of musical instruments.

Modern technology has provided an alternate method to vary timbre in music. No longer are acoustic instruments required. With the aid of the sound synthesizer, it is now possible to generate an unlimited variety of complex sounds, those that are familiar in nature and those that have never been heard before. A new understanding of timbre, derived from computer technology, permits the composer to write music for synthesizer in which the timbre of the music replaces melody and rhythm as the principal feature of the music. Imagine a musical composition that is based upon variations of tonal color rather than on variations of pitch. Such music bears no resemblance to traditional music in which the melody is the principal feature, and we can no longer expect to hum the music as we are accustomed to hum a melody or the theme of a symphony. Listen to Ligeti's 'Artikulation' (Wergo, WER 60059) for a very early example of this kind of music. Though some critics might claim that variations in timbre are too subtle to form the basis of enjoyable music, psychologists have pointed out that all of us depend upon the different timbres of vocal sounds to understand speech. Judging from the growing demand for electronic music, this new focus on timbre will lead to novel musical forms and to new musical idioms, indeed to a new musical genre.

Electronic music has won a growing audience. Pioneers in the field include Vladimir Ussachevsky and Otto Luening. Both helped to found the electronic studio at Columbia University in New York. In more recent years, Milton Babbitt has worked there.

To follow these developments in our understanding of timbre and its application in musical composition, we must first review the concepts of resonance, harmonic structure, and the principles that govern the experience of consonance and dissonance.

RESONANCE AND HARMONICS

Strike a tuning fork against a tabletop and you will hear it vibrate to produce a thin wisp of sound. At a distance of three or four feet from your ear, you may not hear it at all. But if you place the stem of the vibrating tuning fork firmly on the tabletop, the sound will be amplified substantially and the tuning fork will seem to buzz. The reason is that the tabletop is made to vibrate in sympathy with the tuning fork. Compared to the thin wisp of the tuning fork vibrating in air, this sympathetic or *resonant* sound is more nearly like that of familiar musical tones. All modern musical instruments, strings, wind

142   *Sound and Music*

and percussion, have a body or surface (such as the sounding board of the piano) that resonates to the sound generated by the performer.

If you pluck one of two adjacent strings tuned to the same frequency, you will find that the other is thrown into sympathetic vibration. The string will resonate even if its tuned frequency was sounded on another instrument, such as an organ or a horn. All objects have a particular set of resonant frequencies: that is, they are likely to be thrown into sympathetic vibration by a limited number of sounds. It was well known by the seventeenth century that a crystal glass object might crack at the sound of a trumpet playing a tone in unison with the resonant frequency of the object. It may be that the sounds of Joshua's trumpets made the walls of Jericho resonate and that is why they came tumbling down. The great tenor, Enrico Caruso, was reputed to shatter a wineglass with his powerful voice when he sang a tone that approximated the resonant frequency of the glass.

Fig. 9.1. Glass goblet vibrating. That a solid object can be made to vibrate is easily demonstrated. Here, a glass goblet has a number of lightweight balls hanging around it so that they just barely touch the rim. When the rim is stroked with a violin bow, the goblet is set in vibratory motion, as indicated by the violent motion of the balls. A glass goblet can even be shattered if it is made to resonate to an intense sound.

It was already noted in the seventeenth century that plucking the higher-pitched of two strings placed side by side might cause the lower string to vibrate in parts. By wrapping a bit of paper around a vibrating string and moving it to different positions on the string, you can actually see the amplitude of vibrations vary along the length of the string, and you will satisfy yourself that vibrating strings always divide into simple fractions -- into halves, thirds and quarters, to produce the octave (or second harmonic), the twelfth (or third harmonic), and the double octave (or fourth harmonic, see Fig. 6.7)

Harmonics can easily be demonstrated on the piano. Raise the damper for middle C by silently depressing its key. Then forcibly strike the C below middle C and release the key at once. Though the struck C will immediately be damped, the higher C (middle C) will clearly be heard; the struck C has thrown it into sympathetic vibration. Similarly, raise the dampers for the shorter strings matching the various upper harmonics of the C below middle C (such as the G above middle C and the E above that), and you will hear each of these harmonics by just striking the low C. The explanation is that the upper harmonics produced by the low C will generate sympathetic vibrations of the shorter strings. Sometimes music teachers demonstrate the phenomenon of resonance to their pupils by depressing the damper pedal and singing a specific note loudly into the piano, which, in turn, echoes the note.

The presence of harmonics in complex tones was already recognized by the seventeenth century. In 1636, Mersenne noticed that a vibrating string produces a number of high tones (overtones) that become audible as the fundamental pitch fades out. Descartes suggested that these overtones result from the string vibrating in parts, and he proved to be right. Today, we apply the term 'fundamental' to the lowest frequency heard, and reserve the term 'harmonic' for the overtones that are integer multiples of the fundamental. The harmonics can be brought out by lightly touching a vibrating string at a node (the point that divides the separately vibrating parts of the string). For example, if the string is touched at one-third of its length, its fundamental frequency is damped and its third, sixth, ninth, etc., harmonics become audible. All intervening harmonics are damped. Virtuosity on the violin includes the ability to play harmonics by lightly touching the string at a node without fully depressing it.

In short, the listener hears the total vibration of the string, which is composed of the sum of all the harmonic vibrations sounding simultaneously. Although the upper harmonics are not ordinarily identifiable in the total mass of sound, they come out clearly when the lower components have been damped, and they can be identified by a *Fourier* analysis, as we shall see.

Compared to complex tones, pure tones or sine waves have unambiguous pitches that are directly related to their frequencies. But they sound bland and uninteresting; they lack color. Complex tones, the tones we are accustomed to hear in music, contain perhaps six or seven audible harmonics. They sound brighter and warmer, even a bit tremulous, and sometimes buzzy or raspy. (Theoretically, a complex tone has an unlimited number of harmonics but most listeners cannot identify them. The first sixteen are listed in Fig. 11.2.)

The listener can sometimes be trained to distinguish the first few harmonics. Once trained, his attention can then be drawn to their presence. However, a complex tone is ordinarily heard to have a single pitch, that of the fundamental component. This singleness of pitch is an example of tonal fusion, a phenomenon to which we will turn presently.

Harmonics, together with the fundamental frequency of a complex tone, were named partials by Helmholtz, the great nineteenth century physiologist, to call attention to the fact that a complex tone may contain inharmonic as well as harmonic components. Unlike harmonics, the inharmonic components are not related to the fundamental frequency as integer multiples (e.g. 2/1, 3/1, etc.). It is the inharmonic components that give instruments like the gong and cymbals their unique color.

The writer of traditional music specifies just the fundamental frequencies of complex tones, not the harmonic or inharmonic components. (The musical staff is not designed to indicate the timbre of each individual tone. Composers indicate timbre by specifying particular instruments or voices.) These fundamental frequencies range from about 25 to 4,500 *Hz* (the range of piano strings and organ pipes). However, humans can hear up to 20,000 *Hz*, but these very high frequencies provide very little in the way of definite pitch sensations.

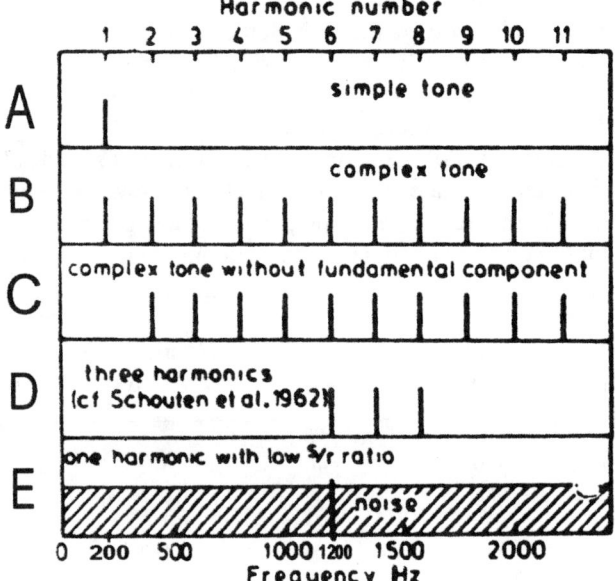

Fig. 9.2. What composition of frequency components is required for the perception of the pitch of a fundamental frequency? The answer is not as simple as you might guess. It goes without saying that the fundamental frequency alone, as emitted by a tuning fork, will suffice (A). It is also clear that a series of natural harmonics will fuse with the fundamental to yield the same pitch (B). More surprising is that the fundamental frequency may be missing from the series of harmonics without affecting the apparent pitch of the tone (C). Even more baffling is that a limited number of upper harmonics, as few as three (Schouten et al, 1962), will suffice (D). It has even been suggested that one harmonic will suffice to produce the same fundamental pitch (E). Houtgast (1976) succeeded by sounding the sixth harmonic and filling the region of the fundamental with noise. To work, he found that the harmonic must have a low signal-to-noise ratio, and attention must be directed to the fundamental frequency by prior stimuli. (Adapted from Rasch and Plomp, 1982).

Above 5,000 *Hz* or so, high tones have the character of a thin 'sss...' sound. Low tones, in the audible range of 20 to 40 *Hz*, have the character of a rumbling or rattling sound. Transitions to and from definite musical pitch are gradual at both the high and the low ends of the audible spectrum. It is a remarkable fact that pitch can be recognized after just a very few waves of the sound have been presented, less than a millisecond of sound.

A comparison of the harmonic composition of sounds of two acoustic instruments, bassoon and clarinet, is shown in the table below. Note the differences in the proportion of energy present in the fundamental frequency and in the second and third harmonics:

Harmonics	Bassoon: E=329 Hz		Clarinet: $D^{\#}$=622 Hz	
	Frequency (Hz)	% Energy	Frequency (Hz)	% Energy
Fundamental	329	40	622	93
2nd	658	29	1,244	0
3rd	987	25	1,866	2
4th	1,316	5	2,488	1
5th	1,645	0	3,180	3
6th	1,974	0	3,732	1

Since Helmholtz, the timbre of complex tones was thought to vary solely according to the proportion of energy in the various harmonics, as illustrated in the table. However, the attempts to synthesize complex musical tones in recent years have made it plain that timbre has a more complex physical basis. The distinguishing characteristics of piano and flute tones depend also upon the rise and decay times of each of the component partials. We will have more to say about this later.

Fourier Analysis

In 1822, Baron Fourier reported that any continuous function or curve, no matter what its shape or how irregular, can be represented by the algebraic sum of a series of sine waves. Each of these sine waves has its own frequency and amplitude and together they bear certain phase relationships to one another. Fourier proved, first, that there is one and only one solution to the analysis of a complex waveform, and second, that the original complex function can be reconstructed from its constituent sine waves and will approach any degree of approximation by adding enough harmonic components to the series.

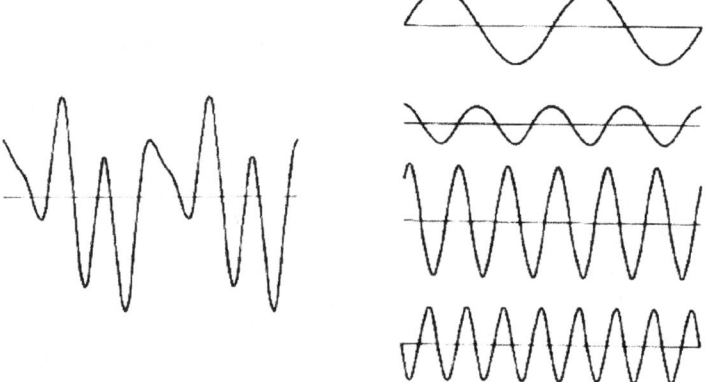

Fig. 9.3. Fourier's theorem is illustrated here. A complex waveform, left, is in fact the sum of the simple waveforms on the right. The sinusoidal waveforms on the right are referred to as the first harmonic or fundamental, the second, third and fourth harmonics.

A Fourier analysis can be made of the complex waveforms generated by musical instruments. If the form of the complex sound wave is known, the analysis can be made mathematically, or the components can be identified by resonance, provided that an adequate number of resonators is made available. In short, any complex tone can be represented by a series of sine waves that bear a certain phase relationship to one another, each having its own frequency and amplitude. The sine waves that result from a Fourier analysis can be displayed on an oscilloscope screen, as shown in Fig. 9.3.

The Fourier principle is synthetic as well as analytic; this means that one should be able to create a complex tone by the addition of its harmonics just as one could analyze any complex function into its harmonic components. Modern synthesizers of complex musical tones make use of a series of sine wave generators and the Fourier principle to determine the proper proportions of component sine waves.

In 1843, Ohm (of 'Ohm's Law' fame) gave the Fourier analysis a physiological meaning. Ohm argued that the inner ear performs the same harmonic analysis: it 'resonates' to each of the various harmonic components. This acoustic law of Ohm implies that it should be possible to pay separate attention to the simple harmonic components of any complex tone although musically untrained people are unaware that separate harmonics exist in a complex tone.

Ohm's law provided the basis for Helmholtz's resonance-place theory of pitch perception. This theory proposes that the basilar membrane in the cochlea is tuned to respond in parts to different pitches - high tones at the basal end of the cochlea and low tones closer to the apex. In Chapter 13, we will review the contributions of von Békésy who showed that high tones do, in fact, produce local perturbations in the cochlea, but that low tones throw the entire basilar membrane into motion thus raising the question whether the place principle can account for the discriminability of low tones.

TONAL FUSION

As discussed earlier, complex musical tones are obtained by combining sine waves of different frequencies. The modern synthesizer can generate recognizable musical tones by sounding together the frequencies of the harmonic series: f, 2f, 3f, 4f, 5f, 6f, and so on, in proper proportions. Such a combination of frequencies produces the impression of a single musical tone in which the components have intimately fused, and which can be described as having a certain pitch and loudness and a certain timbre or tonal quality. Yet, when we hit the C major triad on the piano, we hear a chord of three distinct tones, C, E, G, not one fused tone, though we are actually playing the fourth, fifth, and sixth harmonics of a C two octaves below. Why do we not get the unitary impression of a single fused complex tone when playing a major triad?

A number of factors are involved. First of all, it is clear that sine waves are required for fusion to take place. Piano tones do not qualify, since they are all complex tones. Second, a little vibrato helps to fuse the components into a single tone, the same vibrato for all harmonics. In short, if we want to produce a single fused tone using the C major triad as components, we need to use sine wave generators

- tuning forks, for example, rather than piano tones - and play the three tones with a little vibrato.

It was Helmholtz who pointed out that harmonics fuse so intimately with each other that they cannot be heard separately. However, once the listener knows what to listen for, he can frequently learn to hear the harmonics in a tonal complex provided that they are sufficiently intense. Stumpf, a turn-of-the-century psychologist, recognized this fact in 1890.

According to Stumpf, there are different degrees of tonal fusion, depending on the frequency of the components. The octave produces the best fusion. Stumpf's untutored subjects mistook the two tones of the octave for a single tone most of the time. The fifth produces the next best fusion, being mistaken for a single tone about half the time. The fourth comes next, followed by the third and sixth, and, finally, the seconds and sevenths.

In the course of this experiment, Stumpf noted that the degree of fusion is not greatly affected by slight mistunings. The 'equal tempered' intervals are as subject to fusion as are the 'just' intervals. For example, the equal tempered third, having a frequency ratio of about 1.26/1, fuses to the same degree as the just third, having a frequency ratio of 1.25/1 (5/4). Moreover, tonal fusion occurs under conditions of dichotic listening, that is, when one tone is presented to one ear and another to the other ear, proving that tonal fusion takes place in the brain and not in the cochlea.

At one time, theorists of tonal fusion described the octave as 'smooth,' the fifth as 'hollow,' the fourth 'coarse,' the third 'mellow,' the sixth 'luscious,' the seventh 'astringent,' and the second 'gritty'! No wonder modern psychologists have been disposed to dismiss the early theories of tonal fusion. But the problem of understanding tonal fusion persists. Contemporary composers of electronic music, such as Chowning, have made important contributions to the understanding of tonal fusion.

But to tackle the problem of why tones fuse, we have to raise the question, why is the pitch of the complex tone ordinarily the pitch of the fundamental? This is true even when the second and third harmonics are more intense than the fundamental, and even when the fundamental is actually missing from the acoustic signal. The physiological basis for tonal fusion is not yet understood, but those concerned with sound synthesis have explored its conditions, as we shall see.

CONSONANCE AND DISSONANCE

The Pythagorean Intervals. When played together, certain tones are said to produce an agreeable or consonant effect on the listener, while others are said to produce a less agreeable or dissonant effect. There has been a great deal of debate as to which intervals are consonant and which are dissonant. But, despite numerous efforts, no agreement has been reached on the definition of consonance and dissonance, nor is there likely ever to be agreement, since this matter is, ultimately, a subjective judgment. It's like asking, which do you like better, apples or oranges?

In traditional Western culture, most people judge the octave, perfect fifth and fourth, and major and minor thirds and sixths, as consonant. These intervals are supposed to carry the feeling of smoothness and harmony, while the other intervals in the octave, carry the feeling of roughness and tension. This was not always so. The truth is that standards change, and what was dissonant for one generation becomes consonant for another.

The Pythagorean intervals, 2/1, 3/2, and 4/3, were the consonances of antiquity. During the period of early polyphony, around 900-1100 A.D., the fourth was the preeminent consonant followed by the fifth. By the end of this period Guido of Arezzo, the great innovator of musical notation, had proposed four consonances: the perfect fourth, the major second, and the major and minor thirds, thus excluding the fifth. By the thirteenth century, the unison and the octave were accepted as 'perfect' consonances; next came the fourth and fifth; and finally came the 'imperfect' consonances of major and minor thirds. The major and minor sixths were regarded as dissonant intervals, as were the seconds and sevenths.

But it was already becoming clear that consonance was not only a matter of the particular interval played, but also depended upon the musical context. An interval that sounds dissonant in one context might be quite consonant in another if properly resolved, for example. When played together, an F and adjacent G form the interval of a major second. In the absence of a musical context, most listeners of traditional music would describe this as a tension-provoking sound and would call that interval dissonant. But if a second interval, a minor third composed of the same G and the E below, followed the first (as in the novice pianist's 'Chop Sticks'), most listeners would accept that as an agreeable cadence. Beethoven began his First

Symphony with a dominant seventh chord that was dissonant to his contemporaries, but it was promptly resolved, and the result is quite agreeable, certainly to our ears. It must have sounded strange to many of Beethoven's contemporaries when first performed, for they were not accustomed to such sequences of sounds at the beginning of a piece.

Those who have sought physical objectivity in the matter of consonance and dissonance have offered a number of interesting suggestions. According to the classic Pythagorean theory, the smaller the numbers that express the ratio of frequencies, the more consonant the interval appears to be. The ten intervals cited below are listed in order of increasing complexity of frequency ratio. The same order of intervals is obtained (more or less) when the listener is asked to list them in order of decreasing consonance:

Unison	1/1
Octave	2/1
Perfect fifth	3/2
Perfect fourt	4/3
Major sixth	5/3
Major third	5/4
Minor third	6/5
Minor sixth	8/5
Major seventh	15/8
Minor seventh	16/9

The trouble with this theory of consonance is that it fails to take into account that the corresponding well-tempered intervals having complicated frequency ratios are still judged to be consonant. For example, the well tempered fifth, represented by the ratio, 439/293, sounds as consonant to most listeners as the harmonic fifth, 439.5/293 (3/2).

Let us concede that there are degrees of consonance and dissonance. According to Stumpf, the degree of consonance of an interval can be measured by the degree of fusion of the two constituent tones. The percentage of listeners reporting the perception of one tone, when there were indeed two, was used by Stumpf as a measure of consonance. Based on a large-scale experiment, Stumpf's results were as follows:

Octave	75%
Fifth	50%
Fourth	33%
Third	25%
Tritone	20%
Second	10%

If you accept these data as relevant, where would you draw the line between consonance and dissonance? At 50%? This would make the fifth barely consonant, and the fourth decidedly dissonant. Most contemporary listeners would challenge this conclusion.

According to Helmholtz, when two non-unison tones are played together, the degree of consonance depends on the number of coinciding harmonics. Helmholtz showed that the simpler the ratio, the greater the number of coinciding harmonics and the greater the consonance. The most consonant interval is the octave, 2/1: all the harmonics of the upper tone coincide with the harmonics of the lower. The next is the fifth, 3/2: two of the harmonics of the upper tone coincide with two of the harmonics of the lower tone (see Fig. 10.3). The tritone, 45/32, is more dissonant: only 1/32 of the harmonics of the upper tone coincide with 1/45 of the harmonics of the lower. In defining consonance, Helmholtz eschewed esthetic considerations in favor of mathematical ratios in the tradition of Pythagoras. Ultimately, however, consonance and dissonance reside in the realm of esthetics and this is where our search must take us. Nevertheless, many authorities still believe, along with Helmholtz, that dissonance is associated with the presence of unpleasant beats.

Beats. If two pure tones having equal frequencies and amplitudes are played together, they fuse into one tone whose intensity is the sum of the two and is steady if the two tones are exactly in phase. If the two tones differ slightly in frequency, they still fuse into one tone, but one that now fluctuates in intensity, throbbing at a rate equal to the difference between their individual frequencies. When played together, two sine-wave tones, one G tuned to 196 *Hz*, the other mistuned to 198 *Hz*, sound like one tone that pulsates at a rate of twice per second, the difference between the two frequencies. The throbbing is called beats and is due to amplitude variation, which can be displayed on an oscilloscope screen. If the two tones differ by less than 20 Hz or so in the lower range of audible frequencies, the beating can be heard distinctly, and, if the difference is less than 8 Hz, the beats can even be counted.

When the frequency difference is more than 20 Hz, the listener can no longer follow the individual beats as loudness fluctuations and the experience becomes rattle-like or jangly and is frequently described as rough and harsh. For many contemporary listeners, this experience is judged to be unpleasant only if the interference between the two tones is not resolved in some way. If the frequency difference is further increased beyond a minor third or so (the critical bandwidth), no fusion takes place, and the two tones are perceived individually and distinctly with no rough interference between them.

When beats are created by mistuning tones that have complex waveforms, not only are their mistuned fundamentals responsible, their non-coinciding harmonics are responsible as well. For example, if the fundamentals of a fifth are mistuned, their harmonics will also be mistuned and these, too, will cause beats. This has practical consequences. As an aid in tuning their instruments, violinists play two strings at the same time and listen for the beating of harmonics.

Have you ever watched a piano tuner at work? He starts by striking an octave in the middle register, and uses his tuning wrench to increase or decrease the tension of the mistuned string. He tunes the octave by decreasing the rate of beating, and he knows that the octave is perfectly tuned when the beats cease. Actually the piano tuner listens for beats between the second harmonic of the lower tone and the fundamental of the upper tone, and it is when these beats disappear that the octave is in tune.

Intervals other than octaves are also tuned by listening for beats, this time adjusting for a specified slow rate of beating (if the tuning is equal-tempered). Once all the tones of an octave are tuned, they can be used to tune the corresponding tones of octaves above and below, again by listening for beats.

As pointed out earlier, intensity fluctuations are the basis for the perception of beats. In order to understand how these intensity fluctuations are generated, it is necessary to examine the way two simultaneous tones interact with each other. In addition to their respective frequencies and amplitudes, two tones bear a certain phase relationship to each other. Consider two pure tones that are identical in frequency and amplitude, and suppose that they are exactly in

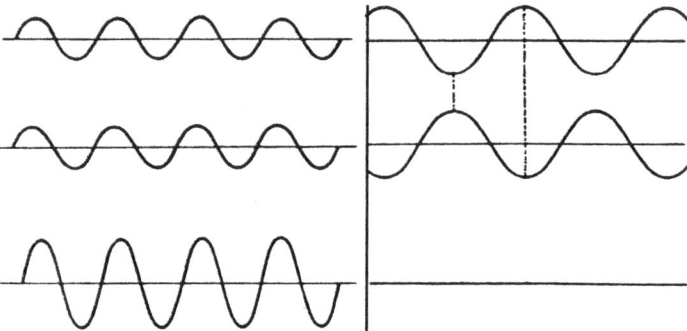

Fig. 9.4. Phase relations. On the upper left, two identical waveforms are shown exactly in phase. When played together, the two summate and the amplitude of the resultant is twice that of the two constituents. On the upper right, two identical waveforms are shown exactly out of phase. A sum of their amplitudes results in a cancellation of one waveform by the other. The resultant waves are shown at the bottom of the figure.

phase. Under normal circumstances, these two waveforms will summate to produce a waveform equal in frequency and double in amplitude. Because its amplitude is that much greater, the resultant tone will sound much louder than each constituent tone alone. This is diagrammed in Fig. 9.4. Now, suppose the same two tones are exactly opposite in phase. In an acoustically controlled environment, they will cancel each other out, and nothing will be heard. This is also diagrammed in Fig. 9.4.

If the two simultaneous tones differ in frequency, their phase relationships will vary continuously, from exactly in phase to exactly out of phase, back and forth. When the discrepancy in frequency is small, the phase relationship of the two tones will shift slowly: when in phase, their amplitudes will summate and the resultant sound will be that much louder; as they move out of phase, the resultant amplitude will diminish, and the sound will get softer; when exactly out of phase, the two tones will cancel each other completely and nothing will be heard. As they move back in phase, the resultant amplitude will increase, and the sound will get louder. In short, there will be an alternation of summation and cancellation of amplitudes as the two tones move in and out of phase. Fig. 9.5 shows how the amplitudes of two sine waves of slightly different frequencies interact with each other. On the oscilloscope screen, the resultant waveform waxes and wanes in amplitude and the resultant experience is the throbbing of beats.

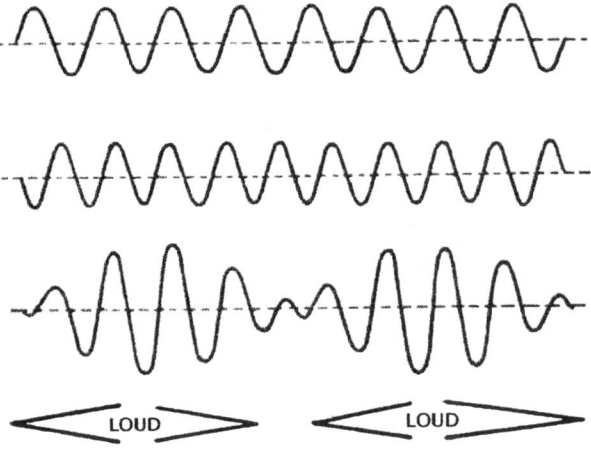

Fig 9.5. *The generation of beats. Consider two simultaneous tones whose frequencies do not quite match. The two frequencies will necessarily move from positions of exact in-phase relationship to exact out-of-phase relationship, at a rate determined by the precise difference between the two frequencies. As the two waveforms move toward an in-phase relationship, the waves will summate, the amplitude will progressively increase, and the sound will get louder. As the two waveforms move toward an out-of-phase relationship, there will be a progressive reduction in the amplitude, and the sound will get softer. The result is a fluctuation of loudness, called beats.*

In line with his resonance theory of pitch perception, Helmholtz suggested that beats occur when two similar frequencies act on the same resonator in the cochlea. However, it is now thought that beats must involve mechanisms beyond the cochlea, in the brain itself, since beats can be heard with dichotic stimulation: when the two mistuned tones are presented individually, one to one ear and one to the other. Since beats are still heard under these dichotic conditions, they cannot be generated within one cochlea, as Helmholtz thought they always were, but must be the result of an interaction of neural activity upstream where the inputs from the two cochleas converge, that is, somewhere in the auditory part of the brain.

Now, to relate the phenomenon of beats to consonance and dissonance. According to Helmholtz, intervals are consonant if no disturbing beats are produced by the fundamentals of two complex tones, or by their higher harmonics. If beats are produced, the intervals are dissonant. Since the most disturbing rate of beating is in the neighborhood of 33 beats per second, this theory predicts that the third, C to E (131 to 164 *Hz*, generating 33 beats per second), should sound as dissonant as the second, C to D, (261 to 294 *Hz*, also generating 33 beats per second). Needless to say, this is not what most people experience. Thus, we are entitled to question Helmholtz's theory as the sole explanation of consonance and dissonance. This matter will be investigated further in the Chapter 10.

Chapter 10

PERSPECTIVES ON TONAL COLOR

CRITICAL BANDWIDTH

We have seen that Helmholtz tried to explain dissonance entirely in terms of beats. He suggested that dissonance is experienced when two complex tones that differ slightly in pitch are played at the same time. Under these conditions, the fundamental frequencies and upper harmonics interact to produce the experience of throbbing beats.

Plomp (1976) has challenged the generality of this view. The relation between the experience of dissonance and beats is not always predictable. For example, slow beats do not ordinarily generate the experience of dissonance but merely a tremolo, a rising and falling of loudness. Conversely, a disagreeable roughness is heard even when the frequencies of pure tones are so far apart that no beats are reported (i.e. no fluctuations in loudness). Since loudness fluctuations can be too slow or too fast to produce the throbbing of beats, there must be a range of frequencies between these extremes that do produce the experience of beats. This range of frequencies within which we hear beats is called the *critical bandwidth*. When two frequencies lie outside the critical bandwidth, no beats are heard and the effect is

158   Sound and Music

smooth and consonant. This concept of critical bandwidth is really a specification of the limits of Helmholtz's theory of beats underlying consonance and dissonance. But it can also be invoked to account for other auditory phenomena, such as the perception of noise and the masking of sound.

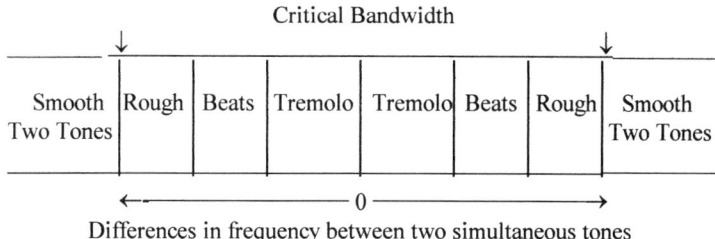

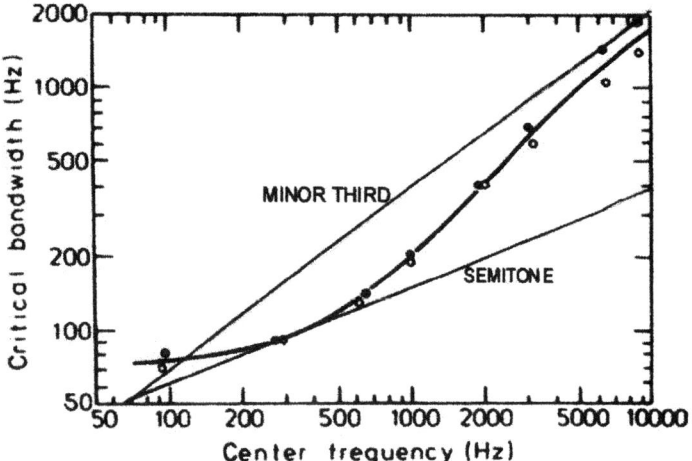

Fig. 10.1. Critical bandwidth. The smallest difference between two frequencies that sounds consonant, plotted as a function of frequency. Above 500 Hz, critical bandwidth is roughly proportional to frequency. Below 500 Hz, critical bandwidth is roughly constant. The frequency difference for the minor third and for semitone, also plotted as a function of frequency, are shown for comparison. The rough match with the minor third curve suggests that two pure tones above 500 Hz will sound consonant if a minor third or more separates them. Adapted from Rasch and Plomp, 1982

In order to predict what intervals would prove to be consonant, it is necessary first to determine how critical bandwidth varies with frequency. This is shown in Fig. 10.1. Above a frequency of 500 Hz, the critical bandwidth is roughly proportional to frequency. For frequencies below 500 Hz, however, the critical bandwidth is roughly constant.

To estimate the size of the interval corresponding to critical bandwidth, the frequency differences of a semitone and of a minor third are plotted in Fig. 10.1. In the frequency range, 500-5000 *Hz*, the critical bandwidth lies just below a minor third and well above a semitone. For frequencies below 500 *Hz* or so, the critical bandwidth is greater than a minor third and remains more or less constant beginning at 100 *Hz* and down toward the lower limit of hearing. This means that two frequencies below 500 *Hz* would have to be more widely separated than higher frequencies in order to achieve consonance. Indeed, composers frequently separate the component notes of chords in the bass range more widely than the notes of chords in the treble range.

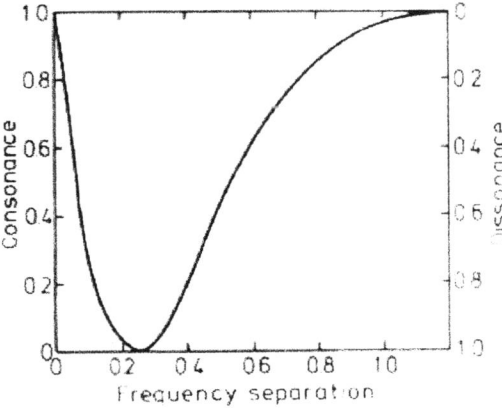

Fig. 10.2. Consonance as a function of bandwidth. The degree of consonance of two pure tones, played simultaneously, as a function of their frequency separation. The curve shows that consonance is greatest when the two frequencies match (when the two tones are in unison) and when the two frequencies are separated by a critical bandwidth (a minor third) or more. At about one-quarter of the critical bandwidth, the two tones are as dissonant as they can be. Most listeners deny that this is always so when pairs of complex musical tones are sounded together. Nor should it be, since upper harmonics interact as well as the two fundamentals Adapted from Plomp and Levelt, 1965.

According to the theory of critical bandwidth, any interval a minor third or greater should be judged to be consonant, however complex the ratio of frequencies. Fig. 10.2 shows how consonance and dissonance vary in degree as a function of the frequency separation of two tones. Maximum dissonance occurs at about one-quarter of the critical bandwidth. As frequency separations increase beyond this point, consonance increases and becomes optimal when separations of a critical bandwidth or greater are reached, however complex the ratio of frequencies (e.g. 3.1/2)

The concept of critical bandwidth refers specifically to intervals of *pure* tones. When complex musical tones containing many partials replace pure tones, the relationship between critical bandwidth and dissonance becomes more complicated. Let us examine the interval of the perfect fifth made up of two complex tones. Next to the octave, the perfect fifth is the most consonant interval. Fig. 10.3 suggests why this is so.

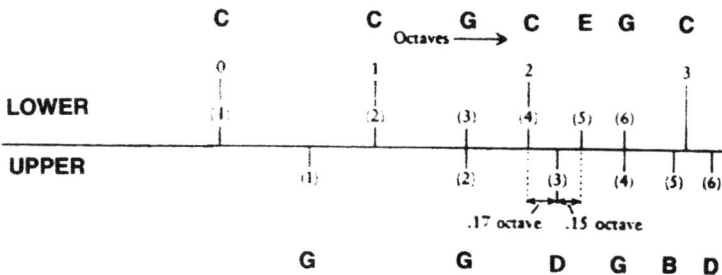

Fig. 10.3. Two complex tones a fifth apart are diagrammed here. Each has six harmonics (a fundamental and five overtones). If coincidence of harmonics accounts for the perception of consonance, the interval of a fifth should sound relatively consonant because a number of the harmonics of the two tones coincide. As demonstrated in the figure, the third and sixth harmonics of the lower tone coincide with the second and fourth harmonics of the upper tone. Though the other harmonics do not coincide, they are separated by a critical bandwidth (a minor third) or more.

In this figure, three successive octaves are represented along the horizontal line. Two tones, a fifth apart, are represented on this octave line so that the relationship of harmonics can be examined.

The six harmonics of the lower tone are shown above the line and the six harmonics of the upper tone are shown below the line. Note that two harmonics of the lower and upper notes coincide. Most of the others are separated by more than a quarter of an octave, that is, by more than a minor third or critical bandwidth. Only the third harmonic of the upper tone, falling as it does between the fourth and fifth harmonics of the lower tone, creates two separations of about a tone apart, somewhat less than the critical bandwidth. Since most separations between harmonics are at least a critical bandwidth apart, these two tones, a fifth apart, sound consonant when played together.

If additional upper harmonics are added to either of the two tones, the higher harmonics will be less than a minor third apart and each of the two tones will have a sort of internal dissonance. We perceive this as a buzzing quality on the piano and a jangling quality on the harpsichord. To the modern ear, these tones are frequently described as 'colorful,' not as dissonant. In short, the more complex the instrumental notes, the more colorful they sound when played individually. But they tend to sound dissonant when played together.

The concept of critical bandwidth explains the dissonance of the traditional dissonant intervals, such as the semitone (the minor second), the tritone (the augmented fourth), and major and minor sevenths. In these intervals, many harmonics lie much closer together than a minor third. According to critical bandwidth theory they should sound rough and dissonant, and they do. However, critical bandwidth theory is not always so successful in predicting consonance and dissonance. Pierce's experiment of 1966 is instructive and fascinating.

Suppose that, instead of basing our music on the normal octave with a frequency ratio of 2/1, we use a computer-generated stretched octave whose frequency ratio is 2.4/1. Let us also stretch the intervals between all notes that are played in a given piece to the same relative degree, including all harmonics belonging to those notes. In this tonal system, each complex tone will have non-harmonic partials (harmonic components whose frequencies are not integer multiples of the frequency of the fundamental frequency), and the equal-tempered 'semitone' of the stretched chromatic scale will have a frequency ratio of 1.0757/1 instead of the 1.0595/1 of the keyboard chromatic scale. Let us now play a familiar piece of music in four-part harmony, using the tonal system of the stretched octave. If any harmonics coincided in the unstretched version of the piece, they will coincide in the stretched version. Harmonics that do not coincide in the unstretched version will be farther apart in the stretched version, sometimes beyond the critical bandwidth. According to the critical bandwidth theory, the stretched version should sound more consonant than the unstretched version, because many more harmonics are now separated by more than the critical bandwidth. But it doesn't. Quite the contrary.

Among the subjects in Pierce's experiment was Pierre Boulez, the renowned composer of electronic music and former conductor of the New York Philharmonic Orchestra. Boulez reported that all the familiar harmonic effects vanished and he recognized no melody. Other subjects who heard the unstretched or normal version first still barely recognized the melody in the stretched version, and it was difficult for them to follow the inner voices. Furthermore, the stretched perfect cadence (dominant to tonic chords) produced no sense of closure or finality. As a matter of fact, all cadences, including those ending on the dominant chord or chord of the sixth, seemed equally strange and equally dissonant.

You may well wonder whether non-harmonic components in a complex tone *ever* fuse to produce the experience of a single tone. There are, in fact, many natural sounds with non-harmonic components that are well fused, such as the sounds of bells, gongs, drums and even wood-knocking. Each has a distinct and identifiable timbre. The auditory system does not analyze these sounds into separate components. Yet Pierce's computer-generated tones with stretched intervals are analyzed and broken apart. The ear refuses to hear such a collection of harmonics as a distinct tone with a single, fused pitch and a single timbre. Instead, the ear (the brain) pulls apart these synthesized stretched tones. Because the component frequencies do not fuse, several notes are heard, not as a chord, but rather as a confused collection of sound. And this is why the listener in Pierce's experiment could perceive no organic design in the stretched four-part piece even though the usual mathematical structure was present. By the rules of critical bandwidth, consonance and dissonance should have been preserved, but they were not. Everything sounded dissonant. It seems clear that any theory of consonance and dissonance that is based solely upon critical bandwidth is limited in predictive value.

Past Experience and Context

Aside from the question whether consonance can be perceived in the presence of harmonics that lie too close together in frequency (within a critical bandwidth), this discussion of consonance and dissonance must be expanded to include the contributions of the past experience of the listener and of musical context.

Consider the effects of musical training on the experience of consonance and dissonance. Musicians frequently judge the consonance or dissonance of pairs of pure tones by first identifying the interval and then calling the pairs of tones either consonant or dissonant on the basis of what they have been taught. Thus, musicians are likely to identify thirds, fourths, fifths and sixths as consonant, but will report sevenths, and seconds, as dissonant. The interval of seconds, yes, but why sevenths? Critical bandwidth theory cannot explain the dissonance of the seventh produced by two pure tones. In this case, there are no harmonics to interact. The answer must lie in the realm of past experience. Sometimes the musician will be puzzled by a sequence of chords and identify the effect as dissonant even though each chord in the series is consonant. When queried, the musician will say that it sounds wrong. Why? The answer, in each case, suggests that there is a transmitted culture regarding the normal sequence of chords, and that contextual unfamiliarity breeds the experience of dissonance.

Consider also how important context is in determining consonance and dissonance. The familiar cadence, dominant seventh to tonic, sounds consonant to most everybody today even though the dominant seventh itself is a dissonant chord. It is the resolution produced by the tonic chord that makes the experience a consonant one.

It is quite evident from the history of musical taste that the standards of consonance have changed with the passage of time and the acquisition of experience. The sounds that appeared dissonant in Beethoven's music in his time are now likely to be accepted as consonant, despite the presence of beats and the violation of the rule of critical bandwidth. Those who remember learning to enjoy Le *Sacre du Printemps* by Stravinski can attest to the power of repeated exposures in the shaping of musical experience and preference. As we mature, our ears (our brains) become attuned to the musical sounds that earlier appeared to be dissonant.

Whether it has a physical basis or not, dissonance is an important experience in music and cannot be dismissed. A piece of music consisting entirely of consonant intervals would be judged by the standards of the contemporary listener as bland and uninteresting. Dissonant intervals bring a restlessness and tension to the music that composers of traditional music ultimately resolve to produce the experience of consonance. As a matter of fact, even the resolution is no longer demanded in modern composition. Just as suspense and conflict bring tension to drama and fiction, so does dissonance bring tension to music. Without this tension, the successive consonances would be empty of feeling and meaning.

The truth is that music has become increasingly dissonant over the ages, by any definition of dissonance. This is because the subjective standards of dissonance seem to loosen with time. A new tonal combination can strike the musical audience of one age as harsh and jarring. But with time and repeated listening, the audience gets accustomed to it. What began as a dissonant experience becomes more and more consonant with time. The result is that each new generation of composers has had to create new combinations of tones to sustain the same degree of tension and restlessness as their predecessors were able to sustain. Compare the music of Mozart, Brahms, Stravinski, and Berg in this regard. Over the ages, musical audiences have moved inexorably toward the acceptance and appreciation of greater and greater dissonance.

Finally, in the twentieth century, the distinction between consonance and dissonance has become blurred. For composers of atonal and serial music, the distinction has become obsolete. Today, musical enjoyment does not seem to hinge on whether the intervals used in a composition are judged to be consonant or not. We will return to the subject of musical enjoyment in Chapter 18.

Noise

A sound comprising very many unrelated frequencies, or inharmonic components, is frequently referred to as noise. If all frequencies in the audible range are equally represented, we speak of 'white noise.' No periodicity is detectable in the sound-pressure record of sound that people call 'noisy.' So might read a dictionary definition of 'noise.'

However, both musical tones and noise are types of sound. From a physical standpoint, they belong to the same category: they result from complex patterns of vibrations of air particles. It is just since Helmholtz that musical sounds have been described as periodic or tonal, while noises have been described as aperiodic or atonal. Indeed, a piano tone does have a periodic waveform when displayed on the oscilloscope screen, while a thud does not. No one will dispute that a jet engine sounds noisy compared to a major or minor chord on the piano and, obversely, that the piano chord sounds musical compared to the jet engine. But if you would like to classify sounds as noisy simply because they have no identifiable pitch, consider the following noises: the thud, rumble, bang, pop, rattle, and hiss. These noises have been ordered in pitch, from low to high. Isn't a pop higher than a thud, and a rumble lower than a hiss? Is it any easier to identify the pitch of the roll of a snare drum compared to the popping of firecrackers? These examples should make it plain that the presence or absence of an identifiable pitch does not distinguish musical tones from noise.

What people accept as music and reject as noise varies enormously. How would you vote on a series of chords taken from Berg's opera Lulu, or, for that matter, on a series of chords taken from contemporary rock? We seem to be led to extreme relativity when it comes to distinguishing noise from music, at least from a perceptual point of view. What about the physical distinction?

Let us start with the proposition that noise is a complex fusion of many waveforms. But so is musical sound, and there is no clear discontinuity between noise and music on the basis of waveform. We have already agreed that many noises have some of the characteristics of tones. The sound that most people agree appears noisy can also be built from legitimate musical tones, as by striking a large number of adjacent keys on the piano at once. Or try the following little experiment. Shape eight strips of wood so that they will each vibrate to give the eight notes of the diatonic major scale. The way to accomplish this quickly and easily is to vary their length, or their thickness, or both. When they are thrown together on a bare table, the result is a clatter with no identifiable pitch. Traditionally, this would be called a noise, not a musical sound. But, if dropped individually in proper sequence, a simple and recognizable melody can be produced, and most people would call that musical.

Every elastic object produces its own sound when struck. Its dominant pitch depends on where the blow is applied. A wooden pencil, held at one end and struck on the edge of a table at the other end, produces a relatively low principal pitch. The farther up toward the fingers that the pencil is struck (thus effectively shortening the pencil), the higher the principal pitch. A tune can be played in just this way.

It seems clear that there are intermediates between noises and tones. When the spokes of a slowly rotating wheel are permitted to hit a sounding board, the successive sounds are likely to be classed as noises, but when the wheel is rotated rapidly, an unmistakable musical pitch is perceived. Tonality begins to enter before noise disappears. Again, there seems to be no discontinuity between noise and musical tones.

In short, the labeling of certain sounds as music and others as noise cannot simply reflect the difference in physical properties of the two sounds. From a physical standpoint, the sound of a rock group may have more in common with the sound of a jackhammer than with the music of Mozart. By the same token, the music of Philip Glass may be more closely related to industrial sounds than to conventional music. Whether a sound is classed as noisy or not depends not only on the physical properties of the stimulus, but also on the past experience of the listener, his expectations, what he thinks are the intentions of the sound-maker, and even whether he perceives others as admiring the sound or not. Any unwanted sound may become annoying, and an annoying sound is frequently taken to be noisy. When a musical tone has a sharp onset, it will start with a click. Does this disqualify the sound as a candidate for a piece of music? It depends on the context and on the effect the composer wants to achieve.

In this view, it is the listener himself who determines whether it is noise or music. It might be said that one person's noise is another person's music. These two people may even be one and the same, at different stages of esthetic development.

COMBINATION TONES

When two loud tones that differ in pitch are played together, we frequently hear a third tone whose pitch is related to the two generating tones. This third, or combination tone, can be of two types. The frequency of one type is equal to the difference between the two generating frequencies, as 100 *Hz* is the difference between 200 and 300 *Hz*. This is called the *difference* tone. The frequency of the other is the sum of the two generating frequencies, as 500 *Hz* is the sum of 200 and 300 *Hz*. This is called the *summation* tone.

Modern psychoacoustic research has shown that the pitches of combination tones agree with the frequencies predicted by non-linear transmission in the auditory system. Six theoretical combination tones, three difference and three summation tones, generated by playing a high (H) and a low (L) tone together, are listed below:

Generating Tones		Combination Tones	
High (H)	Low (L)	Difference	Summation
H	L	H - L	H + L
L	H - L	2L - H	
L	H + L		2L + H
2L - H	H - L	3L - 2H	
2L + H	H + L		3L + 2H

As an illustration of a difference tone, if D and B, a sixth apart in the frequency ratio 5/3, are played together loudly, a difference tone may be heard, equal to the difference between the two frequencies (5-3 or 2). Since the interval between the difference tone and the generating D is 2/3, or a fifth, the difference tone must be G below the generating D. The same two notes, D and B, may also generate a summation tone that is equal to the sum of the two frequencies (5+3 or 8). Since the interval between the summation tone and the generating D is 8/3, the summation tone must be G, the interval of an eleventh above the generating D.

Although combination tones were discovered by musicians (Tartini described the difference tone in 1714), their significance for music listening is not great for they contribute little to the tonal color of the piece. Difference tones can be produced by playing loud tones in a high register, as Tartini discovered when he played double stops on the violin. However during normal listening the loudness of combination tones is usually too low to attract attention. Furthermore, they are masked by lower tones when those are present. Following Tartini, some violinists use combination tones to control the intonation of double-stops and to tune their instruments. This seems to be the sum total of their usefulness and esthetic value.

Because the frequency of the first difference tone is the same as the frequency of beats, the histories of the knowledge of beats and of combination tones are related, even though psychologists since

Helmholtz have had adequate evidence that the two phenomena are distinct. Beats have a physical basis: they can be displayed on an oscilloscope screen. But combination tones have no physical basis; they are not present in the acoustic signal. They result from the physiological processing of sound in the auditory system. In short, they are perceived as though they are present in the signal, thus giving them the status of an illusion. However, they may be cancelled effectively by adding a tone with the same frequency and amplitude, but opposite in phase, thus giving them the status of apparitions.

TONAL COLOR

Vowels and Consonants. What is responsible for the rich and varied tonal colors of musical instruments? An examination of vowel and consonant sounds of the human voice will help us find the answer.

The vowel sounds of the human voice are distinguishable, regardless of their perceived pitch, on the basis of three chief resonances of the vocal tract, called formants. While singing text on a single pitch, say middle C, the singer is able to change the vowel he/she sings, from 'ah' to 'ee,' for example. It is surprising that the change in vowel does not affect the perceived pitch of the vowels. Try singing successively, on one note, the vowel 'u' in 'who'd' and the vowel 'e' in 'heed.' You will hear that the pitch remains the same as you shift from one vowel to the next. This agrees with the fact that the fundamental frequency of the note sung remains constant. Nevertheless, 'heed' sounds shriller than 'who'd.' Studies have shown that differences in timbre, not differences in pitch, are responsible for the discriminability of different vowels.

We distinguish vowels by means of formants, that is, by the particular harmonics above the fundamental that are amplified in the vocal tract. The harmonics that match the resonant frequencies of the vocal tract become the formants and these in turn are determined by the shape of the vocal tract as we sing the various vowels. Whatever the fundamental frequency of the sung vowel 'a' as in 'had' -- whether 200 or 400 *Hz* -- for example, its formant frequencies will be around 660, 1720, and 2410 *Hz*, as can be seen in the table below.

In short, the vowel sounds of the human voice are recognized by the three principal resonances, or formants, of the vocal tract. Near the formant frequencies, the intensities of certain upper harmonics are strong. This is what produces the character of vowel sounds. Fig. 10.4, taken from the article, *The Phonetics of Speech* in the

Encyclopaedia Britannica, fifteenth edition, shows the various configurations of the vocal tract for eight common English vowel sounds. The table below specifies the three principal formant frequencies for these eight sounds.

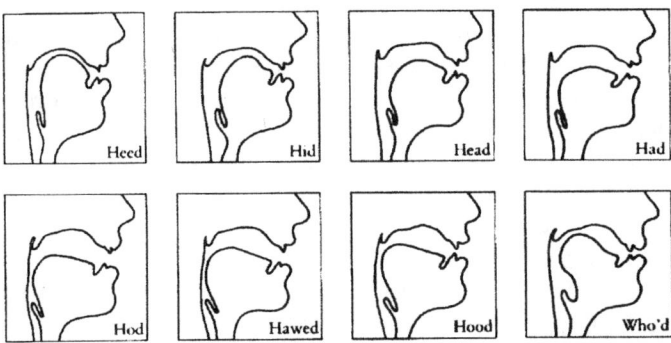

Fig. 10.4. Vocal tract configurations for eight vowel sounds The vowels in heed, hid, head and had are front vowels because the highest point of the tongue is in the front of the mouth. The vowels in hod, hawed, hood and who'd are back vowels, because the tongue is highest in the back part of the mouth. The timbre of the vowel in heed seems shrill while the timbre of the vowel in who'd seems low and dull. Adapted from Encyclopaedia Britannica ,fifteenth edition, © 1974.

	Heed	Hid	Head	Had	Hod	Hawed	Hood	Who'd
f_1	270	390	530	660	730	570	440	300
f_2	2,290	1,990	1,840	1,720	1,090	840	1,020	870
f_3	3,010	2,550	2,480	2,410	2,440	2,410	2,240	2,240

You can make some interesting observations about the perception of vowels. You can sound a vowel for prolonged periods without it changing its timbre. Sing "ah" for as long as you want and it will retain its vowel quality. In contrast, words frequently lose their meaning with quick repetition, a phenomenon called semantic satiation. Try uttering the word 'mother' over and over again quickly, and you will find that it slowly loses its meaning. Instead of being reinforced by quick repetition, the word becomes devoid of meaning.

Since vowel quality is unaffected by repetition, each vowel must be recognized by steady-state cues, that is, by its three principal formant frequencies. Further, it is known that vowel quality is determined primarily by the absolute frequencies of formants, not by their relative frequencies. If the frequencies of the three formants are shifted, keeping them, at the same time, in the same position relative to the fundamental frequency, the vowel quality changes. If the fundamental frequency alone is shifted, the vowel quality remains unchanged. Try it for yourself. Sing 'ah' up and down your vocal range and the quality of this vowel will not be affected. Conversely, you can change 'ah' to 'ee' without shifting pitch.

Finally, you can change the loudness of the vowel without changing its vowel quality. A shouted 'ah' can match a whispered 'ah,' if you want it to.

These observations demonstrate that vowel quality depends on some steady-state properties of the voice and is more or less independent of pitch or loudness. You can demonstrate for yourself that specific vowels are associated with specific upper harmonics (formants). Shout vowel sounds into the piano, all at the same pitch, while depressing the damper pedal. Listen for the resonances to 'ah' and to 'ee.' You will hear different strings resonate to the two vowels, even though the vowels themselves appear to have the same pitch.

Musical instruments vary widely in the relative intensity levels of their harmonics during the period of steady-state playing. As with vowels, the steady-state timbre of many instruments seems to be determined by constant formant frequencies belonging to the harmonic series. But it is to the onset transients that we must turn for a better understanding of instrumental timbre. It will help to return to the human voice for guidance.

While the vowel quality of speech depends on steady state cues, the consonant quality depends on transient patterns during the first 50 ms after the onset of the voice. Any complex tone can vary in a number of ways in the immediate period after the onset of the tone. First, the rise in sound can be abrupt or gradual; second, the onset may be accompanied by varying amounts of noise (inharmonic partials); and third, the relative intensities of harmonics can vary during the initial period following onset.

The vocal sound, 'tah,' and the vowel, 'ah,' differ in the abruptness of onset. The first has a sharp rise time, while the second rises more gradual. They also differ in the amount of noise introduced by the initial release of air by the movement of the tongue. In speech, the presence of such noise bursts distinguishes 'stopped,' 'voiceless' consonants, such as 'p,' 't' and 'k,' from 'voiced' consonants, such as 'b,' 'd' and 'g,' and from other consonants that generate long-duration noises, such as 's,' 'z,' 'f' and 'v.'

These differences between consonances are reflected in the differences between musical instruments. The trumpet's attack is more like the consonant 'tah' than like the vowel 'ah,' and the attack of the bassoon is more gradual. The rise of the trumpet tone is very rapid, reaching a peak within the first 20 ms, while the bassoon tone rises more gradually, taking perhaps 50 ms to reach its maximum intensity. Because the formant frequencies of two different instruments are so similar, we must conclude that steady state patterns of harmonics are not a sufficient basis for the discrimination of timbre. To determine the discriminability of the timbre of different instruments, Soldanha and Corso (1964) made tape recordings of 10 instruments, all playing the same three pitches. Musicians found the clarinet, oboe and flute easiest to identify, and had the most difficulty identifying trombone, violin, cello and bassoon. When the initial portion of each taped tone (the onset transients) was eliminated, the identifiability of all musical instruments dropped markedly, proving that the onset of musical tones contains important cues for identification. In most cases the first 20-50 ms after the onset of the tone contain the critical cues. Thus, the appreciation of the timbre of musical instruments seems to depend on the presence of onset transients.

Strings generally have noisier attacks than brass instruments. When playing the violin, for example, the bow scrapes on a string before the resonance of the instrument begins. Of course, the attack of each instrument varies depending on how it is played. The violin attack can be relatively smooth, but it can also be quite abrupt, depending on the forcefulness of the bow on the string. A forceful attack adds initial noise to the tone.

During the transient phase after onset, the patterns of harmonics of tones of different instruments differ in their relative intensities. Some instruments, such as clarinet and saxophone, maintain similar relative intensities of harmonics during the transient phase, while others, such as trumpet and piano, show a change in the distribution of energy among their constituent harmonics during the transient phase.

We have argued that timbre is relatively independent of pitch, but this is true only within limits. We have already noted that we can sing 'ah' from low bass to mid-soprano, and the vowel quality will remain 'ah.' It will not change to 'ee.' But at higher pitches, beyond the range of the formants, timbre *is* affected. This effect can be heard as the fundamental frequency rises into the region of the formant frequencies (say, above 800 *Hz*). The highest note that sopranos can sing begins to impinge on the region of formants, and differences in vowel quality tend to blur in this register.

Percussion instruments, too, violate the rule of independence of timbre and pitch. Drums, gongs and bells have ambiguous pitches because of the presence of inharmonic partials. Changing the pitch of these instruments is frequently difficult to distinguish from changing their timbre.

Synthesis of Complex Waves. We have seen that a stretched string vibrates as a whole and in parts at the same time. The complex tone is a fusion of pure tones, the fundamental produced by the string vibrating as a whole, plus the upper harmonics produced by the string vibrating in halves (2nd harmonic), in thirds (third harmonic), in quarters (fourth harmonic), etc. The different harmonics vary in intensity (i.e., each harmonic has its own amplitude), and the relative contribution of harmonics depends on the instrument and the way the string is excited. It is the fusion of all these harmonics that is responsible for the timbre or color of the tone. This analysis applies equally to vibrating columns of air.

We have already noted that a Fourier analysis reveals the spectrum of a complex waveform. It shows the relative contributions of the various harmonics to the tonal color of the sound. The technology that makes music synthesis possible today provides the means for confirming our understanding of the composition of complex sounds. By incorporating some of the features revealed by analysis and disregarding others in the process of sound synthesis, it is possible to determine which features are essential in producing what tonal colors. We restrict ourselves here to steady-state waveforms, ignoring the rise and decay time of each synthesized complex waveform.

Starting with simple sine waves, let us see what it takes to create three standard steady-state waveforms: the saw-tooth wave, the square wave, and the triangular wave.

To see how a sawtooth waveform is synthesized, we will start with a sine wave of 100 *Hz*, which we will treat as the fundamental or first harmonic. Let us superimpose a second sine wave of 200 *Hz* having an amplitude one-half the first and beginning in phase with the first. This sine wave is shown in the top left graph of Fig. 10.5. We then add the amplitudes of these two waves and display the resultant waveform in the next graph below. The third harmonic is 300 *Hz* and one-third the amplitude of the fundamental. This waveform is shown superimposed in phase with the earlier resultant in the second graph. We then add the amplitudes of these two waveforms and display the resultant in the third graph, bottom left. In the subsequent graphs, the fourth and fifth harmonics are successively added, with their respective amplitudes in inverse proportion to their harmonic number. As we continue to add the higher harmonics, the waveform representing their sum approaches the theoretical sawtooth waveform shown at the bottom right. This is how a sound synthesizer would generate a sawtooth wave.

To see how a square waveform is synthesized, let us start again, following the same procedure, but this time adding to the fundamental or first harmonic only the odd-numbered harmonics, the third, fifth, seventh, ninth, etc., all in phase, and with their respective amplitudes in inverse proportion to their harmonic number. The resultant waveform approximates the theoretical square wave shown at the bottom right of the series of graphs in Fig. 10.6. (Notice that the final synthesized waveform does not have sharp contours. This is because a small number of component sine waves were used, not an indefinitely large number.)

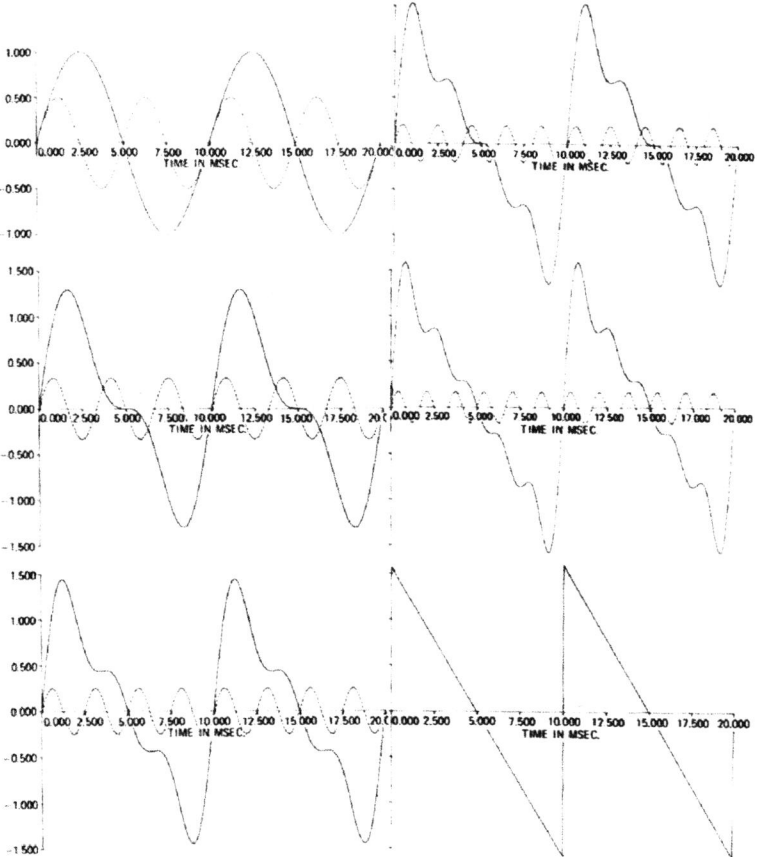

Fig. 10.5. Sawtooth waveforms produced by additive synthesis. The first five harmonics are added with their respective amplitudes in inverse proportion to their harmonic number, and in phase. The theoretical sawtooth waveform is shown at the end (bottom, right).

Tonal Color

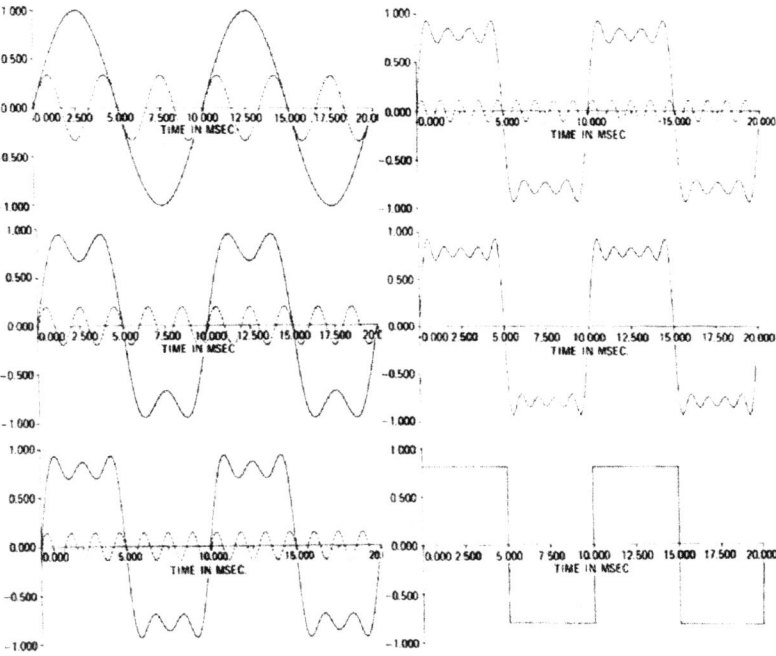

Fig. 10.6. Square waves produced by additive synthesis. The first, third, fifth, seventh and ninth harmonics are added together with their respective amplitudes in inverse proportion to their harmonic number, and in phase. The theoretical square wave is shown at the end (below, right).

What does a square wave sound like compared to its constituent sine waves? Since the frequency of the square wave matches that of the first sine wave (100 *Hz*), they sound the same in pitch. But, unlike the sine wave that sounds thin and wispy, the square wave sounds harsh and raspy.

Finally, to produce a triangular waveform, we add to the fundamental just the odd-numbered harmonics, third, fifth, etc., but this time their amplitudes in inverse proportion to the *square* of their harmonic number, and their harmonics alternately out of and in phase. This is shown in the series of graphs in Fig. 10.7.

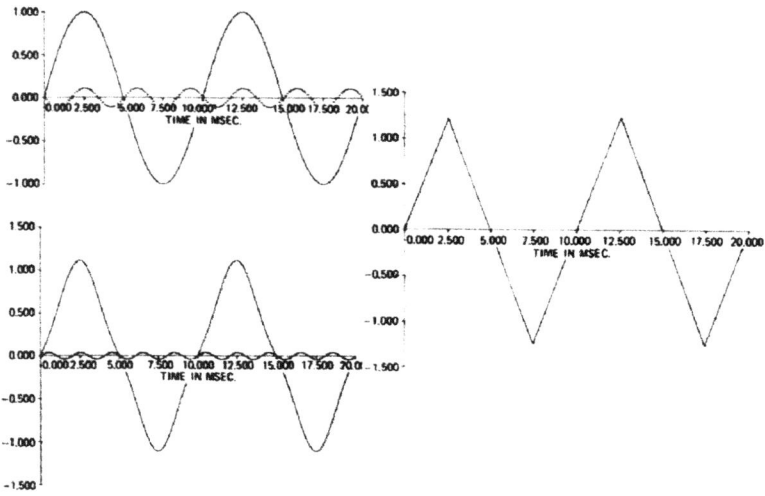

Fig. 10.7. Triangular waves produced by additive synthesis. The first, third, and fifth harmonics are added together, with their respective amplitudes in inverse proportion to the square of their harmonic number, and with harmonics alternately out of and in phase. The theoretical triangular waves are shown on the right side.

Fig. 10.8 summarizes our discussion of the synthesis of sawtooth waves, square waves, and triangular waves. Since waveforms can be described by specifying amplitude and frequency, we can graph each waveform by plotting amplitude as a function of frequency. These graphs are shown on the right side of Fig. 10.8. The height of the lines represents the magnitude of the amplitude of each sine wave, and the position of lines along the abscissa, its frequency. Since the simple sine wave at the top of the figure has all its energy concentrated at just one frequency, only one line can be shown. (This representation neglects the phase relationships of successive harmonics.)

As more and more harmonics are added to the individual fundamentals, the higher harmonics will be less than a minor third apart (less than a critical bandwidth), and the resultant complex tone will have a sort of internal dissonance, giving it a buzzy or jangly sound, as is normal for square and sawtooth waveforms.

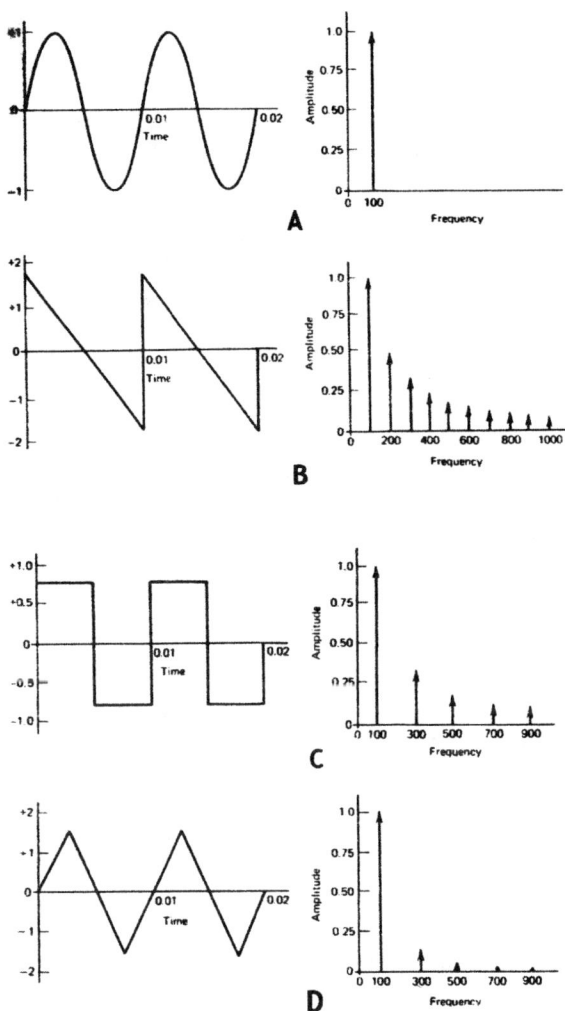

Fig. 10.8. *A summary of synthesized waveforms. It can be shown mathematically that any periodic waveform can be analyzed into a series of sine waves of multiple frequencies, of varying amplitudes, and in varying phase relationships. We can represent these waveforms on a graph of amplitude as a function of frequency. These graphs show sine, sawtooth, square and triangular waveforms in both the time domain, on the left, and in the frequency domain, on the right. The graphs in the frequency domain are frequently referred to Fourier spectra. Phase relationships of sine waves have not been indicated in these graphs.*

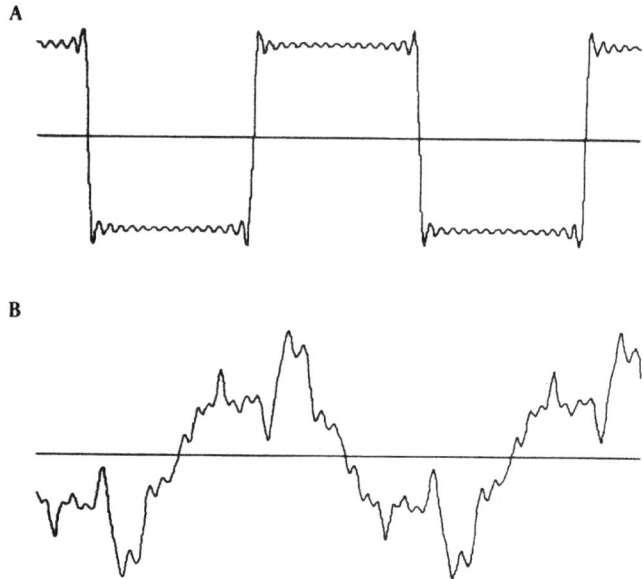

Fig. 10.9. A comparison the two synthesized waveforms. They are composed of the very same sine wave components, but their phase relationships differ. The upper waveform is the result of a systematic relationship of phase of constituent harmonics. In the synthesis of the lower waveform, phase relationships were randomly varied.

Since Helmholtz, the lore has been that the phase relationships of harmonics in a complex tone are not analyzed by the ear or brain and do not contribute to the color of the tone. But experience with sound synthesis casts doubt about this view. Suppose we vary phase relationships and study the effect on complex waveform and on timbre. For example, we might randomize the phases of the very same harmonics that were responsible for the square wave. The resultant waveform, shown below the corresponding square wave in Fig. 10.9, certainly does not look square, though it retains the periodicity of the square wave. Its pitch is unaltered, but it sounds less raspy compared to the square wave. Experiments of this sort lead us to conclude that phase relationships do affect the waveform and the resultant tonal color, but not the pitch.

The Vibrato. Vibrato is a pulsation of pitch, frequently accompanied by synchronous pulsations of loudness and timbre. It is used to enrich and enlarge the sound of each individual tone, particularly when feeling and emotion are to be expressed. During the romantic era, the vibrato was cultivated to intensify the emotional tone of the music, sometimes to such an exaggerated extent as to sound maudlin.

Though vibrato is frequently thought of as a musical ornament, it is really a special way to enrich and strengthen an otherwise thin and uninteresting tone. Our ears have now grown accustomed to the vibrating of pitch (as we have grown accustomed to the beats of equal-tempered intervals), for the western music of the nineteenth and twentieth centuries is nearly always played in this way. Because of these expectations, an unvibrated musical tone generated by strings and winds sounds thin and uninteresting to most of us. There is no mistaking when a violinist plays a sustained tone on an open or unstopped string, because he must play it without vibrato, and it sounds 'flat' when compared to the tones around it. Sometimes the composer takes advantage of this effect as when he deliberately writes for the open G-string on the violin, which has no alternate fingering, as Sibelius did in the first movement of his violin concerto. Musicians playing and singing music of the Renaissance, before the age of vibrato, have struggled to get modern audiences to appreciate the sustained unvibrated tone as it must have sounded hundreds of years ago.

Nevertheless, it is likely that vibrato was used in the emotional expression of primitive speech and tone. The truth is that there seems to be a certain universality to vibrato: you can hear it in the cooing of the dove, in the crying of the baby, and in the laughter of the adult. Vibrato has been found in music all over the world. Modern professional singers make use of vibrato in order to express depth of feeling, particularly on sustained notes. As soon as the child begins to sing with genuine feeling, he is apt to inject vibrato into his singing.

Instrumental vibrato is not very different from vocal vibrato. Performers of stringed instruments tend to use vibrato on sustained notes although not all instruments allow for it. The frets on the fingerboard of stringed instruments, like the guitar and the viola da gamba, limit the use of the vibrato. For this reason, the style of Renaissance music is violated if it is played on modern unfretted instruments with vibrato.

There are two principal variables that influence the quality of the vibrato: the amplitude of the excursion of pitch from an average value and the rate of the vibrato (frequency and amplitude mosulation). Professional singers average 0.4 to 0.6 of a tone in total excursion-amplitude (or about a quarter of a tone above and below the average value). The average vibration rate is 6 to 7 per second, with a range of about 3 to 8 per second. However, there is a tendency to deepen and quicken the rate of vibrato in order to convey emotional intensity and to slow it down as the feeling subsides. At the same time, it should be noted that high pitches can sustain higher frequencies of vibrato.

The mean pitch of the vibrated tone tends to match the notated pitch. It is interesting that the perceived excursion of the pulsations of vibrato is less than the actual excursion. Since deep vibrato can be annoying, perhaps it is this illusion that renders the large-amplitude vibrato more tolerable.

Computer Music. Early attempts to generate the sounds of musical instruments with the aid of a computer proved to be disappointing. Those attempts involved converting simple waveforms such as sine waves and sawtooth waves into patterns of numbers, which were then used to produce sounds delivered through an audio system. The disappointment lay in the fact that the computer sounds tended to be bland (the sound of sine waves) or buzzy (the sound of sawtooth waves). Specific timbres were simulated by additive synthesis to produce complex waveforms, but the results were again disappointing, and it became clear that all the important ingredients of timbre had not yet been identified. The prevailing view at the time was that a musical tone could be described completely by its waveform which was believed to remain constant through the duration of the tone. For example, the timbre of the clarinet was thought to be determined completely by its odd-numbered harmonic components. But that was not enough to produce a reasonable facsimile of the clarinet's timbre. What was missing was the beginning or attack of the waveform and its end or decay. The total contour of a waveform, from attack through its steady-state, to its decay, is called its *envelope*. An example of an envelope, one with a steep attack and a gradual decay, is the sound of a plucked or struck stringed instrument. The tonal fluctuations that take place during its steady-state seem to be of minor importance in determining the timbre of the tone.

In 1965, at the Bell Laboratories, Jean-Claude Risset attempted to synthesize trumpet tones by specifying just the relative amplitudes of the trumpet's harmonics, but he was disappointed with the result. Later, in analyzing the tones of a real trumpet, he discovered that the spectrum of harmonics changed during the playing of the tone: the high-frequency harmonics had a larger amplitude in the middle than at the beginning or end of the envelope. By incorporating this variation in its harmonic composition, Risset succeeded in synthesizing tones that could not be distinguished from recorded trumpet tones. Risset's experiment revealed that one must know how the sound's harmonic spectrum varies as the tone is played on a musical instrument in order to simulate its sounds.

During those early years, Risset used the method of additive synthesis: the individual harmonics of a given musical sound were synthesized separately, allowing each to have its own independent frequency and envelope. Only then were they added together to achieve a realistic simulation of the musical sound. Risset learned that inharmonic components of certain sounds (components that are not integer multiples of the fundamental frequency) are of great importance, for these must also be incorporated in the wave complex in order to achieve an authentic-sounding musical tone. These inharmonic components are required for the simulation of piano, gong, drums and other percussion instruments.

Unfortunately, additive synthesis is expensive and slow. Each harmonic of each complex tone has to be generated separately, and a great deal of computation is required. Since each harmonic follows its own course, many envelopes need to be generated for each complex tone. Synthesizing the tone of a trumpet typically requires ten separate audio-oscillators and ten envelope generators. Sometimes a million computations per second are required for a large-scale musical composition. A convenient short-cut was proposed by John Chowning. He showed that sound synthesis can be accomplished by frequency modulation, a method now employed in most good-quality sound synthesizers.

The violin sound is still difficult to reproduce accurately by sound synthesis. Though a sawtooth wave produced by a sound synthesizer is similar to the sawtooth wave produced by bowing a violin string, it sounds unnatural, unpleasant and buzzy, not rich and mellow like the sound of an authentic violin. The reason is that the body of the violin has certain resonant frequencies and it is these frequencies that are emphasized by the authentic instrument. Until recently, these resonant frequencies were not included in the program for the violin. New developments in the speed of integrated circuits now make it possible to simulate by computer the resonant frequencies of the acoustic violin.

The tonal color of the piano has received considerable attention in recent years. The warmth of piano tones seems to depend, in part, upon the constituent inharmonic components. When these inharmonic components are omitted from synthesized piano tones, the sound becomes bland and unlike the piano. The wavering quality of piano tones seems to be caused by the continual shifting of phase, creating beats between harmonics. Traditional piano design places the striking point of the hammers at one-seventh of the way along the string. This has important consequences for the tonal color of the piano for it prevents the seventh harmonic from being generated and it enhances the prominence of others. The degree of hardness of the felt on the hammers also determines the composition of harmonics. A hard hammer produces a brighter tone, a soft hammer a mellower tone. Because the harpsichord strings are plucked rather than struck, higher frequency harmonics are generated that are less than a critical bandwidth apart, and the sound is jangly.

The struck or plucked sound of keyboard instruments results from the abrupt rise of the tone and its gradual decay, regardless of steady-state fluctuations. Listen to a tape of a piano piece played backwards. You will likely find the timbre of the piano unrecognizable. This is because the sharp rise and slow decay characteristic of piano tones have been reversed: a slow rise and sharp decay of tones are simply unfamiliar as piano sounds.

We seem to have enough information now about the determinants of timbre to permit accurate imitations of specific musical instruments. Grey's attempt in 1977 to synthesize the tones of acoustic instruments proved to be so successful that they were virtually indistinguishable from the real thing. The parameters he chose were based upon a computer analysis of the sounds of acoustic instruments.

It is now clear that timbre is a multidimensional variable. In order to identify the separate dimensions, psychologists have resorted to multidimensional scaling techniques. A representative effort is that of Grey (1977) who asked trained musicians to rate the degree of similarity of pairs of musical sounds produced by some 15 different acoustic instruments. On the basis of judged similarity, Grey was able to group the instruments into three timbre families, and he drew a three-dimensional space to accomodate all the instruments. In this space, shown diagrammatically in Fig. 10.10, each cube stands for a particular instrument, and the proximity between instruments reflects the similarity of their sounds.

Tonal Color 183

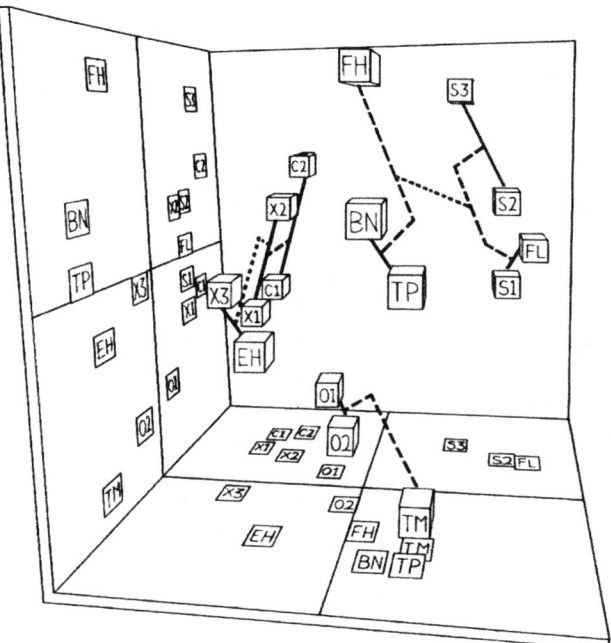

Fig. 10.10. Scaling of timbre. Three-dimensional display of judged similarities and differences between instrumental sounds, based upon a multidimensional scaling technique. In this space, instrument sounds that were judged similar are close together, while those judged to be different are far apart. The squares on the wall and floor are two-dimensional projections of the cubes, showing their relative positions: up-down, left-right, and forward-back. The instrument abbreviations are O1, O2, oboes; C1, C2, clarinets; X1, X2, X3, saxophones; EH, English horn; FH, French horn; S1, S2, S3, strings; TP, trumpet; TM, trombone; FL, flute; BN, bassoon. Adapted from Grey, 1977.

It is important to note that the three instrument families do not correspond to the choirs of instruments in the orchestra, such as strings, woodwinds and brass. In one family are found saxophones, bass clarinet and English horn; in another, oboe and muted trombone; and in a third, bassoon, French horn, cellos, trumpet and flute. Grey argued that the up-down dimension in his three-dimensional space seems to represent the spectral distribution of energy. The left-right dimension seems to reflect whether harmonics rise and fall at the same time. And the forward-back dimension seems related to the noise burst at the onset of the sound.

This analysis indicates that at least three physical aspects of sound contribute to the discriminability of musical instruments. Spectral energy distribution between harmonics enables us to distinguish steady-state sounds such as vowels. The asynchrony in the onset of harmonics plays an important part in the identification of brass sounds. And the initial burst of noise is necessary for the identification of flutes and strings. More generally, the quick rise and gradual decay are characteristic of plucked or struck strings.

Standard musical notation indicates the pitch, duration and loudness of individual notes. But there is no way to indicate timbre on the five lines of the musical staff. Timbre can only be indicated by specifying the musical instrument to be played or the voice to be sung. Since they do not specify acoustic instruments, composers of electronic music have no means of notating timbre on the standard musical staff. Only by specifying each and every component harmonic, its relative intensity and envelope as well as vibrato, can the timbre of each note be determined. This makes the notation of electronically synthesized music extremely complex. There is, as yet, no simple way to encode timbre.

Early computers did not have the capacity to synthesize music in real time. For this reason, composers had to synthesize music by recording a number of sounds on separate channels of magnetic tape and then combining them by means of dubbing and mixing. Although fine music was composed in this laborious way, the recording process eliminated the live performer and the joy of performing music in public. In addition, the unique interpretations of individual performers were no longer available. General-purpose computers having enough power for live performance are now becoming available, but they are still too expensive and too cumbersome to serve as practical musical instruments for concert performance. With time, however, special-purpose chips, such as those that are already built into the Yamaha sound synthesizers, will be incorporated in digital musical instruments, and this development will usher in an era of new musical sounds and a new performer, the musician-engineer.

In summary, timbre has proved to be a complex attribute of musical sounds. It is not possible to rank-order sounds on a single scale with respect to timbre. Even more than pitch and loudness, timbre has turned out to be a multidimensional attribute of music.

PITCH OF MUSICAL INSTRUMENTS

Each musical instrument can be regarded as a complex sound generator having its own characteristic range of pitches. Of all acoustic instruments, the piano produces the widest range of pitch, seven and one-third octaves. Considering just the fundamental frequencies generated by the 88 keys, this represents a range of 27.5 to 4,186 *Hz*.

The limits of audibility of the young ear, usually given as 20 to 20,000 Hz, encompass about 10 octaves. These limits could accommodate perhaps another half-octave beyond the low end of the piano and there are organ pipes that generate these very low notes. Though nothing can be heard below the lower limit of 20 *Hz*, one can feel the vibrations of lower notes. The audible range of frequencies above the highest fundamental of the piano, 4,187 to 20,000 *Hz* or about two and one-half octaves, accommodates the overtones of the high piano notes. There is a good deal to hear within this range, because the overtones generated by the fundamental tones of the piano extend to, and well above, the upper limit of hearing.

In Fig. 10.11 on p. 188, we can examine the considerable variation in the range of pitches of different musical instruments. The human voice is a good place to begin. Although there is some variation from one singer to the next, both male and female voices have a range of about two octaves. Consider the vocal choir of soprano, alto, tenor, baritone and bass. Like the instruments of the orchestra belonging to a single choir, the voices overlap.

The soprano's lower limit is around middle C; the alto's is G below middle C; the tenor's is D, almost one octave below middle C; the baritone's is A, over one octave below middle C; and the bass' is E, almost two octaves below middle C. From lowest to highest, the vocal choir encompasses a frequency range of about 82.4 to 1,046 Hz or close to four octaves. Compare that with the seven and one-third octaves of the piano.

Now consider the quartet of strings of the orchestra. The violin, viola and cello all have a range of some three and one-half octaves, and the double bass is usually tuned to have a range of a little over two and one-half octaves. The violin's lowest note is the G below middle C (reported to be heard though not actually present in the acoustic signal. This is the so-called missing fundamental), and its highest note is shown in the figure as the C three octaves above middle C. Descending a fifth, the viola's lowest note is the C one octave below middle C. Descending one octave below that, the cello's lowest note is the C two octaves below middle C, and the double bass' lowest note is the E below that. From lowest to highest, the quartet of strings encompasses a frequency range of 41.2 to 2,093 *Hz*, or just over five and one-half octaves. Compare this again with the seven and one-third octaves of the piano.

The double bass, or bass viol as it is frequently called, retains many features of the early viol family of strings: the sloping shoulders, the flat back, and the shape of the bow, which is sometimes still held in the manner of a viol bow, underhanded. Together with the other modern orchestral strings, violin, viola, and cello, the double bass has evolved from a six-stringed instrument to one with four strings. Since the spread of the fingers in stopping the strings is necessarily great for such a low-pitched instrument, its four strings are tuned, as the old double base viol was, in intervals of fourths (E, A, D, G) rather than in fifths. This restricts the compass of the instrument considerably. To overcome this limitation, a fifth string is sometimes added (or a mechanical device is attached to the low E-string) to extend the range down to C=33 *Hz*.

The woodwind quintet of bassoon, clarinet, oboe, flute and piccolo encompasses a frequency range of 58.3 *Hz* (the bassoon's B Flat just over two octaves below middle C) to 3,729.3 *Hz* (the piccolo's B Flat almost four octaves above middle C), or a total of six octaves. And the brass quartet of tuba, trombone, French horn, and trumpet, encompasses a frequency range of 55 Hz (the tuba's A over two octaves below middle C) to 932.3 Hz (the trumpet's B Flat just less than two octaves above middle C) or a total of four octaves.

(The range of individual wind instruments is as follows: Bassoon, B Flat, 56.3 - E Flat, 622.3; Clarinet, G, 98 - B Flat, 932.3; Oboe, B Flat, 233 - G, 1,568; Flute, C, 262 - C, 2,093; Piccolo, D, 587.3 - B Flat, 3,729.3; Tuba, A, 55 - E Flat, 311.1; Trombone, E, 88.4 - B Flat, 466.2; French horn, F, 87.3 - F, 698.5; Trumpet, E, 164.3 - B Flat, 932.3.).

Finally, the tympani have a frequency range of 87.3 to 174.6 *Hz*, F up to the F below middle C, or a total of one octave.

If we plumb to the very lowest notes produced by orchestral instruments, we find that the harp makes it down to the C Flat three octaves below middle C. But the B Flat contrabassoon (not shown on the figure) does even better. Sounding an octave below the bassoon, it beats the harp by one tone. Its lowest fundamental frequency is 29 *Hz*. To accomplish this, it needs to be 12 feet long internally and is bent four times to facilitate handling. Of course, the piano beats them both.

Tonal Color

Just as the harmonics of complex tones increase the frequency range generated at the high end, so also do combination tones increase the range of frequencies sounded at both the high and the low end. When two or more loud notes are played together, the sum and differences of their individual frequencies may be heard, and these frequencies could conceivably range all the way down to the lower limit of hearing.

Each instrument generates its own characteristic series of harmonics and this contributes to the recognizability of each instrument. Though the fundamental frequencies of two notes sounded by two different instruments may be exactly the same in pitch and loudness, the harmonic structures are different. This is in part responsible for the differences in tonal color of musical instruments. The upper limits of sounds generated by each instrument, quoted earlier, specify just the fundamental frequencies. They do not include the harmonic series, which sometimes extends all the way up to the limits of audibility.

Compared to other musical instruments, the timbre of the organ is unique. Organ pipes are arranged in stops, or ranks, of pipes. A stop contains one pipe for each key of the keyboard and is referred to by the length of its longest pipe. Thus, all the pipes of the 16-foot stop are twice as long as the corresponding pipes of an 8-foot stop, and all their pitches are an octave lower.

The pipes of different stops differ not only in length but also in shape and composition, which gives them different timbres of sound. Mutation stops are designed for just this purpose: the nazard, or 2 2/3-foot stop, produces pitches an octave and a fifth above those of an 8-foot stop; the tierce, or 1 3/5-foot stop, produces pitches two octaves and a major third above those of an 8-foot stop; the larigot, or 1 2/3-foot stop, produces pitches two octaves and a fifth above those of an 8-foot stop. By playing these stops together with 8-, 4-, or 2-foot, stops, organists can produce sounds that are strange and colorful, and that may appear to the uninitiated like a lot of wrong notes going along with the melody.

The pitches emphasized by any instrument are determined not so much by the frequencies of the notes played, but by the resonances of the soundboard. If a resonance of 2,200 *Hz* is excited by the tenth harmonic of a note of 220 *Hz* (the A below middle C), it will also be excited by the fifth harmonic of 440 *Hz* (one octave higher). Thus, tonal color depends on the relative intensities of particular harmonics. Closed organ pipes have a 'hollow' sound because only odd harmonics are present. Open pipes have a 'fuller' sound because they include both even and odd harmonics (see Chapter 6).

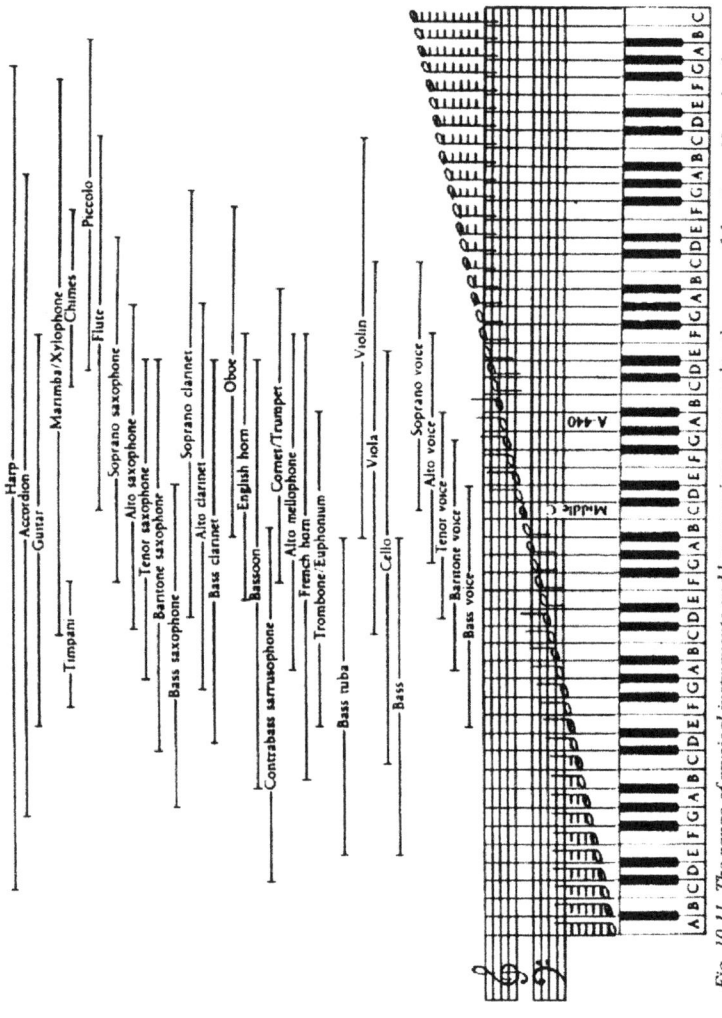

Fig. 10.11. The range of musical instruments and human voices compared to the range of the piano. Note the eleven line great staff and the large number of ledger lines needed to accommodate the total range of musical instruments.

Chapter 11

THE DEVELOPMENT OF MUSICAL SCALES

The major and minor scales of the Western world form familiar patterns of sounds. Many people first encounter these musical scales when they begin to play a musical instrument in childhood. Others come to recognize the pattern of consecutive notes when they learn the seven musical syllables of solfège in school, 'do, re, mi, fa, sol, la, si (or ti)' and back to 'do.' Even those who have never had these learning experiences find that the musical scales are familiar because the music they listen to is based on these scales.

Students learning to play a musical instrument frequently complain about having to practice scales all the time. Many tacitly assume that scales were concocted simply as exercises to torture them. It is true that scales are excellent exercises to learn to play the 'runs' frequently found in musical compositions, but they were not invented for this purpose. Western scales consist of a limited number of notes, seven in each octave, for example. These notes are drawn from a vast number of possible notes in the audible spectrum, to which musical instruments are tuned. The main purpose of scales is to provide composers with a defined pool of notes that can be used in musical compositions. The vocabulary of pitch in music consists of such a pool of notes, and the melodic grammar of music is based upon the intervals between these notes. Melodies are frequently written in a single key, which means that all the constituent notes of the melody belong to a single scale. Many people do not recognize this fact when they listen to the melody. It is only when these notes are re-arranged and played consecutively in ascending or descending order that they are recognized as forming the pitch pattern of the familiar scale.

It comes as a surprise to many people that the seven steps, or intervals, between the eight successive syllables of the octave are not all equal to each other. Those who are musically untrained do not realize that the interval size in the major scale between 'mi' and 'fa' and between 'si' and 'do' are exactly half the interval size between all the other syllables. The two half-step intervals are called *semitones*, the remaining five whole-step intervals are called *tones*, and these seven intervals together make up an *octave interval*. Normal human hearing encompasses perhaps ten such octaves.

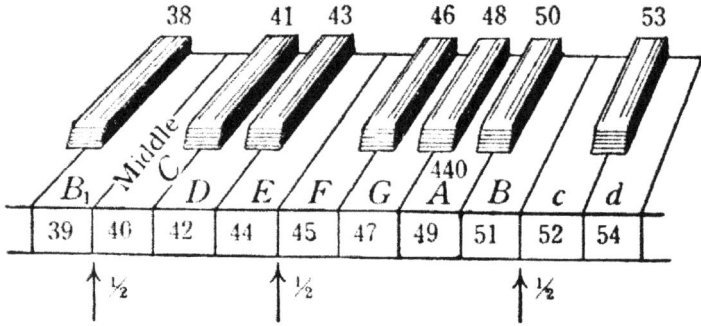

Fig. 11.1. One octave of the piano keyboard, from middle-C to the C above. Note the arrangement of black and white keys. The interval of the semitone is found between all adjacent keys, be they black or white. The keys are numbered from the lowest key on the piano. The fraction 1/2 is meant to remind you that the interval of a semitone is found between adjacent white keys (as well as between white and black keys).

If you examine the keyboard of the modern piano, you will see that there are 12, not seven, *different* keys within each octave, (seven white keys and five black keys). When these 12 keys are played in consecutive order, many people recognize the pattern of notes as the chromatic scale. This is the octave pool of notes from which composers can select for their piano compositions. Most of the music known to people of the Western world is limited to this pool of 12 different notes in the octave even though other musical instruments, stringed instruments such as the violin, are capable of producing many more sounds.

On the modern piano tuned in equal temperament, the chromatic octave encompasses 12 *different* piano keys, with 12 equal semitones between successive keys. This octave is reduplicated seven and one-third times giving the pianist a total of 88 keys (12 x 7 1/3) on which to play. It also provides composers of piano music with a total pool of just 88 different notes from which to draw for their compositions. This is still true today, as it was for Gershwin earlier in the twentieth century, for Chopin in the nineteenth century, and even for Mozart in the eighteenth century.

How did Western music get to be built on this chromatic system, 12 different notes in the octave (equally spaced on the modern piano, as we shall see)? The pitch spectrum is, after all, continuous. Draw a bow across a violin string while progressively shortening the string. Since there are no frets on the fingerboard of the violin, a glissando is produced: the pitch is raised continuously, and the number of different notes that can be derived from such a glissando is many more than the 12 we are accustomed to hear in the piano octave. However, Western musical tradition set a limit on the pool of notes used in musical compositions, and that limit is exactly 12 in the octave and a total of 88 on the piano.

In defining a pool of notes, early composers might have permitted themselves all the notes that are audibly different. This would have included notes one-eighth tones apart, since these notes are all discriminably different over most of the audible spectrum. In this way, composers would have had 48 different notes in the octave instead of 12, and would have needed 352 keys on the piano to encompass the 7 1/3 octaves (48 x 7 1/3). From the viewpoint of the pianist, such a keyboard would have been impossible to master with only 10 fingers. And the texture of the resulting music would have been too complicated for comfort. Instead, the interval unit of traditional Western music became the semitone, (12 of them in the octave, or 88 notes on the piano). How was a particular set of 12 notes selected in the first place, and why were the white and black keys on keyboard instruments arranged in the manner shown in Fig. 11.1?

Actually, the pool of notes was restricted still further. In composing melodies, Western composers frequently selected seven different notes from the chromatic scale of 12. We now refer to these seven notes as belonging to a diatonic scale. The two principal diatonic scales of Western music are the major and minor scales. There was a long period of musical development before these scales were codified. The evolution of the various arrangements of tones and semitones in Western scales is the subject of this chapter.

In order to tune the early instruments in a consistent way, a series of discrete pitches had to be defined. A continuum of pitches, like the continuum of hues that can be prepared on the painter's palette, would not do. The ancient Greeks had to tune the seven strings of the lyre and the seven pipes of Pan to seven specific pitches. The question has been raised whether the selection of these pitches was determined solely by the esthetic qualities of the intervening intervals. This question has been debated for a very long time. Some modern musicologists believe that the intervals that emerged from the selection of these specific pitches are not native or inevitable, not absolute in any sense, but quite arbitrary. In support of this view, they note that the specific pitches of Occidental music (the 'do, re, mi,' of our scales) were fixed only after centuries of experimentation. Their cross-cultural comparisons reveal startlingly different scales. They believe that African and Eastern music possess unit-intervals unlike ours. (An example of an Indian scale will be given later.)

Other musicologists have noted that some musical intervals are found universally, and they have concluded that these intervals could not have been selected arbitrarily. There does seem to be something special in all musical cultures about the relationship of two notes an octave apart, two notes whose frequencies are in the ratio 2/1. Aristotle remarked that voices in different registers tend to sing an octave apart when singing the same melody. The note you sing when asked to match a particular note on the piano will depend on your pitch range: the soprano will sing in a high register, the bass in a low. You may, in fact, sing up or down an octave and not realize it. Even people who possess perfect pitch who almost never mistake one note for another, do occasionally confuse octaves. In short, there is a feeling of great similarity of pitch, or even of identity, when the frequency of one note is just twice or half the frequency of another.

Musical Scales

It was Pythagoras who taught us that musical intervals are ratios of frequencies of vibrations, and that different intervals are produced by changing the length of stretched strings. If you pluck the lowest string of the violin, you will hear the G *below* middle C. In our modern tuning system, this pitch corresponds to a frequency of 196 *Hz*. If you 'stop' the string by pressing a finger exactly in the middle of the string and pluck either half, you will hear the G *above* middle C, corresponding to a frequency of 392 *Hz*. In short, a stretched string half its normal length produces a frequency twice its unstopped frequency (2/1 is the inverse of 1/2), and the upper octave is heard.

Pythagoras believed that there is something special about the interval of the fifth, for he used it as the basis for his musical scale, as we shall see. To produce a fifth, stop the G-string of the violin by pressing a finger exactly two-thirds of the way down the string and pluck the longer part. You will hear the D *above* middle C corresponding to a frequency of 294 *Hz*. A stretched string two-thirds its normal length produces a frequency three-seconds higher (3/2 is the inverse of 2/3), and a fifth, G to D, or 196 to 294 *Hz*, is heard. What made the interval of the fifth so special to Pythagoras was that its frequency ratio, 3/2, was composed of small whole numbers like the octave. Similarly, a fourth, G up to C, is produced by shortening the string to three-quarters its normal length, and the frequencies of the two notes making up the fourth are in the ratio 4/3 (the inverse of 3/4, or 262/196 *Hz*). The same logic is applicable to all seven intervals of a diatonic scale.

Is there any reason to believe that the interval of the fourth is primary and native? In descending form, the fourth is said to be the natural drop of the voice in ending a statement. The operatic recitative was originally based on the descending fourth, giving the feeling of finality and repose.

In summary, Western tradition leads us to conclude that certain intervals are indeed special, particularly the octave and the fifth. In addition, the descending fourth seems to be the first interval to be fixed in Western music. The ancient Greeks used the fourth as the limit in tuning the tetrachord, and all other intervals seem to be based on it.

THE GREEK TETRACHORD

The beginnings of Western musical scales can be traced back to the musical practices of the ancient Greeks. Our music has inherited the fixed pitches of their two musical instruments, the lyre and the pipes. Had it been possible with the seven-stringed lyre to get intermediate notes by plucking two strings at the same time, as orange is obtained by mixing red and yellow, the development of music would have taken a different course.

Pythagoras investigated musical intervals using a primitive instrument called the monochord, a stretched string whose length could be altered with a movable bridge. It was when he played intervals such as the descending fourth on the monochord that he discovered the relation of pitch to the length of the stretched string. (Pythagoras oversimplified. Today, we know that its mass or thickness, and tension also influence the pitch of a stretched string). Pythagoras established the intervals of the octave as 2/1, the fifth as 3/2, and the fourth as 4/3. These simple ratios seemed to him to yield the most pleasing combinations of tones, the so-called Pythagorean consonances. Today, it seems clear that the properties of numbers were more important to Pythagoras than the sensations. Only later did sensations validate the rules of numbers. The fact is that the perception of consonance and dissonance depends on a number of non-mathematical variables, including the past experiences and expectations of the listener, and is thus much more complicated than Pythagoras imagined.

The tetrachord was a four-stringed instrument having a range of a fourth, 4/3. It was tuned to A, G, F, E, approximately. Our best guess is that the three consecutive intervals that resulted from this tuning were tone, tone and semitone. This tuning was a milestone, for it created the three-interval fourth that we have incorporated in our diatonic scales. The movement of pitch is downward, and the final semitone, F to E, contributes to the feeling of finality and repose. Some time later, a second tetrachord was added with one note of overlap, to produce a heptachord. The second tetrachord was tuned so that its three consecutive intervals were something like: tone, semitone, tone. This resulted in a scale of seven notes with six intervening intervals:

Musical Scales 195

```
1 2 3 4 5 6 7
[D C B A]
      [A G F E]
```
('A' is the note common to the two tetrachords)

The musicians who adopted this scheme of two overlapping tetrachords found themselves limited to seven notes ranging from D to E, thus leaving out the octave note, D! Recognizing the deficiency, some Greek musicians tried to increase the lyre's strings from seven to eight to complete the octave, but they met with opposition from the Spartans, who had a law against more than seven strings, perhaps because there was something magical or sacred about the number seven. In this scale system, the middle note of the series, A, became the orienting note, or 'final' (or tonic, as we refer to the orienting note today).

Pythagoras finally succeeded in stretching the scale from seven to eight notes, to complete the octave. He accomplished this by adding an eighth string to the lyre and interposing the seventh interval, the interval of disjunction, between the two tetrachords:

```
              [Interval of
[E    D   C    B] Disjunction] [A    G    F    E]
[         4/3         ] [ 9/8 ] [        4/3        ] = 2/1
```

In this system, the interval of disjunction turns out to be 9/8. How was this determined? Since the two tetrachords were each 4/3, the two combined made an interval of 16/9 (4/3 x 4/3 -- intervals are combined by multiplying their separate frequencies). To complete the octave, 2/1, the interval of disjunction had to be 9/8 (2/1 divided by 16/9) and the interval of the fifth became 3/2 (4/3 x 9/8). We are less sure of the frequency ratios of the other intervening intervals. For example, we can only guess at the frequency ratios, E to D, at the beginning of the scale, or F to E, at the end of the scale. Nevertheless, we have here an example of an early diatonic scale, a scale consisting of eight discrete notes and seven intervals in the octave. As we shall see, this became one of the scales on which plainsong, or Gregorian chant, is based. During the early Christian period, this scale became known as the Phrygian mode, one of eight Ecclesiastical modes.

Put yourself in the position of the ancient Greek musician who had to tune the eight strings of his lyre in some consistent and rational way. Naturally you would want to tune your instrument so that your music would sound consonant. You would be especially concerned about this whenever you plucked two or more strings or blew two or more pipes at the same time because a mistuning would create the throbbing of unpleasant beats. What scheme could you use for the tuning of your instrument? One scheme that would avoid these unpleasant beats would be to tune your strings to tones derived from the harmonic series. This series of tones, reviewed below, provides a rational basis for the subdivision of the octave into a sequence of precisely defined notes.

As we proceed in this chapter, we will note how the Pythagorean sequence of notes slowly evolved into the notes of our eight-tone diatonic scale with C as the tonic of the C major scale: C, D, E, F, G, A, B, C, instead of the A string providing the orienting note or final. We have grown so accustomed to the sound of seven intervals in the octave that a deviation to six or five intervals (as in the blues and pentatonic scales) seems strange and needs some getting used to. We have also grown accustomed to the sound of semitones (between E and F and between B and C in our system of notes), that produce a release of tension and the feeling of finality. In the modern C major scale, B has come to be known as the leading tone, leading to the tonic, C. Since descent to the bottom semitone, F to E in the ancient Greek musical scheme, was so obviously the way to gain the feeling of finality and repose, it is curious that the scale came to be reversed with the leading tone, B, pointing upward to the tonic, C.

THE HARMONIC SERIES

All musical instruments produce complex tones consisting of many constituent pure tones, called harmonics. This is because the elastic body of the musical instrument, the stretched string or the column of air, vibrates not only as a whole but also in parts. The lowest frequency of any complex tone is called the fundamental tone (or first harmonic). It is the fundamental that gives the name to the tone because it is usually more intense than the upper harmonics (also called overtones). We are not ordinarily aware that so many different sounds are present in a complex tone because they are so well fused together, but they are there nevertheless. The frequencies of the upper harmonics are exact multiples of the frequency of the fundamental tone: if the frequency of the fundamental is f, the successive harmonics have frequencies of *2f, 3f, 4f,* and so on. The sequence of the first 25 harmonics generated by a complex tone having a fundamental frequency of 33 *Hz* (approximately C, three octaves below middle C) is as follows:

Harmonic Name	Frequency Number	Frequency in *Hz*	Fraction of String	Corresponding Interval Ratio	Corresponding Interval Name
Fundamental	1	33			
C	2	66	1/2	2/1	Octave
G	3	99	2/3	3/2	Perfect Fifth*
C	4	132	3/4	4/3	Perfect Fourth*
E	5	165	4/5	5/4	Major Third
G	6	198	5/6	6/5	Minor Third
Bb	7	231	6/7	7/6	
C	8	264	7/8	8/7	
D	9	297	8/9	9/8	Major Tone
E	10	330	9/10	10/9	Minor Tone
F-F#	11	363	10/11	11/10	
G	12	396	11/12	12/11	
Ab-A	13	429	12/13	13/12	
Bb	14	462	13/14	14/13	
B	15	495	14/15	15/14	
C	16	528	15/16	16/15	Semitone
Db	17	561	16/17	17/16	
D	18	594	17/18	18/17	
Eb	19	627	18/19	19/18	
E	20	660	19/20	20/19	
F	21	693	20/21	21/20	
F#	22	726	21/22	22/21	
Gb	23	759	22/23	23/22	
G	24	792	23/24	24/23	
Ab	25	825	24/25	25/24	

*Historically, the intervals of a fifth, fourth, unison, and octave came to be called 'perfect,' while the intervals of a second, third, sixth and seventh came to be called 'major.'

Fig. 11.2. All musical instruments produce complex tones that consist of a fundamental tone and many harmonics or overtones. The quality of the complex tone is determined, in part, by the relative prominence of these harmonics. The frequencies of harmonics are exact multiples of the frequency of the fundamental tone.

Here is an attempt to notate the harmonic series, starting with the fundamental C, two octaves below middle C, and the 15 harmonics above. The attempt cannot be fully successful because musical notation does not provide a note somewhere between F and F# and between A and Ab The result is no more than an approximation.

The harmonic series of tones has played an important role in the development of the musical scale. To understand why, we must turn our attention to the phenomenon of beats.

If two tones differ slightly in frequency, they fuse into one tone that fluctuates in intensity and produces an unpleasant roughness or throbbing sound, called beats. If two tones an octave, fifth or fourth apart are similarly mistuned, they also combine to produce beats. However, the harmonic series of tones has the feature that no beats are produced when any of their constituent tones are played together. If composers restricted themselves to the tones of the harmonic series as a pool of notes from which to draw, they would avoid generating unpleasant beats. This is why there has been a preference through the ages for discrete notes that are related to each other in the ratio of small whole numbers, such as 3/2 for the fifth rather than, say, 3.02/2 producing two beats per second, which some would judge as unpleasant.

Now we can define a musical scale based on the harmonic series of tones. We can draw from this series as many notes as we like. For example, we might decide to have five in the octave (as in the pentatonic scale), or six (as in the blues scale), or seven (as in the diatonic scale), or 12 (as in the chromatic scale), or even 22 (as in the SA-grama scale). However many we choose from the harmonic series, we can be assured of consonant intervals. The number of intervals in the octave is now engraved in ivory (12 on the piano) and cannot be changed, but many musicologists believe that the original selection was really quite arbitrary.

The harmonic series demarcated by the two lines in the middle of the table above provide us with an interesting scale consisting of eight intervals in the octave. These are the harmonics numbered 8 through 16: C, D, E, F-F$^{\#}$, G, A^{b}-A, B^{b}, B, C. To illustrate this harmonic scale, the eight intervals in the octave were laid out horizontally in the diagram below.

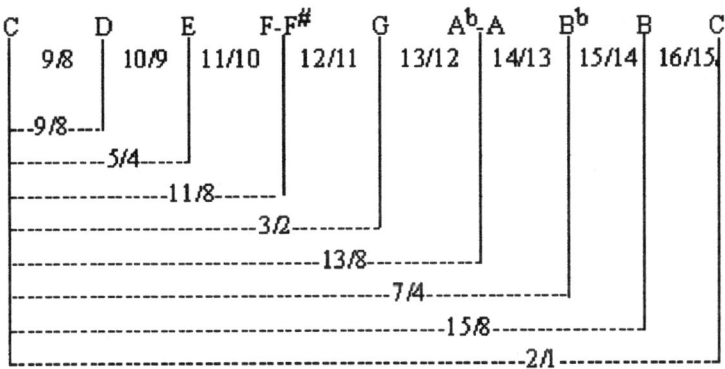

In this diagram, the octave, from C to C, is divided to yield the nine notes of the harmonic series in the middle of the table above. These notes are shown separated from each other by the eight interval ratios of the harmonic series, 9/8, 10/9, 11/10, etc. The ratios enclosed by the dashed lines in the diagram show the same eight intervals cumulatively, starting from the basenote, C: first to D (9/8), then to E (9/8 x 9/8 = 5/4), then to F (9/8 x 10/9 x 11/10 = 11/8), and so on, all the way to the upper C (9/8 x 10/9 x...x 16/15 = 2/1). To combine two or more intervals, their separate frequency ratios must be multiplied. (It should be noted in passing that upper harmonics, 16 through 25, carry the names of the chromatic scale and that enharmonic intervals are among them, such as F$^{\#}$ to G^{b}. Two notes make up an enharmonic interval if they share the same key on the modern piano.)

The harmonic series provides a rational basis for a system of discrete notes that can be used for musical composition. Using this set of notes, composers could avoid the production of unpleasant beats in their music. This series of nine harmonics did serve as the basis for the development of musical scales, but it was never adopted practically as a scale itself. Why was there a need for other scales?

Although esthetically pleasing from a harmonic standpoint, a scale composed of nine consecutive tones derived from the harmonic series is quite unsatisfactory in a practical sense. The eight intervals are all different from each other: 9/8, 10/9, 11/10, 12/11, 13/12, 14/13, 15/14 and 16/15. As you can see from the diagram, there is no standard whole tone and no standard semitone -- in fact, no standard interval at all. The F is distinctly too sharp and the A is distinctly too flat compared to the corresponding tones in the Western scales that we are accustomed to (the equal-tempered scale). Finally, it is impossible to transpose melodies from one register to another and retain the precise relationship of notes. This will be elaborated later.

The intervals of the harmonic series are nevertheless 'natural' in the sense that no beats are produced when any of the constituent tones are played together. The lore until quite recently was that the more perfectly harmonic the intervals of the musical scale (approaching 2/1, 3/2, 4/3, etc.), the more consonant the intervals when used in harmony. The history of musical scales is a history of compromise between the desire for consonant, pleasant-sounding intervals, on the one hand, and the practical need for equal intervals within the octave, on the other. The ultimate aim of this musical evolution was a system of tuning musical instruments that permits the substitution of one note for another, as $G^{\#}$ can be substituted for A^{b} on the modern piano. But there was a long struggle before this result was attained. A number of compromise scales were proposed, including the 'just' and 'meantone' scales, but they did not survive to the modern period for the tuning of keyboard instruments. The end product of this evolution was the equal-tempered scale, which abandoned the principle of consonances in favor of equal intervals between successive notes of the scale.

Before we turn to the modern systems of scales, we will examine how Pythagoras himself constructed a musical scale. Though his scale has no practical importance in Western music, the method he used to arrive at it illustrates how one simple mathematical ratio, 3/2, can be used to determine all the intervals in a scale of discrete notes. The pattern of seven intervals in the Pythagorean scale has served as the prototype of the scales that have followed, as we shall see.

Pythagorean Intonation

Pythagoras is said to have invented a musical scale that encompassed seven intervals in the octave. Its principal feature is that only two unit-intervals are needed in the octave: a whole tone, 9/8, and a limma (or small semitone), 256/243. The successive intervals are: tone, tone, limma, tone, tone, tone, limma. This is shown in the diagram of the scale below. Note that the Pythagorean ratios, 2/1, 4/3, and 3/2 are preserved in this scale, making the octave, fourth and fifth consonant intervals. A comparison with the scale based on the harmonic series reveals that the two scales differ in one important respect: the Pythagorean scale displays just two unit-intervals among its seven, the whole tone, 9/8, and the limma, 256/243, while the harmonic scale contains eight different intervals, no two exactly alike.

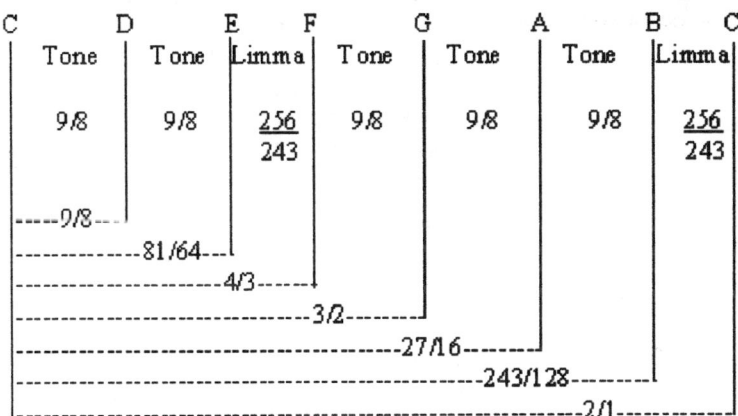

How did Pythagoras derive his two unit-intervals, whole tone, 9/8, and limma, 256/243? And why did he arrange the two unit-intervals so that the limmas would appear between the third and fourth degrees, and between the seventh and eighth degrees, of the scale? Although the whole tone, 9/8, appears in the harmonic series, this is not where Pythagoras got it. In order to derive all the successive intervals in his scale, Pythagoras began with the ratio of the consonant fifth, which he knew to be 3/2, and he played a little mathematical game. Let us repeat what he did.

Starting with C, at the beginning of the scale, let us move up in successive fifths, combining the intervals as we proceed: the initial fifth, C to G, is 3/2; the next fifth, G to D, is also 3/2. Combining these two intervals yields the interval C to D, 9/4 (3/2 x 3/2). This ratio is greater than 2/1, indicating that we have exceeded the octave. We can eliminate the octave interval, 2/1, by multiplying 9/4 by 1/2. This gives us the first interval of the Pythagorean scale, between the C we began with and its adjacent D, the whole tone, 9/8.

If we continue our ascent in successive fifths, the next fifth is D to A. To determine the interval of the sixth, C to A, let us combine the fifth, 3/2, with the whole tone that we just determined, 9/8. This ratio turns out to be 27/16 (9/8 x 3/2). By repeating this process twelve times, combining the intervals as we proceed, and eliminating the octaves as they are exceeded, we can derive all the intervals of the Pythagorean scale (including the chromatic intervals called augmented in the table below), just as he did. This process of moving from one fifth to the next, twelve times, is shown on the piano keyboard in Fig. 11.3, and is summarized in the table below.

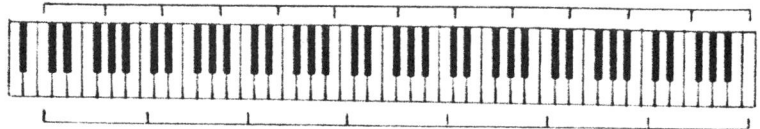

Fig. 11.3. The Pythagorean ascent in 12 successive fifths is shown above the piano keyboard, starting with the lowest C, compared to the seven successive octaves, shown below the piano keyboard. Since the same key is reached, the highest C, we might conclude that 12 successive fifths are equivalent to seven successive octaves. This is true for the piano tuned in equal temperament, as you can see in this figure, but it is not true for the piano tuned in the Pythagorean consonance of the fifth, 3/2. The ascent of 12 successive fifths ends in B♯, not C, and the combined interval, low C to high B♯, equals $(3/2)^{12}$ or 129.75/1. In contrast, the ascent of seven successive octaves ends in C, and the combined interval, low C to high C, equals $(2/1)^7$ or 128/1.

Successive Fifths Name	$(3/2)^n \times 3/2$	Octaves Eliminated $(\times 1/2)^n$	Scale Intervals Ratio	Name
*F-C	$(3/2)^{-1}$	$(\times 1/2)^{-1}$	4/3	C-F: Perfect fourth
C-G	$(3/2)^{1}$	$(\times 1/2)^{0}$	3/2	C-G: Perfect fifth
*G-D	$(3/2)^{2}$	$(\times 1/2)^{1}$	9/8	C-D: Major second
D-A	$(3/2)^{3}$	$(\times 1/2)^{1}$	27/16	C-A: Major sixth
*A-E	$(3/2)^{4}$	$(\times 1/2)^{2}$	81/64	C-E: Major third
E-B	$(3/2)^{5}$	$(\times 1/2)^{2}$	243/128	C-B: Major seventh
*B-F#	$(3/2)^{6}$	$(\times 1/2)^{3}$	$3^6/2^9$	C-F#: Augm. fourth
*F#-C#	$(3/2)^{7}$	$(\times 1/2)^{4}$	$3^7/2^{11}$	C-C#: Augm. first
C#-G#	$(3/2)^{8}$	$(\times 1/2)^{4}$	$3^8/2^{12}$	C-G#: Augm. fifth
*G#-D#	$(3/2)^{9}$	$(\times 1/2)^{5}$	$3^9/2^{14}$	C-D#: Augm second
D#-A#	$(3/2)^{10}$	$(\times 1/2)^{5}$	$3^{10}/2^{15}$	C-A#: Augm. sixth
*A#-E#	$(3/2)^{11}$	$(\times 1/2)^{6}$	$3^{11}/2^{17}$	C-E#: Augm third
*E#-B#	$(3/2)^{12}$	$(\times 1/2)^{7}$	$3^{12}/2^{19}$	C-B#: Enharmonic

There are actually 13 consecutive fifths in this table, not 12. The entry for the first fifth, F - C, the fifth below the base note C, was added to derive the perfect fourth, 4/3.

**By adding successive fifths, the octave of C was reached or was exceeded. To remain within a single octave, successive octaves were eliminated by multiplying the interval-ratio by 1/2.*

There are serious problems associated with the Pythagorean scale. Ascending twelve successive fifths starting with C should bring us back to C, seven octaves higher; that is, twelve fifths, $(3/2)^{12}$, should be equivalent to seven octaves, $(2/1)^7$. But this is not so: $(3/2)^{12} = 129.75/1$, while $(2/1)^7 = 128/1$.

The last note of the Pythagorean series of successive fifths is B#, not C. Though these two notes are enharmonically related to each other, that is, the two share the same key on the modern piano, they are not identical in frequency. The last interval-ratio in the table, $3^{12}/2^{19}$, should equal a unison, 1/1, but the ratio is actually 1.0136/1. This interval is called a *stretched unison*, sharp by a Pythagorean comma (the interval between the major tone and the minor tone which we will encounter in just temperament). The end result is a stretched octave, 2.0273/1, that produces annoying beats and must be replaced by the harmonic octave, 2/1, to retain the harmonic consonance of the octave.

One way to overcome the problem of the stretched octave is to begin the Pythagorean game with a slightly flatted fifth, flatted just enough to insure a perfect unison when the twelfth fifth is reached. Had Pythagoras played his game of 12 consecutive fifths using the ratio of 2.9966/2 for the fifth (derived by subdividing seven octaves into 12 equal fifths, $^{12}\sqrt{(2/1)^7}$), instead of 3/2, he would have anticipated the equal tempered semitone, 1.05946/1, two millenia before the equal-tempered scale was actually introduced in Europe. Unfortunately, Pythagoras was preoccupied with the beauty of simple ratios. (The mean-tone temperament, which we will encounter later, was derived by the same principle, using the flatted fifth.)

The Pythagorean scale does not appear to have enjoyed much popularity in the past, and is not remembered except as a historical curiosity. Its major advantage is that beats are minimized when its constituent notes are played together. Its major disadvantage is that the whole tone is too large to encompass two limmas exactly. As a consequence, starting the Pythagorean scale on a note other than C changes the serial order of intervals. As with the harmonic series, accurate transposition of melodies is not possible. However, the use of seven intervals in the scale and the location of the two limmas between notes 3 and 4 and between notes 7 and 8 presages the pattern of intervals later fixed in the major scale.

JUST INTONATION

Around the beginning of the Christian era, Didymos worked out an elegant scale of eight notes in which the Pythagorean consonances were cleverly preserved. He made each of the two tetrachords, C,D,E,F, and G,A,B,C, consist of just three intervals derived from the harmonic series: one major tone, 9/8, one minor tone, 10/9, and one semitone, 16/15. Between the two tetrachords, between F and G, Didymos interposed another major tone, 9/8 (the interval of disjunction), to complete the octave. This scale is called the *major scale of just intonation:*

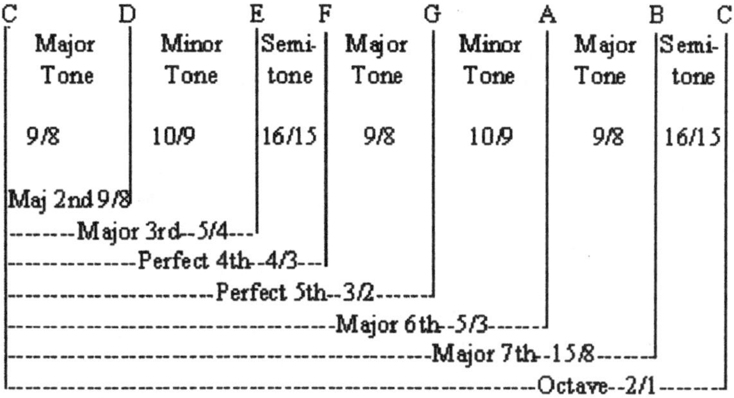

Musical Scales

C	D	E	F	G	A	B	C
Major Tone	Minor Tone	Semi-tone	Major Tone	Minor Tone	Major Tone	Semi-tone	
9/8	10/9	16/15	9/8	10/9	9/8	16/15	

```
|Maj 2nd 9/8|
|-------Major 3rd--5/4---|
|-------------Perfect 4th--4/3---|
|----------------------Perfect 5th--3/2------|
|--------------------------------Major 6th--5/3------|
|-----------------------------------------Major 7th--15/8------|
|-----------------------------------------------Octave--2/1------|
```

As before, adjacent intervals are combined by multiplying their separate frequencies. For example, the major third, 5/4, is produced by combining the major and minor tones (9/8 x 10/9). Similarly, the octave interval, 2/1, is produced by combining all seven individual intervals, 9/8 x 10/9 x 16/15 x 9/8 x 10/9 x 9/8 x 16/15.

The major chord includes the third, fifth and eighth notes (or degrees) of the scale. Referring to these intervals in the diagram above, the major chord on C turns out to be:

Tonic	Major Third	Perfect Fifth	Octave
C	E	G	C
1	5/4	3/2	2/1

Multiplying by 4 to eliminate fractions, we get

| 4 | 5 | 6 | 8 |

This is the chord that is frequently described as sounding bright and happy.

By changing the order of intervals in the first of the two tetrachords, major tone, minor tone, semitone, to major tone, semitone, minor tone, a corresponding minor scale can be constructed. This minor scale in just intonation is diagrammed as follows:

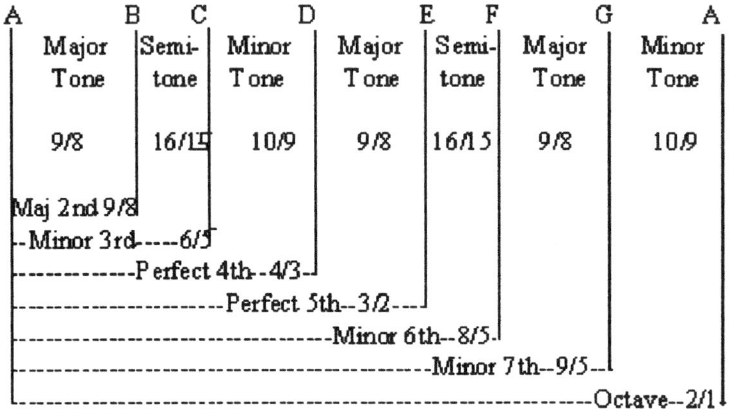

```
A       B    C      D        E    F     G        A
Major  Semi- Minor  Major   Semi- Major    Minor
Tone   tone  Tone   Tone    tone  Tone     Tone

9/8    16/15 10/9   9/8     16/15 9/8      10/9
```

| Maj 2nd 9/8 |
| -- Minor 3rd ---- 6/5 |
| ------------ Perfect 4th -- 4/3 ⌐ |
| -------------------- Perfect 5th -- 3/2 --- |
| ----------------------------- Minor 6th -- 8/5 |
| -------------------------------------- Minor 7th -- 9/5 -- |
| --- Octave -- 2/1 |

Like its major counterpart, the minor chord includes the third, fifth and eighth degrees of the scale. Referring to these intervals in the diagram above, the minor chord turns out to be:

Tonic   Minor Third   Perfect Fifth   Octave

A	C	E	A
1	6/5	3/2	2/1

Multiplying by 10 to eliminate fractions, we get

| 10 | 12 | 15 | 20 |

The minor chord is frequently described as sounding sounding melancholic and/or solemn.

Using the system of just intonation, the octave can be subdivided to yield twelve intervals. The major tone, 9/8, and minor tone, 10/9, each contain one semitone, 16/15. The residual of the major tone is the limma, 135/128, and the residual of the minor tone is the diesis, 25/24. By subdividing the major and minor tones in this manner, each into two fractions, a scale of 12 consecutive intervals can be constructed. Consisting of just three intervals, semitone, limma, and diesis, this is the prototype of the modern chromatic scale:

C		D		E	F		G		A		B	C
	Major		Minor		Semi-	Major		Minor		Major		Semi-
1	2	3	4	5	6	7	8	9	10	11	12	13
semi tone	limma	semi tone	diesis	semi tone	limma	semi tone	semi tone	diesis	semi tone	limma	semi tone
16/15	135/128	16/15	25/24	16/15	135/128	16/15	16/15	25/24	16/15	135/128	16/15

```
|--16/15-|
|--------9/8--|
|----------------6/5--|
|-------------------------5/4--|
|-------------------------------4/3--|
|-----------------------------------45/32--|
|------------------------------------------3/2--|
|-------------------------------------------------8/5--|
|--------------------------------------------------------5/3--|
|---------------------------------------------------------------16/9--|
|----------------------------------------------------------------------15/8--|
|-------------------------------------------------------------------------------2/1--|
```

The major scale of Didymos in just intonation persisted for a long time. It is called the natural scale because it is mathematically elegant, in that all the large intervals are in the ratio of small whole numbers. Instruments tuned in the just intonation produce beautifully consonant intervals. And instruments that are not limited to fixed pitches can be played in just intonation at any time. The human voice is such an instrument. Singers can produce an indefinite number of different pitches even in their limited range, perhaps a hundred or more. Just intonation is particularly valuable to skilled singers when they sing polyphonically or in harmony, for they can adjust their voices to produce intervals that ring out purely, without the sound of beats. Just intonation is frequently considered ideal for *a capella* music, which is sung without instrumental accompaniment.

Just intonation received the sanction of Ptolemy around 130 A.D. Later, Newton championed it. Today, this scale is chiefly remembered as the ancestor of the modern eight-tone major scale. Despite its attractive feature, that it is excellent for harmony since no beats are heard, the great limitation of the just intonation is that its seven consecutive intervals can be played in one major key only. In the scale beginning with C, the fifth, C to G, has its proper ratio, 3/2, but in the scale beginning with D, the fifth, D to A, has a ratio of 40/27

(10/9 × 16/15 × 9/8 × 10/9). Similarly, the fourth, C to F, has its proper Pythagorean ratio, 4/3, but the fourth, A to D, has a ratio of 81/60 (9/8 × 16/15 × 9/8). The tritone F to B is 45/32 (9/8 × 10/9 × 9/8), but its inverse, the tritone B to F is 1125/1024 (16/15 × 9/8 × 10/9 × 16/15). Though close, they are not identical. Finally, combining two semitones to make a whole tone produces 256/225 (16/15 × 16/15), which matches neither the major tone, 9/8, nor the minor tone, 10/9.

The end result is that it is not possible to play accurately in more than one key without having to re-tune instruments that are fixed in pitch. Starting a melody in a new register throws the successive notes out of pitch. To obtain just intonation in all twelve of the modern major keys would require 21 notes in each octave, a complication much too great for the playing of keyboard and wind instruments in which the pitches are fixed. Think of constructing an organ with that number of pipes, and then playing it!

Over the centuries, a number of compromise scales were proposed and attempted in order to achieve satisfactory transposition from one key to another, but as long as the composer and listener demanded that the music sound pure, without annoying beats, no satisfactory solution could ever be found. It took a long time before this demand was abandoned, but, when it was relaxed during the seventeenth and eighteenth centuries, two satisfactory systems did emerge: mean-tone and equal temperament.

During the medieval period, before polyphony was invented in the West and before the new scales began to appear, the problem of beats was avoided by the adoption of a system of notes that required no transposition and therefore no accidentals. These were the modes upon which the church chants were based.

ECCLESIASTICAL MODES

The early church chants were monophonic, that is, they consisted of a single melody unadorned with harmony. These chants were sung in unison and had no instrumental accompaniment. Since the singers were free to begin the chant on any note, they did not have to contend with the problem of transposition from one key to another. Nor did they need to use accidentals in their music. All they needed was a pattern of notes to follow, such as those found in the scale of just

Musical Scales

intonation. Each ecclesiastical mode provided them with just such a pattern of notes.

Over the ages, 14 ecclesiastical modes were proposed. Eight of them are credited to St. Ambrose in the fourth century and St. Gregory in the sixth century. Six more modes were proposed in the sixteenth century, but two of them were never used by the church (locrian and hypolocrian). Once the equal-tempered scale was adopted in the nineteenth century, the church modes fell into disfavor, particularly in the tuning of musical instruments. But they survived in folk melodies, and they have seen a remarkable revival in the twentieth century, in music influenced by the traditional European folk idioms. The church modes have also been adopted in modern jazz, of all places.

Modal scales designate some tones as more important than others and establish dynamic patterns of expectation. Any of the seven different pitches of the scale of just intonation can be taken as the starting point yielding a total of seven modes.

Actually, there are seven '*authentic*' modes and seven corresponding '*plagal*' modes. To illustrate the seven authentic modes, let us select just the white keys on the piano, the eight in the octave, as our pool of notes. It is the succession of tones and semitones in the octave that defines the mode. If we play the white keys in ascending order starting on D, we will have played the Dorian mode. In this mode, the semitones fall between the second and third notes, E and F, and between the sixth and seventh notes, B and C. If we had started on E instead, we would have played the Phrygian mode, in which the semitones fall between the first and second notes, E and F, and between the fifth and sixth notes, B and C.

We have now defined the Dorian and Phrygian modes. As you can see, the starting key of the sequence of white keys on the piano defines the modes. If we repeat this process, starting with F, then G, then A, then B, and finally with C, we will have defined all seven authentic modes. They are listed and named in the table below. No black key, that is, no accidental is normally needed in the ecclesiastical modes.

Each of the seven 'authentic' modes has a corresponding 'plagal' mode that begins the interval of a fourth below its authentic equivalent. Literally, the term *plaga*l means sideways or oblique and, in this case, plagal means 'to accommodate' or to provide those singers whose voices are in a different register with an octave range that better matches their voices. The plagal modes are listed and named in the table, beside their corresponding authentic modes.

Each mode includes a 'final' note on which the piece ends, and a 'dominant' note, which is used as the pitch for the monotone recitation of the Psalms. The authentic and plagal modes are each governed by a rule. For the authentic modes, the dominant is normally a perfect fifth above the final (e.g. D to A in the Dorian mode). For the plagal modes, there is normally a perfect fourth between the first note and the final (e.g. A to D in the Hypodorian mode), and the dominant is a third below the corresponding authentic dominant (e.g. A down to F again in the Hypodorian mode). In the table, the 'dominant' note in each mode is shown in parentheses, and the 'final' note is underlined.

Authentic Mode		Corresponding Plagal Mode	
Dorian	D E F G (A) B C $\underline{D}$	Hypodorian	A B C $\underline{D}$ E(F) G A
Phrygian	E F G A B(C) D $\underline{E}$	Hypophrygian	B C D $\underline{E}$ F G (A) B
Lydian	F G A B(C) D E $\underline{F}$	Hypolydian	C D E $\underline{F}$ G (A) B C
Mixolydian	G A B C (D) E F $\underline{G}$	Hypomixolydian	D E F $\underline{G}$ A B(C) D
Aeolian	A B C D (E) F G $\underline{A}$	Hypoaeolian	E F G $\underline{A}$ B(C) D E
Locrian*	B C D E F (G) A $\underline{B}$	Hypolocrian*	F G A $\underline{B}$ C D (E)F
Ionian	C D E F (G) A B $\underline{C}$	Hypoionian	G A B $\underline{C}$ D (E)F G

The 'dominant' note is shown in parentheses. The 'final' note is underlined.
*These modes were never used by the church.

Two of the authentic ecclesiastical modes have survived unaltered into the modern period, and they flourish in equal-temperament. Originally introduced by Glareanus in the sixteenth century, these are the Ionian and Aeolean modes. They can be recognized as our major and minor scales. They are the offspring of the modal system. The other modes are still heard in folk music and in the ethnic idioms of such composers as Debussy, Kodaly, and Bartok. One version of the celebrated early English melody 'Greensleeves' is in the Dorian mode. Sometimes it is played with a flatted sixth degree of the mode which transforms it into the Aeolian mode or the modern minor scale. As pointed out earlier, the ecclesiastical modes can be heard in modern jazz.

By the seventeenth century, the requirement to avoid beats was relaxed and, in this atmosphere, two satisfactory scale systems emerged. The first was mean-tone temperament.

MEAN-TONE TEMPERAMENT

Around 1500, a compromise temperament was proposed. It was designed to make the whole tone a mean, or average, between Didymos's major tone (9/8) and minor tone (10/9), thus equalizing them. In the resulting scale, the unit interval is the 'mean-tone,' approximately 8.94/8.

To derive mean-tone temperament, we will once again play the Pythagorean game of successive fifths, but this time we will ascend in slightly flatted fifths, 2.992/2, the fifth that results from the mean-tone, 8.94/8. This fifth is barely perceptibly flat, and the resultant beats are slow and not disturbing. Playing the Pythagorean game as we played it earlier, the first four successive fifths, C to G, G to D, D to A, A to E, lead us to a major third, C to E, that is perfectly tuned, 5/4. (In contrast, the third in the Pythagorean scale, 81/64, is significantly larger, and it produces annoying beats.) The sequence of intervals of the major scale in the mean-tone temperament will be summarized along with the equal-tempered sequence of intervals later in this chapter.

The mean-tone scale was widely adopted in the seventeenth century. In keys with no more than three sharps and two flats, the mean-tone scale is quite satisfactory, both melodically and harmonically. For example, the mean-tone C major triad (C, E, G) sounds purer and more consonant than its more familiar equal-tempered counterpart owing to the perfectly tuned third and almost perfectly tuned fifth. However, a further continuation of our game of successive mean-tone fifths (E to B; B to F#; F# to C#; C# to G#) leads to very noticeable discrepancies between sharped and flatted notes, up to a difference of a quarter tone for enharmonic pairs of notes (two notes that share the same key on the modern piano), such as G# and Ab.

Using the mean-tone system, organ builders kept the octave down to twelve different notes in the octave, C, C# (no Db), D, Eb (no D#), E, F, F# (no Gb), G, G# (no Ab), A, Bb (no A#), B. As a result, tuning musical instruments in mean-tone temperament permitted limited transposition from one key to another: only six major keys were possible, C, G, D, A, F, Bb. Since Ab did not exist in this twelve note scale, G# had to be played instead in the Ab major scale. This difference between G# and Ab was known as a 'wolf' and the playing of the Ab major triad with a G# instead of an Ab (G#, C, Eb) was referred to as 'the howling of the wolves,' so jarring was the effect on the listener. Until it was displaced by the second of the new temperaments in the nineteenth century, organs, claviers, and pianos were almost universally tuned to the mean-tone scale.

Equal Temperament

The second compromise temperament, called the equal or well-tempered scale, is used at the present time in the tuning of all fixed-pitch instruments such as keyboard and wind. With the adoption of this scale, the Pythagorean consonances were compromised in favor of one standard interval, the semitone, approximately 15.89/15 instead of the harmonic 16/15. Twelve of these semitones are found in the equal tempered chromatic scale.

Known to have been used in Chinese music for a long time, the equal-tempered scale was not favored in the West until Johann Sebastian Bach championed it in the eighteenth century. We have now become so accustomed to the sound of this scale and accept it so thoroughly that we ignore the beats that are produced by the slight mismatches from the Pythagorean consonances. This scale is diagrammed below. The intervals are expressed as ratios so that they can be compared with their counterparts in just intonation (see p. 207; note that the equal-tempered tone turns out to be a compromise between the just tempered major and minor tones).

Musical Scales 213

C	D	E	F	G	A	B	C
Tone	Tone	Semi-tone	Tone	Tone	Tone	Semi-tone	
$\frac{8.98}{8}$	$\frac{10.10}{9}$	$\frac{15.89}{15}$	$\frac{8.98}{8}$	$\frac{10.10}{9}$	$\frac{8.98}{8}$	$\frac{15.89}{15}$	

|--8.98/8--|
|-----------5.04/4-|
|------------------4/3--|
|--------------------------3/2--|
|--------------------------------5.05/3--|
|--15.1/8-|
|--2/1--|

Note that the intervals of the major third (C to E), the major sixth (C to A) and the major seventh (C to B) are slightly stretched by the process of equal temperament, compared to their counterparts in just temperament. Rounding of figures obscures some slight differences.

How was the size of the unit interval, the semitone, determined? Consider the octave interval, 2/1. Between the first note and the last note, eleven different notes have to be fitted such that the 12 resultant intervals are exactly equal. Call the unknown semitone interval X and remember that musical intervals are ratios of frequencies. Since each successive semitone must equal X, it is necessary to multiply each successive frequency by the interval X. If X^0 (=1) is the first frequency in the octave, X^1 ($X^1 \times X^0$) is the second, and X^2 ($X^2 \times X^1$) is the third, all the way up to X^{12}, which is the thirteenth or octave note. The entire sequence of 12 semitones in the octave is shown in the third column of the table below:

Derivation of the Equal Tempered Chromatic Scale

Note Number	Theoretical Frequency X^n	Theoretical Interval X^1	Calculated Frequency $(1.05946)^n$	Transformed Logarithms $\text{Log}(1.05946)^n$	Transformed Cents $\dfrac{1200 \text{ Log}(1.05946)^n}{\text{Log } 2}$
1	X^0		1.00000	0	0
2	X^1	X^1/X	1.05946	0.025	100
3	X^2	X^2/X	1.12246	0.050	200
4	X^3	X^3/X^2	1.18920	0.075	300
5	X^4	X^4/X^3	1.25992	0.100	400
6	X^5	X^5/X^4	1.33483	0.125	500
7	X^6	X^6/X^5	1.41421	0.151	600
8	X^7	X^7/X^6	1.49830	0.176	700
9	X^8	X^8/X^7	1.58740	0.201	800
10	X^9	X^9/X^8	1.68179	0.226	900
11	X^{10}	X^{10}/X^9	1.78180	0.251	1000
12	X^{11}	X^{11}/X^{10}	1.88774	0.276	1100
13	X^{12}	X^{12}/X^{11}	2.00000	0.301	1200

To determine the value of the semitone interval, X, recall that the octave interval, $X^{12}/X^0 = 2/1$

therefore, $X^{12} = 2$

and, $X = \sqrt[12]{2}$

or, $X = 1.05946$

With the semitone X as the unit interval, each successive higher frequency in the equal tempered scale is 1.05946 times higher than the previous frequency. Keep in mind that the successive powers of 1.05946 give the frequencies of the chromatic tones that belong to the equal tempered scale. For example,

$C = (1.05946)^0 = 1.00000$
C# or Db $= (1.05946)^1 = 1.05946$
$D = (1.05946)^2 = 1.12246$
D# or Eb $= (1.05946)^3 = 1.18920$, and so on up to
$C = (1.05946)^{12} = 2.00000$

This is shown in the fourth column of the table above.

For the first time in the history of western music, the enharmonic intervals, such as C to C#, and C to Db, became equal and the notes C# and Db became one and the same key on the piano.

Some people are uncomfortable with intervals because they are ratios of frequencies and not arithmetic differences. By converting the equal-tempered interval of 1.05946 to a logarithm, the successive intervals become part of a linear scale and are additive. A table of logarithms to the base 10 reveals that log 1.05946 = 0.025. If the first note of the chromatic scale is

$$\log (1.05946)^0 = 0$$
the second note is $\log (1.05946)^1 = 0.025$,
and the third note is $\log (1.05946)^2 = 0.050$, and so on.

The entire sequence of 12 semitones in the chromatic octave is shown transformed into a linear scale in the fifth column of the table above.

In this transformed equal-tempered scale, the differences between successive intervals are arithmetically equal, and they are additive instead of multiplicative. The only disadvantage is that the frequencies are decimals ranging between 0 and 0.301 rather than between 1 and 2. A more convenient range, 0-1200, can be obtained by multiplying each decimal by the constant, 1200/log 2 (or 3986). In this range, the unit of measurement is called the cent. There are 1200 cents in the octave, and each chromatic semitone equals 100 cents exactly. This is shown in the last column of the table above.

To compare the corresponding intervals of the various temperaments, each can be converted to one measured in cents. As an example, the Pythagorean fifth, 3/2, is converted to cents by multiplying the logarithm of 3/2 by the constant, 1200/log 2. It turns out to equal 702 cents.

The modern equal-tempered chromatic scale, together with just intonation, the harmonic series and mean-tone temperament, are given below. Note the universal correspondences to the harmonic ratio of perfect fifths and the discrepancies of perfect fourths. A comparison of mean-tone and equal temperament tuning of the major third, major sixth, and major seventh, reveals that mean-tone intervals approximate more closely the corresponding intervals of just intonation.

Interval Name	Note Name	Harmonic Series		Just Intonation		Mean-tone Temperament		Equal Temperament	
		Hz	Cents	Hz	Cents	Hz	Cents	Hz	Cents
Unison	C	261.6	0	261.6	0	261.6	0	261.6	0
Minor 2 (Semitone)	D^b $C^\#$	278.0	105	279.2	112	(279.6 273.8	115) 79	277.2 277.2	100 100
Major 2 (Tone)	D	294.3	204	294.3 290.7	204 182	292.7	194	293.6	200
Minor 3	E^b $D^\#$	310.7	298	314.0	316	312.8 (306.3	309 273)	311.1 311.1	300 300
Major 3	E	327.0	386	327.0	386	327.4	388	329.7	400
Perfect 4	F	359.8	551	348.8	498	349.8	503	349.3	500
Tritone	G^b $F^\#$			367.9 372.0	590 610	(373.9 366.2	618) 582	370.0 370.0	600 600
Perfect 5	G	392.5	702	392.5	702	391.3	697	392.0	700
Minor 6	A^b $G^\#$			418.6	814	(418.2 409.6	812) 776	415.3 415.3	800 800
Major 6	A	425.2	841	436.1	885	437.7	891	440.0	900
Minor 7	B^b $A^\#$	457.9	969	464.9 470.9	996 1018	467.8 (458.2	1006 970)	466.2 466.2	1000 1000
Major 7	B	490.6	1088	490.6	1088	489.6	1085	494.0	1100
Octave	C	523.3	1200	523.3	1200	523.3	1200	523.3	1200

For some time now, it has become customary to take the frequency of the note 'A' above middle C as the standard of pitch reference. Before the Renaissance there was no universal standard for tuning instruments. Bach frequently had to transpose his instrumental and choral parts because organs in different churches were variously tuned. His compositions as well as those of Haydn, Mozart and Beethoven, sounded as much as a semitone below what they sound today. It was not until the tuning fork was invented (by John Shore, a contemporary of Handel) that a convenient standard could be made available. By the middle of the eighteenth century, the frequency of 'A' settled upon somewhere in the range 415-430 Hz. Handel's fork was 422.5 Hz.

Over the centuries, the frequency of the standard has risen. It appears that strings that can tune to any pitch gain an advantage in brightness if they are tuned sharp with respect to fixed pitch instruments like the woodwinds. Toward the end of the nineteenth century, the standard had risen to 455 Hz in England and even to 461 Hz in the U. S.

A change in the standard of pitch imposes considerable difficulties on musicians and craftsmen of musical instruments so a universal standard is essential. Various attempts were made to establish such a standard. In 1859, the Paris Academy selected 435 Hz. Then, at a congress of physicists at Stuttgart in 1934, the standard pitch, A=440 *Hz*, was adopted. This standard was used above in computing the frequencies of the equal tempered scale. Stuttgart pitch, as it is frequently called, is used widely by many orchestras all over the world as the standard of tuning, at least since 1939 when it was recommended for universal use at a conference sponsored by the International Standards Organization. This was confirmed in 1953 when the International Standards Organization again recommended the universal adoption of A=440 Hz.

Mean-tone temperament deserves one last comment, since it is no longer the system used in the tuning of fixed-interval instruments such as the piano and it is important to inquire why. To seventeenth century composers, mean-tone temperament provided a large pool of notes from which to draw for their compositions. It was eminently successful in preserving the consonances of thirds, fifths and sevenths, which means that the chords in this temperament were, for the most part, harmonious and pure. As examples, the intervals of the major chords, C, E, G, C; G, B, D, G; and, F, A, C, F approximated the intervals of the just temperament, 4, 5, 6, 8. Why, then, was mean-tone temperament abandoned in favor of equal temperament?

The only serious limitation of mean-tone temperament seems to be that only six of the 12 possible major keys were properly tuned. Looking at the problem in hindsight, it seems like a minor shortcoming. However, composers like Bach felt hampered by this limitation. With the adoption of equal temperament, the Pythagorean consonances were compromised in favor of the larger pool of keys and freer modulation. There are nuances of timbre that are influenced by the choice of key, but these nuances differ from one instrument to another and sometimes favor one temperament, sometimes another. Unfortunately, the purity of sound was compromised when equal temperament came to dominate the musical scene. The course of musical history was affected by this choice. Having become accustomed to the buzzing of beats created by the equal-tempered intervals, Western ears (and brains) have never been the same. Maconie (1997) summarized the compromise very well: "The price of freedom of key movement was the loss of the harmonic principles on which music had been based, not to mention the sin of embracing scale divisions based on an irrational number (the square root of two)."

In 1722, Bach wrote his celebrated Well-Tempered Clavier. To demonstrate the power of the new grammar of music, Bach included 24 Preludes and Fugues, one in each of the 12 major and 12 minor keys. However, the general adoption of equal temperament waited until the mid-nineteenth century.

In summary, the great advantage of the equal-tempered scale is that a melody can be shifted, or transposed, to any register without becoming distorted. You might want to transpose a melody if it makes excessive demands on your vocal range. For example, if *Three Blind Mice* goes too high for you to sing, you might want to shift it to a lower register in order to manage the whole tune more comfortably. As long as you sing it in equal temperament (which you will do automatically because you are accustomed to that sound), transposing it to a lower register will not distort it in any way. Similarly, all fixed interval instruments will do so automatically.

An interesting consequence of the adoption of equal temperament is that each pair of adjacent semitones can be summed to produce six successive whole tones in the octave as, for example, C, D, E, $F^{\#}$, $G^{\#}$, $A^{\#}$, C, the so-called whole tone scale.

Fig. 11.4. Frère Jacques *played enharmonically. On a keyboard instrument tuned in equal temperament, Frère Jacques in F# major and Gb major are identical.*

THE INDIAN SA-GRAMA SCALE: AN EASTERN EXAMPLE

It is instructive to compare the Western scales with those of non-Western musical cultures such as the Indian, Chinese, and Arab-Persian. These Eastern systems approximate the Western diatonic scales in that they have a distribution of intervals that are not all equal to each other (like the intervals, tone and semitone, in the Western tradition). In these Eastern systems are also heard the Pythagorean consonances of octaves, fifths, and fourths. As an example, consider the classical Indian scale, SA-grama, which developed about 2,000 years ago.

There are seven different notes in the SA-grama scale, SA, RI, GA, MA, PA, DHA, and NI. The interval between each of these notes is measured by 22 unit-intervals in the octave, called sruti, each roughly equal to a quarter tone (actually 1.032/1 or about half of the smallest interval on the piano, the semitone, 1.05946/1). While the seven-note equal tempered scale of the West, derived from the 12-note chromatic scale, has just two interval steps, semitone and tone, the seven note SA-grama scale has three interval steps, two intervals made up of two sruti, two of three sruti, and three of four sruti. The intervals in the rising form of the SA-grama scale are diagrammed as follows. In this form, it can be compared directly with Western scales.

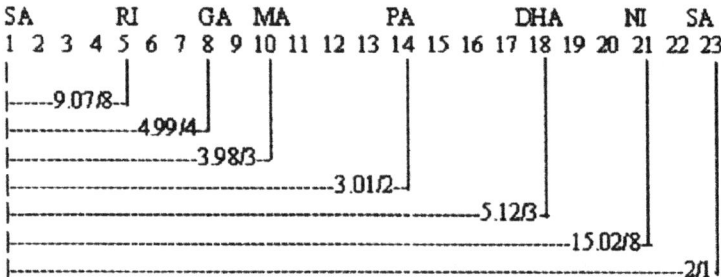

The frequency ratios show how similar this Indian scale is to the Didymic scale of just temperament. Of course, a miss is as good as a mile, for each mismatch with just temperament intervals is responsible for beats, but the mismatches are small and comparable to those of the prevailing Western equivalent, the equal-tempered scale. The near coincidence of Indian and Western scales is startling when one considers that the two systems apparently developed independently of each other.

Chapter 12

PERSPECTIVES ON THE SIGNIFICANCE OF MUSICAL SCALES

CIRCLE OF FIFTHS

Once the equal-tempered scale was adopted and instruments were tuned to it, composers were able to transpose their music from one register to another without changing the pattern of intervals in the scale. The semitone interval is 15.89/15 wherever it appears in the scale, and the whole tone is always the square of that ratio, 8.98/8. Now we are prepared to consider the mechanics of transposition from one key to another.

Tonal music is written in a particular key, such as C major and A minor. We have already seen what this means: composers of tonal music are limited to just seven different notes per octave, out of the 12 in the chromatic scale, as a pool of notes from which to draw. On the piano that has a range of seven and one-third octaves, composers have available a maximum of 51 notes (7 x 7 1/3) in each key. Of course, composers modulate from one key to another, thus increasing their pool of available notes. When composers shift temporarily from C major to G major, they add F# to their pool of notes, as we shall see.

Sound and Music

The key is defined by a succession of whole tone and semitone intervals. The major mode is defined by one succession of tones and semitones, and the minor mode is defined by another. There are 12 keys in the major mode and 12 keys in the minor mode. Each key is generated by starting on one of the 12 different notes of the chromatic scale. Since all semitones are equal to each other, the pattern of intervals can be duplicated exactly in each key.

Consider first the major mode. This mode is defined by the succession of the seven diatonic intervals in the C-major scale, tone, tone, semitone, tone, tone, tone, and semitone. This succession of intervals is duplicated exactly in all the other major scales by using sharps and flats as necessary to change the interval size from semitone to tone, or vice-versa.

Pool In Ascending Order	C	$C^\#$ / D^b	D	$D^\#$ / E^b	E	F	$F^\#$ / G^b	G	$G^\#$ / A^b	A	$A^\#$ / B^b	B	C
Definition of Major Scale	1	Tone	2	Tone	3	4 Semi-tone	Tone	5	Tone	6	Tone	7	8 Semi-tone
No Accidentals	C		D		E	F		G		A		B	C
1 Sharp	G		A		B	C		D		E		$F^\#$	G
2 Sharps	D		E		$F^\#$	G		A		B		$C^\#$	D
3 Sharps	A		B		$C^\#$	D		E		$F^\#$		$G^\#$	A
4 Sharps	E		$F^\#$		$G^\#$	A		B		$C^\#$		$D^\#$	E
5 Sharps	B		$C^\#$		$D^\#$	E		$F^\#$		$G^\#$		$A^\#$	B
6 Sharps	$F^\#$		$G^\#$		$A^\#$	B		$C^\#$		$D^\#$		$E^\#$	$F^\#$
1 Flat	F		G		A	B^b		C		D		E	F
2 Flats	B^b		C		D	E^b		F		G		A	B^b
3 Flats	E^b		F		G	A^b		B^b		C		D	E^b
4 Flats	A^b		B^b		C	D^b		E^b		F		G	A^b
5 Flats	D^b		E^b		F	G^b		A^b		B^b		C	D^b
6 Flats	G^b		A^b		B^b	C^b		D^b		E^b		F	G^b

Though there appear to be a total of thirteen major keys, there are actually just twelve, including C major, which has no sharps or flats. We can count the enharmonic F# major and Gb major keys only once, because they share exactly the same keys on the equal tempered keyboard and are therefore identical.

The sequential order of major keys, shown above, starting with C major, followed by the keys containing sharps, G D A E B F#, and by the keys containing flats, F Bb Eb Ab Db Gb, should be noted. Each successive scale containing sharps starts a fifth above the previous one, and each scale containing flats starts a fifth below the previous one. In addition, each successive scale shares all but one of its notes with the preceding scale. Composers of classical music treated the scales adjacent to each other in the series as closely related. For example, the scales of G major and F major are considered close to the key of C major because both share all but one of their notes with C major. In contrast, the scale of B major is considered remote from C major because it shares only two notes with C major.

Now consider the minor mode, which is also built on the same 12 equal-tempered chromatic intervals. This mode is defined by the succession of seven diatonic intervals in the A minor scale: tone, semitone, tone, tone, semitone, tone, tone. This succession of intervals is duplicated exactly in all the other minor keys by using sharps and flats, as needed, to adjust the size of the intervals. (Melodies in the minor mode often use a different set of pitches for ascending and descending sequences. The ascending set is more like that of the major mode on the sixth and seventh degrees of the scale. The ascending and descending branches of the A melodic minor scale are as follows:

```
1   2   3   4   5   6   7 8   7   6 5   4   3 2   1
A   B   C   D   E   F#  G#A  G   F E   D   C B   A
```

In our discussion of the minor mode, we restrict ourselves to the descending branch of the melodic minor scale, which we will consider, for convenience, in ascending order. Though there appear to be a total of 13 minor scales, there are actually just 12, including A minor, which has no sharps or flats. We can count the enharmonic minor keys of D# and Eb only once, since they share exactly the same keys on the equal-tempered keyboard and are therefore identical.

Note that the first notes of the successive minor keys are also a fifth apart, starting with A minor: rising in successive fifths for the keys containing sharps (E, B, F#, C#, G#, D#), and falling in successive fifths for the keys containing flats (D, G, C, F, Bb, Eb). And, again, each successive key shares all but one of its notes with the previous key. Adjacent keys are regarded as more closely related than more remote ones. For example, the keys of D minor and E minor are considered close to the key of A minor because they share all but one of their notes. In contrast, the Bb minor key is considered remote from A minor because it shares only two notes with A minor.

Pool In Ascending Order	A	B^b / $A^\#$	B	C	D^b / $C^\#$	D	E^b / $D^\#$	E	F	G^b / $F^\#$	G	A^b / $G^\#$	A
Definition of Melodic Minor Scale	1 Tone		2 Semi-tone	3	4 Tone	Tone		5 Semi-tone	6	7 Tone	Tone		8
No Accidentals	A		B	C		D		E	F		G		A
1 Flat	D		E	F		G		A	B^b		C		D
2 Flats	G		A	B^b		C		D	E^b		F		G
3 Flats	C		D	E^b		F		G	A^b		B^b		C
4 Flats	F		G	A^b		B^b		C	D^b		E^b		F
5 Flats	B^b		C	D^b		E^b		F	G^b		A^b		B^b
6 Flats	E^b		F	G^b		A^b		B^b	C^b		D^b		E^b
1 Sharp	E		$F^\#$	G		A		B	C		D		E
2 Sharps	B		$C^\#$	D		E		$F^\#$	G		A		B
3 Sharps	$F^\#$		$G^\#$	A		B		$C^\#$	D		E		$F^\#$
4 Sharps	$C^\#$		$D^\#$	E		$F^\#$		$G^\#$	A		B		$C^\#$
5 Sharps	$G^\#$		$A^\#$	B		$C^\#$		$D^\#$	E		$F^\#$		$G^\#$
6 Sharps	$D^\#$		$E^\#$	$F^\#$		$G^\#$		$A^\#$	B		$C^\#$		$D^\#$

Let us examine once again the succession of major keys. In ascending by fifths, the 12 scales contain sharps, and in descending order, the 12 scales contain flats. These two sets of scales are the same on the piano, in the sense that they are related enharmonically:

$$C \quad G \quad D \quad A \quad E \quad B \quad F^\# \quad C^\# \quad G^\# \quad D^\# \quad A^\# \quad E^\# \quad B^\# = C \quad \text{(Read left-to-right)}$$
$$C = D^{bb} \quad A^{bb} \quad E^{bb} \quad B^{bb} \quad F^b \quad C^b \quad G^b \quad D^b \quad A^b \quad E^b \quad B^b \quad F \quad C \quad \text{(Read right-to-left)}$$

Note that the two keys in each column are related enharmonically. Since C and B# are related enharmonically at one end, as are C and Dbb at the other, we end where we began, on C. This permits us to arrange the twelve scales in a circle, called the circle of fifths. This is diagrammed in Fig. 12.1. If the circle is read clockwise starting with C at the top, the keys follow each other in the sequence of added sharps. If the circle is read counterclockwise, the keys follow each other in the sequence of added flats. The same circle of fifths can be consulted on the order of accidentals, as required in the major and minor scales. The sequence of sharps, in ascending fifths, can be read clockwise: F# C# G# D# A# E# B#, and the sequence of flats, in descending fifths, can be read counterclockwise: Bb Eb Ab Db Gb Cb Fb.

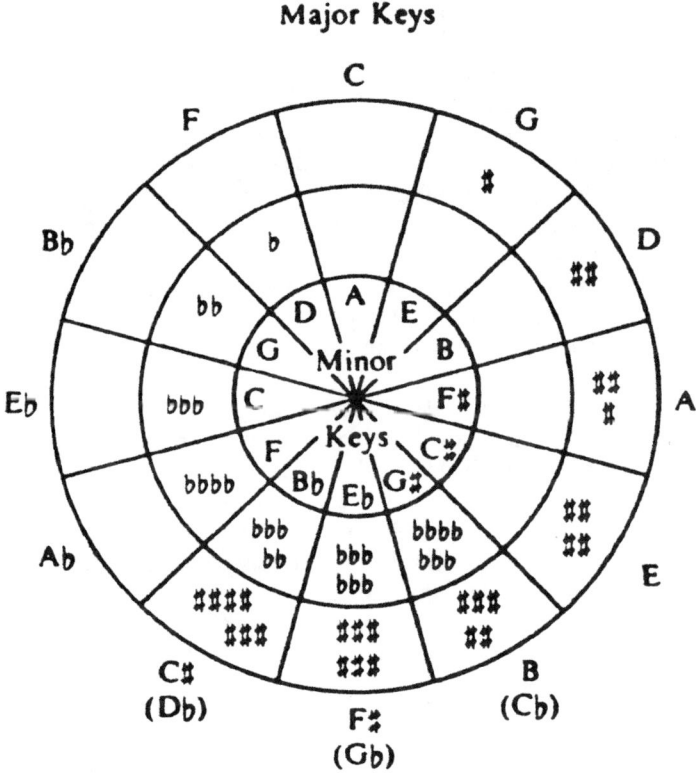

Fig. 12.1. The circle of fifths. The keys containing sharps are read clockwise from the top, while the keys containing flats are read counterclockwise. The major keys are shown along the periphery of the outer circle; the minor keys along the periphery of the inner circle.

CROSS-CULTURAL COMPARISON OF SCALES

Both the diatonic scale of the West and the SA-grama scale of the East contain unequal interval-steps: two in the case of the Western scale (tone and semitone) and three in the case of the Eastern scale (2-sruti, 3-sruti and 4-sruti). Two or more intervals steps in the scale seems to be a cross-cultural rule. In recent years, however, ethnomusicological studies have uncovered a number of musical cultures that have evolved scales containing just one interval step. Both five and seven equal-interval scales have been described. Measured in cents, their intervals are 240 and 171 cents, respectively (assuming, of course, that they retain the octave of 1200 cents). These two systems should be compared to our equal-tempered scales having semitones of 100 cents and tones of 200 cents. Morton (1974) measured the tuning of a Thai xylophone and found that it approximated an equal tempered, seven-interval scale. The Java and Bali gamelan, as well as the Uganda harp, seem to be tuned approximately to an equal tempered, five-interval scale. What makes these five- and seven- interval scales so intriguing is that they contain fifths and fourths that are substantially mistuned from the harmonic values of 3/2 and 4/3. In these Eastern cultures, there seems to be nothing special about the Pythagorean intervals of fifth and fourth.

In contrast, consider the startling ethnomusicological report of Boiles in 1967. He studied the equal tempered musical scale of the Tepehau Indians and found that their unit-interval measured 175 cents. Because there are seven equal intervals in their scale and a perfectly tuned fifth, the octave is stretched to 1225 cents (175×7). How bizarre for Westerners to contemplate a grossly mistuned octave! The Tepehaus seem to believe that the fifth is a special musical interval, but not the octave. Wasn't it Pythagoras, 2,500 years ago, who constructed his scale on the harmonic fifth, and ended with a stretched octave?

But these are all isolated instances of single-interval scales. The rule worldwide seems to be that musical scales have unequal intervals such as tones and semitones, and this must have some functional significance. Does it mean that unequal intervals serve some fundamental psychological function? Sloboda (1985) suggested that unequal interval-steps in the musical scale help listeners get their tonal bearings from a limited sample of notes. In the C major scale, for example, the interval F-B (the tritone) is unique: no other pair of tones belonging to this scale forms this interval (except its inversion, B-F). So the listener, hearing the sequence F-B-C, feels the tension generated by the first two notes, and immediately identifies the last or resolving note as the tonic. In the Indian SA-grama scale, the interval from MA to DHA containing eight sruti is unique, resulting in a feeling of tonicity of SA. Shepard (1982) pointed out that the obverse is also true: the regularity of intervals of the equal-tempered chromatic and whole-tone scales means that every tone has the same status as every other, and this limits any sense of tonality. That is why these scales have never achieved any wide popularity as a basis for musical composition.

TONALITY AND MODULATION

We have just noted that practically every culture seems to confer a special importance on one tone of the scale, making this the tonal center to which all the other tones are related. All the scales used in familiar melodies are 'tonal,' meaning that there is a tonic or home pitch on which the melody ordinarily starts and ends, and to which the music returns repeatedly. Sing through your favorite hymn or anthem and see whether this is true. Try *My Country 'Tis of Thee* and the round, *Frère Jacques*. Since *The Star Spangled Banner* starts on an upbeat, on the word 'Oh,' you don't get to the tonic until the downbeat, on the word 'say,' and the anthem ends on the tonic. In addition to the tonic, the third and fifth notes of the diatonic scale are relatively stable, in the sense that the melody can rest on these notes without the feeling of tension to move away from them.

Other notes in the diatonic scale are less stable. In the context of a melody, they tend to pull in the direction of the more stable notes. The seventh or leading tone of the major scale is such a note. When reached from below, it wants to move up a semitone to the tonic, the most stable tone. In addition, the second, fourth and sixth notes of the scale are less stable, tending to pull toward the third and fifth, the more stable notes. If you play all the unstable notes together on the piano, as a chord, followed by all the stable ones, again together as a chord, you will have played an acceptable cadence or musical ending. We can thus think of a cadence as a sequence of two or more chords that ordinarily move from the unstable to the stable or from tension to resolution and repose. An even more familiar cadence consists of the dominant seventh chord (5, 7, 2, 4) followed by the tonic chord (1, 3, 5, 8). Notice that the two chords share one note, the fifth, or 'dominant' note. It is this sharing of notes among chords that makes a succession of them so natural-sounding.

Modulation refers to a change of key in the course of the development of a piece of music. There are seven different discrete notes in any diatonic key that are available to the composer. The remaining five of the chromatic scale are foreign in the sense that they do not belong to that key. In C major, for example, the foreign notes would be all the sharps and flats. If any were used in the context of the key of C major, they would create tension. Sometimes these foreign notes are used only in passing from one member of the key to another, and they heighten the interest of the piece. But foreign notes in one key belong to another. F#, for example, belongs to G major. Thus, a more elaborate use of F# may take advantage of its instability in C major to lead the music into the key of G major. This is a modulation from one key to another, and it heightens the interest of the music. Modulation between two specific keys is simplest when the two keys share all their notes but one, as in the modulation from C major to G major which requires just one change, from F to F#. The modulation can be executed smoothly by introducing the F# in passing and then by leading it emphatically to G. Suitable harmony helps the transition from one key to the other.

A chord consists of a number of notes played together. When a sequence of chords is played, the listener will ordinarily *shadow* the top note of each chord, thus creating a melody. The remaining notes serve as the harmony. Harmonizing a melody means playing chords that sound harmonious or pleasant with the melody notes. The most stable chords in C major are those built on the tonic, C, E, G; the fifth, G, B, D; and the fourth, F, A, C. These three chords contain all the notes of the C major scale. Every accompanist knows that any melody can be pleasantly harmonized by using just these three chords.

The apparent universality of tonality raises a number of questions. What is it that makes the note C the home note of the set of notes, C D E F G A B? Why does this particular note sound any more central than F, or E, or D for that matter? The traditional answer is that the listener has learned to recognize the pattern of notes in the prevailing scales of the day and judges which note is the tonic from a sample of notes heard earlier in the piece. For example, the ascending major scale is recognized by the characteristic three successive tones and one semitone that precede the tonic, the final semitone representing the upward movement from leading tone to tonic. This rule establishing tonality can be applied deliberately by those trained in music, and it can just as well be applied quite unwittingly by untutored listeners on the basis of past listening experience. But the existence of a rule is not a satisfactory explanation for the perception of tonality. What remains unanswered is why a tonic needs to be established in the first place. If we could show that C is, in fact, the most central of the notes in the series C D E F G A B, this would help explain the phenomenon of tonality.

Consider the following spatial distribution of notes. Each of the 12 notes of the chromatic octave is assigned coordinates on the horizontal and vertical axes of a two dimensional space. The notes are ordered in successive perfect fifths along the horizontal axis and in successive major thirds along the vertical axis.

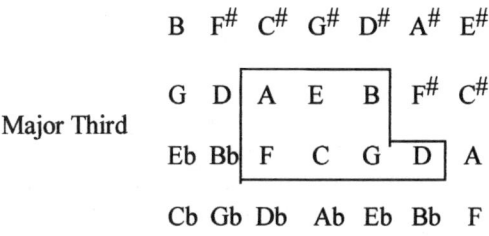

Perfect Fifths

The matrix shows the seven notes of the C major scale in a space bounded by a solid line. In this space, C can reach all the other notes of the scale in a maximum of two moves (diagonal moves are not permitted). No other note belonging to the C major scale can do so. For example, it takes four moves to reach D from A. This game originated with Longuet-Higgins (1978) and was reviewed by Sloboda (1985). It can be played with the seven notes belonging to each of the 12 major keys: they can be bounded in the same-shaped space and, in every case, only the tonic of each key can reach all the notes of that key in a maximum of two moves. As another example, the seven notes of the scale of F major are bounded in the same-shaped space one degree over to the left from C major, and only the tonic, F, can reach all the notes of that key in a maximum of two moves. In short, when the notes are ordered and displayed in a matrix of perfect fifths x major thirds, it is the unique proximity of the tonic to all the notes of the key that accounts for the centrality of the tonic.

The next matrix shows the seven notes of the A minor scale in a space bounded by a solid line. In this space, A can reach all the other notes belonging to the A minor scale in a maximum of two moves. (Again, diagonal moves are not permitted). No other note belonging to

A minor can do so. A similar space can be delineated for each of the 12 minor scales.

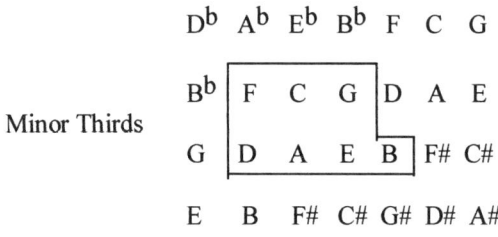

Perfect Fifths

These two matrices of notes were designed to reveal the property of tonicity or centrality exhibited by a particular note in a set of seven notes in the diatonic scale. But these matrices also provide an explanation for the degree of relationship of keys in modulating from one key to another.

The principal chords or triads are obtained from these matrices by selecting a note within a bounded space together with its two immediate *upper* neighbors along the horizontal and vertical axes. The triad that emerges lies in a compact L-shaped space. Whenever chords of this kind are heard, they suggest particular keys to the listener. Consider the C-E-G triad in the matrix of major keys. If you examine the matrix, you will see that this triad is included in just three different keys, F major, C major, and G major. This leads us to predict that there will be ambiguity in tonality when the C-E-G triad is played: the listener will not be able to determine to which tonic, F, C, or G, this triad belongs, unless the triad is heard in a revealing musical context. This prediction is borne out empirically.

Some chords produce less tonal ambiguity than the principal triads. This is because the notes of the chord are bounded in the space of only one key. The dominant seventh chord, G-B-D-F, for example, is bounded in the space of C major only. If the key is shifted, one or more of the notes of the dominant seventh chord will necessarily fall outside the bounded space. This leads to the prediction that the dominant seventh chord will establish the tonic unambiguously, and this turns out to be true. In contrast, some chords cannot be fitted into any one key space (for example, C-E-G#), and we could predict that these chords would be ineffective in establishing the key of the music in question. And again we would be right.

Distributing all the notes of the chromatic octave in a two-dimensional matrix, as we have suggested to account for the perception of tonality, may seem like a lot of hocus-pocus. And it may well be. Keep in mind, however, that there is something special about the interval of the perfect fifth, and using this interval for explanatory purposes may not be as far-fetched as you might imagine.

TONAL EXPECTATIONS

There is a hierarchy of expectations of all the possible sequences of tones in the scale. The most frequent note in Western music is generally the tonic, around which the melody revolves and on which it frequently starts and ends. The next most frequent note is the dominant or fifth above the tonic. In an ascending sequence of tones, the leading tone is most often followed by the tonic. At the beginning of a melody, the dominant-tonic sequence is quite common.

When we hear a piece of music, we are quickly sensitized to the scale and to the probabilities for the occurrence of certain notes and note sequences. This applies to harmony as well as to melody. As a result, there are strong expectations in chord progressions. In the traditional grammar of music, the chord of the tonic, (I), is likely to be followed by the chord of the dominant, (V), or subdominant, (IV), less likely by the chord of the submediant, (VI), and even less likely by the chord of the supertonic, (II), or mediant, (III).

These expectations play an important role in remembering musical pitches. The verbal introduction, "ladies and ...", is likely to elicit the word, "gentlemen", and such a sequence is easily recalled. But suppose the sequence were actually, "ladies and tradesmiths," a sequence never encountered before. This sequence could not have been anticipated. It is the same in music. It is easier to recall a sequence of pitches in a familiar tonal system compared to one that selects tones at random. What chance would you have of remembering a randomly selected sequence of notes compared to a clichéd sequence or, at least, one that you have had some experience with?

Much of modern music discards the familiar grammar of tonal music, and our expectations no longer provide the framework for memory and enjoyment. For example, modern serial music includes all twelve semitones of the chromatic scale. In this music, tonality is lost. Each composition is based on a particular ordering of the twelve semitones (called the basic set, or row). The melodic and harmonic material of the piece is drawn from this basic set, and it is then transposed and transformed in a variety of ways, according to the musical grammar of the composer. The net result is that each piece of music establishes its own set of expectations. This requires work on the part of the listener, work that is not easy to perform, and his memory is likely to be taxed far beyond that required by tonal music that is familiar.

Examples of transformations used in serial music are sequential inversion and retrogression. Inversion involves a reversal in the direction of successive intervals: all ascending intervals become descending intervals, and vice versa. Retrogression involves a reversal in sequence, that is, the music is read backwards.

Are these transformations equivalent in any sense? Despite avant-garde opinion to the contrary, melodies transformed in these ways are not likely to be perceptually equivalent for most listeners. The eminent American composer-educator, Walter Piston, expressed his own compositional practice in 1949: "Retrograde forms are rarely employed, since it is very difficult for the ear to recognize a motive played in this fashion." Other modern composers believe, along with Piston, that retrograde motion in composition is more an intellectual stunt than a purely musical effect. There are, of course, dissenting opinions such as that of the composer, Schoenberg (1951), who compared the equivalence of retrogression to that of the mirror image reversal in visual shape perception. However, Schoenberg's visual analogy is not apt, as anyone who has tried to read print in mirror-image can attest. In short, the weight of the experimental evidence is on the side of Piston: there is little to support the view that either sequential inversions, or retrogressions, are perceptually equivalent for most listeners. Of course, the possibility must be entertained that such equivalences might develop slowly as a result of exposure to, and experience with, these transformations.

ARE SCALES REALLY NECESSARY?

In the present century, Western composers have begun to experiment with systems of notes that depart radically from the traditional seven-note scale. One example is the pentatonic scale, which includes just five notes in the octave, related to each other as are the black notes of the piano. Other examples are the six-tone major and minor scales used in blues music and the 12-tone chromatic scale, perhaps the scale most widely experimented upon today in the composition of serious music, as we have just seen.

Four technological innovations of the twentieth century have contributed to the recent revolution in musical composition. These innovations have exposed the musical scales to the danger of becoming obsolete. The first was the invention of sound-recording techniques. With this tool, it became possible to compose music that no longer requires the traditional music-makers, the voice or the acoustic instrument. Instead, the sounds of nature could be recorded and used as ingredients of musical compositions: the sounds of birds and other animals, the peal of thunder, the splash of water, and the crackling of fire are examples.

The second innovation was the magnetic tape recorder, which eased the constraints of traditional sound-recording, and permitted the transformation of recorded sound by such techniques as splicing of magnetic tape, dubbing, mixing and filtering. The sounds of nature could be sped up, slowed down, played backwards or upside down, etc. The genre that developed out of the early experiments with the tape recorder was called by the Parisian school, '*musique concrète*,' to emphasize that the sounds used by the composer-engineer had their origins in the familiar noises of the physical world. These sounds could be manipulated and transformed in new sound studios. For an introduction to this genre, listen to a fragment entitled 'Dripsody' by Lecaine, in which the drip of a raindrop was recorded on magnetic tape, and then the tape was manipulated and the sound transformed in various ways. This piece did not require the notes of the musical scale for its composition or its performance.

In the course of transforming the sound of acoustic instruments, such as the piano recorded on magnetic tape, a new understanding emerged of the properties of musical sound. One transformation resulted from the playing of tape recordings backwards. Piano tones played backwards could not be recognized as piano tones. The explanation was really quite simple. The piano is a percussion instrument; its tone rises sharply in intensity as the hammer hits the strings, and then decays slowly. Played backwards, these parameters are reversed: the rise is slow and the decay abrupt and the tone is strangely unfamiliar. This new understanding of the 'sound envelope' of each sound led to a deeper and more realistic analysis of musical tones than was possible earlier.

Once the sine-wave generator was invented, the third innovation was at hand. This was the assemblage of sine-wave generators called the music synthesizer. With this electronic instrument, any complex tone could be created from scratch, by combining the appropriate number of pure tones in proper proportions. The early efforts at sound synthesis were remarkably successful. Realistic copies of the tones of acoustic instruments such as violin and piano could be created, as well as the sounds of nature. This genre is called electronic music. If you are not already familiar with Carlos' work, listen to *Switched on Bach* for an early example of this genre.

Finally came the computer, which could be used by the composer-engineer as his command center, thus eliminating the musical performer altogether. The composer-engineer writes the computer program of a musical composition, specifying all the parameters of sound (frequency, amplitude, phase relationships and duration of each component). These programs are stored on disk or tape and used to activate the bank of sine-wave generators, whose signals are fed into an audio system located in the concert hall, sound studio, or living room. Talented composers in the movement of computer music include Boulez, Chowning, Stockhausen, and Ussachevsky, and Risset. With the aid of the computer, Boulez and Stockhausen have admitted the element of chance events into their compositions.

It is interesting to note that the new sound of electronic music has influenced composers of acoustic music. These composers write for the traditional orchestra but their music has an unmistakable resemblance to the sound of electronic music. Examples are Xenakis and Penderecki.

As a result of these exciting innovations, it is possible, for the first time in the recorded history of music, to treat the audible frequency spectrum as a continuum, and to draw from it an indefinitely large array of notes. Musical scales are no longer required. Are they obsolete?

Before we bury the musical scales with honors and sing them a lofty requiem, let us not forget that all acoustic keyboard and wind instruments are still tuned to the equal-tempered scale, and our hearing is attuned to them. Composers overwhelmingly write for them. Because there is not yet a generally accepted new musical vocabulary or grammar for synthesized music, even the most sophisticated listeners are frequently puzzled by the variety of strange sounds. Perhaps in the future a whole new system of tuning musical instruments will evolve, based upon principles derived from the computer. In the meantime, however, we will continue to listen to Bach, Beethoven and Brahms played on acoustic instruments. It is a safe bet that many composers of the future will continue to be bound by the constraints of equal temperament. And it will be a long time before the chromatic scale is replaced. In fact, the principle of the musical scale as a basis for composition and tuning may never be abandoned.

PART C:
THE PSYCHOLOGY OF MUSIC

Chapter 13

HOW WE HEAR AND WHY WE DON'T

THE QUALITY OF SENSATION

What is it that determines the quality of sensation, whether it is visual like a color, or auditory like a tone, or some other sensory experience? The traditional answer is that the stimulus energy is responsible for the particular sensory experience: that light is responsible for visual sensations, and sound is responsible for auditory sensations. In 1824, Johannes Müller raised the issue whether a particular physical energy is, in fact, the determinant of the quality of sensation. Müller suggested, instead, that it is the excitation of a particular nerve, optic or acoustic, that determines whether the sensation is visual or auditory. This view is referred to as the *doctrine of specific nerve energies*.

    Was Müller right? Contemporary neuroscientists subscribe to his doctrine, though the locus of specificity has been shifted from the peripheral nerve up to the corresponding part of the brain. This revision is called localization of function in the brain. The part of the brain excited by light or by sound, or by any other form of physical energy, determines the quality of the sensation, whether it is visual or auditory.

A 'thought experiment' might clarify this doctrine. Suppose, by some surgical miracle, we could rearrange the connections of eye and ear to the brain so that the eye now projects to the auditory part of the brain and the ear projects to the visual part. The peripheral end-organs, themselves, would be unaffected by the rearrangement. The eye would still be excited by light and the ear by sound. But the information about light and sound would be conveyed to the opposite parts of the brain, to the auditory and visual parts, respectively. How would our sensory experiences be affected? Would we now see the crash of thunder and hear the bolt of lightning?

Try a little experiment on yourself. Press on a corner of your eyeball with the tip of a finger as far back in the orbit behind the eyeball as you can. You will experience a visual sensation, a pressure phosphene, that is roughly circular. What you are actually doing is stimulating a small part of your retina by applying pressure to it. If you stimulate the nasal side of your right eye, you will experience a visual sensation in the opposite right peripheral field. In this case, it is not light energy that is responsible for the visual sensation but finger pressure. In the operating room, neuroscientists have shown that a tiny electric current to the optic nerve or visual cortex also produces a visual sensation, and the same tiny electric current to the acoustic nerve or auditory cortex will produce an auditory sensation. Müller was right. It doesn't matter what form of physical energy is used to excite a particular sensory modality: *any* stimulus that is capable of exciting the visual system will produce a visual sensation and *any* stimulus that is capable of exciting the auditory system produces an auditory sensation. Our experimental subject should indeed see the flash of thunder and hear the crash of lightning.

At the same time, we must remember that the eye is designed to receive light and the ear sound, and this is why we need our eyes to see and our ears to hear. However, it is the pattern of neural activity in the part of the brain corresponding to the sensory modality that determines the sensory experience, whether we see lightning and hear thunder, or vice versa.

AUDITORY MECHANISMS

All mammals possess an ear and a neural mechanism to receive and appreciate sound vibrations. As long as animals live in an environment filled with sounds that have significance for survival, there is adaptive value in an auditory system that provides the animal the capacity to receive and process sonic information. In the course of evolution, each species has developed an auditory mechanism best suited to its needs, considering the environment in which it lives. Some insects, rodents, bats, dolphins, and whales can hear frequencies as high as 100 *kHz* and even higher. These high-pitched sounds are easier to pinpoint in space than low-pitched sounds. With rather limited vision, many of these species have evolved an object-localizing system akin to sonar, and this system requires the reception of sounds that are ultrasonic to humans. Perhaps the hearing of animals like bats, dolphins and whales evolved to facilitate locomotion by species that possess primitive vision. The songs of humpback whales, probably related to echolocation, have captured the attention of the public and recorded samples are now available commercially.

With an audible upper limit of 20 *kHz* or so, we humans have rather restricted hearing, compared to some of our mammalian relatives. Language may have been the principal evolutionary requirement for us. As a consequence, we have developed an auditory mechanism that is specialized to receive and process speech sounds that range from about 300 *Hz* to 5000 *Hz*, precisely the range of frequencies to which we have proved to be most sensitive. Perhaps hearing evolved in the human to better receive the sounds emitted in speech. And a natural byproduct of the development of speech is music, which seems to have stretched the audible frequency band a couple of octaves or more, at both the low and the high ends of the sound spectrum.

Despite some functional differences, the hearing mechanism itself is remarkably similar in all mammalian species. By any audio standards, it is a masterpiece of engineering. In brief, it begins with the visible ear that captures the sound waves and conducts them via the eardrum and mechanical transducer system in the middle ear to the receptors in the cochlea. This receptor system converts the vibratory movement that it receives into electrochemical impulses in the neurons of the acoustic nerve. No commercial components can match the cochlea in its miniature size, or its sensitivity and versatility. If we try to construct the equivalent from state-of-the-art stereo components, we would need a frequency analyzer, an amplifier, and a device to convert mechanical signals into coded electrical impulses virtually free of distortion, all contained in the space of less than a cubic inch. As far as the series of way stations in the brain and the auditory part of the cerebral cortex to which they lead, we have no idea how to construct their equivalents.

A surprising amount of acoustic processing takes place in the receptor system itself. The cochlea analyzes the sound vibrations for frequency and intensity and sends coded messages of this analysis to the brain. Lower centers in the brain integrate the stereo information originating in the two ears to reveal where the sound is coming from. The highest center, the auditory cortex, is concerned with decoding the signals provided by language and communication. In short, the auditory cortex determines the significance of sounds, stores them in memory, colors them in emotion, and determines when they should have access to the motor system.

Now, let us examine the hearing mechanism more closely. The pinna is the only visible portion of the ear in most mammals. It is designed to collect and deflect sound. In many lower mammals, the pinna reflex aids in orienting the animal with respect to sound sources, such as predators. The ridges, valleys, and folds of the pinna play an important role in sound localization, for they introduce time delays in arrival of direct sound and sound reflected from the folds. In humans, however, the pinna is vestigial. It no longer moves reflexly and plays a minor role, at best, in sound localization. It should be viewed as an ornament (and it frequently is, as is portrayed in Fig. 13.1).

The external meatus or canal leads from the opening inside the pinna to the tympanic membrane or eardrum, which is cone-shaped with the apex directed forward.

Hearing

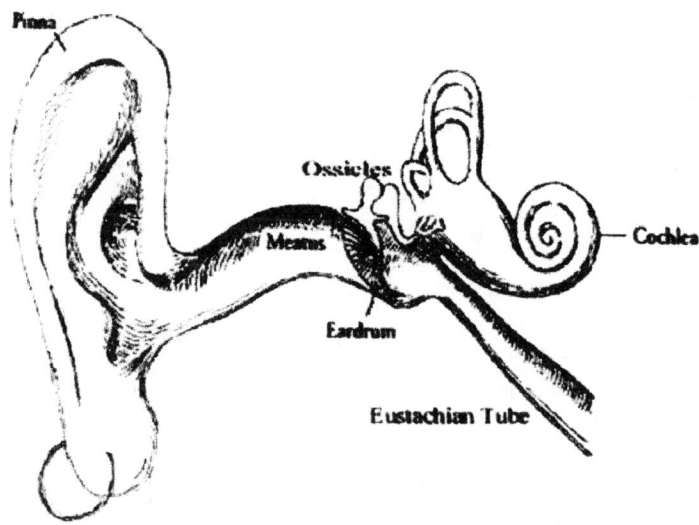

Fig. 13.1 The outer ear, consisting of the pinna (or auricle) and meatus, serves to funnel the vibrating air particles to the eardrum. In the human, the pinna serves as little more than an ornament. The three tiny bones, or ossicles, of the middle ear, hammer, anvil, and stirrup, articulate with each other and transmit the vibrations of the eardrum to the oval window of the cochlea. Note that the apex of the cochlea faces forward. The air-filled middle ear communicates with the throat via the Eustachian tube. Not until the vibrations are transmitted to the fluid-filled cochlea is hearing initiated. (The semicircular canals in the inner ear, as well as the remaining vestibular apparatus, are concerned with the sense of balance, not hearing.)

Beyond the tympanic membrane is the middle ear, which is an air-filled chamber housing three articulating ossicles: hammer, anvil, and stirrup (maleus, incus and stapes), collectively known as the ossicular chain. At one end of the chain, the hammer is attached to the eardrum, and at the other end the footplate of the stirrup is inserted in an opening in the cochlea known as the oval window. Interposed between hammer and stirrup is the anvil (see fig. 13.2). This articulating chain of ossicles transforms vibratory energy into mechanical energy, which is then transmitted to the cochlea. The proper functioning of the tympanic membrane and the associated ossicular chain depends on the relative air pressure on either side of it. As a result of metabolism, oxygen is absorbed in the middle ear, thus producing a negative pressure inside, as compared to the outside. This becomes a problem because of the discomfort produced by the streching of the eardrum.

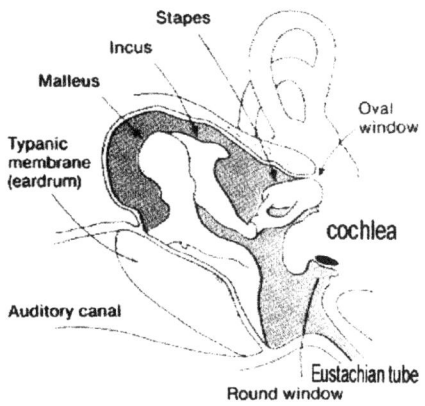

Fig.13.2. The middle ear shown in gray. The three ossicles in the middle ear articulate with each other to convey vibrations from the eardrum to the membrane covering the oval window which, leads to the cochlea in the inner ear. With air pressure on the eardrum, the malleus and incus move to exert pressure on the stapes that acts like a piston on the oval window thus producing perturbations of fluid within the cochlea that stimulate the sensitive hair cells on the basilar membrane.

The chamber of the middle ear communicates with the pharynx, or throat, via the Eustachian tube. When we swallow, the slender Eustachian tube tends to open, thus ventilating the middle ear cavity and equalizing the air pressure inside the middle ear with that outside. If we find ourselves in an environment where the atmospheric pressure is low, as on a mountain or in an airplane, we experience discomfort because of 'pressure in our ears.' To relieve the pressure, we must swallow or otherwise succeed in opening our Eustachian tubes. This will equalize the pressure on both sides of the bulging eardrum. We experience the same kind of mounting discomfort when the atmospheric pressure increases, as we descend from a mountain or come down for a landing. Ordinarily, this is no problem; various maneuvers, including yawning, chewing, blowing the nose, coughing, or sneezing, can open the Eustachian tube. When we get a cold and the mucous membranes of the oro-pharyngeal passages become inflamed and/or congested, the Eustachian tube is blocked. The resulting pressure difference causes discomfort, or even pain, and a temporary hearing impairment. A middle ear infection can be very annoying for these reasons. Before the era of modern broad-spectrum antibiotic therapy, the mastoid bone behind the external ear frequently became involved and the infection could linger for many weeks, sometimes leading to permanent damage to the auditory system.

Up to now, we have reviewed the mechanical sound-conducting part of the hearing mechanism; it has nothing to do with the actual reception of the sound signal by the nervous system. Not until the receptor cells in the fluid-filled cochlea are stimulated is there excitation of the fibers of the acoustic nerve leading to the brain.

The peripheral mechanism of hearing is an incredibly miniaturized sound system. It is contained in a volume of about one cubic millimeter, and it is designed to convert fluid vibrations into electrochemical neural impulses. This organ of hearing, containing the receptor cells, is housed in the bony labyrinth located in the temporal bone behind the external ear. The labyrinth consists of three parts: the vestibule (saccule and utricle), the semicircular canals, and the cochlea. The first two are concerned with balance, the sense of head orientation, and the sense of acceleration and deceleration. The last part, the cochlea, is concerned with hearing. However, all three communicate with each other, and it is not uncommon to find deafness accompanied by disorders of balance, as in Menière's disease in which the symptoms include attacks of dizziness, imbalance and deafness.

The cochlea is a spiral-shaped tube, about one and one-half inches in length that is wound so that it makes two and one-half turns in humans. It resembles a snail's shell; hence its name. This long and narrow tube is divided along its length into two tubes by the basilar membrane, one called the scala vestibuli, and the other, the scala tympani. These two canals are filled with perilymph and communicate with each other at the apex of the cochlea by way of an opening called the helicotrema. The scala vestibuli begins at the base of the cochlea with the oval window in which the footplate of the stapes sits. The scala tympani has a similar window, also at the base, called the round window, which can bulge with increased fluid pressure.

The basilar membrane is fibrous, with its fibers running transversely, across the membrane. Its width varies, being five times greater at the apex than at the base. Helmholtz thought that this arrangement resembles the shape of a harp with stretched strings. These structural properties led him to propose his place-resonance theory of pitch perception. Like the strings of a harp, each fiber, he thought, is tuned to resonate to a particular frequency: the low tones activate the longer fibers near the apex, and the high tones activate the shorter fibers near the base. Though some form of resonance activity does seem to take place in the cochlea, Helmholtz's conception of cochlear function was a fanciful one, as we shall see.

The vital structure responsible for the transduction of hydraulic vibrations in the cochlea into nervous impulses is the organ of Corti, which lies along the entire length of the basilar membrane. It is bathed in endolymph, which is separated from the perilymph by a delicate sheet of cells called Reissner's membrane. With the basilar membrane on one side and Reissner's membrane on the other, the cochlear duct or scala media is formed in which the organ of Corti is located. The cochlear duct thus lies between the scala vestibuli and the scala tympani.

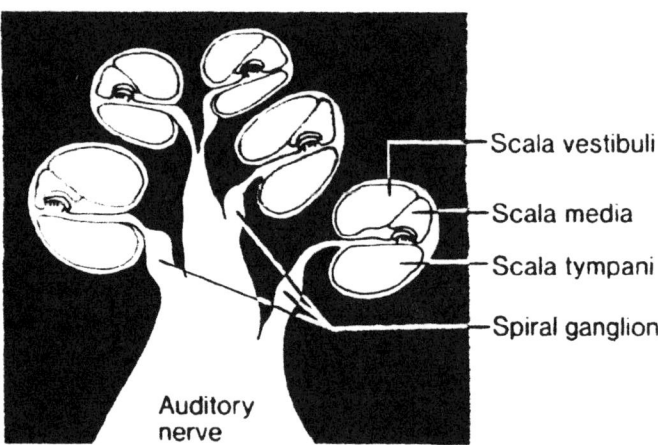

Fig 13.3. Schematic cross-section through the cochlea. Since the cochlea makes 2 1/2 turns as it coils from base to apex, its ducts show up 5 times in cross-section Note the spiral ganglion, composed of nerve fibers emerging from each section of the cochlea. These merge to form the acoustic part of the auditory nerve, which projects into the brain.

Hearing 245

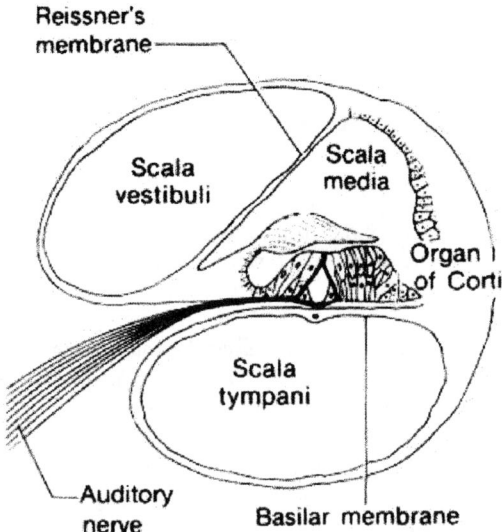

Fig. 13.4. One cross-section of the cochlea magnified to show the organ of Corti on the basilar membrane where the auditory receptor cells are located. Disturbances of lymphatic fluid in the scala media produced by movements of the stapes cause the hairs of the receptor cells to bend, thus exciting them.

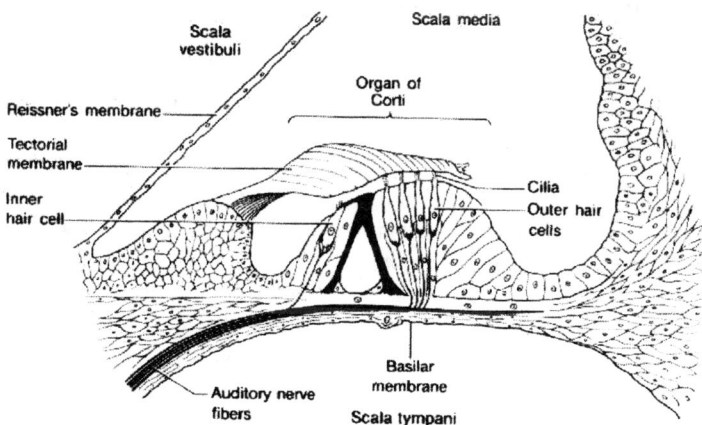

Fig. 13.5. The Organ of Corti itself magnified in cross-section. Note the hairs of the three outer hair cells and one inner hair cell embedded in the gelatinous tectorial membrane.

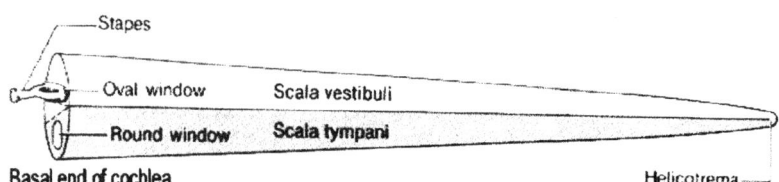

Fig. 13.6. A diagram of the cochlea unrolled, showing the length of the basilar membrane in the tapered cochlear tube. The stapes transmits its vibrations to the oval window, creating waves of disturbances of the lymphatic fluid that deform the springy basilar membrane. A movement inward causes the round window to bulge outward, and vice-versa. What does not show in this figure is that the basilar membrane itself tapers, surprisingly, from wide at the apex to narrow at the base.

The organ of Corti is composed of arches, in which are embedded the auditory receptors or hair cells. There are three rows of outer hair cells and a single row of inner hair cells running the entire length of the basilar membrane. In all, there are about 15,500 hair cells in each cochlea. These connect at their base with the acoustic nerve fibers, about 40,000 of them, which cross the basilar membrane to reach the axis of the cochlear spiral where they collect to form the acoustic nerve. The tufts of hairs of the receptor cells are embedded in a gelatinous membrane called the tectorial membrane. Vibrations cause the hairs to bend against the tectorial membrane and this triggers neural activity.

When the stapes is set in motion, inward movement gives rise to an increased pressure of the perilymph that is relieved by the outward bulging of the round window. These movements are reversed with outward movement of the stapes.

Helmholtz believed that the hair cells in the cochlea are spread rather evenly along the length of the basilar membrane and this permitted him to conclude that each receptor is stimulated by resonance of individual fibers of the basilar membrane. But vibrations of the basilar membrane are very different from vibrations of harp strings. The 'fibers' of the basilar membrane are tied together; they do not resonate independently of each other. The basilar membrane resonates as a whole. Also, unlike harp strings, the basilar membrane stops vibrating very soon after the sound stimulus ends. This is because of the damping properties in the cochlea. Without damping, we would have an incessant ringing in our ears from constant stimulation that doesn't die away. This damping factor is required for normal hearing, but it presents a problem for Helmholtz's place theory of pitch discrimination. The more damping increases the greater the spread of vibratory activity in the cochlea, and the more likely we are to perceive a smudge of pitches rather than a specific pitch.

Our modern conception of the place principle in hearing is credited to von Békésy, the Nobel prize-winning psycho-acoustician. He was the one to observe that the basilar membrane is not composed of independent resonators, as Helmholtz believed, but vibrates as a whole. When a sound stimulus is received in the cochlea, a wave of displacement of the basilar membrane travels from the base toward the apex of the cochlea like a wave along a taut rope. Because the stapes is in continuous oscillation during a sound of any duration, there is a steady succession of travelling waves along the basilar membrane. The precise shape of these travelling waves is determined by the differences in stiffness along the length of the basilar membrane and the damping properties of the fluid-filled cochlea. Each frequency of stimulation produces a maximum displacement at a different point along the basilar membrane, between base and apex, and pitch discrimination is based upon these differences in maximum displacements. He believed that the hairs of the receptor cells are bent at the place of maximal displacement, and it is the deformation of these hairs that excites the neurons leading to the brain

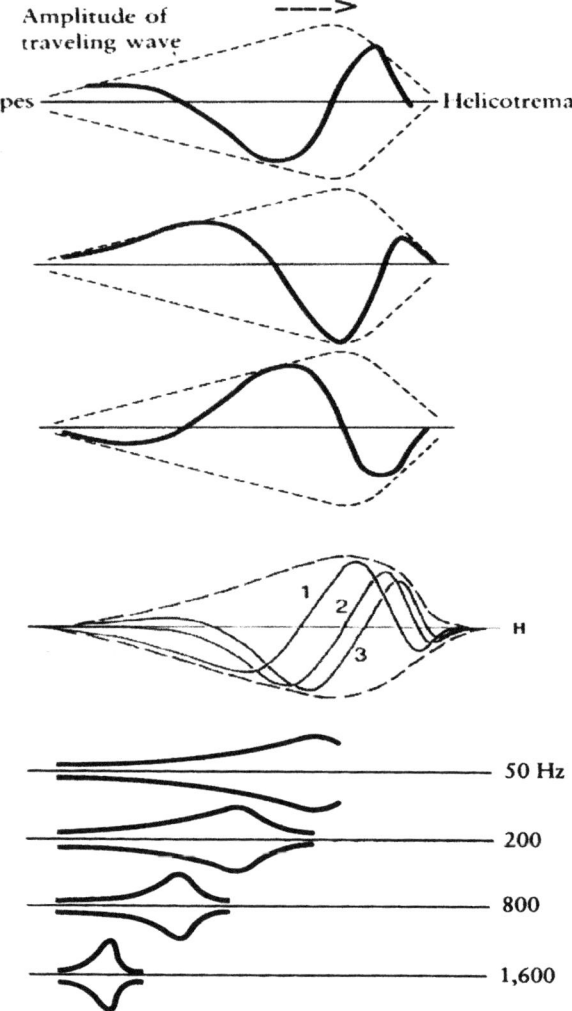

Fig. 13.7. (Above) A wave travelling from left to right along the basilar membrane is shown at three points in time. The envelope of these waves summarizes the maximum displacements at different loci along the basilar membrane. (Center) Composite of three waves obtained at three points in time. (Below) Four different envelopes generated by four tones differing in frequency, 50, 200, 800, and 1,600 Hz. Adapted from Békésy, 1960.

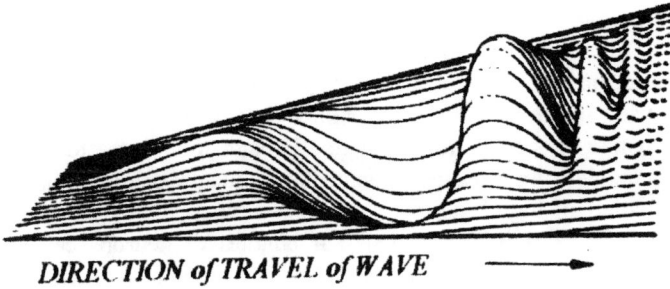

Fig.13.8. A three-dimensional representation of the basilar membrane deformed at a point in time. The broad displacement suggests that a low tone is responsible. Note the tapered basilar membrane. Adapted from Tonnedorf, 1960.

The higher the frequency of the sound, the closer the maximal displacement is to the base of the basilar membrane; the lower the frequency, the broader the maximum displacement. Theoretically, each of the higher frequencies in the audible range can be mapped onto one particular place on the basilar membrane and each of the higher frequencies excites different receptor cells. This is called tonotopic organization inside the cochlea.

However, even in von Békésy's version, the place theory does not work for sounds below 1000 *Hz*, because the displacement maxima are too wide to serve as a pitch-differentiating mechanism. Whereas high-pitched sounds set only basal parts of the basilar membrane, near the oval window, in motion, too large a part of the basilar membrane is set in motion by these low-pitched sounds. In short, even in its modern form, place theory has proved to be limited by the evidence that low tones generate broad displacements of the basilar membrane. Yet, we discriminate pitches that produce these broad displacements, leaving unexplained the specificity for which place theory was designed to account.

What, then, accounts for our ability to discriminate the low tones, 1 *kHz* and below? In the late 1920s, E. G. Wever suggested that all auditory nerve fibers, no matter what part of the basilar membrane they feed, are capable of responding at a frequency that matches the frequency of the sound. For example, a tone of 100 *Hz* can generate

100 impulses per second in the acoustic nerve fibers, and a tone of 200 *Hz* can generate 200 impulses per second, and so on up.

This mechanism, often referred to as the frequency principle, can operate up to a limit of a few hundred impulses per second--no faster, owing to the fact that, once a fiber fires, it takes some time to recover before it is ready to fire again. Though this seems to be an insurmountable limitation in applying the frequency principle to the discrimination of high tones, Wever pointed out that this limitation can be overcome if it is assumed that bundles of neurons can act together, taking turns in firing at some low frequency (say, 100 impulses per second to a tone of 2 *kHz*) but out of synchrony with each other. If the bundle of neurons is processed as a whole, and all the impulses are added together in the brain, the resultant total might amount to, say 2000 impulses per second, matching the frequency of a 2000 *Hz* sound. Wever applied the term, the *volley principle*, to this mechanism of extending the frequency of firing in bundles of neurons.

Thus, we have two mechanisms of pitch discrimination, both limited, but with an overlap in their effective frequency ranges: a place mechanism that operates from about 200 *Hz* to 20,000 *Hz*, the upper limit of hearing, and a frequency mechanism that operates from, perhaps, 2000 *Hz* down to 20 *Hz*, the lower limit of hearing. It seems not coincidental that our most acute pitch discriminations, in the vocal range, fall in the range of overlap.

The bending of hairs of the receptor cells at the site of maximal displacement of the basilar membrane triggers the transduction process, that is, the conversion of mechanical energy to electrochemical energy in the auditory neurons. Technically, the bending of the hairs generates ion currents, and these currents cause the release of transmitter substance at the base of the hair cells, thus stimulating the acoustic neurons to fire.

Each neuron in the acoustic nerve (part of the auditory or eighth cranial nerve) originates in a narrowly circumscribed region of the cochlea. Because certain sites along the basilar membrane are excited by certain frequencies above 1 kHz or so, each neuron is fired most readily by a particular frequency. If the ear is stimulated by other frequencies, this particular neuron is not likely to be fired.

We have discussed how pitch is encoded in the auditory neurons. If a sound contains several frequencies, the neurons responding to all these frequencies are excited. The duration of a sound is encoded in the duration of the neural activity and its intensity by the discharge rate and by the total assembly of neurons firing.

The highest level of acoustic processing in the brain seems to be the auditory cortex of the cerebral hemispheres. This tissue is found in the first gyrus of the temporal lobes. Most of it is concealed in the depths of the sylvian fissure.

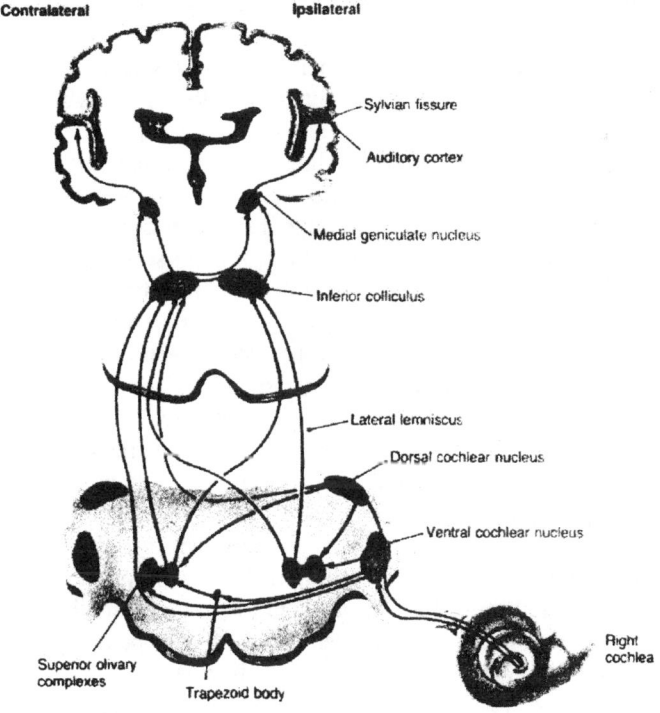

Fig. 13.9. Auditory pathways ascending from the hair cells in the cochlea; the cochlear nuclei; the olivary complex; the lateral lemniscus; the inferior colliculus; the medial geniculate; to the auditory cortex in the temporal lobe. (Descending tracts from the auditory cortex to the cochlea, via similar way stations, are not shown.) Note that the contralateral projection is stronger than the ipsilateral one. However, each cochlea is represented bilaterally in the brain so that a lesion on one side of the brain anywhere above the cochlear nuclei never produces profound deafness in either ipsilateral or contralateral ear.

Each ear projects to the auditory cortex via six or more relay stations in the brain stem. Their names need not concern us here. However, there are three principles of projection that should be noted. First, the strongest projection is contralateral, that is, the information originating in one ear is transmitted, for the most part, to the opposite cerebral hemisphere. Second, the tonotopic organization already described for the cochlea is preserved at all the relay stations of the auditory system including the cerebral cortex. There is, nevertheless, an enormous spread of activity. At each of the several relay stations on the way to the cerebral cortex, each axon makes contact with the dendrites of many neurons. The resultant spread of activity is so great that it seems strange that we hear anything but cacophony. Third, the more peripheral acoustic neurons, those closest to the receptor cells, are excitable by pure tones; but neurons at the higher levels, those closest to the auditory cortex, are not. The further upstream from the cochlea toward the brain, the more complex the sound patterns that activate the neurons. In general, the information contained in a sound is recoded a number of times as the excitation passes the various relay stations up the auditory pathway. In the process, neurons extract more and more complex properties of the sound.

In everyday life, we are almost never confronted with pure tones. The sounds we are exposed to contain many frequency components. The amplitudes of such sounds vary as do their durations. They begin and end abruptly or gradually. They may be repeated or not. Their source may be nearby or far away, left or right, moving or stationary, and so on. These are all discriminable properties and there must be neuronal processes that mediate these discriminations. In the auditory cortex, neurons have been found that respond only to the onset of sound, others to its termination. Still others fire only when the sound continues for a certain time, and others are excited only by repeated sounds. Some can be activated by broad frequency-band noises, others are finely tuned to respond to specific frequencies. Most cortical neurons are activated by the contralateral ear, but some respond to ipsilateral stimulation, and a few only when both ears are stimulated simultaneously. A few neurons cannot be excited at all during the course of an experiment. Presumably, these neurons are highly specific, responding to sound too complicated to be reproduced in the laboratory.

The neurons in the auditory cortex are evidently involved in auditory pattern recognition, a process essential for the understanding of speech and the recognition of music. In this connection, neurons have been found in the cerebral cortex of monkeys that respond to the sounds monkeys emit when they communicate with each other. In humans, brain lesions involving the temporal lobes sometimes cause difficulties in understanding speech, in finding words to express meaning, in localizing sounds in space, and in identifying sound patterns. However, such injuries rarely affect the ability simply to discriminate different pitches and loudnesses. Chapter 19 deals with hemispheric specialization and the effects of brain damage on the perception and performance of music.

SOUND LOCALIZATION AND STEREO

As for our ability to localize sounds in space, we know from everyday experience that the direction of sound can be perceived quite accurately (except in the median plane). Since sound waves are bent and reflected by dense objects in the environment, it is not possible to determine the source of sound from its direction on entering the ear. Light waves cannot be bent in the same way, and visual localization of objects in space is based on a topographic correspondence between the place on the retina stimulated and visual space. There is no such correspondence between place on the basilar membrane in the cochlea and auditory space. Instead, there is a tonotopic correspondence between sound frequency and locus of excitation on the basilar membrane, as we have seen. How, then, are we able to judge the location of a sound source? It is, after all, the same sound, whether it originates to the left or right of us. Yet we are quite good at localizing sound.

Visual localization of objects in space can often be determined with just one eye, but directional hearing ordinarily depends upon stimulation of the two ears. We know that the position of the two ears, on either side of a large-sized head, provide us with important cues that we use quite unconsciously and automatically to localize sounds. If the source of sound is not visible, we respond to these cues to pinpoint the direction of the sound. Whenever the sound source is displaced from the midplane, one ear is farther from the sound source than the other, and this provides us with two unequal aural signals. By integrating in the brain the two disparate signals that originate in the two ears, sound is located in space.

We will use Stumpf's terminology to distinguish two kinds of binaural stimulation. When the two ears are stimulated simultaneously, we refer to identical stimulation of the two ears as *diotic*, and different stimulation of the two ears as *dichotic*. At any point in time, the complex auditory stimulus can be both diotic and dichotic. For example, the binaural stimulus may be diotic as to frequency and duration, but dichotic as to intensity, phase, and time of onset. As we shall now see, it is these dichotic cues that are used to localize sound in space.

Because of its relatively slow conduction velocity, the sound arrives later at the more distant ear (it takes about three-quarters of a millisecond to travel the 23 cm between ears), its intensity is lower, and the phase of the sound waves at the two ears may not match. Since we are able to detect intensity differences of 1 dB under optimal conditions, a sound source $2°$ from the midline can be localized. Sounds that have a sharp onset and offset, such as clicks and chirps, are more accurately localized than steady tones. These bursts are called transients. A more compelling stereo effect is obtained with transients than with steady tones.

If the subject's head is fixed in position, directional hearing can be shown to depend upon differences in time of onset (called onset asynchrony), intensity, and phase, at the two ears. When earphones are used for independent stimulation of the two ears (dichotic stimulation), a lag in time of onset at one ear, or a reduction of intensity of the signal to that ear, or a phase lag, all produce the sensation of a sound displaced toward the other ear.

When the sound source is in the midplane, it is more difficult to determine whether the sound source is immediately in front of the head, behind it, above or below. Animals take advantage of their mobile pinnas which are shaped to capture the sound signal according to its direction. But the pinnas of humans are fixed and have a limited function in hearing. To localize sounds in the midplane, we must move our heads in order to provide ourselves with those binaural differences, in time of onset, intensity, and phase.

Suppose we blindfold you and have you listen to pure tones of various frequencies, out in the open air where there are no walls from which sound could bounce, and no traffic noises. The tones would be presented over a loudspeaker that could be moved to various unpredictable positions, and we would ask you to point to where the sound seems to come from. If your hearing is more or less normal, you would be likely to do very well.

Stevens and Newman conducted such an experiment in 1936. Under these conditions, their subjects pinpointed the source of sound most accurately if the pure tones were below 1000 *Hz* and above 3000 *Hz*. Why was this so? The answer illustrates how the binaural cues to sound localization operate.

Suppose the sound originates on one side. It will arrive at the nearer ear about 0.5 ms before it reaches the further ear. This disparity in onset serves as a lateralizing cue for low-pitched sounds. These sounds travel more easily around obstacles like the head without being reflected. Under these conditions, the sound that reaches the two ears is likely to be out of phase, and this disparity will also serve as a localizing cue. If you don't hear the onset of the sound, you will miss the delay of onset at the two ears, and you will need the out-of-phase cue to pinpoint the source of the sound. But at 2000 *Hz*, the delay between the two ears produces an exact match of phase, and that cue is not available. Without onset asynchrony and without the out-of-phase cue as the sound frequency approaches 2000 *Hz*, sound localization accuracy deteriorates.

Higher frequency sounds are more apt to be reflected by the head, and this means that the nearer ear will receive a more intense signal than the farther ear. This begins to happen at about 2300 *Hz*. The wavelength of these sounds, about 15 cm, matches the diameter of the head, and the onset disparity is lost.

In short, lower frequency sounds, 1000 *Hz* and below, are well localized on the basis of onset asynchrony and the phase cue. These sounds, having long wavelengths, are conducted around the head without much interference and are almost equally intense at the two ears. High frequency sounds, above 3000 *Hz*, having shorter wavelengths, are more apt to be reflected by the head, thus creating a difference in intensity at the two ears. These sounds are less likely to provide onset-asynchrony and phase cues. Between these low and high frequencies, in the vicinity of 2000 *Hz*, none of these cues are available and sound localization is very imperfect.

Now, let us consider the spatial dimension in music. The distribution of musicians on the stage at a concert can be perceived aurally because we have two ears located on either side of the head. Seated at an orchestral concert around the middle of the hall, the listener gets slightly disparate auditory images of the sound at the two ears. With the usual distribution of orchestral musicians on stage, the left ear, being closer to the left side of the stage, favors the sound of the violins, while the right ear favors the sound of the cellos. The brain is responsible for integrating the two auditory images into the one that is actually heard, and that reflects the actual spatial distribution of sound, and the acoustic properties of the hall.

It is difficult to attend to individual instruments when a large ensemble is playing together. This is ordinarily not a problem unless a soloist is playing and we want to hear him above the thick texture of orchestral sound. How do we do it? Increasing the intensity of the sound of the soloist is obviously effective, but auditory masking frequently reduces the perceptibility of sound. Sometimes the soloist is simply not heard without amplification. It would help if the soloist could be located in space. Even a soft solo part can be made to stand out if localization cues are provided. One possibility is to have the soloist move back and forth in front of the ensemble. Many singers do just that: they move across the stage and they know that their voices are more apt to stand out in the mass of sound.

The same problem is encountered in listening to recorded music. The information on the position of instruments and voices is lost in monophonic recording. The only cues the listener has available to differentiate the various voices of sound derive from their pitch, loudness, timbre, and rhythm.

The principle of stereophonic sound was added to musical recordings in the 1950s to approximate the distribution of sounds heard in the concert hall, that is, to provide the spatial dimension and 'presence.' The principle involves recording the two disparate auditory images at the two ears on two separate channels, by using two microphones. The channels are then fed to two loudspeakers properly placed in the listening room, and the brain integrates the two signals to produce one to which the spatial dimension has been added.

Ideally, the recording should be made with the aid of a listener, real or dummy, seated at some optimal position in the concert hall. Two microphones, one at each ear canal, record the sound signals after they have been modified by the acoustic properties of the hall. These signals are then filtered and mixed properly and fed to two loudspeaker systems. These loudspeakers can only be listened to in an anechoic chamber, because the acoustic properties of a normal room would add unnatural reverberation. If this method of recording and playback is carefully followed, the sounds from the two loudspeakers would re-create in the ear canals of the live listener precisely the same sound pressures that had been recorded when the head was exposed to live sound during the recording session. Needless to say, these ideal conditions are never met, not in making the recording, and certainly not in the playback. Those hi-fi buffs who seek absolute fidelity will always be disappointed.

This is not to disparage modern stereophonic recording. The multi-miking, repeated takes, splicing and mixing features of modern recording techniques are responsible for a new art medium. Some modern recording artists will not compare their records and tapes against the standard of a live performance. The recorded sound is simply different from the live sound. One such artist is the late Canadian pianist, Glenn Gould, who gave up a career of playing in the concert hall in favor of capturing the performance in the recording studio.

HEARING IMPAIRMENT

Hearing difficulties, especially deafness, greatly change the life of the affected person. With severe hearing impairment, it becomes difficult to get around. There is the hazard of being unaware of approaching danger. Speech is not accurately heard, and paranoid feelings tend to develop ("people are talking about me"). And, of course, music can no longer be enjoyed in the same way. Let us review the reasons why hearing is impaired. To do this, we must re-examine the mechanical properties of the ear.

Though deeply embedded in the skull, the cochlea is very vulnerable to damage. If the pressure level of the sound is slowly increased, eventually there will be a sensation of pain. Experiments have revealed that pain begins when the intensity level reaches 120 dB or so. Such intense sounds cause a temporary reduction in hearing (or rise in audibility threshold). If exposure is prolonged, a permanent hearing loss can result. This is called stimulation deafness or sound trauma. High-frequency noise is the most damaging; microscopic examination has revealed that the hair cells and blood circulation near the base of the cochlea are destroyed by the loud sound. In fact, sound trauma can be caused by sounds at considerably lower intensities if the exposure is sufficiently prolonged. It has been found that long-term exposure will cause injury if the intensity is no more than 90 dB. The hearing of people regularly exposed to sounds exceeding this level is therefore endangered and should be protected by sound-damping devices such as earplugs. Without this precaution, people become hard of hearing in a matter of years. Our urban environment is badly polluted by loud sounds. No wonder many of us can't hear much above 12 *kHz* by the time we are in our thirties.

Apart from sound trauma, that is, physical damage to the inner ear, sound can have a variety of harmful effects ranging from objective symptoms, such as elevated blood pressure and insomnia, to the experience of annoyance. Which disturbances are caused by sounds depend a great deal on a person's psychological attitudes and make-up. For example, a tenant in an apartment may feel seriously disturbed by the piano playing of another tenant, even though they live two floors apart. Other tenants have no complaints and the actual intensity level of the music in the apartment of the aggrieved person is not high. It is difficult to hit upon rules to prevent annoying everybody, and the guidelines offered in civil regulations are often unsatisfactory compromises.

The process of testing hearing is called *clinical audiometry*. A variety of tests are designed to demonstrate the nature of the hearing loss and to suggest the site of the damage, whether in the conduction mechanism in the middle ear, or in the receptor cells, or in the brain.

To plot a threshold audiogram, various tones are presented to one ear at a time via a single earphone. Initially sub-threshold, the intensity of the tone is gradually raised until the person finally reports hearing the tone. This is repeated using frequencies ranging from perhaps 100 *Hz* to 15 *kHz*. These threshold sound pressures are plotted on audiometric graph paper. When the threshold is a certain number of dB above normal threshold, the person is said to have a hearing loss of that many dB within a specified frequency range. Try shutting both ears with your fingers. You will experience a hearing loss of about 20 dB for the sound about you.

When earphones are used in clinical audiometry, airborne conduction is being tested. If, instead, tuning forks are placed on the mastoid bone behind the ear, the procedure can be repeated to study hearing via bone conduction. By comparing the threshold curves for air and bone conduction, it is possible to distinguish between middle ear hearing loss, on the one hand, and receptor or nerve hearing loss, on the other.

Hearing 259

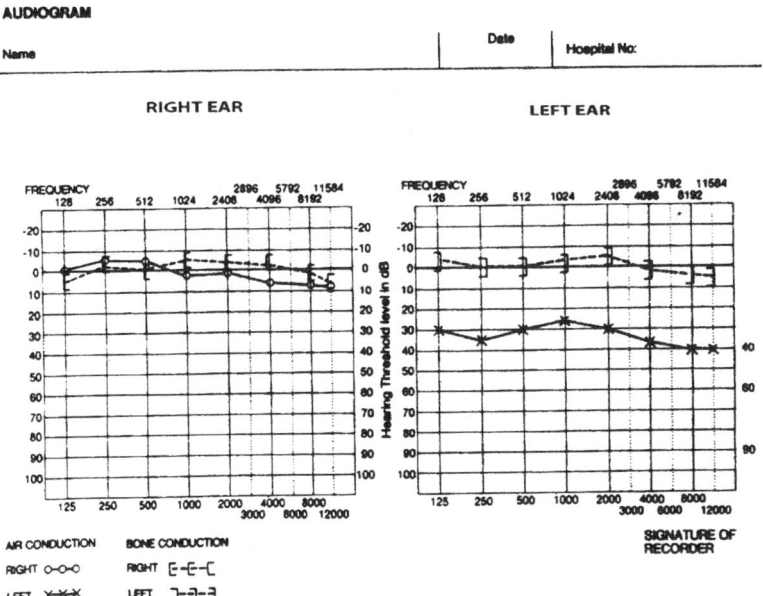

Fig. 13.10. The audiogram is a plot of thresholds, expressed in dB, at tonal frequencies ranging from 125 to 12,000 Hz. The curve of normal hearing is expected to follow the horizontal 0 dB line. A hearing loss is indicated by a curve that deviates below the 0 dB line. The audiograms shown here are of a patient that proved to have impaired sound conduction on the left side.

Hearing losses can be classified as follows:

1. *Disturbances of sound conduction.* The damage is in the sound-conducting mechanism in the middle ear. In cases of inflammation, for example, the ossicular chain does not transmit the normal amount of sound energy to the cochlea, and hearing is impaired even though the inner ear is intact. Since conduction through the bones of the skull is unaffected, the person continues to hear himself quite well when he speaks. Also, since the inner ear is not damaged, bone conducted sound is perceived normally, because the sound arrives at

the hair cells without the aid of the impaired middle ear. This conduction impairment is shown in the illustrated audiograms.

2. *Inner ear damage.* Deafness arises from damage to the hair cells so that the process of transduction is disturbed. This condition may be caused by noise trauma, by disease or age, and by ototoxic drugs such as certain antibiotics and diuretics. Audiometric testing reveals raised thresholds to both airborne and bone-conducted sounds, since both must be transduced by the same damaged hair cells.

Noise-induced hearing loss frequently results from impulsive sounds such as explosions and gunfire. A characteristic audiometric configuration has been described, the so-called acoustic trauma notch. As a rule, hearing becomes poorest in the range 3 to 10 *kHz* during the acute phase of hair cell damage. Since recovery often occurs above 7 *kHz*, a notch in hearing is seen on the audiogram between 3 and 7 *kHz*, with the sharpest drop at about 4 *kHz*. This pattern suggests damage around the basal turn of the cochlea, a fact verified by post-mortem microscopic examination of that organ.

Of course, the precise pattern of hearing impairment depends upon the frequency composition of the traumatic noise. Considering the composition of frequencies in rock music, mostly in the range of speech, listeners are advised to limit their exposure.

People with an acoustic trauma notch frequently complain of a ringing in the ears (*tinnitus*) that can be matched to frequencies in the 3 to 6 *kHz* range. Many of these people are not aware that they suffer a hearing loss, because this range of impairment does not affect their hearing and understanding of speech.

Exposures to jet engines, pneumatic hammers, subways, and even computers, have been documented as causing hearing loss. Hunters, target shooters, and snowmobile drivers are a particularly difficult group because of their reluctance to wear hearing protectors or to limit their sport.

3. *Retrocochlear damage.* This includes damage to the left and/or right acoustic nerves, the auditory pathways, and relay stations in the brain. This type of damage may be caused by trauma to the head, by a cerebrovascular accident such as a stroke or hemorrhage, or by an expanding lesion such as a brain tumor. In these conditions, the middle and inner ears may be intact, but conduction leads to a damaged central auditory system. Like inner ear deafness, retro-

cochlear damage raises the threshold for both airborne and bone-conducted sound. Sometimes a ringing in the ears accompanies neural damage. If the brain damage is restricted to just one side, the hearing impairment is rarely profound.

Whether a hearing aid is useful to those who have suffered a hearing loss depends upon the nature of the injury to the auditory system. If there is a disturbance in sound conduction in the middle ear, the amplification provided by a hearing aid will benefit the victim. However, no currently available device or treatment will benefit those who have suffered permanent destruction of receptor cells, neurons, or brain areas.

In the February, 1985 issue of the *Scientific American*, a prosthetic implant in the cochlea to overcome receptor deafness was described. The prospect sounds exciting, for it means that hearing may be restored, but the current device provides the hard-of-hearing with little more than clangs and buzzes, certainly nothing remotely resembling speech or music.

In our society, there seems to be a stigma attached to the wearing of a hearing aid. We celebrate having defective vision by ornamenting our faces with oversized glasses. Yet we hide the evidence that we have a hearing impairment by wearing a miniaturized hearing aid and, many of us, if sufficiently embarrassed, will not wear one at all. Since there is a tendency to turn a bit paranoid when we cannot hear others, it seems foolish to resist wearing a hearing aid if it will help us hear.

With the aid of a tuning fork (customarily 256 *Hz*), anyone can quickly distinguish conduction impairment from inner ear or nerve damage, if just one ear is affected. The stem of the vibrating tuning fork is set firmly on the middle of the skull. The person with inner ear damage reports hearing the tone displaced toward the healthy side whereas, with middle ear damage, the sound is heard on the affected side.

Hearing frequently becomes impaired as people get older. This condition, called presbycusis, first shows up in the high frequency range. A 60-year old large-city dweller can expect a hearing loss of about 40 dB at 8 *kHz* and about 30 dB at 4 *kHz*. The damage is of the inner ear-retrocochlear type, and sometimes extends to frequencies between 250 *Hz* and 4 *kHz*, a range important for the understanding of speech and the appreciation of music. Whether this condition is the result of the normal aging process, or is caused by the noise pollution of jet engines, subways, rock music, and the like, is debatable. It is probably both.

Otosclerosis is a disease of aging. Hearing is impaired because the stapes becomes locked in the oval window of the cochlea and cannot vibrate back and forth to produce the perturbations of the lymphatic fluid that are necessary for hearing. Surgical attempts have been made to free the stapes, but the disease process of sclerosis promptly re-immobilizes the stapes. A generation or so ago, a New York surgeon named J.Lempert devised a microsurgical procedure that involved drilling a tiny hole in the bony cochlea and inserting a metal ring to prevent the hole from closing. This procedure, called *fenestration*, has benefited many older people. Since the stapes remains immobile after surgery, the mechanism by which hearing is re-established in these people is not well understood.

TUNE-DEAFNESS OR MELODY APRAXIA

People who cannot sing a tune or say whether a note is high, low or out of tune, sometimes complain that they 'have no ear.' Music teachers frequently confirm that these persons have no ear or are 'tone deaf.'

But is it right to describe these people as 'tone deaf'? A person who really could not discriminate between different pitches would be unable to understand speech and would confuse Luciano Pavarotti with Beverly Sills. In this sense, nobody is tone deaf unless he is deaf--that is, unless he is unable to hear.

What some people have difficulty doing is carrying a melody. We might call that condition, 'tune-deafness,' or more accurately, singing apraxia. This inability is shown when a person cannot sing a melody in tune, or sings in a monotone, sometimes admitting sheepishly that it doesn't sound right or that it is out of tune. Such a person may not be able to sing even a single pitch accurately.

The explanations range from poor registration by the sensory apparatus, to faulty perception because the signals have not been properly elaborated in the brain, to poor short-term memory for tones, to inability to sing because of a motor impairment.

Experiments have shown that tune-deaf people can usually discriminate between two different pitches in normal fashion. This has been interpreted to mean that it is the inability to sing that is the proper explanation for tune deafness. However, singing in pitch can be improved with suitable practice and this has led to a developmental explanation of tune deafness. Frequently, songs are sung in school in an unsuitable register for some children. Unless the child is able to move easily from one octave to another, he is likely to find himself lost when trying to match his voice to the pitch of the song sung by the teacher. A good way to convince someone that he is tune deaf is to make him sing when the conditions make it well nigh impossible. Such children frequently stop in embarassment and say, "No, that's not right." This suggests that children can recognize a melody more easily than they can reproduce it, which places the problem in the motor realm of singing rather than in the perceptual realm of hearing.

There is very little reason to hold the ear responsible for the explanation of tune deafness. Certainly the ear is not the seat of musical talent. The differences between musical and non-musical individuals must involve differences in the coding and decoding of tonal information as well as the storage and retrieval of blocks of sound. It is true that the ear is essential for the musical enterprise (though consider the case of Beethoven). But the ear itself does not organize the tonal ingredients of music. The very essence of music, and indeed the essence of any art, is organization. Consider whether the secret of reading lies in having good eyesight. The secret of musicality seems to depend not so much on good hearing as on effective organization imposed by the brain.

Chapter 14

ACTIVE LISTENING

Everyone recognizes that music can be very stirring. It seems curious then that listening to music may involve no overt activity. The listener may sit motionless, with expressionless face. This should not be taken to mean that he is passive inside. As he sits listening impassively, many thoughts may run through his head. His brain has been stirred. He is also *feeling* the music and this means that his autonomic nervous system, his limbic system in his forebrain, and some of his glands have been activated. Measurements like pulse rate, blood pressure, galvanic skin response, stomach motility, blood epinephrine and EEG all reveal the extent of his bodily activities while he sits impassively listening to music. In short, there is a veritable explosion of activities inside the body, though nothing shows overtly.

But frequently, the listener cannot sit still while listening to music. He may engage in all kinds of activities, not just fidgeting. The listener may shake his head to the music, or he may clap, or conduct imaginary musicians or drum his fingers. He may hum, smile or frown, sway or tap his feet. And if he is really listening attentively, his mind is not passive. He is engaged in the cognitive activities of categorizing and organizing involving activity in the cerebral cortex. In this chapter, we will focus on the contributions that the listener makes to his own experiences of music.

Up to now, we have considered the physical dimensions of musical sound in some detail, and you might conclude from the discussion that the music you perceive is a copy of the musical stimulus, exactly as you see it displayed on the oscilloscope screen and perfectly reproduced in your mind. Of course, the sounds emitted by musical instruments or voices form the basis for the music you hear. Without these sounds, you should hear no music and, if you did, we would say that you were hallucinating.

The question we wish to raise here is whether there is a perfect match between the sounds generated by musical instruments and the music you hear. The early psychophysicists of the nineteenth century believed that the nature and magnitude of the response is determined simply by the nature and magnitude of the stimulus. This view prompted the stimulus-response formula (S-R) of the early twentieth century behaviorists. For every response, they argued, there is one and only one antecedent stimulus. But our everyday experiences belie this view, and it has long been abandoned. Modern psychologists recognize that responses are produced not by stimuli but by the organism. Similarly, stimuli do not initiate responses directly; they act on the organism. This more contemporary view is summarized in the following diagram:

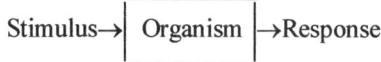

Once the organism entered into the stimulus-response formula, a number of matters quickly became the subject of inquiry. For example, psychologists could ask why a stimulus might be effective in eliciting a response on one occasion and not on another. Here are some obvious reasons why a stimulus may not make an impression on the organism. Let us start with some trivial reasons:

- The stimulus may be too weak to excite the receptors of the sense organs, such as rods and cones in the eye, or hair cells in the cochlea.
- The perceiver may not be oriented properly to receive the stimulus. For example, the person may have his back to the stimulus, or his eyes may be averted or even closed. Or his eyes may not be properly focused on the stimulus.

Less obvious reasons include the following:

- The perceiver may not be properly adapted to receive the stimulus, as when she first enters a darkened theater and cannot see a thing.
- The perceiver may be in a non-receptive state: tired, angry, feeling sick, half asleep, etc.
- The perceiver may not be paying attention to the stimulus.

Is listening to music simply a matter of soaking up the sound? Clearly not. If the match between stimulus and response were, in fact, perfect, then the response to musical sound would not vary as long as the stimulus itself did not vary.

The truth is that we are notoriously fickle about what we perceive. Sometimes we hear a piece of music in great detail; sometimes it passes us by and we aren't even aware of it. Sometimes it is masked; and sometimes we just don't pay any attention to it. Sometimes it grips us and we experience an emotional charge; at other times it seems banal and flat, without a spark of feeling. Sometimes it appears full of meaning and, at other times it seems utterly meaningless. Sometimes we organize it in one way and, at other times in a totally different way. Sometimes we like it; sometimes we don't. In short, we vary greatly in the way we respond to the same music, the very same pattern of sounds. Also, we differ among ourselves in the way we respond to music. How can a hall full of listeners disagree so vehemently about the very same music?

We must conclude that there are many reasons why a stimulus has varying effects on the individual. Leaving aside the two trivial cases, one, where the stimulus is too weak to be sensed and the other, where the individual is simply asleep, we are left with some interesting cases to consider.

ATTENTION AND HABITUATION

As you sit in your chair reading these lines, there are a great many stimuli that impinge on you. Most of these stimuli simply pass you by; you are not aware of them. As you read this, are you aware of the pressure on the seat of your pants? All of you are, now that I have called your attention to it. But were you, before I said anything about it? The pressure was there all along but you were not aware of it. You simply weren't paying attention to the seat of your pants.

Though a stimulus is applied and the receptor cells are excited, the stimulus may not produce its effect on the organism until attention is directed to it. In order to hear something, you must listen for it. I have always marveled at how my children were able to do their homework with the radio blaring. Apparently, they could turn the music off in their heads, and turn it back on, simply by shifting their attention.

It is easy to habituate to a stimulus. When you first sat down to read this, you may have felt uncomfortable because of the pressure on the seat of your pants, and you may have squirmed and fidgeted to relieve the discomfort. But it didn't take long before you habituated to it. Sometimes it takes another bit of squirming to dishabituate so that you feel the pressure again. If repeated over and over again, my query would become less and less effective in directing your attention, but a bit of moving around on your part would bring the pressure back into your awareness. The same kind of habituation and dishabituation occurs at the movies when you hold hands and enjoy the pressure. Sitting quietly this way without fidgeting, you become habituated and you don't feel the pressure any longer. A bit of squeezing is enough to bring the sensation back. In the auditory modality, too, habituation takes place but, in hearing, no amount of 'squeezing' will bring the sensation back. A sudden change in the stimulus, as the early Haydn attempted in the *Surprise Symphony*, might be effective.

AUDITORY MASKING

Masking is said to occur when one sound is obscured by another. The most obvious example of masking is when loud sounds drown out soft sounds; soft sounds are much less likely to drown out loud sounds. There are other variables besides loudness that influence the effectiveness of masking, for example, pitch. Low-pitched sounds more easily drown out high-pitched sounds rather than the other way around.

Everyone who has had the experience of coming out of a darkened theatre into the blinding sunlight knows that it takes a while before she can see normally. Psychologists refer to this as light adaptation. In this respect, the ear differs from the eye. The ear recovers very quickly from noise endured for some period of time (provided that the noise did not damage the inner ear). Also, a loud sound renders only certain frequencies inaudible, while a bright light has a broader spectral effect.

Given two sounds, one obscuring the other, we speak of the obscuring stimulus as the *masker*, and the masked stimulus as the *signal* (or *maskee*). We may liken masking to a temporary impairment in hearing: the *masker* raises the threshold of hearing of the *signal*. This means, in effect, that it is necessary to raise the intensity of the *signal* in order to hear it.

As one moves the masking pitch away from the pitch of the *signal*, there comes a point where the *masker* no longer affects the threshold of the *signal*. When this point is reached, we hear the *signal* just as well with or without the *masker*. The frequency range within which a *masker* raises the threshold of the *signal* is the critical bandwidth of the *masker*. For pure tones below 500 *Hz*, the critical bandwidth interval has been estimated to be as narrow as a major second or so. Above 500 *Hz*, it remains more or less constant at about the interval of a minor third, all the way up to 5000 *Hz* and higher. This is shown in Fig. 10.1.

In actual music, rough estimates show that low tones are more effective maskers over wider musical intervals than are high tones. In the range of bass instruments, a tone as far as an octave above the masker might be attenuated in audibility. In the range of high treble instruments such as the piccolo, tones as close as a major second might not be masked. This has important consequences for the audibility of melodic lines. In polyphonic music with a thick contrapuntal texture, the treble notes are more audible than the bass notes. In a reverberant concert hall or church, bass sounds tend to persist longer after being played, creating a muddy bass sound which becomes all the more effective as a masker.

An early experiment on masking, going back to 1876, involved the use of an organ pipe to generate a low tone, and a tuning fork to generate a high tone. They were sounded together initially so that they both could be heard. But, as the amplitude of vibrations of the tuning fork waned, its sound ceased to be heard because it was masked by the lower sound of the organ pipe. That the tuning fork was still audible was shown by stopping the air to the organ pipe to remove the masking sound, and immediately the tuning fork was clearly heard.

The research by Wegel and Lane (1924) at the Bell Laboratories is classic in the field of auditory masking. Using pure tones, they demonstrated that there is a systematic relationship between the intensity of the *masker* and the threshold of the *signal*: the greater the intensity of the *masker*, from 20 to 100 dB, the higher the shift in threshold of the *signal*. They also showed that the more similar the *masker* and *signal* were in frequency, the more effectively was the *signal* masked. There is an interesting exception to this rule. As the *masker* approaches the *signal* in frequency, auditory beats are generated by the combination of the two sounds. And, as long as the

270   Sound and Music

beating is audible, even a relatively weak *signal* will be detected. That is, the presence of beats gives the *signal* away, so to speak; the threshold of the *signal* is lowered, and we say that the amount of masking has decreased. All this is summarized in the Wegel and Lane graphs, shown in Fig. 14.1.

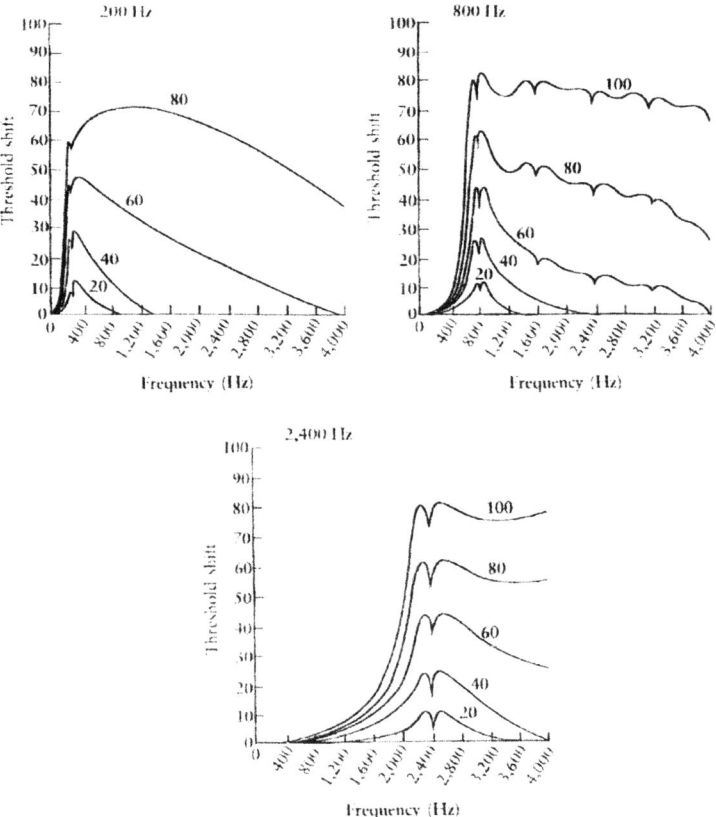

Fig.14.1. Masking curves produced by a masker of 200, 800, and 2,400 Hz on ten signals (maskees) varying from 400 to 4,000 Hz, shown on the horizontal axis. The vertical axis shows the amount of masking in dB, that is, how much more intense the signal must be above normal threshold for it to be heard in the presence of the masker. On each graph, the effects of five masking intensities are shown, 100, 80, 60, 40, and 20 dB above threshold. The signal is heard only if its intensity is above the corresponding curve. A signal having an intensity below its corresponding curve will not be heard. Adapted from Wegel and Lane, 1924.

It has been shown that noise is a more effective masker than is a pure tone. For one thing, there are no dips in masking due to beats. This is because no beats are heard when noise is combined with a *signal*.

Though masking by broad-spectrum noise is an important subject in psychoacoustic research, it is less important in the perception of musical sounds. However, here is one interesting musical example. The ambient noise in a concert hall with a hushed and attentive audience is in the neighborhood of 40 dB. What musical sounds will such a noise level mask? Remarkably little, actually. Musical sounds can still be heard even if they are a few dB *below* the intensity level of the noise. You may find the rustling next to you in the concert hall quite annoying. You may also find annoying the paroxysms of coughing coming from all over the concert hall. But the ambient noise level of 40 dB does not do much to interfere with the perception of music from the stage, and you may be completely unaware of it. Only that part of the audience-noise that is within the critical bandwidth of a pure tone is likely to have any masking effect on that tone.

As we have just seen, masking is of some considerable importance in our perception of music, and masking influences our enjoyment of it. Over an automobile radio, the soft passages in a piece of music may be completely masked by the noise of engine and traffic. In a relatively quiet concert hall, even the subtlest musical nuances may be heard because masking noises are reduced to a minimum.

It is interesting to inquire to what degree sounds emanating from the stage mask each other. Sometimes we are aware of an imbalance of sound in the concert hall. The inner voices in a symphonic work may be masked by the lower voices, or the vocal soloist may not be heard because the accompaniment is too loud. How do opera singers manage to be heard above the din of the orchestra, anyway? Sundberg (1977) compared the distribution of power in the frequency spectrum of the orchestra and the late tenor, Jussi Björling. He found that the intensity level of the orchestra falls off rapidly after peaking around 500 *Hz*, but Björling's voice showed a second peak at around 2,500 *Hz*, giving him an advantage of about 13 dB in that frequency range of upper harmonics.

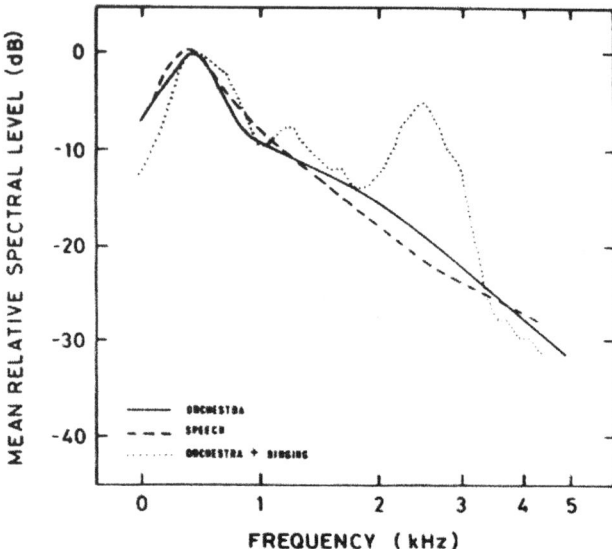

Fig. 14.2. Sound power of orchestra and tenor. A comparison of the frequency distribution of sound power of an orchestra (dashed line) and a tenor (dotted line) over a pitch range of 100 to 4,500 Hz. The curves are adjusted to have the same peak values. Orchestral sound power falls off steadily as the frequency is increased above 500 Hz. In comparison, the tenor's voice has a second peak of power between 2,000 and 3,000 Hz, which overcomes masking in this frequency range. Adapted from Sundburg, 1977.

Masking is also important in reducing the annoying distortions generated by audio equipment. Non-linearity in recording and playback is responsible for frequencies that were not present in the live music. If these frequencies are close to those present in the music (within a critical bandwidth), they are likely to be masked by the music. But if the distortions include frequencies at some distance from the frequencies of the music, they will not be masked, and they can be very annoying, even though the power of these distortions is low. Were it not for masking, a wider spectrum of distortion would be audible and annoying.

Why are low-pitched sounds better maskers than high-pitched sounds? To understand this, we must recall that there are varying loci of maximal displacements of the cochlear basilar membrane in response to varying frequencies of sound. Low frequency tones produce the broadest displacement of the basilar membrane, with a maximum displacement toward the apical end of the cochlea. In contrast, high frequency tones produce a more restricted displacement of the basilar membrane, maximally at the basal end of the cochlea, near the oval window. Since the wave of displacement is initiated at the basal end, the wave generated by a high frequency tone will excite just the basal receptors. But the wave generated by a low frequency tone must traverse the place of high tones to approach the place where low-frequency excitation occurs. As the wave of displacement initiated by low tones travels along the basilar membrane toward the apical end, we might expect that the excitation of the receptors at the basal end would interfere with the perception of high frequency tones. This is one theory why the low-frequency tone would affect the audibility of high-frequency tones, and not vice versa.

ATTENDING TO A MELODY

The world is full of so many things happening at the same time. Such a world should appear to be a blooming and buzzing confusion were it not for the fact that we can narrow our attention to a limited number of items. Many psychologists believe that we are able to attend to just one event at a time. If we focus on reading a book, for example, we cannot watch television at the same time. It is true that some of us can shift easily from one item to the other and so follow them both, but we actually pay attention to just one item at any given moment.

Motor activities are another matter. A number of activities can be engaged in at the same time. We can hold a conversation while driving a car, and plan the day while brushing our teeth. Some of us can play the guitar while singing. In these instances, however, one of the two activities is executed automatically, without thinking. Remember what it was like trying to talk while you were just learning to drive? Having to concentrate on driving does not permit you to do other things at the same time. Only if at least one activity is executed automatically can you engage in two activities at once. This is an important point, because a musical performance ordinarily involves more than one activity at a time. Think of the accomplished organist having to move his ten fingers as well as his feet, all at the same time; or the violinist stopping the strings with the fingers of his left hand while drawing the bow across the strings with his right arm. The secret of their success lies, in part, in the fact that these movements are executed auto-matically, without having to be planned or monitored step by step.

But it is the sensory examples that concern us here, not the motor ones. *Playing cards* vary in suit and value. Does the card player identify the suit and value at the same time? We speak of the 'ace of spades' rather than the '*jibble*,' suggesting that the identification is sequential, not instantaneous; first one dimension, then the other, not both at the same time.

Dichotic listening studies support this view. If two different messages are presented to the ears at the same time, one to the left ear and the other to the right, it is possible to shadow just one of the messages, and almost nothing is learned about the other. For example, it is possible to change the language of the message presented through the non-attended channel without the listener even being aware of it. This dichotic listening study, and others like it, support the view that our perceptual system has a limited handling capacity, so that just one channel is processed at a time. The perceptual system operates like a filter, routing some distinctive material through to consciousness and letting the rest fall by the wayside.

This raises an intriguing musical problem: how many melodies can we attend to at the same time? A large segment of the music literature is polyphonic, that is, more than one melodic line are played at the same time. Clearly the composer expects us to recognize all the melodic lines that he embedded in his musical texture. But is he justified? First we must inquire whether all the melodies are actually heard.

Let us assume that the music is played by a string quartet. If this is a first listening, the naive listener does not yet know what to listen for. Where is the melody? In one of the violin parts? In the viola or in the cello? Is there more than one melody being played at the same time? The composer resorts to attention-getting devices to cue his listener. For example, he frequently writes the melodic line in the highest register, because he knows that his listener is likely to focus his attention there. If you play the piano, try the following little experiment on your friends: play the melodic line of a well-known hymn, chorale or anthem in the lowest voice, adding the harmony in the upper voices. You will find that your friends will frequently fail to recognize the familiar melody. Try the same exercise on yourself with the aid of a piano-playing friend.

In the music of the Western world, the high-pitched instruments ordinarily state the themes; the subsidiary materials are usually relegated to the instruments of lower register. The right hand usually plays the melody on the piano; the left hand plays the harmony. This may be an arbitrary convention, but we should ask why this convention developed in the first place. One reason has to do with auditory masking.

Most listeners are attracted to the two outer lines of a piece of music: the highest and the lowest lines are the most salient, the highest comes first, then the lowest. The inner lines seem to be part of the texture of the music and are difficult to follow. The explanation usually offered is that the inner voices are partially masked by the higher and lower voices on either side of them. In contrast, the highest and lowest lines are partly protected from the effects of masking: nothing higher to mask the highest line and nothing lower to mask the lowest line. Though this explanation may be correct, it does not account for the saliency of the highest voice.

We noted earlier that low-pitched sounds are better maskers than high-pitched sounds. In a multi-voiced piece of music where masking can be expected to play an important role in the perceived organization, it is the higher-pitched tones that will be more audible than the lower-pitched tones because they are less subject to masking. Hence the perceptual prominence of the uppermost melodic line.

But there are other reasons for the prominence of the uppermost melodic line. First, low tones tend to reverberate longer, to persist in a 'live' room long enough to interact with the low tones that follow. This combination of sounds creates a muddy, low-pitched noise that renders the lower lines less discriminable. Second, we must not forget that the upper harmonics are responsible for the timbre of tones. For low-pitched instruments, these harmonics will overlap the range of high-pitched instruments and are likely to be masked. The harmonics generated by high-pitched instruments are not masked in the same way, for there is nothing at the high end to mask them. Finally, it is possible that experience with music that always carries the melodic line in the upper register has resulted in a learned disposition to pay attention to the higher pitches and organize them into a melodic whole.

Of course, a melodic line can capture the attention of the listener because it is distinctive in some way. It may be played louder than the other lines, for example, or in a very different pitch register. It may enter suddenly with a flourish, or it may introduce a new element into a repetitive and otherwise uninteresting texture.

How many melodies can we attend to at the same time? Perhaps just one when the music is unfamiliar. But, as we become acquainted with the strategies and tactics of the composer, we learn to respond to his cues and know when and where to listen for his melodies. Perhaps we never really hear more than one melody at a time. What we do learn in the face of multiple melodies is to shift our attention quickly and effortlessly from one melodic line to another, and gain the illusion of hearing a number of melodies at the same time. The contrapuntal texture that captures our fancy seems to be perceived in just this way.

ORGANIZING PRINCIPLES IN AUDITORY PERCEPTION

Anyone who has ever attended a cocktail party has noticed that he can hear what someone nearby is saying over the babble of others no farther away. It is a bit mysterious that we are able to do so. Sometimes, this is a matter of paying attention and listening to a particular voice. Sometimes we become aware, over the din of the party, that someone spoke our name. Though we have not been listening for this, it means that the sounds making up our name must have registered in the brain. It also means that, in order to be recognized, these sounds must have been organized and compared to the file of other names stored in the brain. Finally, it means that the sounds were salient and drew our attention.

Of course, there is more to the 'cocktail party phenomenon' than just paying attention. The most interesting aspect of it is how the sounds in the babble are organized so that meaning can be extracted. The gestalt psychologists, during the early part of the twentieth century, have studied this phenomenon most intensively in vision.

Here is a little experiment you can try on yourself. How would you describe the following display?

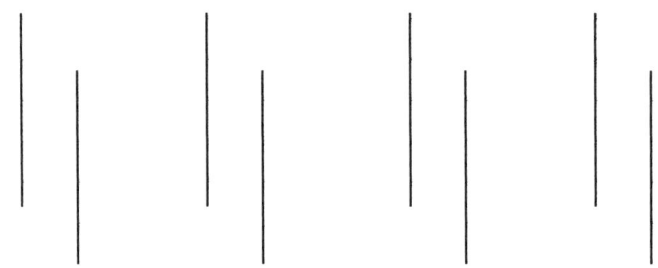

Did you describe the vertical lines as organized into four pairs? If you did, the gestalt psychologists would have invoked one of their laws of perceptual organization, the *law of contiguity* to account for the pairing in perception of the closer lines.

Now, shift your attention to the next display. What do you see now?

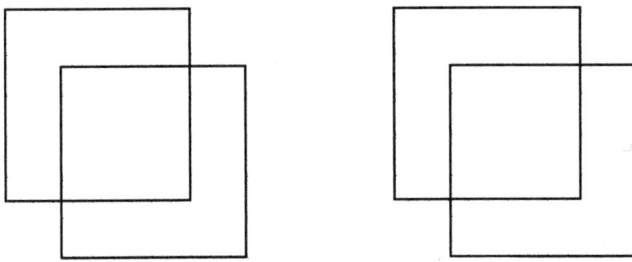

Though the very same eight vertical lines are present in this display, the perceptual organization has changed. Most viewers describe two sets of overlapping squares. What is important to note is that the vertical lines, the same lines described earlier as organized in four pairs, now stand apart. To account for this, the gestalt psychologists invoke another of their laws of perceptual organization, the *law of good figure*, which seems to override the law of contiguity.

Finally, shift your gaze to the next display. What do you see?

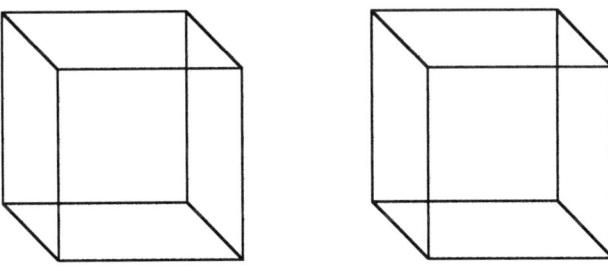

The very same eight vertical lines are present in this display, but the percept is now very different. Most viewers describe two isometric cubes, figures in three dimensions, and many viewers will notice periodic reversals in perspective. These are known as reversals of the *Necker cube*. These reversals provide further evidence of the contribution of the observer to perceptual organization and illustrate once again the gestalt principles of perceptual organization.

Now, let us return to the auditory modality and inquire whether there are laws of musical organization. For example, when *pitch* and *location* are available as organizational cues, which of the two is the more salient? Will the listener group musical sounds according to their location in space or by pitch? In nature, the location and the pitch of sounds often act together: sounds that come from the same place are likely to have a similar pitch. In 1975, Deutsch deliberately set the grouping cues of location and pitch in opposition to each other and found that pitch won out over location as the organizing principle. Listeners wearing stereo earphones were presented dichotically with two sequences of pitches simultaneously, one set of pitches to the left ear and another set to the right ear. These two sequences of sounds are illustrated in A of Fig. 14.3

Fig. 14.3. Deutsch's scale illusion. Shown above (A) are the two dichotically presented melodic lines. Shown below (B) is the reported perception of most subjects. This illusion can be heard only with earphones. Adapted from Deutsch, 1983.

What do listeners report hearing in the two ears? Not what is actually presented. The sounds are reorganized to be coherent in pitch, thus forcing a relocation in each ear. See B above. Most listeners report hearing, in each ear, a coherent ascent and descent of notes. Furthermore, the higher notes are usually reported in the right ear, and the lower notes in the left. Following the gestaltists, we might consider this illusion the result of the operation of a law of perceptual organization that we might call the *law of ascending and descending pitch*. A recording of this illusion can be found on the LP disc cited in the Note to Readers in the Prologue of this book. Of course, you will need stereo headphones to perceive this illusion.

RHYTHM

By musical rhythm we mean the arrangement of repetitive patterns of accents in a sequence of notes. Accents are given primarily by variation in intensity, but also by variation in duration, pitch and even timbre. These patterns are repeated over and over again, creating expectations in the listener. This is the essential feature of rhythm. How fundamental rhythm is in our system of music is indicated by the fact that we frequently succeed in recognizing familiar tunes that are tapped out, leaving only the rhythmic patterns as cues.

Tempo is an aspect of rhythm. It refers to the number of perceived elements, including pauses per unit time. It can be lively or slow. However, when tempo is too slow, rhythm tends to disappear.

Is there a natural or spontaneous tempo in music, one that seems easy and right? Surprisingly enough, it turns out that there is a preferred rate of finger tapping. Musical pulses at that preferred rate are relatively easy to execute and to remember accurately. The best evidence suggests that the preferred pace is about 1.3-1.7 per sec., which means that the beats are spread 0.6-0.75 sec. apart, on the average. This translates into a metronome setting of 80-100 beats per min. (in the *andante* range). At this tempo the listener makes his most accurate time judgments.

How does tempo influence rhythmization? A frequency of 8 elements per sec. seems to require grouping and a frequency of 0.8 per sec. is difficult to group. Rhythmic units or measures have a duration range of about 1.25 to 5.5 secs. Perhaps this reflects the 'phenomenal present' referred to by William James.

The two most fundamental rhythmic patterns are 2/1 and 3/1, | o o | and | o o o |:

| — -| — -| — -| — -| etc., two beats per bar.

| — --| — - -| — - -| — --| etc., three beats per bar.

The beat marked ' - ' represents unaccented movement, or the upbeat. The beat marked ' — ' represents the arrest of movement or the accented downbeat. If beats are played at equal tempos, as indicated above, the piece in duple time hits the downbeat more frequently than the piece in triple time. Conversely, the piece in triple time has more upbeats than the piece in duple time. Traditional dances such as the waltz and minuet are in triple time while the march is in duple time (or quadruple time). Up to 90% of notes in the works of composers like Beethoven and Bartok contain two note durations standing in that 2/1 ratio. So fundamental is that 2/1 ratio that the 3/1 ratio is frequently distorted and assimilated toward 2/1. This effect is well known to music educators who must teach their pupils to guard against the drift of a 3/1 rhythm to 2/1. For example, the biting rhythm of 'dotted eighth and sixteenth' (3/1): | ♪.♪ | is spontaneously transformed to the more bland 'quarter and eighth' triplet (2/1): | ♩ ♪ |. If you've had music lessons, you may remember the problem. Listeners, too, experience the drift from 3/1 to 2/1.

Rhythm is a universal experience in nature. All organisms perceive the rhythms of natural phenomena, such as the successions of day and night, and the seasons, all reflecting the movement of the planet. Even the periodic pulses of light and sound, that we call stimulus frequency (hue and pitch) might be viewed as sensory rhythms. All organisms also experience their own biological rhythms and those of others, such as the diurnal and nocturnal events associated with wakefulness and sleep; hunger and thirst; the variations in body temperature and glandular secretions; the more constant rhythms of heart beat and respiration; and the longer rhythms of menstruation, sexual activity, and even life and death. The term, 'circadian rhythm' was coined to encompass the regular recurrences of daily events.

How early in life can rhythmic activity be observed in the human baby? Voluntary rhythmic behavior is not seen until the child is able to sit unsupported and can grasp objects. By eight months, or so, the baby will engage in repetitive manual banging and babbling (echolalia) that seems rhythmic. However, we might debate whether there is a rhythmic intention in this behavior. Each repetition is executed as soon as the earlier one is completed and the sequence of repetitions is more or less fixed and not modulated in tempo. Because it takes roughly the same time to perform each repetition, a regular pulse seems to be generated. Before ascribing rhythmic intention to the baby, Sloboda (1985) suggests that the following behaviors be seen:

Active Listening   281

- The subdivision of a beat or regular pulse into two or more fractions.
- The omission of a beat, and resuming it after a pause without losing the meter.
- The imitation of a rhythmic pattern, or moving in time to the music. This last item is frequently observed by the time the baby is able to sit unsupported.

Once the child is running or even walking, a definite rhythmic pattern can be observed. Like the automatic rhythms found in nature, a temporal ordering of events is involved. But, now, the behavior is clearly voluntary or intentional. If we focus on the running of an animal like the horse, we may be struck by a remarkable feature of rhythm, namely, the periodic shift in the ordering of the events, as when the horse shifts from a two-beat trot to a three-beat canter. Like the curious shifts in the perceived patterns of floor tile, rhythm is subject to reversals of stress patterns.

How does the listener identify the rhythmic pattern in a piece of music? Usually by the stresses imposed by the composer and executed by the performer. These stresses are given by the regular variation of intensity, duration and pitch of notes, as noted earlier. The composer usually communicates his intention ahead of time by specifying the value or duration of each beat in the denominator of a fraction and the number of beats per rhythmic cycle (called a bar or measure) in the numerator. 3/4 time means three quarter notes in each measure. But, if the listener is presented with a series of equally accented notes of equal duration and pitch, then there is no sense in which the rhythm is said to be present physically. Under these circumstances, the listener is likely to impose some sort of rhythmic grouping of her own.

Thus, musical rhythm can be generated subjectively and idiosyncratically. Even when there is no variation in the sequence of sounds, such as the regular sounds of metronome beats, the listener imposes his own periodic accents. This seems to be a property of all perceptual systems that respond to temporal and spatial events.

Traditional Western music is limited, for the most part, to regular two-, three-, four- and six- beat rhythms. However, five- and seven- beat rhythms do appear in Western music as well, but they are usually treated as beat-complexes of alternating twos, threes, and fours: two- plus three- (or three- plus two-) alternating, to produce the five-beat rhythm; three- plus four- (or four- plus three-) alternating, to produce the seven-beat rhythm.

Sometimes the beat set by the composer is intricate and hard to determine with certainty, and the listener is likely to impose his or her own rhythm on the music. For example, as the pulse reaches faster and faster tempos, the listener combines successive pulses and follows a slower rhythmic pattern. Whenever there is ambiguity in the beat, the listener is likely to impose one. Sometimes we find ourselves imposing a rhythm, as on the drip, drip, drip, of a leaky water faucet.

To summarize, repeated sounds tend to be grouped even when the groupings are not based on objective variation of sound intensity or duration. An interesting property of these groupings is their reversibility. The tile floor of a bathroom seems to consist of repeated groupings and the groupings vary from time to time. An example of visual reversals in perspective was shown above under *Organizing Principles in Auditory Perception*. The figure changes in perspective though the stimulus does not vary. In the same manner, the rhythmic beat of a piece of music may vary, though the objective beat is unaltered. Listen to the clicking of a metronome, the periodic drip of raindrops or a leaky faucet, or the swiping of windshield wipers back and forth, and see if you don't naturally group the sounds in a variety of different ways. It is almost impossible to avoid imposing a grouping on repeated sounds.

On some of the older musical instruments such as the recorder and harpsichord, little or no dynamic variation is possible. Nevertheless, rhythmic accents can still be expressed, primarily through articulation and phrasing. For example, the stressed note can be held for its full length while the unstressed notes are released early. In the absence of notated stresses, the performer is responsible for indicating the rhythm of the piece.

There are a number of conventions that arose in early Western music regarding the distribution of stresses in a piece. The relationship between performer and listener depends on a knowledge of these implied rules that they share. Among these rules are the following:

- A stress is likely to occur at the beginning of a note, not some time later during the course of it.
- While unstressed beats may be subdivided into fractions of beats, stressed beats should not.
- Patterns of note duration (such as one long note followed by two short) tend to fall in the same part of the rhythmic cycle or measure, when repeated.
- Patterns of pitch (such as an ascending series of notes repeated every three notes) tend to subdivide by pitch pattern into rhythmic units.

These rules are part of the grammar of rhythm to which listeners in the Western world become accustomed. But they are frequently broken and this creates interest in the listener.

The dyadic relationship between speaker and listener depends upon a strict adherence to explicit rules. When communicating, both speaker and listener abide by the grammar of the shared language. The speaker's intention is to provide unambiguous messages, which the listener is supposed to interpret as intended. In music, the composer abides by a grammar in a looser sense. He creates expectations in the listener by following the rules for a time, and then thwarts the listener's expectations by breaking the rules. If a piece is generated totally by a grammar, it is likely to turn clichéd and dull as it proceeds. If the rules are violated in an intelligible way, the listener is more likely to be captured by the music. Examples of such violations in rhythm are the hemiola, syncopation, and cross rhythms when two or more voices are heard together.

Let us now consider subordinate groupings of beats. Each beat can be divided into units of two, three, and four, sometimes into five or six or more. But the overall rhythm remains the same. 6/8 time, where two beats in a measure are each divided into three, is an interesting case. Compare that with 3/4 time in which the three beats can each be divided into two. These two rhythms are actually equivalent in the total number of notes per measure, but the accent is different. During the baroque period, rhythmic interest was occasionally heightened by the hemiola which occurred when a measure or two of one rhythm (say, 6/8) appears in the context of the other rhythm (3/4). A hemiola is revealed in the following two illustrations:

6/8 | ♪♪♪ ♪♪♪ | ♪♪ ♪♪ ♪♪ |

3/4 | ♪♪ ♪♪ ♪♪ | ♪♪♪ ♪♪♪ |

Leonard Bernstein's memorable line from *West Side Story*, 'I like to be in America,' is an interesting example of a hemiola in modern music: | ♪♪♪ ♪♪♪ | ♩ ♩ ♩ |

If you see the accent in a measure shift from a note that is normally accented, like the first note in a bar, to one that is normally not, like the second, then you have an example of syncopation.

If the listener encounters music that lacks a definite rhythm, he is likely to extrapolate from the preceding meter and continue it as long as the music allows. Syncopation occurs when the stress is shifted to a beat that would not normally carry it, at a time when it is unexpected and could not be predicted on the basis of the previous beat. If the meter is to be heard as syncopation and not as a permanently changed meter, the listener must be persuaded not to abandon the previously established meter. Composers frequently exploit the listener's reluctance to abandon his expectations in order to create rhythmic interest.

The traditional rhythms of Western music tend to be relatively simple as compared to those of Africa and Asia. Occasionally, however, the beat set by the Western composer is more intricate and hard to determine with certainty, and the listener is likely to impose his own rhythm on the music. For example, as the pulse reaches faster and faster tempos, the listener combines successive pulses and follows a slower rhythmic pattern. Whenever there is ambiguity in the beat, the listener is likely to impose one.

To heighten musical interest, the composer may impose two different accent patterns at the same time. Performers sometimes have to struggle to execute such a rhythm accurately. For example, pianists must learn how to play the two hands together when one hand plays two beats while the other plays three. We call this poly-rhythm, two against three. To experience this struggle yourself, try slapping your left thigh twice with your left hand while slapping your right thigh three times with your right hand. You must start both hands together and end both hands together, repeating the pattern rhythmically, over and over again. It is not easy for the untrained, and it takes the piano student a while to get the hang of it. You may be helped by reciting the phrase, 'poor lit-tle girl' rhythmically and repetitively as you slap your thighs, coordinating each syllable with a slap. First, try three slaps with you right hand alone, reciting the phrase with accents on 'poor,' 'lit-,' and 'girl.' When you have mastered this, add two slaps with the left hand on 'poor' and '-tle.' Remember to slap both thighs at the same time whenever you recite 'poor.' Continue as follows:

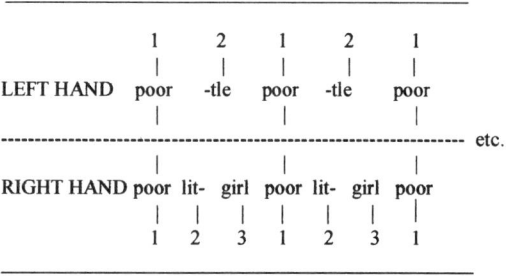

If you succeed, you might want to try another poly-rhythm, three against four. This time, recite the phrase, 'pass the bread and butter,' carefully coordinating each syllable with a slap. First try three beats with your left hand alone reciting the phrase with accents on 'pass,' 'bread,' and 'but-.' Make sure that 'bread' comes quickly after 'the,' and '-ter' comes quickly after 'but-.' When you have mastered this, add the right hand on 'pass,' 'the,' 'and,' and '-ter.' Both hands slap together on 'pass.'

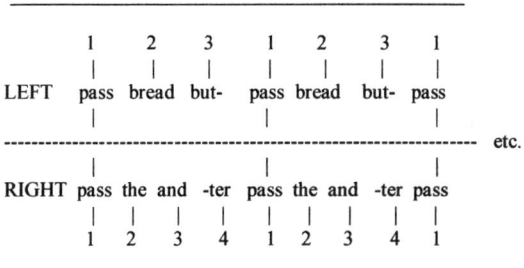

Want to try 'four against five'? See if you can find a ditty that will help you. If you can't, try the phrase 'sing a song of sixpence, Annie.'

In these examples, you are experiencing the motor rhythms of the performers, and those include the instrumentalist, the singer, the poet and, of course, the dancer. Mach (1865) placed motor activity at the center of the experience of rhythm.

Consider for a moment the codified rhythms of poetry. The metrical foot, corresponding to the musical measure, varies principally in twos and threes. The iamb is a metrical foot consisting of one unaccented syllable followed by an accented one:

("iambics march from short to long," Coleridge).

The trochee is the reverse: one accented syllable followed by an unaccented one:

(trochees speak in accents clear).

If the accented syllable is given a duration twice that of the unaccented syllable, these two meters turn out to be in triple time | ♩ ♩ | and | ♩ ♩ |.

In contrast, the dacyl and anapest each consist of three syllables. The dactyl has the accented syllable first followed by two unaccented ones:

— – –   — – –   — – –   —

(dactyls consist of one long and two short).

Finally, the anapest has two short syllables followed by one long:

– – —   – – —   – – —   – – —

(anapest is a need, to the poet give heed).

Again, by increasing the duration of the accented syllable, these two meters turn out to be in quadruple time | ♩ ♩ ♩ | and | ♩ ♩ ♩ |.

There seems to be a continuum in the realm of sound periodicity, ranging from a strict beat at one end, called isochronous repetition, and illustrated by the pulse of the body, the tick-tock of a clock and the click of a metronome. At the other end are the arrhythmias of random sequence, illustrated by the heart condition and certain compositions of modern music. Free verse lies toward this end of the continuum. It is interesting in this regard that a principal feature of Western rhythm is its inexorable repetition. With familiarity of the idiom, the accent is fully predictable and the succession is anticipated with pleasure.

To conclude, musical rhythm is largely a matter of the temporal ordering of tones and rests. Where repeated time intervals are of a precise length, the beat is consistent and predictable. The elements of rhythm are marked by differences in duration and loudness (or pitch and timbre) conferring periodic stresses or beats. This is the periodicity of 'objective rhythmization.' In addition, there is a contribution by the listener that renders rhythmic even the most accentless sequence of sounds. And this is 'subjective rhythmization.'

By the age of two or three months, the baby responds to rhythmic groupings, thus indicating that the *gestalt* laws of organization operate at that age or even earlier. It seems unlikely, then, that temporal and spatial organization depend upon the prior execution of voluntary activity, or even require motor accompaniment. There seems to be an innate quality to rhythmization.

Finally, regarding the enjoyment of music: we must conclude that enjoyment is enhanced when listening is active. There is no doubt that there is a virtual explosion of activity in the body and in the brain when listening to music. This activity organizes the sounds of the music into musical patterns, which can then be appreciated. The evocation of feelings is not the whole story in the esthetic experience. The activity of the brain contributes the knowledge that adds to the esthetic experience. In the end, we have to acknowledge that music is a science as well as an art.

Chapter 15

SOME PERFORMANCE SKILLS

TRANSCRIPTION

Composers sometimes transcribe for one instrument a piece of music that they originally wrote for another. A celebrated instance is the sonata that Cesar Franck originally wrote for violin which he later transcribed for the cello. Instrumentalists frequently transcribe a piece of music they admire so that they can play it themselves.

But transcription has a broader meaning. Transcription takes place when musical material presented in one mode, such as the auditory or visual, is reproduced in another mode, such as writing, singing or playing. Transcription from hearing to writing, singing or playing forms a good part of the active performance enterprise. These types of transcription are required in formal tests of musical aptitude or achievement. For example, how good are students at notating a melody or rhythm that they just heard played or sung? We will review these tests in Chapter 17.

Transcription from hearing to singing seems to be an innate and universal skill. It occurs when the parent, teacher or friend sings or plays a melody and the child copies it by singing it. Writing it down (musical dictation) and playing it on a musical instrument are examples of transcription skills that are acquired.

Transcription from notation to performance is ordinarily referred to as 'reading music.' Western children ordinarily learn to read music at the start of music lessons. Most professional musicians read the music in order to learn it on their instrument and frequently read the music during performance. However, many skilled musicians are able to memorize the music they wish to perform, and it is not uncommon to observe musicians glancing at their music only now and then during performance. These musicians use the notation to cue recall rather than to provide a full litany of the music. They are then free to communicate and coordinate by looking at each other.

Some music students learn their music without referring to the score, that is 'by ear.' In this case, the transcription is from hearing the music to playing it. The professional musician, though he is likely to be musically literate, may also choose to learn a piece by ear, but sometimes he has no choice because he is unable to read music. It is reputed that Ezio Pinza, the celebrated bass, never learned to read music with any facility. Apparently, he learned his vocal parts by ear, by listening to the music and by imitating it. Blind musicians, too, have proved that reading music is not an essential skill for the development of virtuosity. Although not the usual or efficient mode of learning music, many musically literate performers have to learn a piece by hearing it played because no score is available. Nevertheless, musical literacy should be required of all music students. Ideally all children should learn to read music notation as part of the curriculum in grammar school.

Listeners, too, must 'transcribe' the music in order to enjoy it. First of all, the music must register on listeners in order to be appreciated. Then, listeners must interpret the music. With successive exposures, they may commit it to memory. Listeners who are untutored in music seldom accurately retain the contour, intervals and rhythms of the music they heard. More likely, the music is fragmented, distorted and recombined in idiosyncratic ways, and listeners end up remembering something quite different from the original. It is sometimes quite amusing to hear children's rendition of a song that they learned in class, because of the distortions that result from incorrect registration and interpretation during group singing or recitation. Without the child really understanding what is being sung, the lyrics are apt to become garbled. Have you ever heard a child sing: "gladly the cross-eyed bear?" Or recite ". . . and lead us not into Penn Station?"

SIGHT-READING

Fluent sight-reading of music by the performer involves reading notes while in the process of executing other notes read earlier. A good sight-reader reads ahead, that is, he executes a series of notes as much as two or more seconds after he has finished reading them. How many notes can a good sight-reader execute after the score is removed from sight? That depends on the nature of the music, whether there are clichés in it (familiar patterns of sound that have been heard repeatedly, such as a scale or *arpeggio* passage) but six or seven notes certainly is not uncommon. Skill in sight-reading is facilitated by learning to 'chunk' the music into larger and larger units. Chunking is facilitated when there are familiar clichés in the music and deteriorates when the piece is written in an unfamiliar musical idiom. Like readers of text, fluent readers of music increase their reading span by improving their ability to organize and perceive superordinate structures. As the performer becomes more and more experienced in reading, he forms performance plans that he is able to execute without frequent cuing.

When learning a new piece of music, musicians typically pick up the contour of the music very quickly, though not the exact notes, which are encoded much more slowly. The fact that many sight-readers miss typographical errors indicates that they do not read every note (just as copy editors miss proofreading errors).

Musicians know that sight-reading is an essential skill. To play in a group, such as a quartet for the sheer fun of playing music together with others certainly requires sight-reading skill. Readers of literature do not have to practice their reading before they start to read a new book. Nor do they have to plod through the book with great effort, worrying all the while whether they got each word right. Yet many amateur musicians try to get by in an ensemble without any fluency in sight-reading music. The struggle to read each note takes much of the pleasure out of music making, and is an imposition on skilled sight-readers in the ensemble who must slow down to accommodate their unskilled colleague, and even repeat whole passages.

When we read a book, we ordinarily read it silently and, of course, we sight-read it. Since we ordinarily expect to read the book just once, we must learn to read the language fluently and with understanding. This means that we must extract the meaning from the words as we read, and go on. To achieve this level of competence, the child is subjected to an extended period of instruction.

By the time we are teenagers, reading an unfamiliar passage or text is no problem; we don't have to practice reading the passage in order to read it fluently. It is true that the pace varies depending on what we are reading: multiple ocular fixations slow us down; backtracking and rereading slow us down still further. Sometimes we have to review a passage because we didn't catch the meaning the first time and want to check whether we missed anything. When we read to ourselves, these variations in pace are normal and expected. But if we are required to read together in a group, we need to coordinate the pace with others. Timing becomes critical as, on the theater stage, actors must coordinate and cue each other.

Compare this with the reading of musical notation. Unless we have learned to sight-read, an unfamiliar passage poses problems. A quick succession of notes is difficult to read, and we have to practice the passage to play it in a satisfactory way. If we play by ourselves, we can tolerate delays, but not in an ensemble where coordination is essential.

Let us now review the circumstances that usually prevail when we learn to read music. Most children are required to learn to play a musical instrument at the same time as they learn to read music. The task is more demanding than most children can tolerate, and so they frequently fail to learn to read music fluently. And they frequently give up entirely. Some modern training methods, such as the *Suzuki* method of violin instruction, involve attaining a certain level of instrumental competence before the introduction of music notation. Another method, advocated here, involves learning to read musical notation by singing it before the musical instrument is begun. This method, called solfège, treats singing like speaking: you learn to speak before you learn to read. The voice is a built-in musical instrument requiring very little formal instruction on how to use it.

But the ultimate task is to read music and to perform in public in a competent manner. The only comparable linguistic task is the recitation of a fine piece of literature with emphasis on the sound of it, including nuance of voice, expression, rhythm, timing, etc. Most of us are rarely put in this position linguistically, yet many amateurs quite unrealistically expect to achieve it musically with little or no effort.

Chunking of musical notation has been examined by monitoring eye movements. The nature of the music dictates the direction of the eye movements. Contrapuntal music tends to elicit more horizontal movements, while homophonic music tends to elicit more vertical movements.

This raises the question, what constitutes a musical unit? The proficient reader has learned to chunk in larger and larger units. He can then scan a lengthy musical unit instead of having to sample a number of short musical units in haste. This is the optimal strategy for efficient sight-reading.

In our society, the contrast between learning to read English as a child and learning to read music is striking. Starting in infancy, we are subjected to an extended period of informal instruction in English. By the time we reach kindergarten, we have already learned a great deal about language. We understand speech, and we can already speak quite fluently. After three or four years of schooling, we have mastered silent reading, that is, we can sight-read text. We ordinarily read a book just once, and so we must learn to read fluently, with understanding. This means that we must extract the meaning from the words, phrases, and sentences as we read, and go on.

However children manage to acquire the skill, the ultimate aim is to read and to perform unfamiliar music in a competent manner. No normally seeing child should be permitted to learn to play a musical instrument without acquiring the skill of sight-reading.

IMPROVISATION

In some respects, improvisation is analogous to spontaneous speech. In the course of music making, a novel piece of music is generated on the spot, according to some explicit or implicit rules.

Excellence in improvisation results from having at one's fingertips a large repertoire of options to accomplish some end result, and being able to select one particular option rapidly, effortlessly, and even automatically. It is like fluent public speaking, or like rapid logical thinking. Each step in a series of acts depends upon the previous step, and one step leads to another. The less skilled improvisor makes false starts and meanders, not knowing where to proceed, as might an unpracticed public speaker. Sometimes he uses clichés to avoid embarrassing pauses, and the result is uninventive and uninteresting.

The good improviser is adventuresome, choosing from options that yield a less repetitive and more inventive effect. Some expert improvisers have a style that reflects the way they choose their options. And sometimes the improvisation serves as a vehicle for a display of virtuoso playing.

Many classical and romantic composers of the eighteenth and nineteenth centuries provided the performer with vehicles for improvisation, such as the *cadenza* of the concerto. Unfortunately, this skill seems to have been lost among modern musicians schooled in the classical tradition, for they tend to play the *cadenzas* that were written down by the celebrated performers of bygone days, such as the great violinist Joachim. Variations on a theme was another vehicle to display the talents of the improviser. And, during the sixteenth, seventeenth and eighteenth centuries, there was the ornamentation that the composer of baroque music frequently omitted in notation, meaning it to be added in an improvisational manner by the performer as he played the music. In the twentieth century, jazz musicians have revived the art of improvisation. To be a great jazz musician means to be able to improvise. Improvisation in a jazz ensemble depends on a style and a grammar of music more or less agreed upon by the participants.

MUSICAL EXPRESSION

To be successful, the musician must transport his audience on a wave of feeling. When he does this in a personal way, we call it expression or interpretation. This personal way of playing involves a subtle understanding of the music. The ingredients of expression are embedded in a precise way in which the music is played. What does the performer actually contribute, beyond that which is made explicit by the composer in his notation?

Which of the six principal dimensions of musical tones -- pitch, loudness, timbre, duration and articulation -- are varied during the interpretation of a musical piece? On keyboard instruments, pitch and timbre are fairly well fixed. No variation in key depression will affect these two dimensions in any significant way. It must be the variation in loudness, duration and articulation that the keyboard artist depends on to shape his/her musical phrase. Compare this to the singer and string players, who have available all six dimensions for the expression of feeling and interpretation. In addition to loudness and duration, nuances in pitch and timbre are available to shape the musical phrase. But for the most part, it seems clear that all musicians depend on variation in loudness, duration and articulation to confer a unique shape to the music.

The modern music synthesizer provides a valuable lesson on the nature of musical expression and interpretation. Electronic music is a very analytic art. Whatever features are heard in synthesized music must have been put there deliberately by the composer. There is no room for expression in an inanimate sound source, except to the degree that a prescription for it has been included in the compositional program. And then, of course, it will be repeated verbatim every time the piece is played.

Beyond virtuosity, expression is what distinguishes the outstanding instrumentalist and vocalist. The teacher is frequently puzzled as to how this is to be conveyed to the budding musicians. It is common for the teacher to exhort the student to imitate him or her: "Let me show you what it should sound like." Unfortunately, sheer mimicry stifles the development of individuality of expression.

In the case of wind and bowed instruments, non-linear mechanisms are responsible for the quality of tones, and here the musician and instrument are so intimately coupled that it is impossible to separate musical expression from the timbre of the instrument. Once again, the synthesizer is devoid of musical feeling, and cannot express itself in a creative way. The composer of electronic music must write expression into the composition if the music is not to sound mechanical. But, even with such a prescription, the piece will never possess the spontaneity and freshness of human creative expression.

It is true that synthesizers of electronic music have helped us understand expression a little better. It is the tiny variations in dynamics, timing, attack and decay (envelope) and even pitch that are responsible for the individuality of musical expression.

Attempts to synthesize the sound of the violin have revealed that vibrato plays a large role in generating musical feeling. Vibrato ordinarily grows in depth and frequency with increasing duration of the tone; also there is a tendency to let the notes grow in loudness as they are sustained, and then to ebb. In synthesizing piano tones, it was discovered that the attack must be gate-limited. Otherwise, once triggered, the tone will always complete its course, giving the note the same attack regardless of the length of time the key is depressed. The use of the envelope generator has revealed how important the attack and decay times are in generating specific timbres. As noted earlier, the piano tone has a swift attack and a gradual decay. Reverse the tape recording of such a tone so that there is a gradual attack and a swift decay, and you lose completely the piano quality of the tone.

Rhythm

Observing the rhythm of a piece of music is a very important performance skill. Without this skill, musicians cannot play in ensembles. The reader is referred to Chapter 14 on Active Listening for an extended consideration of rhythm as an attribute of music.

On Musical Notation

Musical activity must have had distinct survival value for people of the ancient world. Before the development of writing, music provided a mnemonic framework for the storage of knowledge, information and events. With the aid of sing-song and rhythmic gestures, preliterate people were able to form a repository of knowledge. Such ritualized sequences of behavior are easier to remember than those dry accounts later recorded in chronicles. The epics, myths and tales of the ancient world were thus codified in a vocal and gestural tradition. These were the mnemonic devices that evolved into song and dance as we know them today.

But with the invention of chronicles, it became clear that music too should be notated in order to preserve it and the church Fathers fostered that development. We have already seen in Chapter 2 that Guido of Arezzo took the initiative.

Words and symbols in musical notation: There are four principal qualities of musical sounds: pitch, duration, loudness and timbre. By tradition, words describe two of the four qualities, loudness and timbre. The other two, pitch and duration, require those special musical symbols we call notes. With a combination of words and symbols, then, the composer is able to specify all four qualities for the benefit of the performers who must carry out his or her dictates; otherwise, performers must imitate the playing of others in order to learn a musical piece.

Pitch is the quality of sound that is described as 'high' or 'low.' The octave seems to be the basic interval of pitch perception. When singing a melody, men and women usually sing an octave apart, automatically, without any special instruction. To many of us they sound like they are singing 'in unison.'

The duration of a note is its length in time. The unit of duration is the beat, or perceived pulse of the music. Tempo refers to the rate at which beats occur, fast or slow; and meter is the accented organization of beats, as in three-quarter time (ONE, two, three; ONE, two, three).

The loudness of a sound is based upon its intensity. Loudness is usually notated by abbreviating the Italian words for loud, soft, and medium: '*f*' for *forte*; '*p*' for *piano*; and '*m*' for *mezzo*. Though theoretically continuous, the dimension of loudness ranges in discrete steps in musical notation from '*pppp*' which is very soft, through '*ppp*' '*pp*' '*mp*' '*mf*' '*f*' '*ff*' '*fff*' and '*ffff*' which is very loud. It is very important not to confuse loudness with intensity. Loudness is a perceptual dimension (the sound level we hear), while intensity is a physical dimension (the sound level that is produced). The decibel scale is a scale of intensity, not of loudness. Since it is a logarithmic scale, a small increase in decibels means a large increase in intensity. For example, 60 decibels means 1,000,000 times the intensity of a barely audible sound. For one listener, 60 dB of intensity might be quite loud, but for another with less acute hearing 60 dB might be quite soft. And none of us will hear a sound played at 60 dB that is outside the audible frequency range, 20-20,000 *Hz*. Since the dB scale of intensity will not do for loudness, psychologists have devised scales of loudness, like the '*phon*' and '*sone*' scales, but they are of no consequence in reading music. (In the audio industry, the intensity level control is frequently labelled '*volume*.' Psychologists adopted this term in the 1930s to describe an alleged fifth quality in music, which listeners were able to judge with some consistency. Experiments have shown that the quality of *volume* in music is a joint function of frequency and intensity: sounds lower in pitch and louder have a greater *volume* than sounds higher and softer. Furthermore, a high and loud sound might have the same *volume* as a lower and softer sound. Considering this history of the term *volume*, it is misleading for manufacturers of audio equipment to use that label for a control that varies intensity alone. It is especially misleading because switching on the traditional *loudness control* on a preamplifier *reduces* the bass response as *volume* is increased. Manufacturers should drop the term *volume* for the knob that controls intensity and replace it with *intensity level* or some equivalent.)

The dynamic changes in a musical composition refer to the transient shifts in loudness and accent during the piece. Sometimes a passage gets progressively louder up to a certain point and then returns to its original level. This is the *crescendo*, shown by the symbol over the relevant notes ◁▭▭▭▭▭▭ ▭▭▭▭▭▭▷ and the *diminuendo*. If a single note needs to be accented, a small version of the crescendo symbol is placed directly over that note ♩.

Timbre is perhaps the most complicated dimension of music. It refers to the color and richness of the sound, its harmonic structure and envelope. Timbre distinguishes a cello playing a sequence of pitches from a baritone singing the same sequence. The vowels of speech also vary in timbre ('oo' vs. 'ah,' for example). In traditional musical notation, the composer indicates the timbre of sound simply by specifying the instrument, the voice, or the syllable.

Today, we hear new and unfamiliar timbres, created by modern sound synthesizers. These timbres are difficult to notate because the harmonic composition of each tone of a piece has to be specified individually. Composers of new timbres, like Pierre Boulez in Paris, are struggling with this problem today.

Duration is specified by the stem of the note, and whether it is blacked in or not. Traditionally, the basic unit of duration, or beat, is the quarter-note, represented by a blacked-in note with a stem ♩. Half notes are twice as long as quarter notes, represented by an open note with a stem ♩. Whole notes are twice as long again, represented by an open note without a stem 𝅝. The shorter notes are formed by adding tails to the stem: eighth notes are half as long as quarter notes and look like quarter notes but with a single tail added to the stem, ♪. Each additional tail divides the duration in half: for example, ♪ with two tails is a sixteenth note. A dot beside the note adds half as much to its duration. For example ♩. is equal to ♪♪♪ and ♪. is equal to ♬♬♬.

The numerical fraction found at the start of a composition is its meter or time signature. The fraction 3/4 indicates that three quarter-notes (or their equivalent) are found between successive bar lines, e.g., | ♩♩♩ | ♫♫♫ | ♬♬♬ |. The fraction 6/8 indicates that six eighth-notes (or their equivalent), are found between successive bar

Performance Skills

lines, e.g., | ♫♫ ♫♫ |. As you can see, eighth notes are frequently grouped by connecting their tails: 6/8 meter consists of six eighth-notes organized to two groups of three eighth notes each, showing that there are two beats in the bar, | ♫♫ ♫♫ |. In contrast, 3/4 meter may also consist of six eighth notes but this time they are in three groups of two, |♫ ♫ ♫|. In Renaissance and Baroque music, such a change of meter during a piece, for a bar or two, is called a *hemiola*.

The anthem *My Country 'tis of Thee* is notated below to show the time signature and the beats in each bar. In this example, the overall tempo of the piece is specified at the beginning by the Italian word, ADAGIO, which means *at a slow pace*. Here again, discrete steps of tempo are specified with words, usually in Italian. The most important, in order of slowest to quickest are, *largo* (slow and broad), *lento* (slow), *adagio* (slow, but at ease), *andante* (walking pace), *moderato*, *allegretto* (moderately fast), *allegro* (fast and cheerful), *presto* (very fast), *prestissimo* (as fast as possible). Sometimes the tempo markings are in other languages, like *nicht schnell* (not fast) or *tres vite* (very fast). Not infrequently, composers resort to metronome markings for accuracy of tempo, like '60' which means 60 beats per minute (a fast *largo*); '100' (a fast andante); and '160' (a fast allegro). However, this accuracy sacrifices character and style, which can only be expressed linguistically (as in *allegro vivace* or *andante cantabile*).

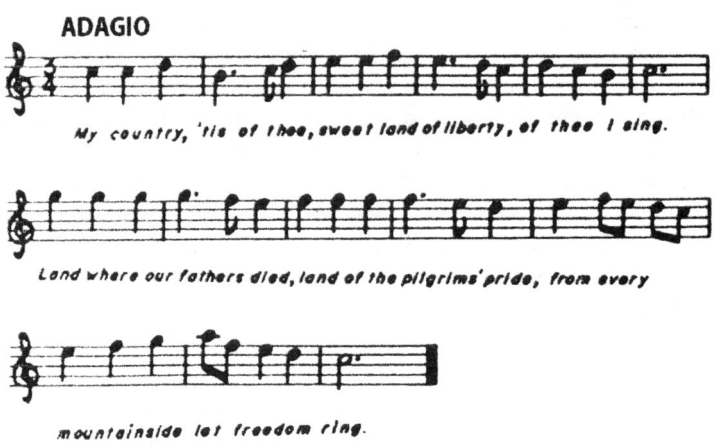

Fig. 15.1. The musical notation of the anthem America *or* My Country 'tis of Thee. *Music by Henry Carey. Lyrics by Samuel Francis Smith.*

Pitch notation and the great staff: Though there are theoretically an unlimited number of pitches, composers of Western music have a limited pool of pitches to choose from for their compositions. On the piano, the octave contains 12 different pitches and the octave is repeated 7 1/3 times to yield exactly 88 discrete pitches. These and only these are available to composers of keyboard music.

The 12 different pitches in the octave are frequently referred to as the chromatic scale. When seven of the 12 are selected, we refer to the diatonic scale, major or minor (see Chapters 11 and 12 for a discussion of the musical scale). Familiar melodies like *Frère Jacques*, *Three Blind Mice*, and *Yankee Doodle* are composed of these particular pitches. The English names given to the seven different pitches of the diatonic scale are derived from the first seven letters of the alphabet, A, B, C, D, E, F, G. They are the same notes octave after octave, that is to say, there is a C in every octave, a D in every octave, etc.

In the musical score, the up-and-down motion of a melody is represented graphically by the position of notes on a staff of lines and spaces (see the notation of *My Country tis of Thee*, in Fig. 15.1). The convention is to use a staff limited to five lines and six spaces (four between the lines, one above the staff, and one below). Together, the lines and spaces provide for 11 different notes, which frequently suffice for the range of the untutored voice and the popular song. If the range of pitch exceeds 11 different notes, ledger lines can be added above and below the staff. With three ledger lines added below the staff and three above, almost three octaves of notes can be accommodated, enough for most musical instruments.

However, instruments vary widely in their pitch registers. As extreme examples, the bass viol plays in a low register while the violin plays in a high register. These registers do not overlap and the same five lines of the staff cannot accommodate both instruments. If only there were a way to have just five lines represent different registers for different instruments: low for the bass viol and high for the violin!

The problem is solved with the aid of the great staff, a system of 11 lines and 12 spaces, and seven signs or *clefs*. The uppermost five lines, called the treble staff, always starts with the treble *clef* 𝄞. This *clef* is really a fancy G, and its curlicue indicates that the note on the second line is G above middle C. This staff of five lines provides for the highest range of pitch. The lowest five lines, the bass staff, always starts with a bass clef, 𝄢. This is really a fancy 'F': the two dots are the cross-bars of the F and are positioned on either side of the fourth line, which is the F below middle C. The '*clef*' (French for 'key') tells the musician which five lines he is to read, the upper or the lower. The violinist will find his music notated on a treble staff of five lines, while the bass viol player will find his music notated on a bass staff of five lines. Those of you who know the names of the five lines as E,G,B,D,F, and the spaces as F,A,C,E, should now realize that these names refer to the treble staff only, not to the bass staff or to any other staff described below.

Keyboard instruments require the entire great staff to accommodate their wide range of pitch. The piano range is from the A, over three octaves below middle C, all the way up to the C, four octaves above middle C. For such a wide range of pitch, the piano requires not just 11 but 26 lines! This is accomplished by using as many as six ledger lines below the great staff, and nine ledger lines above, to accommodate the lowest and highest pitches (see Fig. 10.11). The middle line of the great staff on which middle C appears is omitted, unless middle C is notated, in which case a ledger line is used between the staves. Look at a piano score and you will see two sets of five lines, the upper set beginning with the treble *clef* and the lower beginning with the bass *clef*. A bracket at the very beginning connects the two sets. The space between is meant to accommodate the ledger line for middle C.

Fig. 15.2. The seven clefs. How the five-line staff is derived from the Great Staff. Each clef specifies five adjacent lines derived from the great staff of 11 lines.

Like the bass viol and the violin, other non-keyboard instruments, including voice, require just five lines of the 11 for notation.

But the registers of musical instruments differ, and this dictates which five lines of the 11 are required.

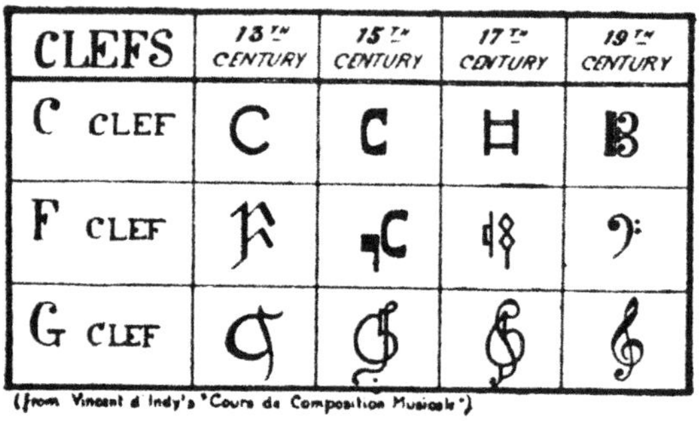

CLEFS	13TH CENTURY	15TH CENTURY	17TH CENTURY	19TH CENTURY
C CLEF	C	C	H	B
F CLEF	⨍	⌐C	⨅	𝄢
G CLEF	⊂	⌀	𝄞	𝄞

(from Vincent d'Indy's "Cours de Composition Musicale")

Fig. 15.3. The evolution of the three symbols that make up the seven clefs. According to Vincent D'Indy.

Instruments and voices with intermediate registers require five intermediate lines. The particular five lines are selected to minimize the need for ledger lines. Consider the viola as an example. Its lowest note is the C one octave *below* middle C. By using the treble *clef*, as many as four ledger lines are required below the staff. Instead, viola music is written using the middle five lines of the great staff. The alto *clef* 𝄡 is the sign at the beginning of this staff of five lines, indicating that middle C is on the middle line; that the lowest line is F below middle C; and the topmost line is G above middle C. The alto *clef* really represents a fancy 'C' that indicates that the middle line is middle C.

There are three additional C-*clefs*, each specifying another set of five lines drawn from the great staff: the soprano *clef* specifies that the first line is middle C; the mezzo-soprano *clef* specifies that the second line is middle C; and the tenor *clef* specifies that the fourth line is middle C. There is also one additional F-*clef*, the baritone *clef*, which specifies that the third line is the F below middle C.

In this way, any adjacent five of the 11 lines can be selected to best accommodate the range of any instrument or voice. Shown above are the 11 lines of the great staff and, on them, the seven *clefs*: treble, soprano, mezzo-soprano, alto, tenor, baritone, and bass, that indicate which five of the 11 lines are to be read. If an 8 appears immediately above or below the treble or bass clef, the notes are to be read exactly one octave above or below those written.

Having concluded our survey of some essential performing skills, let us now ask what recommendations have been made as to how these skills can be acquired efficiently.

Chapter 16

MUSICAL TRAINING

Children everywhere possess the basic abilities to engage in musical activities. As long as they can hear and sing, and as long as they can respond emotionally, they can be taught to play a musical instrument. Of course, not every child can become a virtuoso. But every child can become a competent musician. The differences between children lie principally in the realm of motivation. Whether children crave to engage in musical activities depends upon their temperament and upbringing. Only those children who are adequately motivated will endure the hard work that is required to become a competent musician.

THE IMPORTANCE OF EARLY TRAINING

There are many reasons why young children should be encouraged to engage in musical activities. Music is part of the cultural heritage of the human species and it provides a great deal of pleasure to both children and adults alike. Music is also a valuable means of communication between individuals and deserves to be taught just as the child is taught to speak and read his or her native tongue. One reason that has been overlooked has to do with the need of the child to develop feelings of competence and control.

Learning that what you do has an effect on you and on your environment is a lesson that is important to all children from infancy on. The effect or consequence may be instantaneous, as when:

- you let go of an object and it falls down (the balloon and kite are novelties in this regard)
- you strike a mobile in the course of trying to grasp it and it moves
- you blow air through your vocal cords and you hear a sound
- you touch a part of your body and you feel a tactile sensation

The effect or consequence may also be delayed as when:

- you call for attention and you have to wait to get it
- you eat and you eventually feel sated
- you reach for an object, feel it, and eventually grasp it

This is how a child learns that he can gain control over his environment. One of his first lessons is that crying in an attempt to relieve the gastric discomfort of an empty stomach gets him the bottle. His actions have consequences.

But consider the child who is offered the bottle in anticipation of his crying. In this instance, he never gets to cry and does not experience the feeling of control. Bettelheim has argued that repeated experiences of affecting the environment are essential for the normal development of personality. The child whose every need is anticipated is a child who is deprived of the experience of gaining control. Beware the oversolicitous parent. He or she may be responsible for raising a child who grows up to be passive and unresponsive. With such rearing practices, the danger is that the child will learn that nothing he does seems to have any consequences.

Singing and playing a musical instrument are activities that produce immediate consequences. What a pleasant way to learn this lesson: first and foremost, there is the feedback of hearing the sounds produced. Then there is the bonus of satisfaction if the sounds are pleasing. And finally, there is the further reinforcement that comes from approbation and applause. Musical activity is a pleasant way to experience competence and control, and it should be encouraged for that very important reason.

LEARNING SOLFÈGE IN CHILDHOOD

To create sounds on a keyboard instrument such as the piano requires no more than the trivial act of depressing a series of keys. The piano quality of tones is determined by the acoustic and mechanical properties of the instrument and very little by the way the keys are depressed. The performer does not have to know how the piano works in order to play it. A piano note will always sound more or less the same as long as the key is struck each time in the same way and the piano is not damaged or modified. Nevertheless, it takes years of training and arduous practice to achieve proficiency on the piano.

Consider how complex the task when the child, otherwise untutored, begins to play the piano. Here are some examples of the knowledge and skills that need to be mastered:

- the position of the keys; their relative distances along the keyboard; the difference between white and black keys, and their names
- the need to strike the keys with specific fingers the coordination of the fingers of each hand,
- the coordination of the two hands
- the posture of fingers, trunk and legs

This is just a sampling of problems specific to the piano. To these, we must add the problems that the child will encounter no matter what instrument he chooses to play:

- reading musical notation and transcribing it into a musical performance
- music theory including the major, minor and chromatic scales, the circle of fifths, etc.
- the appreciation and performance of duple, triple, and quadruple time
- the execution of the requirements specified by the musical notation, the pitch, loudness and rhythm of the piece; all at one time
- the understanding of musicality, including the syntax of phrasing and dynamics

Taken together, these requirements form a highly complex task that taxes even the most gifted children to the very limits of their capacity. Put in the situation of having to learn it all at once, most children experience 'task overload,' an inability to cope with all of it because the going is rough and early successes are very modest, at best. Most children do not find it easy to tolerate delayed gratification, but the complexity of the task demands it. To make matters worse, it is well recognized that immediate reinforcement facilitates learning. How can the child accept praise from his elders when he knows full well, from the auditory feedback that he received, that his performance left much to be desired?

Many piano teachers recognize this problem and try to divide the task into manageable proportions, but the progress is slow and the feedback is, at best, marginally gratifying. If only there were a way to delay having to cope with the complexities of the musical instrument in order to focus on the skills common to all instruments. We will see that there is.

Try to match a note within your vocal range with one given to you by someone else. Unless you are tune (or tone) deaf, you will probably succeed quite well, without having to search all over your vocal range for the note. Choir members learn how to retain a tonal standard given to them by the choir leader or accompanist before the start of a song. A good singer will sing accurately even after many seconds of waiting to start the song, indicating that a vocal adjustment had been made.

To succeed, you need to adjust your vocal cords and the shape of your vocal passages before you let the air pass from your lungs through your lips. How did you manage to do it? Did you have to think about making the adjustment? Unlike the keys of the piano, or the strings over the fingerboard of the violin, your vocal cords are invisible to you; they always have been and they always will be. This means that the tension of the vocal cords cannot be adjusted with the aid of vision. Neither is auditory feedback required, since the adjustment of vocal cords (at least, the gross adjustment) is completed before you hear yourself sing.

If both vision and hearing are not required, what cues remain to guide us to a proper adjustment of the vocal apparatus? The best guess is that it is the sensation of stretch from the muscles in the vocal apparatus. It is the same stretch of muscle spindles and receptors in the joints that athletes use to set their muscles at the start of a sporting event and to monitor their performance as it unfolds. Some of us seem to need no special training to pay attention to these motor-feedback cues. This is illustrated by the untutored child who is able to throw a ball more or less accurately the first time he tries. Others of us seem to have little or no talent for these motor adjustments. Part of the difficulty seems to lie with the inability to pay attention to motor-feedback cues.

Singing seems to come naturally to most children. We have this biologically given musical instrument that can be used as a vehicle to acquire many of the skills needed to play a human-constructed musical instrument. By the age of four, most children are able to hum a tune more or less accurately. By the time he or she has begun to read, the child is able to sing songs tolerably well without any special tuition. Children's choirs show how successful this enterprise can be. Why not use the voice of the child as the initial instrument to acquire many of the skills necessary to play a musical instrument? This is not a novel idea. Such a program has been in existence in the form of *solfège* for many years, particularly in Europe.

It is difficult to understand why singing is neglected in American homes and schools. Modern educational priorities simply exclude music and the other arts as routine activities during the early grades. If the child begins early, he can learn to sing as he learns to talk, and he can learn to read music as he learns to read English. All children are eager to learn to talk and read. Very few need to be persuaded. This is because language learning begins early. By the same token, no child should have to be persuaded to learn to sing and to read music. When the time comes to start learning a musical instrument, at the age of seven or eight, many of the musical skills listed above would already have been mastered. The child is now free to enjoy playing his musical instrument without being overwhelmed by the complexities of the task. Many children would be able to sit down at the piano and play without much coaching at all.

The curriculum suggested here follows that published by André Gedalge in 1924. His ten booklets of delightful solfège exercises and music theory, *L'Enseignment de la Musique*, can be closely followed or can be used as a model. An instructor, seated at the piano for the most part should conduct formal solfège classes of 10-15 children. One or two three-quarter hour sessions per week will suffice. The aim of the instructor is to teach the children to sight-read musical notation using the voice as the musical instrument.

In the course of this 'ear training,' the child learns the great staff, notes and rests, dynamic markings, major and minor scales including the difference between tone and semitone, to read by interval and to sing specific intervals on demand (that is, to acquire relative pitch), chromaticism, rhythms of duple, triple, and quadruple time, including the dotted note, slurring and syncopation. A feature of this method is learning to read notes on a staff without a clef in order to foster reading by interval. As he masters this skill, the child is able to read all seven clefs (see Chapter 15) without special training on each clef alone.

To be admitted into the class, the child must show that he has a small repertoire of songs, learned in school or at home, and that he can sing them more or less accurately. He must also show that he can imitate short phrases of an unfamiliar melody more or less accurately. And he must be able to read English at an early grade level. That is all. No prior musical instruction is required or even recommended. Most children can meet these requirements by the age of seven or eight years.

At the completion of such a course of instruction in *solfège*, each child will be sight-reading three-part rhythmic melodies written in any of the seven clefs and involving any number of sharps and flats. Not only that, he will be having a lot of fun at it. After a year of instruction, each child will be ready to begin playing a musical instrument.

In the twentieth century, three other European methods of musical instruction for young children have been introduced into the American musical scene: those of Emile Jaques-Dalcroze, Zoltan Kodaly and Carl Orff. These methods are related, though each has its own stated purposes and practices. Both Kodaly and Orff have been influenced by Dalcroze and both recognize their close mutual relationships. Kodaly has visited the Orff institute in Salzburg and leaders of the Orff and Kodaly movements have exchanged ideas in Europe and America. Though the hand signs that are basic to Kodaly's method of teaching note reading were originally observed in England, the body movements that have proved to be such useful components of Orff's method were first introduced by Dalcroze. Finally, the Suzuki method of early violin instruction, first introduced in Japan, represents another approach to musical education. All four methods deserve to be reviewed and evaluated.

Dalcroze and Eurhythmics

Early in his career, around 1910, Dalcroze struggled with the fact that his pupils experienced difficulties in performing rhythms correctly even though the physical movements of daily life were executed in easy and smooth rhythmic fashion. The prevailing view had it that one must learn the mathematical relations of time symbols in order to learn rhythm. The teacher shows how the whole note can be subdivided into two halves or four quarters, just as a pie can be subdivided. He explains that a half note plus two quarter notes equals one whole note, and that a dotted eighth note plus a sixteenth note equals four sixteenths or one-quarter note. These are exercises in arithmetic, however, and teachers should not have been surprised that there was little or no carry-over to the understanding and execution of musical rhythm. Yet many teachers were grieved to discover that so many of their pupils could not manage rhythms any better than before they received this instruction.

Out of these observations of failures in instruction grew Dalcroze's method of music training, based on the idea that musical rhythms originate in the natural rhythms of the human body -- locomotion, heart rate, respiration, etc. Dalcroze insisted that rhythm must be taught as movement, not as arithmetic. Every child responds physically to music heard or sung and these responses need to be fostered and channeled. Today, many people refer to this method as eurhythmics but in this system of instruction the pupil also studies singing, ear training, harmony, counterpoint, form and analysis, and music history and participates in vocal ensembles. In short, he acquires all the skills offered in a comprehensive program of musical instruction.

The Dalcroze method begins with three areas of study: *solfège*, aimed at developing an ear for intervals and learning to read music; improvisation, aimed at developing the ability to invent music freely and to express oneself; and eurythmics, aimed at developing a feeling for musical rhythm through body movements.

At the same time, the Dalcroze method represents a thrust toward comprehensive musicianship. Dalcroze recognized the limitations imposed by the subdivision of musical studies into arbitrary parts. Instead, he sought to synthesize and relate experiences derived from composition, performance, analytic listening and theory. He fostered musicianship that included not only accuracy in performance of the musical score, but also a sensitive expression and interpretation involving dynamics, phrasing, nuances, and shading. At the same time, he discouraged starting a musical instrument before many aspects of musical training had been initiated.

According to Dalcroze, rhythm is of primary importance in early musical experiences. The pupil is also exposed to dynamics and tempo from the very first lesson. Pitch and texture are added quickly thereafter. Through body movement, the pupil experiences the symmetry and the tension of the musical phrase, the qualities of the rising and falling of pitch, the feeling of greater and lesser intensity, the pull of the music, etc. Dalcroze was especially concerned that instrumental study not be initiated before ear training and the exposure to rhythmic movement are well under way. In his view, an amateur should learn music rhythm and experience improvisation before he touches a musical instrument.

Dalcroze emphasized learning in groups. There are distinct advantages when pupils get together to experience musical sounds. Rhythmic body movement in particular lends itself to group expression, in open spaces where visual as well as auditory experiences can be had. Few textbooks need be used. Many of the principles of music theory, form and vocal expression are learned through active participation.

The teacher's ability to improvise on the piano is essential. This includes the ability to create a feeling, through music, for each movement, since pupils must learn to let music move their whole bodies. The music must be appropriate for each quality of movement, to teach *crescendo*, or *largo*, or *staccato*, or the rise and fall of the musical phrase.

Eurhythmics can be presented in the classroom to teach practically every aspect of music. Even exercises in *solfège* and improvisation are introduced through rhythm. Standard classroom percussion instruments such as sticks, wood blocks, triangles, tambourines and drums are offered to adults as well as to children. With rhythmic movement as the basic mode of instruction, musical concepts such as melody, harmony, dynamics, form and phrasing are gradually internalized. Actualizing the music as it is heard is essential for musical comprehension, and rhythmic movement is the means by which the flow of music is realized. Students of the Dalcroze method are taught that rhythm is really motion, and they learn to hear motion in music.

Here is an illustration of what takes place in a Dalcroze class when the lesson is *'accelerando.'* The teacher builds the concept gradually in the mind and in the body of the pupil. The process may begin with the movements of a person in the act of gaining speed. These movements can be executed first without music, for they are movements familiar in daily life. Then the pupil listens to music in which the *accelerando* is unmistakable, and he is likely to discover that the movement in the music corresponds to what he has just executed. He will then synchronize his movements to the music. In this way, the meaning of *accelerando* is built into mind and muscle, all before the pupil has laid a hand on a musical instrument. Later, when the pupil is introduced to the notated symbol for *accelerando,* he will feel it in his muscles, and he will be able to improvise music using *accelerando* as an ingredient.

Another principle of the Dalcroze method is that time, space and energy are interrelated as are tempo, dynamics and pitch. By synchronizing his movements with the music he hears, the pupil experiences these interrelationships. For example, the pupil realizes a crescendo by walking in a crouched position, first on his toes, taking small steps initially and gradually stepping more forcefully, stretching upward and forward, and finally increasing his stride to his limit.

In eurhythmic classes, students move freely to music improvised by the teacher. In bare feet and loose clothes, class members walk, skip, run and leap through imaginative movements that are evoked by the music. There is a spontaneous quality to the movements for they are not prescribed. The teacher encourages individual interpretation so that each student can express himself in his own way. Individual styles of expression inevitably emerge. The body itself becomes the expressive instrument of the music.

Sometimes the teacher will ask the pupil to improvise and, watching the tempo and intensity of the improvisation, will play music to match the tempo and dynamic level of the unfolding movement. As a musical instrument, the body is called upon to respond in complex ways. The arms may conduct in duple time while the feet beat a syncopated tattoo and the head nods on alternate beats. An observer of an entire class of pupils has the unusual experience of actually seeing children feel music.

Dalcroze greatly increased the possibilities of gesture by having people experiment with space, moving different parts of their bodies in different spatial planes. These relationships of movement and music were naturally valuable to dancers. A freer kind of interpretive dance emerged, a dance no longer constrained by rules, no longer stereotyped and mannered, as was the classical ballet. Isadora Duncan and other American dancers became leaders in the movement called modern dance. Among those who explored the possibilities of Dalcroze's principles and applied them were Nijinsky and Balanchine.

KODALY AND MUSICAL LITERACY

The major goal of Kodaly's method of musical instruction is to provide the pupil with skills in the reading and writing of music. Kodaly believed that every child in his native land, Hungary just before World War II, should receive such training beginning at a very early age, just as he received training in the reading and writing of his native tongue. To carry out this goal, Kodaly initiated a program of public instruction called sol-fa or choral musicianship. This program stresses sight-singing and musical dictation.

Like Dalcroze, Kodaly believed that musical instruction should be accessible to everyone, not just to the talented few. Although Kodaly was familiar with the work of Dalcroze and recognized the importance of rhythmic movement as part of musical training, he emphasized the reading and writing of music. Rhythmic and melodic concepts, key signatures and other notational symbols are integrated into the course of musical studies.

Kodaly shared with Orff the belief that singing and movement go together. As early as nursery school, singing games become an important part of Kodaly's instructional plan. As they learn about the basic pulse of music, children walk, run, march and clap in rhythm to the beat. Kodaly felt that an important part of the Hungarian child's education should be knowledge of his national heritage in music, both folk songs and folk dances.

But it is for the sol-fa method of teaching music that Kodaly is best remembered. Unlike Dalcroze and most other European music teachers, Kodaly used the movable 'do' system of solmization, which he called *relative sol-fa*. This system uses the syllable 'do' for the home-note or tonic for each and every key. In C-major, C is do; in D-major, D is do; In E-minor, E is do, etc. Thus, all major and minor keys are solmized in identical fashion so that, without perfect pitch, all keys sound exactly the same. This system has the advantage of fixing in the mind the relationships between the tonic and the other notes of the scale. Using modern terminology, those relationships between the seven different syllables and the degrees of the diatonic scale are shown in the table:

Syllable	Degree in the Scale
Do	Tonic
Re	Supertonic
Mi	Mediant
Fa	Subdominant
Sol	Dominant
La	Submediant
Si	Leading Tone
Do	Tonic

In this system, 'si - do' is always 'leading tone - tonic' regardless of the letter names of the notes. On musical notation, 'do' can be placed on any line or space of the staff. (Another system, the *fixed 'do'* system, which is the one taught by Gedalge and which I learned at the *Provincial Conservatoire* in Montreal in the 1940s, uses 'do' for the note C, 're' for the note D, etc., whatever the key might be. For example, D-major is solmized: re, mi, fa-sharp, sol, la, si, do-sharp, re. Its tonic is 're.')

Using relative sol-fa, Kodaly taught a vocabulary of rhythmic and melodic patterns. These patterns are analogous to the words and phrases of a language. The pupil encounters these rhythmic and melodic patterns through hearing and singing them. They can be abstracted from the flow of music and practiced over and over again. The pupil recognizes them first as sound patterns, then in concrete visual terms. Individual notes can be represented by the pupil standing alone. With arms linked, pupils begin to represent sound patterns. Gross body movements describe the melodic line. These are made more discrete until finally each note is described by a hand signal and later by staff notations. Only after the pupil is familiar with rhythmic and melodic patterns is he formally introduced to staff notation. In this way, the earliest experience with music notation, like learning to read words, comes after the pupil is ready to apply musical ideas, and notation becomes a practical means to record these ideas.

Syllable names and their interval relationships are introduced in a prescribed order. The descending minor third, sol-mi, is introduced first, then la-sol-mi, then la-sol-mi-do. 'Fa' and 'si' form a tritone together; they are last because they are the hardest to sing. Once the chromatic syllables, fi, si, and ta are learned, the pupil is prepared for modulation from one key to another.

The basic mode of instruction is singing. Kodaly believed that the voice is the most immediate and personal way of expressing oneself in music. Since musical instruments are frequently not available anyway, it is through vocalizations that the ear can best be trained to distinguish intervals and accurate intonation can be fostered. Like Dalcroze, Kodaly urged that this training precede instrumental study.

Kodaly believed that voices are best accompanied by other voices rather than by instruments. In this way, the pupil learns the skills of choral singing, to blend with other voices, and to sing in tune. For early part singing, one voice moves while the others are stationary. These exercises are initiated from the hand signs of the teacher. Later the notes can be read from staff notation.

There is a great deal of practice of melodic patterns that become part of the pupil's musical vocabulary. The minor third interval, sol-mi, is identified in as many familiar songs as possible (e.g., the first interval of *The Star Spangled Banner*). Pictorial representations of melodic patterns are used both with and without the musical staff to illustrate which tones are higher and which are lower. Body movements and hand signs represent the pitch relationships.

It is the hand signs with which Kodaly is usually credited, but he borrowed them from John Curwen in England. These signs represent the pull of the tones toward the tonal center of the scale. For example, 'si' is shown by pointing upward (to the tonic), and 'fa' is shown with the thumb down (tending toward 'mi'). All these hand signs are shown in the accompanying chart, Fig. 16.1.

Many ear training exercises are directed toward the development of inner hearing or audiation. Pupils are taught to recognize intervals and then to sing them silently. As early as kindergarten, children can be taught to interrupt their singing of a song at a signal from the teacher and to sing silently until the signal is given to resume singing out loud. To develop audiation, pupils may be asked to memorize a song silently from the blackboard. It is then erased, and the pupils must sing it aloud from memory.

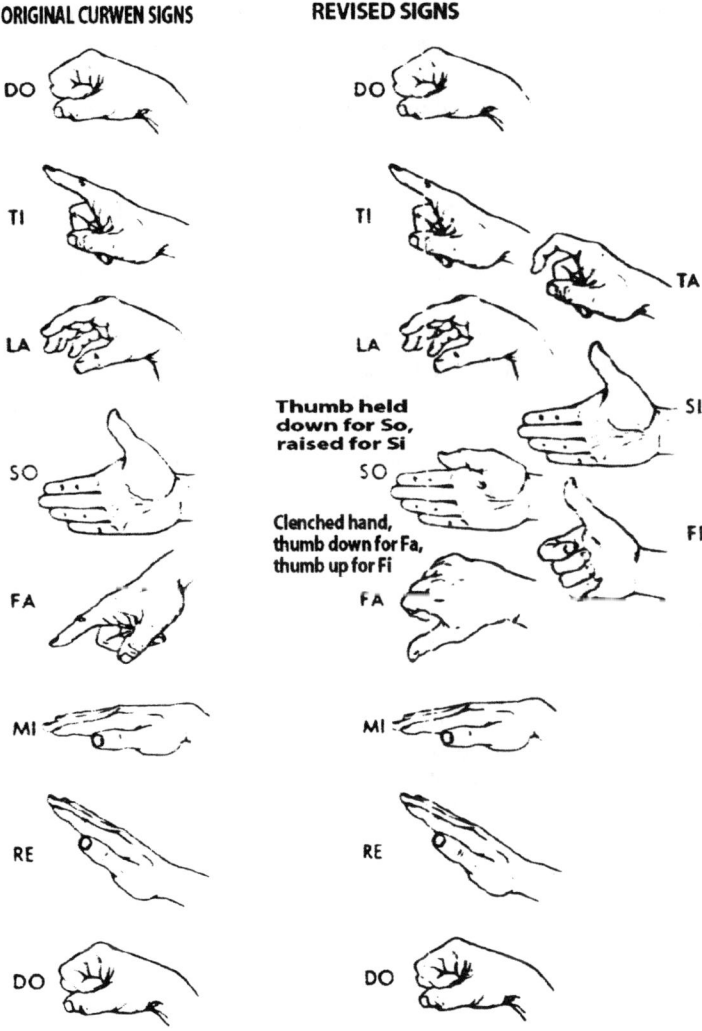

Fig. 16.1. The sol-fa hand signs originally introduced by Curwen, shown on the left, and the hand signs modified to add accidentals, shown on the right.

Kodaly recommended that the first instrument be a xylophone with removable tone bars. Beginning with just two tone bars that sound sol-mi, tone bars are added to the pupil's repertoire. The recorder is the second instrument to which the pupil is introduced. Through it, the pupil learns absolute pitches and their corresponding names on the musical staff. The study of piano is deferred until the pupil has a good background in vocal music and can audiate and sight-sing.

ORFF's INSTRUMENTS AND METHOD OF INSTRUCTION

When expressing themselves in natural every-day situations, children seem to use music, movement, and speech together. A child who is dancing often sings along, and when he sings he will move in rhythm to the music. Carl Orff made these observations and concluded that music, movement and speech must be treated as a primitive unity which he called elemental music. The unity is primitive because untrained and unsophisticated people in the early stages of their cultural development expressed themselves through music, and this always involved movement and speech.

Orff accepted the evolutionary view that ontogeny recapitulates phylogeny and applied it to the realm of music: the historical development of music is reenacted during the course of musical development of each individual. The child is considered a primitive person whose responses resemble those of early peoples.

In his method of musical instruction, Orff begins with the simplest concepts and the simplest songs. As learning proceeds, the material is presented in a series of small increments from the simple to the complex. Instruction begins in early childhood and utilizes the child's own backlog of past experiences: his own name, familiar words and quotations for rhythmic chanting. For example, the child hears his name spoken rhythmically, then chants it, and later reads and writes the rhythm in musical notation. Melodic intervals and rhythmic patterns are learned by singing them, saying them, moving to them, and playing them. Orff's instruments are used from the very first training session.

In many respects, Orff's philosophy of music teaching resembles those of Dalcroze and Kodaly: rhythm is the prime element and the starting point in musical instruction. Since speech and movement have in common the element of rhythm, it is a logical starting point. This belief led to the development of a special ensemble of musical instruments. Orff maintained, along with Dalcroze and Kodaly, that the study of piano, violin and other standard instruments should be deferred until the skills produced by ear training as well as the ability to sing prescribed intervals and rhythms have been developed.

Orff, too, pays special attention to creativity. Children are urged to explore the sounds of words, melodies and instruments. They learn to improvise, and this leads to the invention of rhythmic and melodic fragments, perhaps even whole songs. Early instruction is built upon traditional games. The task of the teacher is to evaluate the musical product, to relate it to conventional forms of music, and to help notate it in order to remember it.

The concept of elemental music includes the assumption that the child relives, in his musical education, the musical development of his species. For this reason, Orff fosters the most primordial of musical experiences: cries, grunts, chants, clapping, stamping, snapping and whirling.

Orff preferred the pentatonic mode because he believed it to be the native tonality of children. And, since he believes it to be part of the heritage of the human species, Orff recommends that the pentatonic mode be introduced early in the musical development of the child so that he can relive it, so to speak. In this mode, children can invent and play several melodic lines together without undue dissonance and without the constant pull of the tonal center of diatonic scales. Major and minor modes are postponed until later. Orff exposes the child to unusual chord progressions thus fostering unfettered improvisation. The child is thus prepared to enjoy contemporary and even *avant garde* music as well as the traditional idioms of the western world.

Like Kodaly, Orff introduces intervals in a planned sequence. Singing begins with the descending minor third, sol-mi, and other tones are added in the following order: 'la,' then 're,' then 'do' to complete the pentatonic scale. 'Fa' and 'si' are introduced last. The earliest singing is in the context of play. Children call back and forth, singing each others names, counting out rhymes, and imitating the teacher's musical phrase and answering it.

As with Dalcroze, movement is fostered from the beginning of training. The enjoyment in running, jumping, skipping and whirling parallels the enjoyment of making music by singing or playing.

Children are thus encouraged to sense rhythm by executing patterns of movement.

It is, of course, his special instruments that are a distinct feature of Orff's approach to musical instruction. With the cooperation of experts in the history and building of musical instruments, Orff developed a kind of xylophone to be played in ensembles that produces mellow and even delicate timbres. The instruments are of excellent quality, produce delightful sounds and are easy to play from the very first class. All the instruments, soprano, alto and bass are played with mallets. There is a resonating chamber on each instrument, and tone bars can be added and removed to create particular scales. With the addition of tone bars for F-sharp and B-flat, three major and three minor diatonic scales become available. Orff added the *viola da gamba*, the lute and the recorder to supplement the ensemble and add color. For percussion, drums, cymbals and triangles can be added as well.

Orff's instruments are not toys. Though they are designed to require only large muscle movements, the playing technique is not trivial and should not be neglected. Today, these instruments are considered in many circles to be indispensable for the early teaching of music. Playing from memory on these instruments is considered far more valuable for the young child than, say, learning the piano or the violin, either of which requires reading of the musical notation as well as familiarity with the requirements of the instrument, all at the same time. Orff's insistence that the child learn to play everything by heart frees him from the demands of concurrent reading, playing technique, and coordinating with others in the ensemble. Notation is introduced only when it is needed, to store the music in order to replay it later. In traditional music instruction, memorizing is required only as a last step in the learning of a piece. For Orff, memorization is a beginning skill and this insures that singing and playing never become dependent on the reading of musical scores. By emphasizing performance as the initial mode of learning, Orff has his pupils playing challenging music from the start.

SUZUKI'S METHOD OF EARLY VIOLIN PLAYING

If you try to learn a foreign language as an adult, you will likely encounter some difficulty. When Shinichi Suzuki came to Germany at 18 to study the violin, he found that it was not easy for him to acquire German. Yet he observed that all German children, by the age of three or four, understand and speak their native tongue quite well. If they can learn to comprehend and to speak such a complicated thing as a language, surely they must have the ability to acquire the musical language and to execute it at a comparable age. Suzuki applied this idea to the teaching of the violin. To the surprise of most everyone but himself, Suzuki found that all children could learn to play the violin regardless of initial talent or heredity.

Up to that time, around 1947, the concept of musical talent frequently meant that a person is endowed by heredity with a musical faculty. According to Suzuki, this is a faulty concept. Just as people acquire their mother tongue with ease, so Suzuki assumes that most people are born with a high musical potential and can develop themselves in a proper environment. What the normal child receives from his parents on the day of birth is not linguistic or musical talent but rather the ability to learn to speak and perform music. Suzuki goes further: he applies the concept of talent to all realms of human attributes and endeavor including morality, character and personality, and esthetic feeling. All must be developed by education and nurturing. Suzuki does not deliberately train prodigies, nor does he necessarily make musicians. What he does seem to succeed in doing is make competent musical performance available to everybody.

Much of what Suzuki advocates is not new or profound; it is simply good common sense. For example, he recommends that parents attend the music lessons of their children. Since the child receives just one lesson per week, there are six days during which a parent would be prudent to monitor practice and even provide instruction and guidance. Suzuki believes that, without a parent's help, many children retrogress during the week. Though many parents are quite ignorant of the musical enterprise, they can still provide supervision and their musical sensitivity will likely develop in parallel with their children's. I know of instances where the parent decided to take violin lessons in tandem with the child.

Since 1964, when Suzuki first demonstrated to Americans the violinistic prowess of young Japanese children, his educational philosophy and methods have spread and thousands of children are now receiving violin lessons in groups according to his prescriptions. As Suzuki sees it, musical education, like language education, begins on the day of birth. The child continues to develop musically by the sheer weight of accumulated experiences just as understanding and speaking a native tongue continue to develop. The child must be helped to acquire an ear for music and he must master each small step in the process of learning to play the violin before he goes on to the next. An ear for music is not innate. It is a human aptitude that must be developed by the experiences of listening and playing. Suzuki invites you to let your baby listen every day to a recording of a good piece of music. After he listens repeatedly for the first five or six months of life, he will begin to recognize the music and to respond to it, and he will develop an excellent musical ear. On the other hand, any baby reared in a family in which melodies are sung off-key by tune-deaf members, or are played out of tune, will develop a poor musical ear.

Some of Suzuki's prescriptions are controversial. For example he recommends that the piece assigned for practice should be heard ahead of time by the pupil by means of a recording of a superior performance, not once but over and over again, even while he learns to play the piece. Many experts, including the eminent American violin teacher, the late Ivan Galamian, would argue that such a practice would result in violinists who are fine imitators of musical performers. The truth is that the role of imitation in creative endeavors is quite imperfectly understood.

Another recommendation by Suzuki is that each step in the learning process must be thoroughly mastered before the pupil is permitted to move on. Most traditional teachers like to move the pupil from one piece to the next as soon as the pupil has learned the elements of playing, but without achieving mastery. This system is based on the assumption that skills develop as the pupil is exposed to more and more pieces of music that are graded in difficulty. Suzuki claims that this teaching method has proved not to be successful. Instead, he encourages the beginner to master each piece before going on to the next. Once the pupil seems satisfied that he is able to play the piece, Suzuki tells him that the lessons can now really begin: "Now your abilities will really develop." He then commences a regimen of intensive training until he is satisfied that the pupil has mastered the piece. Only then will he assign a new piece.

In summary, Suzuki enunciates five conditions for what he calls 'genius' education:

- encourage parents to give their children an ear for music
- educate children as early as possible
- give as much formal training as possible
- create a favorable learning environment

- provide good teachers and adopt a good educational method

Those interested in the details of violin instruction according to Suzuki's method should consult *Suzuki Violin School*, volumes 1 through 10.

There is an interesting progression from Dalcroze, through Kodaly and Orff, to Suzuki on the question when children should be started on a musical instrument. Dalcroze would defer the start until certain basic musical skills are attained through the art of movement. The first musical instrument is thus the body. Kodaly would start the child with ear training through *solfège* and the use of the voice as the musical instrument. Learning violin and piano are delayed. Orff uses his special instruments from the start to teach the elements of music, and recommends that violin, piano, and other instruments be deferred until later. In contrast to these three music educators, Suzuki starts musical instruction directly on the violin or on any other instrument of the child's choice right from the first day.

However, these methods should not be seen as mutually exclusive. Elements of all four methods can be incorporated in a comprehensive music program that is tailored to meet the needs of each child. It is not useful to debate the relative importance of each method considered separately.

SOME PRINCIPLES OF LEARNING TO PLAY A MUSICAL INSTRUMENT

Learning a motor skill requires that you know, to begin with, what it is that you want to achieve. In the case of learning to play a musical instrument, you must first define the behavior patterns that you need to acquire in order to reach the goal you set for yourself. It is these behavior patterns that constitute the ultimate performance. This discussion follows the recommendations of Francis Mechner (1985).

The underlying assumption is that, when you start, you will already have a repertoire of behavior patterns that you will find useful as a basis for the skill you wish to acquire. For example, you will know how to depress any key on the piano using any finger. The ultimate skill will of course be very different from your initial attempts, but the main point is that you can already depress the keys, and this will serve as the basis for your learning how to play the piano.

In order to learn to play a musical instrument, you must start by doing what you ultimately want to do well. But how can you do something before you have learned how to do it? According to B. F. Skinner, the answer is that you learn to play by practicing successive approximations of the ultimate performance. In order to acquire the motor skill involved in playing a musical instrument, the practice material is simplified and fractionated, and practicing begins at a markedly reduced tempo. You start with practice material that is easily mastered, and then you raise the level of complexity in small steps that lead toward the ultimate level of performance, mastering each small step one at a time. It is the skilled teacher who is able to guide the student through the process of simplifying, fractionating, and reducing the speed of the music to be mastered.

As instrumentalist, you must learn a series of movements that are executed first with full awareness of what you are doing and then with greater and greater automaticity as the performance is mastered. Though we speak of discrete movements, we must not forget that each one is embedded in a total musical performance. Its beginning and end are specified for purposes of practice only, for each movement is actually part of the continuous stream of behavior. A movement may be as short as the pressing of a key, the lifting of a finger or the repositioning of the whole hand, or as long as the playing of a run or a whole phrase.

Early in training, many of the movements required in performance are carefully planned and executed deliberately at a slow tempo if need be. Only later, as the performance is mastered with repeated practice, are the movements executed automatically and without awareness. There are, however, many movements that are so small and fleeting that you are never fully aware of them except for their effect on performance. For example, there are individual adjust-ments and micro-movements of the vocal chords in singing that never reach a conscious level of awareness.

As you can imagine, most movements involve many muscles, tendons and joints, all acting synergistically. Though many parts of the body are involved in a single time unit, including fingers, arms, vocal apparatus, torso and feet, all of it can be considered a single movement and can be learned ultimately as a unitary behavioral complex.

Each movement is guided by feedback when it is first tackled early in instrumental practice. This feedback may be visual, as when you guide your hand with the aid of vision; or cutaneous, as when you feel for the piano key; or proprioceptive, as when you feel the stretch of muscle or movements of the limb; or auditory, as when you hear what you are playing. When you do use feedback during the learning of a piece, you are generally not aware of the fact. This does not seem to matter; feedback seems to be effective in learning, whether you are aware of it or not.

That sequences of skilled movements lose their dependence on feedback gradually, with practice, is one of the exciting laboratory findings of recent years. However, it should come as no surprise to the teacher of motor skills that a series of complex movements are actually better executed without feedback. Psychologists had taught in the 1920s and '30s that there is a continuous stream of sensory feedback from muscles, tendons and joints during the execution of a string of movements, and that the nervous system requires this feedback to guide, adjust, and correct skilled movements while they are in progress. However, recent research has shown that monkeys can continue to execute skilled movements in the absence of sensory feedback. (In the work of A. J. Berman and others, these monkeys were surgically deafferented.) After considerable training, it is clear that motor feedback can even become a disadvantage. To judge from the speed and automaticity of skilled musical performance, we must conclude that the movements involved in a carefully cultivated skill are best executed without feedback, which is received too slowly to be acted upon successfully.

Though movements are no longer *guided* by feedback when they become skilled, they continue to be triggered, or aborted for that matter, by feedback. When movements are executed in a sequence, for example, each behavior complex can be triggered by a cue from the immediately preceding behavior complex. The importance of feedback as a cue for the execution of successive movement complexes cannot be overestimated. As learning progresses, the movements are chained in performance; in this way, they tend to become automatic, unguided and ballistic. The chain is initiated by a cue such as a glance at the musical notation, the position of the fingers after the immediately preceding movement, or by an act of will. Once initiated, it keeps going and runs itself off without correction or adjustment along the way, in accord with the motor program that was laid down in the brain by previous practice. It seems clear that skilled motor complexes run one after the other in series, or in parallel -- that is to say, together at the same time.

In short, muscles get their instructions from programs that are stored in the brain. These programs are sometimes activated by a signal that originates outside the organism, such as by musical notation on a stand, and at other times by a signal that originates inside the organism, such as by an act of will. New programs are created in the brain from existing programs that are broken down into shorter programs and reassembled in new sequences to specify new behavior complexes. Examples of new programs are those that specify a run that differs in some way from the well-practiced scale, or those that result from practicing to play with both hands after learning to play with each hand separately.

Musical performance skill, such as playing the piano, can be seen as a member of a family of motor skills that include speaking and typing, whose underlying mechanisms share important features. One of the properties of these skills is something Lashley called response equivalence. In this view, performing a piece of music means translating a cognitive plan of the music into action. The translation involves a specification of what to do and when. In a stereo system, the performance of a piece of music is etched into the phonograph record or the magnetic tape, and each playing is exactly the same as every other. Live musicians, however, do not perform the piece in exactly the same way on each occasion. The skilled vocalist modulates his singing according to his feeling for the piece. This is called singing 'with expression,' and we don't hesitate to identify the song as the same one on each occasion. Furthermore, a person may sing a song from any starting pitch, and the song will retain its familiarity (transposition). Or the vocalist may sing faster or louder without conscious awareness of the change. Having learned to sing the tune, the person may elect to whistle it, hum it, or play it on a musical instrument, all without relearning. He may readily write it in musical notation (transcription), although he never read it before, understanding that it is the same tune that he sang earlier. While the performance has changed, the tune has not.

Since every cognitive plan can be realized in an indefinite number of ways, it must specify something more abstract than the sequence of specific actions, such as the movements of the vocal chords or specific fingers. As the musician becomes skilled, the individual notes become associated with each other, much as letters become words, and words become phrases, and so on. With practice, the cognitive plan consists of larger and larger units, each of which must be translated into a sequence of movements.

Every skilled musician knows that two performances of a musical fragment are never quite the same. There are always small variations in performance, sometimes for the better and sometimes for the worse. Though the program may be fixed in the sense that it permits no variation, the execution of it does vary from one moment to the next. Mechner challenges us to sign our names over and over again without variation, one signature on top of another. Try it; you will find that the lines of your signature become increasingly fuzzy as you add one on top of another, illustrating how variable skilled movements can be.

If skilled movements do vary so much from one instance to the next, it must mean that the underlying programs in the brain do not specify the minute details of movement. Mechner has suggested that it is not the precise trajectory of the limb that is specified by the program, but rather the goal of the trajectory, namely the end-position of hand and fingers. What is stored in the brain, then, is the sequence of positions that all moving parts of the body must find themselves in upon the completion of their trajectories.

Psychologists speak of motor transfer, generalization and equivalence. These terms all refer to the fact that it is not specific movements that are learned or specific muscles that are required to execute the movement. Rather the learning is of patterns of movement. Lashley brought this to the attention of the scientific community in the 1930s. Having learned to write with one hand gives you an advantage with the other hand. You don't have to start from scratch if you must immobilize the trained hand for some reason. You can even write with your feet on the sandy beach, imperfectly to be sure, but remember that you never practiced this feat. You can even write legibly with your nose.

Let us now apply these facts of generalization, transfer and equivalence to the practicing of a musical instrument. If you try to play a well-practiced sequence of notes a little more quickly or a little more slowly you are likely to succeed without additional practice. The same is true if you try to vary the dynamics of the fragment, or its rhythm. Many teachers take advantage of this fact by instructing their pupils to vary the passage they are studying, in rhythm, dynamics, and starting point, in order to free them from a single restricted motor program.

Can a motor program run itself off without being expressed overtly in performance? Many musicians believe that mental rehearsal, or imagining playing a piece, can be an aid in learning to play the instrument. This must mean that the motor program can be cued to run without engaging the muscles that execute the performance. If you imagine yourself in the act of performing and you succeed in firing the very neurons in the brain that mediate the performance, you are, in a certain sense, rehearsing the piece. You may even succeed in firing auxiliary or alternative neurons that serve to improve your performance the next time you engage your muscles.

One of the important strategies in learning to play a musical instrument is to fractionate movement complexes into component parts. Learning each hand separately on the piano is an example of how pianists separate movement complexes into smaller, less demanding, components. In this way, you develop motor programs for each hand as well as those for both hands together. There is a benefit in this, for your performance is less likely to be disrupted: you have built redundancy into the system.

After you have improved the way you play a passage, by eliminating a mistake you used to make, you may sometimes unintentionally revert to the faulty way you used to play the passage. Reversions to an undesired performance may include obsolete limb movements, fingerings, rhythms, dynamics and interpretation. These reversions frequently occur under conditions of stress and anxiety. Every student knows how his performance can deteriorate in the presence of teacher and audience. When practicing alone in familiar surroundings and under relaxed conditions, your performance may be satisfactory. But when experiencing stage fright, you may revert to old and undesired habits of playing. The reader should consult Mechner's *Redundancy Method* (1985) for recommendations on practice techniques that are designed to avoid these reversions.

Teaching Machines

Musical instruments are sound producing machines. Each instrument has been modified over the years, and new instruments have been designed, to meet certain requirements. First is the matter of timbre or quality of sound: each instrument has its own characteristic sound and the instrument was designed to produce it. Equally important, however, is the matter of its technical mastery: what skills are required, not only to play the instrument, but also to master it?

Learning to play a musical instrument is not easy, even after the skills of *solfège* have been attained. We have already reviewed some of the skills needed to play the piano. At the lesson, many teachers of the piano play along with the child, sometimes playing the left hand, sometimes harmonizing. But then the child must go home and practice by himself, again to experience an impossible task that provides meagre if not negative reinforcement.

Or consider a stringed instrument like the violin. In this case, two different techniques are required, one for the left hand and another for the right. Each one is formidable by itself. Imagine how hard it is to combine the two! The left fingers are used to stop (and sometimes to pluck) the strings. Unlike the piano, where the pitch produced by each key is fixed, the violin student must learn to stop the string at just the right place, on just the right string, with just the right finger, in order to prepare to play a particular pitch. At the same time, the student must draw his bow across a particular string with a certain amount of pressure and a certain speed (or, sometimes pluck the string) with his right hand. With all of this to accomplish at one time, no wonder the beginner frequently sounds out of tune, if he is not actually scraping or squeaking. And, no wonder many violin students wash their hands of the whole thing in short order! The learning task is simply too complex.

Why does the student have to learn to play the violin on a violin? No one seems to have designed a teaching instrument that could be used to learn how to play the violin. In this technologically advanced age, it is high time we had such a teaching machine. Since the two hand techniques, left and right, are so different from each other, it seems appropriate to focus on them individually. Imagine if we had a machine that played the right hand for the student while he practiced the left. How much more quickly would he be able to master left hand technique to the point where the intonation is accurate and pleasing to listen to. No squeaking and scraping - the machine is doing the bowing. Remember how important immediate reinforcement is. The reinforcement received from these pleasing sounds should sustain the student's interest as he continues to practice his instrument.

To design a machine that would bow the instrument while the student worked on left hand technique seems not so difficult. Then, why hasn't it been done? Because, you say, there is the matter of coordination of the two hands. If the student practices just one at a time, he will neglect the coordination of the two.

But, learning to play the violin is a very difficult task. The pedagogical challenge is to reduce the problem to manageable proportions. Of course, coordination of the two hands is important, but it can be delayed until each hand attains a certain level of proficiency. Why does the training violin have to be the very same instrument as the performing violin? Consider a new musical instrument, one to be used specifically for practice and training. Before dismissing this suggestion as impractical, we ought to try it.

This discussion is about learning to play the violin, but the problem of 'task overload' applies to the piano and to other orchestral instruments, and the principle of using a training instrument applies to all.

Chapter 17

MUSICAL APTITUDE AND ACHIEVEMENT

Is it possible to determine, at the time when a child presents himself as a candidate for musical training, whether or not he has musical talent or ability? It would be extremely useful to know this before tuition begins so that time and money would not be wasted on a child who has no musical talent or ability. Of course, the highly gifted child requires no special study to reveal his musical ability. Great talent is evident as soon as the child begins to engage in the musical enterprise. Let us restrict our discussion to the child who might have the talent to become a competent musician. Can we predict which child will succeed musically on the basis of test scores?

In the course of this chapter, we will examine the following questions:

- What is musical talent? Is it a global and unitary thing, or, does it consist of a number of unrelated aptitudes?
- How is a test of musical talent constructed?
- Do these tests possess sufficient reliability and validity to be useful?
- Assuming these tests do exist in usable form, what value do they have in our society?

Despite the spectacular advances that have been made in the science of genetics since the structure of the DNA molecule was described in 1953, there is very little that can be stated definitively about the inheritance of any special ability. Most authorities do not doubt that there is a polygenic contribution to musicianship. However, the complex nature of musical ability has interfered with our understanding of its inheritance.

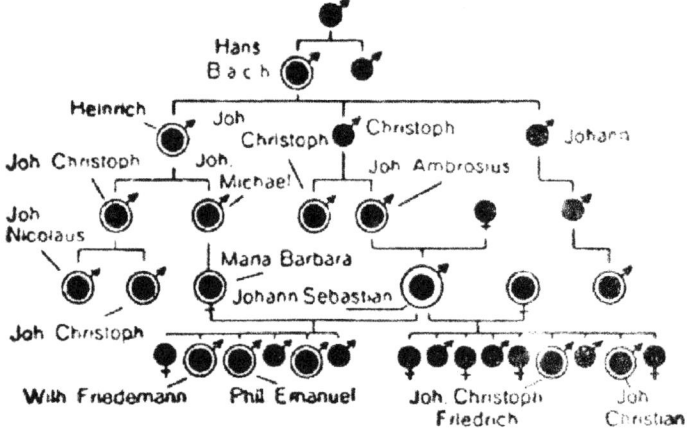

Fig. 17.1. Inheritance of musical aptitude. Genealogical chart of five generations of the Bach family. Seventeen musicians were among the progenitor's 32 descendents. This family is frequently cited as a most extraordinary example of hereditary transmission of musical talent. Scattered throughout Germany, the name Bach became a synonym for musicians. Johann Sebastian had two wives who were musicians. One was a cousin, Maria Barbara Bach, and their offspring included Wilhelm Friedemann and Carl Philip Emannuel. With his second wife, Anna Magdalena Wilkins, a fine singer and daughter of a court musician, he had Johann Christoph Friedrich and Johann Christian who became a musical revolutionary. He made fun of his father by referring to him as 'the old peruke' and he moved to Italy to become a Roman Catholic, which meant forsaking his family's religious tradition. His father must have considered this the work of the devil.

The terms musical *talent* and *ability* are ambiguous in meaning. They confuse musical *aptitiude* with musical *achievement*. This distinction is what we want to examine here. Aptitude refers to potential or capacity to learn and achieve, whereas achievement is the product of learning by an apt or inept individual. Aptitude implies the existence of something like innate capacity. This can be pictured as the volume or capacity of an empty container. Achievement, on the other hand, implies that a learning process is responsible for filling the container with stored experiences. The degree to which the container has been filled indicates the level of achievement. In short, the capacity sets the limits of musical achievement, and the level of achievement can never be expected to exceed capacity.

Let us concede from the start that the distinction is not hard and fast. The view that it is possible to test for innate capacity has been challenged by the recognition that all aptitude test scores really reflect the level of achievement, just as all achievement test scores reflect some sort of initial aptitude for the subject-matter and for learning. The traditional dichotomy between heredity and environment, and their relative influence on behavior, has been modified by contemporary psychologists in recognition of the fact that the environment never operates without a genetic substrate, and that genes never operate independently of environmental influences. There is a continuous interaction between them. Even the fertilized egg is influenced in its development not only by its genetic makeup but also by a buffeting, and chemically variable, environment.

Musical aptitude is as difficult to define as it is to measure. An innate capacity is usually thought of as genetically determined and present at birth. However, it can be argued that musical aptitude continues to develop after birth, over a period of years, and ceases to improve beyond a certain level in spite of continued training. In support of this view, consider two musical abilities, tonal memory, and discrimination of major and minor scales. Tonal memory seems to develop slowly, is exhibited in varying degrees, and does not seem to be directly related to the amount of musical training given. This is an aptitude that expresses itself regardless of length of exposure to music. In contrast, the discrimination of major and minor scales, chords, and *arpeggios* can be learned in a relatively short time by the sufficiently mature and sentient person at almost any point in the life span. Perhaps this is a musical achievement that depends on aptitudes possessed by most people. Although it cannot take place without a certain minimal aptitude, musical achievement also depends on the ability to learn, on the quality of training, on interest in music, and on a willingness to learn. To have reached a certain level of musical achievement means not only that an underlying aptitude was present as a substrate, but also that there must have been present an ability to learn, an emotional responsiveness, an ability to persist and to work hard, and a love for music. A high score on an achievement test means that all these conditions were met. However, it seems likely that musical aptitude, since it is presumed to vary among individuals, sets a limit on ultimate achievement, no matter how favorable the environmental influences or how motivated the individual. At the same time, the possibility needs to be entertained that aptitude itself may not be fixed at birth, but will change with exposure to music. The limits may be set, not by a fixed container as pictured in the past, but by an expanding balloon. Thus, the limits of musical aptitude may expand as the individual acquires more and more experience in music.

The ability to respond to music esthetically, to understand music, and to analyze and interpret it in an enjoyable way, is sometimes referred to as musicality. This ability has never been understood well enough to be operationalized for testing purposes. Here, we approach the realm of extraordinary ability, and this is beyond the scope of present-day knowledge.

There is another way to look at musical aptitude, and that is as the musical counterpart of Chomsky's linguistic competence. As with language, all human beings seem to possess an innate musical competence, that is, the ability to understand the deep structure of the language of music. This competence requires no formal training and is universal.

Musical competence can be interpreted to mean that there is something like an inborn musical understanding and responsiveness. All infants seem to respond to particular tonal patterns. The high-pitched voice of the mother is especially salient, and the infant's responses resemble those to the elements of language. Consider the power of the lullaby in affecting the behavior of the infant; and, later in life, the folk song, the dance rhythm, the anthem and martial strains.

Infants tend to respond to a descending sequence of tones rather than to an ascending one (2000 *Hz* down to 500 *Hz* rather than the other way around). In tests of imitative singing, some two-year olds were already able to hum and even to sing something resembling the rhythm of the model. Singing before speaking seems to be a characteristic of musically talented children. By age four, all children are capable of imitative singing although only some groups of notes are sung correctly.

Although highly talented parents may produce children with little aptitude or interest in music, many musically talented children come from families of musicians, both distinguished and not so distinguished. This has been taken to support the view that there is a genetic factor influencing the incidence of musical talent. However, many authorities are skeptical. A case could just as easily be made that the environment of a musical family, where the child is continuously exposed to music, is the critical factor in the blossoming of musical talent.

In some societies, it is assumed that everyone is capable of making music. Even deaf people are able to dance to imaginary rhythms. In Bali, a person may take his young son on his lap and guide his fingers to the proper keys of the metallophone at the proper time. In Western society, this kind of tuition is not common, and this may account, in part, for the greater prevalence of musical activity among the people of Bali.

In our society, children born in certain families are expected to show ability or talent for music. However, only a few eventually emerge as exceptional. Is this because of a genetic factor, or is it the result of special tuition? It is more likely a combination of both.

We began with the distinction between musical aptitude and musical achievement. However, this discussion is meant to persuade the reader that all aptitude tests are actually tests of musical achievement just as all achievement tests reflect the aptitude of the individual. In addition, achievement tests reflect the quality of training as well as the interest, motivation, emotion, and desire to achieve on the part of the pupil.

In spite of all the effort that has gone into devising items to measure musical aptitude, the truth is that there is very little evidence of success. All tests of musical talent offered thus far seem to require prior musical experience and can only be adjudged to be tests of musical achievement rather than aptitude. As a result, psychologists try to infer aptitude from achievement. It is assumed that a high level of achievement must have required a great aptitude. This assumption may be justified, but consider the obverse assumption, that a low level of achievement must be due to a lesser aptitude. Here lies the possibility of error. Since scores on an achievement test are influenced by many factors other than aptitude, a low score may reflect, for example, limited past experience with music. To the degree that children have been deprived of musical experiences, and the tests have been standardized without including them as part of the pool of subjects, the poor test results may not reflect a limited aptitude at all. For this reason, the test can be unfair to these children. The assumption that achievement scores can be used to estimate aptitude is justified only if there is equal opportunity for all children.

Before we examine the difficulties in devising a test of musical ability specifically, we might inquire whether musical ability is related to other human abilities, such as intelligence. If there is such a relationship, the scores on an intelligence test might then be used to estimate, not just intelligence, but musical ability as well. Unfortunately, intelligence is a concept at least as complicated as musical ability, and the result of using an intelligence test in place of a test of musical aptitude would be a case of the blind leading the blind.

Nevertheless, it is worth exploring, from a practical standpoint, whether musical ability is related to other abilities. Besides intelligence, consider language ability as an example, including reading, writing and spelling; consider the understanding of poetry, art and perception in general; consider mathematical ability and the understanding of spatial relationships; consider, finally, achievement in school as reflected in classroom test scores and in SAT scores. You might guess that most correlations with musical ability are low, frequently bordering on zero. We have no choice, then, but to turn to test items that have a musical content in order to come up with a test of musical ability.

Opinions differ as to whether musical ability is global and unitary or whether it can be divided into a number of unrelated talents, two of which might be a sense of rhythm, and an ability to remember a series of tones. These opinions are reflected in the tests of musical talent that are reviewed here.

Four representative tests that were designed to measure musical aptitude are those of Seashore, Wing, Gordon, and Davies.

Seashore (1938) believed that sensory capacities vary from one person to another, and he proposed that auditory discriminations enter as a major element in tests of musical aptitude. His *Test of Musical Talent*, the prototype of most later tests, include the following auditory discriminations:

- *Pitch*: Is the second tone higher or lower than the first?
- *Loudness*: Is the second tone louder or softer than the first?
- *Rhythm*: Are two rhythmic patterns the same or different?
- *Duration:* Is the second tone longer or shorter than the first?
- *Timbre*: Are two complex tones the same or different?
- *Tonal memory*: Two tonal sequences up to five tones long are played consecutively. Which tone is different in the two tonal sequences?

According to Seashore, this test can be administered to children as young as ten years, and it takes about one hour to administer.

Seashore's assumption that these six subtests reflect talents that are more or less independent of each other has not been borne out by the data. The correlations between subtests range up to 0.5 and even higher, indicating that there is a musical factor common to these subtests, perhaps a 'sensory discrimination factor.'

Though the reliability of each of the subtests seems satisfactory, the question of relevance of sensory discrimination to the enterprise of music performance and enjoyment has never been properly addressed.

Since it is the prototype of later tests, it should be noted that there is little or nothing in this test on musical thought, feeling, motor coordination that bear on instrumental performance, and there is nothing on motivation.

Wing's *Test of Musical Intelligence* (revised, 1962) includes seven subtests:

- *Chord analysis*: How many notes are in the chord?
- *Chord memory*: Have two chords been repeated exactly or has one note been changed?
- *Melodic memory*: Which tone in a melody, 3 to 10 notes long, has been changed on second playing?
- *Rhythm appreciation*: If two rhythms are different, which is the better version?
- *Harmony appreciation*: If two melodies have a harmonic series that is different, which is the better version?
- *Intensity appreciation*: If two melodies have different loudnesses, which is the better version?
- *Phrasing appreciation*: If two melodies are phrased differently, which is the better version?

According to Wing, his test can be administered to children as young as eight years, and it takes about one hour to administer.

Wing assumed that these subtests are significantly correlated and that a general musical ability accounts for this correlation. Wing also believed that these subtests separate people into types, synthetic and analytic, and those depending chiefly on harmony as opposed to melody.

Again the reliability of each subtest seems satisfactory. Also, the test as a whole seems more relevant to the musical enterprise than Seashore's, although the question of relevance is still open to question. And again, there is little or nothing in this test on musical thought, feeling motor coordination that bear on musical performance, and there is nothing on motivation.

Gordon's *Musical Aptitude Profile* (1965) consists of three parts:

- *Tonal imagery*: Is a musical answer a melodic or harmonic variation of the tune, or is it different?
- *Rhythmic imagery*: Is a musical answer played at a different tempo or meter the same or different compared to the tune?
- *Musical sensitivity*: Which of two melodies is performed with better phrasing, balance, and style? The responses of professional musicians were checked to verify the correctness of the testee's responses.

On the basis of the low intercorrelations between subtests, Gordon believed that musical aptitude is multidimensional in nature. Although it is lengthy, this test is intended for children down to the kindergarten level. Its reliability is acceptable and it seems more relevant to musical training. However, musical sensitivity seems culture-bound: what is expected of the child is what professional musicians have learned to select as the better version of a musical fragment.

Davies' *Test of Musical Aptitude* (1971) consists of four subtests:

- *Melodic embedding and location*: A sequence of three or four tones is presented. After a delay of 2 1/2 seconds, a longer tonal sequence of up to six tones is presented. Does the longer sequence contain the shorter sequence? If so, where?

Aptitude and Achievement   339

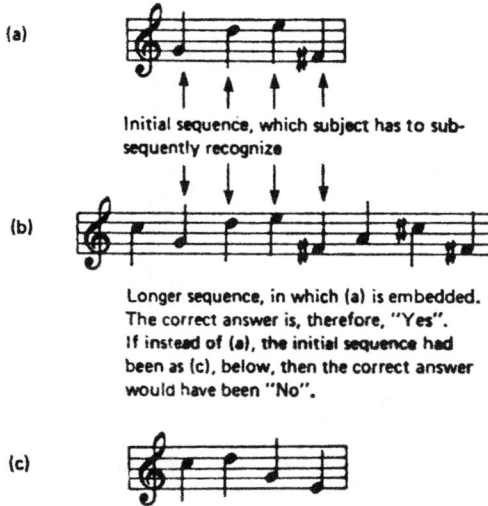

Fig. 17.2. Davies' test of the appreciation of melodic contour. The traditional test of melodic memory requires that the testee detect the pitch change of one note of a sequence of notes. Since one altered note does not make a new melody, Davies (1978) has argued that a more satisfactory test would involve a series of at least three or four notes, one that requires the ability to recognize a melodic contour. In the example given here, the testee is first presented with a sequence of notes that make up a snatch of melody and asked to remember it. This is followed by a longer sequence of notes that might or might not contain the short melody. The testee is required to state whether the melody is contained in the longer series of notes. In the example given, the answer to the sequence is 'yes' if (a) was the snatch of melody presented earlier, and 'no' if (c) was it.

- *Pitch embedding and location*: A sine-wave tone is followed by two 'sweep-frequency' tones. In which of the sweep-frequency tones does the sine-wave tone appear?

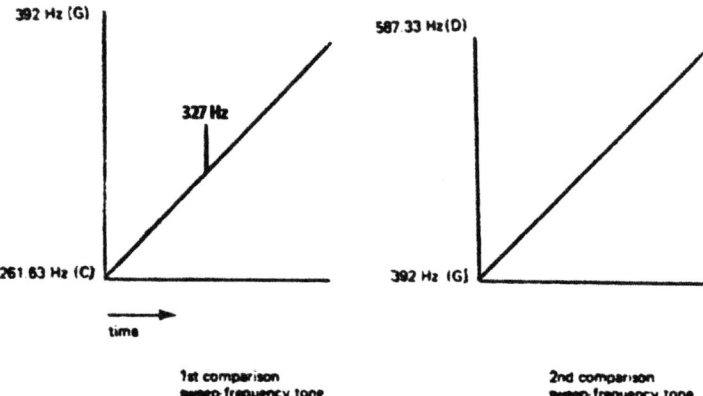

Fig. 17.3. Davies' sweep-frequency. Can the testee retain a tonal image under conditions of interference? This is an ability that seems to be required of musicians who must perform the correct pitch in the face of an array of other pitches all around them. For his test of pitch discrimination, Davies used sweep-frequency tones to embed the comparison pitch, and this test seems to have proved successful in differentiating between musical and non-musical testees. The figure shows two sweep-frequencies, each traversing the interval of a fifth, one from C to G (262 to 392 Hz), the other from G to D (392 to 587 Hz). If the standard tone, presented before the two sweep-frequencies, was 327 Hz, it would be located around the middle of the first sweep-frequency. The testee is required to indicate in which of the two sweep-frequencies the standard tone was heard.

- *Time interval discrimination*: Two pairs of tones are presented. Which pair has the smaller time separation between tones?
- *Rhythmic congruence*: Six bars of a certain meter, duple, triple or quadruple, are presented by a metronome. The first beat is accentuated by a superimposed bell-tone. This is followed by a tapped rhythmic pattern. Do the meter and pattern fit together?

This test is a more interesting one, but its status in the armamentarium of tests of musical aptitude has not yet been established. Its relevance as a test of musical aptitude is also open to question.

Only one test of musical achievement will be cited, that of Colwell (1970). This is because the usefulness of tests of achievement can be challenged, since achievement is conveniently judged on the basis of musical performance. Any test of musical achievement will resemble the test that a music student must take after he or she completes a course of study.

Colwell's *Test of Musical Achievement* consists of four parts:

- The first concerns itself with pitch, interval, and meter discrimination (nothing different here compared to the tests of aptitude cited earlier).
- The second deals with major-minor mode discrimination.
- The third concerns itself with various kinds of musical memory. Examples of items include: Are two chords the same or different? Which instrument is being played solo? Which tone matches the written note? Which member of the trio is playing the melody?
- The fourth part is on musical style and the recognition of chords and cadences. Examples of items are: Which of four composer's styles does the piece you just heard resemble? Is the texture of the piece monophonic, homophonic or polyphonic? Which of the three following chords sounds like the first? Is the cadence you just heard full, half, or deceptive? The purpose of this test remains unclear.

What do all these tests have in common? Pitch discrimination seems to be an essential part of musical perception in Western society. It appears in some form in all test batteries of musical aptitude and achievement. It is revealing to note that pitch discrimination is very difficult for young children. This raises the question whether young children have yet learned to understand the meaning of the responses 'higher' and 'lower' as it relates to pitch perception.

Short-term memory for various aspects of tones and tonal sequences is required by all tests. Drake (1939) believed that memory acts to knit together specific capacities, such as discrimination of pitch, duration, and rhythm. This subtest seems to have a certain face validity with respect to musical talent, and it does, indeed, discriminate between children. The ability to remember long compositions, too, seems to be the mark of distinguished musicians.

Auditory imagery or audiation is a related skill. It involves the capacity to recall music in the mind's ear, so to speak, in the absence of physical sound. For some people, auditory imagery seems to require the support of proprioceptive feedback. To audiate frequently requires singing silently, just as to think frequently requires speaking silently. I met a rather distinguished musician some years ago who had perfect pitch. He played a number of musical instruments, but his first instrument was the double bass. I remember asking him, in the middle of a conversation, to sing the A above middle C. He immediately fell into the posture of holding a double bass and bowed the imaginary instrument as he sang the required tone. I take this to mean that he depended upon proprioceptive feedback and motor outflow for accurate audiation. There is no doubt that proprioception is important in musical performance. And proprioception appears nowhere in the tests we have reviewed.

The ability to feel the presence or absence of a tonal center is still considered important as far as musical talent is concerned. For example, Gordon (1977) considers the sense of tonality to be basic in the development of musical understanding and in the ability to follow modulations. A feature of his test is that the tonic is included in one of the pairs of musical fragments to be judged 'same' or 'different'

It is difficult to take this view of tonicity seriously now that much contemporary music is admired for its atonality. It seems more likely that tonality is an acquired taste. The melodies that Western children sing are frequently devoid of any tonal center. Zenatti (1975) showed that children below the age of eight years could not yet discriminate tonal from atonal melodies. Successful discrimination improves with age. Adults perceive the change of a tone on a second playing more surely with tonal than with atonal phrases. This developmental trend suggests how important is the musical environment in shaping the responsiveness of the individual to particular forms of music.

Some tests include items on tonal movement (e.g., the *Kwalwasser-Dykema Test*) in which the child hears an incomplete pattern of tones and is required to indicate whether the tone that completes the sequence should move 'up' or 'down' in pitch. Individuals raised in an environment surrounded by tonal music would be expected to excel on such items. But the test that includes such items should be labeled, properly, a test of musical achievement. It seems unfortunate to demand from children the responses of their conservative elders. The standards of beauty change and the authors of tests should not be permitted to determine the musical fashion, one way or the other. The same argument applies to the alleged suitability of certain harmonies when the standards of harmonization have changed radically over the years and continue to be in flux. Does preference for conventional harmonies really reflect musical talent, or vice versa?

Tests of music appreciation test are not much different. An original excerpt is paired with a distorted version. The child has to indicate which version he prefers and which element, melody, harmony, or rhythm has been altered. Of course, the child who recognizes the music is at an advantage. Gordon approached this problem by using a piece of music composed especially for this purpose. To begin with, he asked musicians which of two versions they preferred and he used their consensus judgment as the criterion for the 'correct' response. Since these are value judgments, which vary from time to time and place to place, it is unfair to the testee to be judged untalented if he has not yet acquired the expected response in his society. Needless to say, the creative child is at a disadvantage.

Some rhythm tests are concerned with the ability to sustain a steady beat in the face of distracting faster or slower beats. A related ability seems to be motor coordination or movement control. With children, a performance test seems superior to a perception test as a means of testing rhythmic ability. To be able to maintain a steady tempo appears to be a highly specific ability. Igaga (1974) compared the rhythmic abilities of Ugandan and English children. The Ugandan children clearly excelled, particularly the girls, probably because they participate from early childhood in domestic activities accompanied by rhythmic music.

Musical talent, as envisaged by Wing, includes a proprioceptive ability that seems to span tonal memory and rhythm. It has a genetic component as it is understood in contemporary feedback conceptions of skilled behavior. Proprioception enters into more than meter and time. To recall melodies, people frequently have to translate auditory patterns into proprioceptive processes; if the person is forbidden to sing silently, recall is disturbed. Proprioception also plays an important role in the acquisition of instrumental and vocal skills. Many music students have noted the value of performance in orchestra, choir, and as soloist in developing musicality, that is, in grasping the details of a musical idea. Despite the recognition of proprioception as an important ingredient in the musical enterprise, it has received little attention by the test-makers as noted above.

Although tests of musical talent may serve to identify the promising student, questions have been raised in recent years regarding the usefulness of these tests. It has even been suggested that there can be negative after effects of testing a child that should not be ignored.

A low test score tends to pigeon-hole the child as unworthy of musical training. As a result, the teacher is apt to treat the child in such a way as to make this judgment a self-fulfilling prophecy. An optimistic judgment can be a boon but, if the judgment is pessimistic and the child is treated accordingly, he may end up hating music and the entire musical enterprise.

It can be argued that most normal children have the aural and manual skills, which tests are designed to assess, to make perfectly competent musicians. (We must leave aside the problem of predicting virtuosity, because this is an even more complicated problem and is beyond the scope of this discussion.) If this is so, there is no need for tests of musical talent. Any child presenting himself to a music teacher is a *bona fide* candidate for musical instruction. There is, therefore, no need to reject any candidate. The truth is, unfortunately, that most children do not become competent musicians, and this is not for lack of musical aptitude. All young children enjoy music, but most seem to get turned off once a teacher gets hold of them. The fault seems to lie with the teacher and not with the pupil. Perhaps we need tests to weed out the incompetent or ineffective music teachers rather than the incompetent or untalented pupils.

It is true that some children do not have the motivation to endure the rigors of learning a musical instrument. This can best be determined during a short course of training. Sometimes personality factors interfere. The child may be timid. He or she may not be able to sustain interest in the face of protracted practicing. Some children cannot tolerate the absence of immediate success. They may not be able to tolerate competing with others who seem to pick up the same skills more quickly and easily.

Sometimes motor coordination is imperfect. The child does not naturally attend to proprioceptive cues and must struggle to learn how to do so. Again, he or she is at a disadvantage when competing with children who acquire this skill without special tuition.

Sometimes the child does not get the advantage of very early training and is not raised in a milieu of musical activity. There may be a critical period during early development when musical skills are acquired easily. To miss the critical period may make it that much more difficult later to turn the child on to the joys of musical performance, or to interest the child in musical training. Other interests begin to intrude with the onset of puberty. My own opinion is that, if a certain level of competence is not attained by the onset of puberty, the effort is likely to be pointless for most children. The same seems to be true in learning language. Early acquisition seems to be that much easier. Another interesting example of the importance of early acquisition is learning to swim. Most infants seem to act to stay afloat quite spontaneously when placed in water, or will learn quickly and effortlessly. If the early period is missed, many children become frightened and this interferes with swimming acquisition. Later on, it becomes difficult to get the child to enter the water.

The most effective way to train a child on a musical instrument is to offer it as one offers English conversation to the American infant, spontaneously and without any special effort. In this way, preliminary skills are acquired, so that the child is prepared later on for formal musical instruction and is not overwhelmed by the complexities of the task.

Chapter 18

MUSICAL ENJOYMENT AND THE MEANING OF MUSIC

THE MUSICAL SETTING

Serious music listening has become a major activity in the lives of a large segment of contemporary society. To understand what it is that has led to such widespread musical activity, it is necessary to consider the technological and social changes that have occurred in the past century or two.

As late as the eighteenth and early nineteenth centuries, serious music was performed almost exclusively in royal palaces, lofty cathedrals and fashionable salons under the patronage of the wealthy and powerful. As time passed, new concert halls and opera houses were built specially to provide the settings for musical performances attended by the privileged few. There was, to be sure, the popular music of the age, the dance and the march, the lullaby and the folk-song, among the general populace. And there were always occasions, such as weddings and harvest festivals, when music could be heard in modest settings. But for the most part listening to serious music could take place only on special occasions and in special places. These events had to be planned in advance, and there was no way to capture the music for future replay.

In contrast, consider the conditions that prevail today. Nearly everyone owns at least one radio. In most communities local stations play recorded music continuously, and in large cities there are numerous stations specializing in all manner of music, making it available 24 hours every day. Although people have to accept what is offered on radio, the present affordability of audio equipment means that most people can now select what they want to hear when they want to hear it. There are records, tapes and CDs of the most spectacular performances, from Caruso and Heifetz to the Beatles and every other popular favorite. What most people could not hear in a lifetime not so long ago, they can now hear at will over and over again. It is now possible for nearly anyone to contrast the interpretations of musical performers without the necessity of ever attending a single live performance.

Consider the amount of time the average city dweller spends listening to music, in the home, office, automobile, elevator, or just strolling outdoors. The ear is rarely rested, sometimes not even during sleep. People can listen to recordings in the most informal settings, while jogging, for example, or while making love. Subcultures of modern youth revolve around canned music that is used as a mood intensifier together with substances such as alcohol and other drugs.

The prevailing élitist view of what constitutes serious music typically included the music of the classical and romantic periods. Frequently neglected in debates of esthetic experience are twentieth century idioms such as American jazz, blues, and all manner of rock, although the fact is that these forms of music bring a great deal of pleasure to a large number of people. When one considers the arbitrariness of formal definitions of what constitutes serious music, one is forced to conclude that esthetic criteria are quite relative to the society and the age in which one lives. Any theory of music appreciation and choice must consider all forms of music that give pleasure to listeners. It is clear that esthetic experiences result from listening to the most varied of music, from Vivaldi, Purcell, Beethoven, Schubert, Brahms, Stravinsky, Copland, Berg and Webern, to the latest popular hits.. What is needed to understand music is a broad perspective of music and musical appreciation, one that transcends the narrow and élitist definitions of what constitutes 'good' music and takes into account the musical tastes of the age.

THE MEANING IN MUSIC

A remarkably broad range of factors influences the musical enjoyment and preference of listeners. Even without words or a program supplied by the composer, listeners are able to derive meaning in most music. Where does the meaning come from? Clearly, the meaning does not lie in the sound of the music itself but in the listener.

We must seek the meaning in music in two realms: in understanding and in feeling. Understanding involves rational analysis that is swift and discriminating. Its mechanisms involve neural activity, especially in that part of the brain called the cerebral cortex. Feeling is more amorphous, more slow-moving, and less discriminating. Its mechanisms involve activity in the sympathetic and parasympathetic parts of the autonomic nervous system and in the neuroendocrine system. The latter has an arousal function, the former a cue function. When music is played, a large number of biological events are initiated, and these determine the responses of the listener to the music.

The most obvious determinant of the meaning in music is the pattern of the sound itself. The musical experience is, first and foremost, the result of hearing a tonal complex occupying a period of time and played in a particular physical and social setting. When played together, two or more tones sound pleasing to the ear if they are related to each other in a harmonious way, and if placed in a felicitous context. The theory of musical intervals deals with the problem of consonance, dissonance, and tonal fusion. A revolution in the development of tonal complexes occurred when Bach and others in the eighteenth and nineteenth centuries accepted the equal tempered scale as a means of providing twelve equally spaced tones in the octave as elements from which to draw for the composition of tonal complexes. Since then, Western ears have become accustomed to the most complex of musical sounds including the rough, jarring and buzzing sounds of beats (see Chapter 9).

We have already noted that the listener is not a passive absorber of sounds. He/she organizes them and assigns meaning to them. Aestheticians who have restricted their search for meaning to

Pythagorean consonances, or the harmonic series, or the tonal fusion of Stumpf have neglected the remarkable contributions of the listener to the musical experience. What is consonant and what is dissonant to the ear is frequently less a matter of the acoustic relationship of tones and more a matter of the expectations of the listener. Expectations, in turn, depend on the past history of the listener. The tonal complexes that prevailed in the acoustic environment of the listener's past have a profound effect on his later musical appreciation and preference.

Thus, the listener brings to the music:

- His own propensities for responding to sound. As a member of the human species, he shares certain capacities with his fellows. These capacities are partly inherited from his parents and determine the way he tends to respond to sound.
- His transient or momentary state. What is his physical and emotional state? Is he paying attention, or is he distracted? Is he well or ill, fatigued or fresh, anxious or bored? Is he in a state of expectation, is there cognitive uncertainty, or is he fully familiar with what is being played?
- His more enduring state, which is largely determined by his past experiences. What were his early experiences at home? Did he grow up with Mozart and the Beatles? Did he discover Stravinski early in maturity? Did he read Lewis Carroll as a youngster and did it make an impression on him? Has he seen the movie *2001*? Has he experienced the cosmic theme of Richard Strauss' *Thus Spake Zarathustra*? A person's brain is shaped by his myriad past experiences, going back all the way to infancy and even earlier. If the Martian would have to begin listening to the music of the earthling without the benefit of the earthlings past experiences, he would be likely to derive a different meaning from the music. If he has never heard the gurgling of a brook, the singing of the cuckoo, the clap of thunder or the piping of the shepherd, he would be unable to understand many of the sounds like those in Beethoven's *Pastoral Symphony*.

The sounds that produce pleasure in the listener are frequently less a matter of the acoustic relationship of tones and more a matter of the expectations of the listener. Expectations, in turn, depend on the past history of the listener. In short, the tonal complexes that prevailed in the acoustic environment of the listener's past have a profound effect on his later appreciation and preference.

The meaning of the word 'meaning' is elusive. It seemed clear to the British empiricists and associationists of the nineteenth century that meaning is carried by the *context* that surrounds the core idea. Thus the name Voltaire becomes attached to the picture of Voltaire through repeated experiences, and the name Voltaire becomes the meaning of his picture.

For Leonard Bernstein (1976), repetition, redundancy, deletion and ambiguity are the keys to the problem of the meaning in music. Variation in repetition that generates novelty is an important ingredient of meaning, as is deletion that creates ambiguity.

Building on the ideas of Bernstein, Pribram (1982) has suggested that posterior cortical systems in the brain operate to reduce redundancy, acting much as an editor searching for novelty. Reduction in redundancy, the process of information, constitutes one aspect of the aesthetics of music. Further, behavioral habituation to novelty (involving activity of frontolimbic systems) is dependent on the visceroautonomic components of the orienting reaction. In short, repetition results in habituation and recognition, while variation on a repetitive pattern (novelty) evokes dishabituation (the orienting response) which is another aspect of the felt aesthetic.

THE EARTHLING AS LISTENER

The way we perceive sounds depends upon who we are, namely human beings possessing a certain anatomical and physiological endowment, and where we live, namely, in a world that has certain physical properties.

On the one hand, the human as a species is designed to make sense of certain intervals, scales and rhythms, whether that human is a Pygmy, a Maori, a Mongolian or an American. The human brain is designed to organize its input in particular ways, whether that input is words on a sheet of paper, floral scents in a garden, colors on a canvas or sounds in a concert hall. Like the visual mechanism that registers its input in the form of lines, edges and contrasts, the auditory mechanism registers its input according to wave frequencies, amplitudes, and waveforms and rhythms.

On the other hand, nonhuman species like the dolphin and whale, having an upper limit of pitch discrimination that is much higher than ours, and having a sonar mechanism that aids in locomotion, must hear our music in a way that is much different from the way we hear it. Similarly, an ET, possessing a quite different sensory and neural system compared to ours, will respond to our music in a very different way, with different feelings and expectations. Our own earthling children, who have limited musical experiences, have very different feelings and expectations compared to their parents. After going up a certain number of notes, we adults expect the notes to start coming down. We would find it bizarre if they did not ever come down, as in Shepard's endlessly ascending scale (see Chapter 7).

As far as musical tempos are concerned, we experience them by our own time standards, those given by our heart rate, for example. Imagine the bird or the rat, with much faster heart rates than our own, exposed to our music, which must sound maddeningly slow-paced to them. What a colossal bore it is likely to be to them.

On earth, sound sources get louder as they approach us or as we approach them. Imagine if things were reversed and sounds got softer instead: a shout at a distance would be heard as a whisper close up, and vice-versa. Or imagine if we possessed just one ear on the top of our heads, instead of two: our concept of auditory space would be very different, and our experience of stereo would have a different meaning altogether.

On earth, we all experience the force of gravity no matter who we are or where we live. It lends us the weight we know ourselves to have, and it gives us an up-and-down dimension. Imagine what it would be like to grow up on the moon, or better yet, in outer space where there is no gravitational pull at all. In that environment, we probably would have a very different sense of rhythm and phrasing. We would certainly have a hard time understanding what is 'up' and what is 'down.' Objects would float in the air along with us. The idea that it takes energy and tension to run up hills would elude us, and certainly we would miss the feeling of coasting down and of moving back and forth on a swing or in a hammock. Imagine what that would do to our perception of melodic lines: there would be no up or down, no swing, no back and forth, no heaviness or lightness, at least nothing resembling our earth-bound perceptions.

In short, our understanding and appreciation of music would change in fundamental ways if the ears and brain that we inherited were altered, or if our metabolism, including our heart rate, were sped up or slowed down, or if our sense of gravity were interfered with. We are each of us a prisoner of our body, our brain and our planet. It is precisely because we can run up and down hills, feeling the force of gravity and experiencing the rolling on wheels, or swinging like a pendulum, that we come to respond to music as we do. These are inevitable experiences that all of us are subject to as long as we live on earth.

There are sounds that we all share as long as we live on earth. These include the sounds of nature, like thunder, the hoot of the owl, the bark of the dog, the chirp of the cricket, the rustle of leaves, the buzz of the bee, the trickle of running water, the beating of our heart and the gurgling of our stomach. These sounds are an inevitable part of our environment. As earthlings we are subject to an earthly repertoire of sounds as surely as we are subject to the light and heat of the sun and the wetness of water.

Other sounds are man-made and are more variable, like the noises of a jackhammer and a jet engine, or the music of a *celeste* and a *cello*. Our musical responses certainly depend not only on the experiences provided by our natural world but also on the variable experiences of our civilization. Consider the variety of images we earthlings conjure up while listening to a series of waltzes such as those of Johann Strauss, those in Ravel's *La Valse*, in Richard Strauss's *Der Rosencavalier* or in Stravinski's *Petrushka*. We have already remarked that the Martian might hear something very different, never having experienced the sounds of our nature and our civilization.

Development of Musical Taste

Enjoyment of a piece of music is enhanced by knowing its period, the state of the art in that period, the ideals and purposes of the composer and the biological capacities of the listener. To optimize enjoyment, reason must accompany emotion. Furthermore, it is extremely difficult for a person to begin to appreciate a complicated piece of music after he is old enough to have acquired a stock of prejudices and preconceptions. It is so much easier to absorb good music a little at a time in the early years, and to grow up exposed to a variety of music, than to try, as an adult, to start with Bach's *B minor Mass* or Stravinsky's *Rite of Spring* without passing through the intermediate steps.

That responses to a given piece of music change with time is well recognized. Musical tastes evolve, even as gastronomic tastes and other esthetic experiences evolve. The listener who is naive musically is less likely than the experienced listener to derive pleasure from Mozart or Debussy. What is found at an early age to be strange sounding, unorganized and dissonant, can turn out to be a favorite piece of music later on in life. There seem to be no absolutes when it comes to musical tastes.

There are two classes of explanation for this. First, enjoyment seems to depend upon a certain level of maturation. Before that level is reached, the necessary pathways in the nervous system for the processing of auditory input have to be laid down. Or the endocrine system is not yet releasing the levels of hormone that are needed to provide the substrate for certain feelings and emotions. Second, enjoyment requires a familiarity with the particular piece of music in question, a familiarity that comes with repeated exposure. Or exposure to related music is required, a familiarity with the grammar and style of this music.

In this connection, our enjoyment of the classical Mozart will undoubtedly be altered in the light of the later romantic idiom, just as our appreciation of the romantic Rubens would change in the light of Picasso's cubism, or an early friendship would change in the light of a later love. Just as we enjoy the old in the light of the new, so we enjoy the new in the light of the old - Schoenberg, for example, in the light of Bach, Beethoven and Brahms. Heaven help us if we are exposed to a piece by Schoenberg and haven't yet been conditioned by any of the old masters, nothing but folksongs and country music in our background! We would probably hear noise, not music. To understand Schoenberg, we will need a lengthy period of exposure to the Western tradition, proceeding chronologically perhaps, as we might while growing up. Of course, exposure and understanding, by themselves, do not insure enjoyment and preference. But, to be meaningful, a piece of music has to stand on familiar ground so that the listener can have certain expectations about what is likely to come next. *Pari passu*, there has to be enough new material to keep interests high and to communicate something that is not already known.

'Good' pieces of music generally are better appreciated and seem 'deeper' with successive exposures. The 'bad' ones seem shallower and quickly become banal and clichéd. Because we are likely to miss something worthwhile every time we listen to good music, there is always something new and fresh in that piece even after a hundred exposures. The reason we miss some nuance or subtlety is that we do not know where to focus our attention. We are not yet familiar with the myriad of possibilities, or we lack the education to know what to listen for. Acquiring a taste means becoming aware of new possibilities for enjoyment. The subtle seasoning of foods is a gastronomic example, as is the potent olive.

In short, both maturation and experience are required for the development of musical taste. Each society provides certain experiences to its members, experiences that vary from age to age and from one period to another. For example, traditional tonal music required that the musical piece center around a 'home' tone and end on it, while composers of atonal music made it a point not to establish a tonic or any specific reference pitch. Once the brain is accustomed to that *genre* of music, it is better able to handle the task of categorizing and organizing the sounds of that *genre* of music in order to enjoy it.

MUSICAL SYNTAX

There have been attempts to characterize the regularities found in music in terms of rules and rule systems. Is there a universal musical grammar, like Chomsky's deep structure for language that is revealing of the human mind, or better, of the human brain?

People learn to speak grammatically. But even if they do not, the intention is still to communicate propositions that are meaningful to others. Thus if the speaker has good reason to suppose that he will be understood despite his unfamiliarity with the correct grammar and vocabulary of the prevailing language, then he may not pay too much attention to it. The child who reports to his daddy, "Today, I goed to the store" illustrates his knowledge of the rule of the past tense in English. Abiding by that rule, he has violated another, but he will eventually correct it even though he is understood perfectly well.

In musical composition, the intention may be deliberately to violate the listener's expectations with respect to the musical grammar of the day. To succeed, a composer must create interest and enjoyment without depending on denotative communication. The writer, on the other hand, must communicate something meaningful or denotative to his audience. In this respect the verbal and musical languages are really not comparable.

Because the number of rule-abiding sentences is indefinitely large and because people are obviously capable of generating sentences that they never heard before, it follows that people remember the rules for constructing sentences rather than the myriad of sentences themselves. Similarly, to enjoy a piece of music, people must be familiar with the vocabulary and grammar of the music they listen to. This is clear in every age when a new and unfamiliar grammar of music is offered to the listening public. But, in contrast to verbal language, people love to hear the rules violated.

SUBJECTIVE ORGANIZATION

A piece of music is really a series of tonal complexes, one succeeding the other in an orderly way. But its organization is not simply provided by the composer. To a large extent, the listener imposes it himself or herself. When engrossed in a piece of music, the listener does not hear a series of discrete tonal units. If she did, she would be puzzled by the disordered experience. Instead, she hears musical phrases rather than individual notes, she recognizes lengthy tunes and is capable of weaving extended patterns of sound into unified wholes. Though arbitrary and changeable, these patterns are built by the listener according to the grouping principles enunciated by the gestalt psychologists during the early part of this century. Two of these principles are 'proximity' (those tonal complexes that are sounded in close temporal order tend to be heard as belonging together) and 'good figure' (the act of perceiving imposes on the tonal complex the most stable organization, in line with prevailing conditions). See Chapter 14 for illustrations of the Gestalt principles.

The ear registers sounds, but it does not organize them. A good ear is no more central for enjoyment of music than good eyesight is for the appreciation of literature. The very essence of music and other works of art is organization of elements within the artistic medium, and that is imposed by the brain. Although composers are responsible for tonal complexes, it is the listener who makes a melody. Listening to music is thus not a passive process of mere reception but one of active participation. The ear picks up the sound signals; the brain constructs a melody and a rhythm from the raw material. Only when the listener organizes the succession of sounds is there a melody. People do not always agree about the tunefulness of a piece of music and this is a clear indication of the subjective quality of melody perception. Is Alban Berg's or Anton Webern's music tuneful? Whether this question has any meaning can only be judged by individual listeners.

What do we mean when we say that it is the listener that organizes a tonal complex? The answer lies in the listener's ability to make complex units out of a tonal sequence, although the sequence is composed of individual tones. The bathroom floor is made up of many separate tiles, but the viewer sees not the individual tiles but a certain repetitive pattern. The viewer assembles what is merely a collection of units into a whole. This propensity to perceive not individual elements but overall patterns or configurations applies equally for pitch and rhythm, as well as for the other attributes of music.

Now let us turn to the matter of aesthetic preference. People seem to enjoy pieces of music that have a certain unpredictability. As a result of listening, the uncertainty about a sequence of tonal complexes is reduced. This reduction of uncertainty is known technically as 'information.' Extremely high and extremely low levels of information seem to be alike in failing to generate aesthetic pleasure in the listener. One overloads the listener because it is so complex and therefore sounds meaningless or just a jumble of sounds. The other is so simple as to sound banal and uninteresting. The optimal range of information for appreciation is somewhere between those extremes. Of course, this optimal range varies from one listener to another, and even a single listener may change his mind as he accumulates auditory experiences. The music that pleases an adult did not necessarily please him earlier when he was a youngster, probably because it was too complex at the time and overloaded him with information. Conversely, what pleased a child does not necessarily please the grown man for, now, the music has become clichéd and banal; if the music provides no information, it sounds boring. Call on your own experience and you will notice that expectation and a certain modicum of surprise are important determinants of aesthetic enjoyment.

All musical pieces establish expectations, and it is the challenge of the composer to do the expected in unexpected ways, too early or too late, too high or too low, too loud or too soft, or by veering toward the blatantly unexpected. As the listener becomes more and more sophisticated, the amount of deviation from 'home' that he can tolerate increases. 'Home' itself may become a class of tones instead of a single tone such as the tonic. With enough repetition, almost any sound or set of sounds can come to be heard as 'home' and welcomed as familiar.

If musical experience was simply provided for by the reduction of uncertainty of tonal complexes, we could stop here and proclaim that we have an elegant explanation for aesthetic preference. Unfortunately, many other factors enter the equation.

The setting in which the listener finds himself influences aesthetic preference. In your living room, you may elect to listen to Beethoven. Move to the dining room for dinner and your preference may shift to Strauss. You get into your car and you may find yourself bored with both previous selections. The concerts you attend are chosen on the basis of the pre-announced program, and this program is frequently arranged to please the maximum number of listeners.

We have not yet considered the role of the emotions in music appreciation. When the young boy, David, entertained King Saul with his music, he understood the effect that music can have on emotion and feeling. Not only does music affect the mood of the listener, but the mood will influence the choice of music. Imagine the music you might select when you are elated and contrast that with the music that you might select when you feel anxious and depressed, or angry. Consider the influence your physical state may have on your appreciation of music, such as fatigue or illness. The field of music therapy has grown in recent years, as psychologists have come to recognize the important relationship between mood and music (see Chapter 20).

It has also become clear that musical enjoyment and everyday behaviors influence each other, behaviors such as manual work, reading, conversation, eating and drinking, and loving. Music has become embedded in the stream of everyday life. It has been claimed that productivity in the workplace is influenced by certain kinds, and certain tempos, of music. Imagine the music that might accompany the various episodes in a motion picture: patriotic, ecclesiastical, and dance music, lullabies, ethnic and folk music, pastoral and impressionistic music, scary music, etc.

Music can be appreciated at a variety of levels. At a literal level of enjoyment, the listener responds to the meaning made explicit by the composer. In his *1812 Overture*, a programmatic piece, Tchaikovsky made the meaning very plain. It is the conflict between the Russians and the French during the War of 1812. The appeal to the listener is frankly emotional, and Tchaikovsky martialled the forces of all the orchestral choirs, even cannons and church bells, to elicit an emotional explosion. Beyond that, however, there is an intellectual appeal that increases with the acquisition of information about the historical context, such as the victory of the Russians over the French at the *Battle of Borodino*; about the use of particular orchestral instruments to elicit patriotic and religious fervor; about the use of melodic elements derived from the French and Russian past, including the two national anthems; about the technical problems of coordinating, in space and time, the cannons with the orchestra, etc. At the intellectual level, there is always some uncertainty, and pleasure in the reduction of uncertainty.

And then there is enjoyment in performing a piece of music. Those of us who play a musical instrument or sing know the great pleasure when a difficult passage is finally mastered. Subsequently, there is a special appreciation in hearing that piece of music since it is associated with the sense of accomplishment.

Lest we suspect that familiarity always breeds contempt, consider the apparent paradox that one piece of music, so very familiar to some, is preferred over another piece that seems to most others to be so much fresher and more interesting. There are a number of observations to be made about this. We live in an ever-changing world and this, in itself, is anxiety-provoking. As we move around in the world, the objects in our environment are forever changing. We travel from home to work, from one person to the next, from one event to another, and it is a bit frightening. Anything that lends some stability to the world is apt to be anxiety-reducing, and therefore pleasurable. Familiar music provides some stability to our world. It is like coming back home, like returning to the tonic if that makes us comfortable. How pleasant to sit down and listen to something familiar after a day of anxiety-provoking instability!

Sometimes a musical phrase pops into our heads and repeats itself over and over again. Although it may be something we have long enjoyed hearing, it begins to get on our nerves, and we try to get rid of it, but it continues to haunt us. You would think that we would never want to hear that hackneyed phrase again but, strangely, at the next hearing, we may be all the more fascinated by it.

And then there are the pleasant associations elicited by a familiar piece of music. Just as the familiar scent of a perfume can evoke a dreamy recollection of bygone days, so can a favorite musical passage revive the pleasant feelings associated with an earlier experience. You may remember with nostalgia your first kiss that was accompanied by a song. Seated in a restaurant at some later date, you might suddenly recognize that song and, bending over, you might whisper to your love, 'They're playing our song.' The song evokes pleasant feelings whenever you hear it. To everybody else, it might sound hackneyed, but to you and your love, it is very special and evokes pleasure whenever you hear it. Unless, of course, the relationship is lost, and then it may elicit some mixture of pleasure and pain. As we go about our affairs, we develop associations with pieces of music that are quite unique. No wonder each of us has our own idiosyncratic favorites.

Finally, we must not neglect the universal human responsiveness to the rhythm of music. At a concert, we enjoy watching the conductor beat out the rhythm, and frequently we cannot restrain ourselves from doing the same. Rocking appears to be a universal soother. Even sitting in silence, we may beat out a tattoo with pounding fingers, tapping feet and waving head, to the annoyance of others. On the dance floor, couples undulate to the music and they frequently appear mesmerized. Later, the familiar music evokes pleasurable feelings, since it continues to elicit those uncontrollable responses associated with rhythm.

Chapter 19

MUSIC AND THE BRAIN

What do we know of the brain of a Mozart, a Beethoven, or a Berlioz? A gross physical examination is likely to reveal nothing unusual, yet we know that there must have been something in the nervous system to explain the childhood genius that blossomed into Mozart, the musical creativity of the deaf Beethoven, and the virtuosity of the troubled Berlioz. Mozart declared that he conceived a new composition in his mind in such a way that he could survey it, and examine it, like a fine painting. He could then translate the whole imaged auditory fabric of melody, harmony, counterpoint, rhythm and timbre, into the visual symbols of musical notation by a succession of movements of the writing hand. This involved, first, abstracting each of the parts, so that each melodic line could be sung separately, or played as a succession of notes on the keyboard. As a composer, Mozart did all this with apparent ease over and over again during his musical career. As a performer, he was able to move his fingers over the keyboard without the conscious awareness that makes movement effortful. To attend to each movement risks distraction and the introduction of flaws in the performance.

Well-trained musicians can read a whole musical composition silently in their heads, hearing it as they read it; then practicing it on their musical instrument in order to commit it to memory; and finally, playing it as they hear it in their mind's ear and as they feel it in their fingers. Denied access to the score of Allegri's *Miserere*, Mozart is said to have written it down after hearing it in 1770 during Holy Week in the Sistine Chapel when he was fourteen years old. This was a remarkable feat of musical memory, for he could not have heard the work more than six times - more likely, only twice (Farnsworth, 1969). Scored for two choirs and composed of nine parts, the *Miserere* is elaborately ornamented. Though the number of mistakes Mozart made is really not known, this was nevertheless a display of incredible virtuosity.

As a young man, Yehudi Menuhin witnessed a rehearsal by Georges Enesco of a just completed *sonata for violin and piano* by Ravel. After reading through the work once, with Ravel himself at the piano, Enesco asked if they might run through the work once more. Ravel agreed and, to Menuhin's amazement, Enesco put down the score and played every note from memory.

Mozart must have had eidetic imagery in hearing, as Enesco must have had photographic memory in vision. Eidetic imagery is remarkably vivid recall, perhaps hallucinatory, which is seen in some children and usually fades with age. Some conductors, von Bülow and Toscanini are examples, are reputed to have had a photographic memory for musical scores. As with the less dramatic forms of memory, its neural substrate is still unknown.

In addition to eidetic imagery as the explanation of Mozart's remarkable musical memory, he must have been able to categorize and classify extended patterns of music, and remember them as single units. Modern psychologists refers to this as 'chunking.' Speed-readers are alleged to scan the printed page without laboriously moving their eyes between individual words or phrases involving multiple successive fixations. They have acquired the skill to chunk the material of the printed page and move from one chunk to the next with a limited number of eye-fixations.

Similarly, the chess master remembers, not a copy of the chessboard, but a set of relationships between groups of pieces. Through years of experience, he can rapidly categorize and classify frequently occurring strategic patterns, quite automatically (a pawn chain, a fork, a concealed check, etc.). In this way, the chess master can recognize and remember several thousand patterns of pieces.

Music, too, can be subdivided by categorizing and classifying patterns of sound. There are regularly occurring patterns in Western music, patterns that include scales (ascending and descending), chords, cadences, *arpeggios*, *Alberti* accompaniments, and other repeated figures, etc. These are relatively small chunks. But patterning can take place in a hierarchical fashion, leading to ever-increasing chunk sizes such as themes, harmonic progressions, and repetitions, etc. When the performer is familiar with these patterns, there is no longer any need to remember individual notes. As the musical unit becomes larger, fewer and fewer of them need to be remembered. The ability to form higher-order groupings must have contributed to Mozart's prodigious memory.

CEREBRAL ORGANIZATION

The two cerebral hemispheres of the human brain are not much larger than your two fists held together, with knuckles opposite each other. They weigh a little over three pounds, look pink and gray when alive and well-nourished, and have the consistency of thick porridge held in a very fine transparent bag. There are over twelve billion nerve cells, or neurons, in the human brain, holding millions of pieces of information that can be expressed in some mysterious way, when needed. Millions of chemical and electrical events take place in the brain every second during our lifetime from before birth to death, without a moment's respite, even during sleep and coma. The moment all the neurons stop firing is the moment of death. The chemical and electrical events are responsible for every aspect of our thinking, feeling, and doing, from creating our own dreams and aspirations to learning the skills of musical performance and enjoying it.

All twelve billion neurons in the brain are more or less fully formed by the end of the first year of life. The best evidence is that they do not continue to subdivide after birth to create new cells, as our skin cells do during the course of our lifetime. Neither can neurons in the brain replace themselves after an injury. Again, the lore is that there is no regeneration of dead neurons in the central nervous system. Once dead, neurons are gone forever. (This lore has recently come into question as a generality, but it remains true as far as any practical purpose is concerned.) There is a normal death rate of neurons in the adult and it averages perhaps 10,000 per day, every day, until we die. A rough calculation reveals that we lose perhaps half a billion neurons during our lifetime. A startling number perhaps, but still no more than 4% of the total brain. We need not fear for our mental well being because of the loss of 10,000 neurons per day. Our memories, for example, are not likely to be affected by such a small loss. Memory seems to be reduplicated through the many areas of the cerebral hemispheres, and any small loss seems to have little or no effect. It has even been suggested that such small losses of neurons are required for the normal formation of memories; in this way, the patterns of activity of the brain can become unencumbered by the dead weight of redundancy. By discarding excess neurons, memories are shaped, much as the sculptor shapes his art form, by chipping away excess material. The important facts underlying memory loss seem to have little to do with sheer number. Most neurons link up with thousands of other neurons, and a quadrillion of connections is quite possible, more than most of us mere mortals are ever able to use.

A single experience is likely to activate millions of neurons. Listening to a piece of music is such an experience. These patterns of activity in the brain are likely to alter muscle tension, pulse rate, blood pressure, skin resistance, stomach motility, brain waves, and countless other bodily functions. It is now possible to detect which parts of the brain are activated by auditory experiences by scanning the brain. We believe that different parts of the brain process information in different ways, within each of the two cerebral hemispheres, on the one hand, and between them, on the other.

The neurons are kept alive by nutrients and oxygen, delivered to the brain by the circulating blood. While the brain tissue makes up perhaps two percent of body weight, it consumes 20% of the circulating oxygen. Normal intellectual activity and behavior depend upon the requisite amount of oxygen. Activities that promote blood circulation are likely to raise consciousness and improve retention, performance and enjoyment.

The brain is both a receiving and a sending organ. It receives inputs via the various sensory organs such as eye and ear, and it initiates outputs to muscles and glands. Think of the pianist seated at the keyboard, poised to play a piece of music. The two hands are placed in a playing position. The pianist directs his attention to the score. Sensory information is transmitted to the brain areas that decode the information, relate it to stored memories, and interpret it.

Commands are issued to the fingers for the proper execution of the requisite serial movements. The brain monitors these movements as they are executed. This complex of activities include reading, sensory awareness of sound, sight, and touch, emotional experience, physical movement, musical interpretation, memories of past experiences; all are integrated in the making of a smooth performance by the pianist. Various parts of the brain must cooperate in this complex enterprise. The hind parts of the brain are involved in the activities of elemental survival and body maintenance. Above this, the brainstem relays information up to the higher centers and down to the primary apparatus of movement. This system includes the cerebellum, the coordinating and integrating areas for automatic movement. The cerebellum frees the pianist from the constraints of thinking and planning from one moment to the next. In this way, the movements can run themselves off without the intrusions of awareness and volition. At the same time, the upper brain is kept informed of the progress of the piece. The cerebellum controls wrist, hand, finger and leg muscles for smooth and coordinated playing by the pianist.

Ascending the nervous system still further, we come to the limbic system, which is essential for certain kinds of learning, memory and emotional expression. This system is speechless and opinionless, but it has more elemental functions compared to the cerebral cortex above. The urge to make music, to dance and to feel, seems to depend on the activity of the limbic system. Finally, the cortex, or outer layers of the cerebral hemispheres, seems to be involved in knowing, recognizing and understanding. Here, experiences are analyzed and evaluated, and voluntary acts are initiated. Here, too, decisions are made, and logic is formulated and applied. The pianist needs the cortex to interpret the symbols in the printed score, to call on his learned skills and to interpret the music.

Why do we need two hemispheres and not just one? First of all, each hemisphere receives information from, and controls the opposite side of the body. For the most part, the left hemisphere is connected to the right side of the body, while the right hemisphere is connected to the left side of the body. Secondly, each hemisphere possesses its own tendencies and each processes information in its own characteristic way. The two hemispheres communicate with each other primarily through a broad band of interconnecting neurons, a commissure called the *corpus callosum*. Through this commissure, each hemisphere is informed of what the other is doing, and they are able to cooperate in their activities.

How the human brain is organized has been the subject of much speculation. MacLean holds that the human possesses three brains, not one. The product of evolution, the three brains are organized hierarchically. Lying in the core of the brain is the lowest of the three brains. It is the brain possessed by reptiles, such as lizard and crocodile, and is concerned with basic survival functions: possession, territoriality and self-defense. The biological functions of breathing and circulation are coordinated in the reptilian brain.

The second of the three brains is the mammalian brain. It is composed primarily of the limbic system which animals like dogs, cats, rats and monkeys also possess. The limbic system is involved with the feelings and expressions of emotions like fear, anger and joy. This is the brain of hunger, pain and sex, of conviction and challenge, not of logic.

The most recently evolved brain is the cerebral neocortex. Parts of it are uniquely human. It is the brain concerned with abstract thinking and language. The ability to create new ideas resides here. The human is capable of mathematical reasoning and logic because he possesses the cerebral neocortex.

The three brains must cooperate so that the human being can reach his full potential. Like all other forms of human endeavor, the musical enterprise involves learning, thinking, striving, emoting, social interacting and pleasure. Some educators believe that music and the other arts can be used to activate the limbic system, which is frequently held in check by the cerebral cortex. Our socialization dictates that, when the areas of reason in the cerebral cortex are active, the primitive and emotional parts of the limbic system are in a quiescent state. Rather than combine emotion with reason (limbic system excitation together with the cerebral cortex), one is likely to dominate and inhibit the other. Our rearing practices foster this. Modern children are often taught to sit still in order to listen and recite their factual knowledge, with the result that their spontaneity of feeling is suppressed. As a result, some educators advocate training to foster cooperation among the three brains for the sake of achieving a fuller and more satisfying life. Art, music, dance, crafts and literature are used to awaken the limbic brain, to shake it from the inhibitory influences of the cerebral cortex. The result, some experts claim, is an increase in scholastic achievement across the board, in reading, science, mathematics and so on.

Much of the publicity accorded brain research in the 1970's and 1980's is in the area of hemispheric specialization. The recent data have upset the conventional view that the left hemisphere is superior to the right. Since the time of Broca in the 1860's, the left hemisphere was believed to be the language processor and is used in reading, writing and speech. Nothing was known about the specialized functions of the right hemisphere until recently.

Sperry studied patients in whom the *corpus callosum*, the broad band of fibers connecting the two hemispheres, was surgically severed to relieve the seizures of epilepsy. After the separation of the two hemispheres, the left hand, as the saying goes, did not seem to know what the right hand was doing. In one experiment, Sperry exposed a dollar sign to the left side of the left eye, and a question mark to the right side of the right eye. This insured that the dollar sign information would be transmitted via the optic nerve to the left hemisphere, and that the question mark information would be transmitted via the right optic nerve to the right hemisphere. Without the connection between the two hemispheres, these patients seemed to have two streams of consciousness, operating independently of each other, and one hemisphere could not convey to the other what it saw. From studies such as these, Sperry was able to conclude that the right speechless hemisphere, in contrast to the left, is involved in holistic thinking, in intuition, in determining spatial relationships and emotional expression. The right hemisphere is also specialized to interpret the auditory impressions of pitch, and to recognize voices, intonations and musical experiences.

Our culture tends to serve the left hemisphere. We inculcate children with the logical, the grammatical, the analytic, sequential and timed aspects of life. At the same time, we tend to squelch spontaneity, reflection, imagination and metaphoric thinking, all expressions of the right hemisphere.

When we analyze a piece of music by classifying the instruments, the styles, the historical data, etc., we are using the left hemisphere. We think that the more we know about the music, the more we will enjoy it. This may not always be the case. Too much knowledge may actually interfere with emotional expression and enjoyment. Some people know so much about music that they develop unreasonable expectations and cannot enjoy the music because it does not meet their standards. It is thought that art critics frequently have this problem (see Epilogue).

It is clear that musical experiences change with age and education. As the brain matures and is educated, tastes change. The record collection of a teenager is likely to be different from that of a mature adult, and this presages what is likely to happen to the teenager as he gets older. Laboratory experiments have revealed that, as musical knowledge grows and listening experiences increase, the response to music changes from a holistic experience to a more analytic and sequential one, representing a shift from right to left hemisphere processing. But both modes of processing contribute to musical enjoyment. The good music teacher will foster the integration of activity of the two hemispheres. A music teacher who emphasizes left hemisphere functioning may succeed in inculcating a technical vocabulary and a set of sequential skills that promote technical prowess in musical performance, but at the cost of spontaneity, expression and creativity.

To know the modes of neural processing is not likely to make us into better listeners or performers of music. However, I hope that I have challenged your left hemisphere into a debate over what the musical enterprise is - a motor skill, a cognitive process, an emotional resonance or any combination of these activities. Our left hemispheres can ask a myriad of valid and logical questions about musical experiences. Perhaps out of such a quest will emerge the conviction that we must pursue the vague and intuitive possibilities afforded by our right hemisphere. The question then becomes a pedagogical one: how can we train ourselves to experience the activities of the right hemispheres, not just the left?

Brain Damage and 'Amusia'

Amusia is an old medical category that refers to the loss, or impairment, of musical abilities as a consequence of brain damage or neurological disease. Like other syndromes of higher brain function, such as *agnosia, aphasia, and apraxia, amusia* represents a specific disability, not the result of diffuse decay of mental activity, as observed in *dementia* or perhaps in *psychosis*.

The impairment may express itself in musical performance: in loss of ability to sing, whistle, or hum a tune (*expressive apraxia*); in loss of ability to play a musical instrument (*instrumental apraxia*), or to write music (*musical agraphia*). The impairment may also manifest itself in the realm of musical reception: in loss of ability to discriminate between melodies (*receptive amusia*); in identifying familiar melodies (*amnesic amusia*); or in reading musical notation (*musical alexia*). Alteration of emotional responses to music is still another form of amusia (*affective amusia*).

These disabilities may occur singly, or in combination. But the principal question is whether the amusias are associated with speech disorders. This will become clear as we proceed.

In the late nineteenth and early twentieth century clinical literature, there appeared many examples of *aphasic* patients showing various forms of amusia. Here are several, taken from a review by Benton (1977):

- Loss of ability to read music, without impairment in the recognition of songs or ability to sing, play or write music.
- Loss of ability to hum or sing, without losing the ability to play the piano, read notes, recognize melodies or compose music.
- Loss of ability to sing, read and write music, without losing the ability to play the violin, or to discriminate melodies and rhythms.
- Loss of ability (by a skilled musician) to reproduce a sung melody on the piano, without any loss of ability to do the same on the violin.

At the same time, there are reports of aphasic patients retaining all their musical abilities, and also of patients who lost their musical skills and who were not aphasic. One example is that of a trained musician who could not sing, whistle, or read a score, but who could recognize pitch and intensity and had no speech impairment. These are the interesting cases, for they suggest that speech and musical ability do not share the same neural mechanisms.

These early observations have been validated with the use of modern testing techniques and nonclinical subjects. We will return to this issue when we describe these newer techniques.

The assessment of disturbances of musical function is difficult, especially when the impairment is mild or subtle. There is an extremely wide variation in musical aptitude and achievement in the American population. Some people can read and write music with great skill, but the majority are all but musically illiterate. Some people cannot carry a tune. Others cannot distinguish one melody from another, and cannot remember tonal sequences of any length. In short, there are no normal standards to which the musical performance of a patient can be compared. In judging whether or not a change in musical abilities has taken place after brain damage, it is often necessary to rely on the testimony of the patient and his relatives. Unfortunately, the evaluation of premorbid musical ability is rarely accurate, or even available in many instances.

The test battery published by Dorgeuille in 1966, and used in his study of patients exhibiting amusia, provides an example of a systematic examination that is, at the same time, comprehensive and practical. To assess vocal expression, the patient is asked to sing familiar songs that are named; and to sing and whistle tones and melodies by imitation. Rhythmic expression is tested by asking the patient to reproduce a rhythmic pattern tapped on the table. Reading music and writing by dictation are tested if the patient possessed these skills prior to the trauma. Finally, various musical discriminations and identifications are assessed, such as pitch, type of music (dance, martial, and church), and type of musical instrument. In addition, Dorgeuille assessed the premorbid musical abilities by means of a checklist that inquired about musical training, participation in chorus and band, sight-reading, instrumental skills, etc.

Some of the contemporary evidence indicates that disturbances in musical function occur in association with speech disorders. About 70% of amusiacs suffer from one or another form of aphasia. Furthermore, the type of impairment in music tends to conform to the type of impairment in speech. For example, patients with motor aphasia are likely to show an oral-expressive defect in music without concomitant impairment in musical perception or recognition. Similarly, patients with a receptive aphasia are more likely to have problems with musical perception and recognition and not with oral-expressive function. And finally, an amnesic type of amusia is likely to be associated with *amnesic* difficulties in speech.

Expressive amusia, with preservation of receptive abilities, is associated with frontal lobe damage, while defects in the perception and recognition of tones and melodies are associated with temporal lobe damage. The similarity with the expressive-receptive dichotomy in *aphasia* is obvious.

Other contemporary evidence supports the view that musical ability and speech are mediated by separate neurological systems. The observation that patients with severe expressive speech disorders, including stuttering, are able to sing fluently is sufficient proof of this. Many aphasic patients, when singing, retain the capacity to perceive the musical aspects of spoken language, such as voice quality and accent.

Nor is the sparing of musical ability in aphasic patients restricted to simple expressive and receptive functions. In 1965, the Russian neuropsychologist, Luria and colleagues described the case of an eminent composer-conductor and professor at the Moscow Conservatory who sustained a severe receptive aphasia after a cerebrovascular accident at the age of 57. The aphasia persisted until his death four years later. During his period of survival, this musician completed a number of compositions, some begun before the stroke, and he performed them in public to the acclaim of his peers. Post-mortem examination disclosed a massive softening of the temporal and parietal areas of the left hemisphere, a finding that accounts for the severe aphasia.

The obverse, that disturbances in musical function can occur in patients free of *aphasia* is further evidence for the independence of speech and musical ability. Amusiacs with oral-expressive-musical impairments, in particular, are as likely as not to be normal in speech.

HEMISPHERIC SPECIALIZATION

The traditional view is that musical abilities are associated with language abilities, both being a function of the left hemisphere. In this view, amusia results from the same lesion that produces *aphasia*, with the exception of expressive apraxia, such as impairment in piano and violin playing that requires the use of both hands. Another view is that both left and right hemispheres have been damaged in patients who show both impairment in language abilities and musical abilities. To evaluate these possibilities, we must turn to the modern evidence on the topic of hemispheric specialization. This evidence will lead us to conclude that musicality, considered globally, seems to depend on the normal functioning of the right hemisphere, more than has been suspected heretofore.

Viewed as a complex of human skills, language includes speaking, listening to and understanding the speech of others, reading and writing, including the skill of spelling. Various motor and sensory skills are required. Articulation is involved in vocal speech, manual dexterity in writing. Hearing and vision are required for the perception of speech and the printed page. Meaning has to be extracted from the signals of language, signals that have been organized as a system governed by rules called grammar. Words and phrases have referents in the world of objects and events which, in turn, are represented by activity in the nervous system. The symbolizing power of words and phrases opens up the possibility of communication between humans about objects and events.

From the point of view of the nervous system, this complex endeavor that humans call language, and engage in most of their lives, seems to be unitary, for it depends on the integrity of one of the two cerebral hemispheres, usually the left hemisphere in right-handed individuals. We refer to this as the lateralization of speech function in the left hemisphere. After significant brain damage, there is frequently language impairment, and the nature of the disorder depends on the location of the lesion in the left hemisphere. For example, vocal speech is affected by damage in the left frontal lobe, while receptive speech is affected by damage in the left temporal lobe.

Is music a unitary phenomenon, as language appears to be? The list of skills that are involved in the musical enterprise is equally long and there is considerable overlap with language. First, let us consider the similarities.

Both motor and sensory skills are required. Articulation is involved in singing, while manual dexterity is involved in playing a musical instrument. Hearing and vision are required for the perception of music and the printed score. Meaning has to be extracted from the sound signals, signals that have been organized as a system governed by general rules called musical syntax (scales, rules of harmony and counterpoint, etc.) and personal rules called musical style.

Here the similarities end. Musical phrases ordinarily have no referents in the world of objects and events. Represented in the nervous system are the sounds that make up the music. If there is meaning, it is subjective. The music itself has little or no power to communicate information about the external world. If music is a language in any sense of the word, it is a language of feeling and emotion, not of things.

Still, the similarities between music and language are striking. And it seems appropriate to inquire whether musical activities, like language, depend on the integrity of the left cerebral hemisphere. This is the question we will address here.

It was originally believed that *aphasia* (more properly, *dysphasia*, a disturbance in language function) and amusia (more properly, dysmusia, a disturbance in musical activity) are related. If a person suffers an aphasia due to left hemisphere damage, then he is also likely to suffer an amusia. However, the early clinicians focused on musical ability only if the patient had been highly skilled in music. Thus, the early conclusions were based upon observations of sophisticated musicians to the exclusion of patients untrained in music. As we will see, these observations were biased and have resulted in misleading conclusions.

Since that time, a more detailed analysis of the problem has been made. Before we review the contemporary data, here are some of the conclusions:

- A distinction should be made between reception of music and execution of music (between listening and playing). We ought not to speak of a global amusia, since nobody ever loses all musical skills and retains all other skills.
- From the point of view of brain function, music should not be treated as a unitary ability, but should instead be broken into separate skills such as pitch discrimination; rhythm, meter and stress; prosody; word recitation; tonal memory; etc.
- Trained musicians who analyze the musical patchwork will more likely use the analyzing hemisphere (the left in right-handers), while musically untrained individuals, who adopt a more global or holistic attitude toward the musical patchwork, will more likely use the hemisphere that processes the input in a global way (the right in right-handers). The data derived from dichotic listening have revealed that the right hemisphere is more likely to process musical material, especially in musically untrained subjects.
- Among the numerous case reports published in the modern era is the one by Luria et al (1965). This is the dramatic case, referred to earlier, of an eminent composer-conductor who developed an intense receptive aphasia (suggesting that the left hemisphere was damaged) while, at the same time, preserving the ability to conduct and compose in a more or less normal manner. There was not even a question of a lower standard of performance since several musical experts testified to the patient's unchanged creative and executive abilities.

Now, let us turn to the recent experimental data.

First on the perception of melody: B. Milner (1962) studied patients after temporal lobectomies for the relief of epilepsy using the Seashore *Measure of Musical Talents*. Right-sided lobectomies produced rather striking impairment on subtests for timbre and tonal memory.

Kimura (1964) made use of dichotic listening to investigate left-right hemispheric differences in the perception of melodies. Subjects were normal volunteers with no particular musical aptitude. She demonstrated that the left ear was the preferred one for the optimal reception of small snatches of melodies when presented during simultaneous two-channel stimulation. This is interpreted to mean that the right hemisphere processes melodies better than the left.

Shankweiler (1966) repeated Kimura's experiment using temporal-lobectomized patients as subjects. Like B. Milner, he found that right lobectomies produced severe impairments (the extinction of melodies in the left channel).

King and Kimura (1972) showed that non-musical, non-speech sounds such as laughing, crying, moaning and coughing are also processed by the left ear-right hemisphere system. Though vocally produced, these are non-speech sounds in the sense that they are non-propositional.

Gordon's study, published in 1970, revealed another variable that should have been suspected earlier. Gordon used dichotic listening with melodies and chords. In this study, professional musicians were used as subjects. For chords, there was a superior performance by the left ear, as expected, but no differences between ears for melodies. These latter data diverged from all the earlier experimental results. It seems pretty clear that musical training was the key variable that accounted for the different results.

Music seems to be processed differently in individuals with musical sophistication as compared to those without. For example, a melody may be perceived in terms of its over-all melodic contour, as a gestalt, on the one hand, or as an organized arrangement of components, on the other. Listeners untutored in music tend to perceive melodies in a gestalt fashion (mediated by the right hemisphere), while musicians tend to hear the relation between musical elements in a melody (sequential analytic processing is carried out by the left hemisphere). Gordon's use of musicians in his subject group accounts for his discrepant results, and the data, taken together, suggest a dynamic change in the brain with musical sophistication. As capacity for musical analysis increases, the left hemisphere takes over melodic processing from the right.

On musical performance, the data are conflicting. There are two contrasting clinical examples. In the first, the ability to sing was retained by a 46-year-old man after right hemispherectomy to remove a glioma. His melodic reproduction and articulation were normal, in spite of his aphasia. In the second example, Damasio (1975) reported that singing of melodies was distorted in a case of right hemispherectomy. Whether the difference in this case might be due to differences in the degree of musical sophistication is not clear.

By injecting sodium amytal into the carotid artery in the neck, a transient, functional, hemispherectomy can be produced. Gordon and Bogen (1974) studied the singing of melodies by patients after the right hemisphere was knocked out by the injection. As expected, speech was hardly affected, but an expressive amusia was observed. It was the singing in pitch that was affected, not the rhythm. The patients sang in a monotone, but the rhythm was retained. This dissociation of the skills of singing in pitch and in proper rhythm is noteworthy. Oddly enough, both pitch and rhythm were retained after the left hemisphere was injected. An impairment in rhythm was expected. If not in the right or the left hemispheres, where then is rhythm mediated? Whatever the answer, it seems likely that singing in the untutored depends not only on right hemisphere function, but also on the cooperation of the two hemispheres. More on this later.

Borchgrevink (1977) prepared a recording of a right-handed patient singing after a right carotid injection. The patient was able to count as he attempted to sing, but he lost control of pitch and tonality. He counted in a monotone while rhythm and local dialect (prosody, intonation, and stress) were preserved, as were speech comprehension and speaking. In contrast, there was an abrupt loss of speech after left hemisphere injection, while singing was retained.

An objection is sometimes voiced against data such as these when the subjects are epileptic, a condition that might in itself produce an unusual cerebral organization. However, the findings of epileptics prior to temporal lobe and other surgical procedures have been reproduced in non-epileptic subjects, and there is little reason to doubt their validity.

For the most part, recent case studies have tended to differentiate *aphasics* and amusiacs on the basis of which of the two cerebral hemispheres is damaged. The well-preserved ability to perform that some *aphasic* musicians have, such as Luria's celebrated composer-conductor, is also in accord with the view that the right hemisphere is the one essential for skilled musical performance. Whether the normal reception of music is equally dependent on the right hemisphere is not quite so clear.

In summary, the data suggest that musical achievements depend, during their early development, on right hemisphere function. As training proceeds, the dominant activity is slowly transferred to the left hemisphere for analytical processing.

If the right is the musical hemisphere and the left is the language hemisphere, how do we manage to sing a song with words? Do the two halves of the brain cooperate in such an activity? Though this possibility is not at all unlikely, we really do not know the answer. Perhaps cooperation between the two hemispheres is not necessary. Let us assume that the neural processing involved in singing a lyric is very different from the neural processing involved in uttering the very same words outside a musical context. We might speculate that the musical lyrics emerge in a global way from a store of emotion and feeling, while the verbal utterance emerges in an analytic way from a store of propositional language. We might further speculate that the musical lyrics are processed in the right hemisphere where the melody itself originates. In this view, there is no need for interhemispheric cooperation and no interhemispheric conflict. When conflict is produced experimentally, as in patients under the influence of sodium amytal, the correct lyric might be sung, but to a distorted melody. Perhaps language and music do unite in the right hemisphere in order to escape interhemispheric conflict. Consider the following example of conflict and its resolution.

Not so long ago, it was not uncommon to insist that all children learn to write with their right hands. Being naturally right-handed, most children easily complied. But those who were naturally left-handed had a more difficult time, probably because their left cerebral hemisphere was not their language-processing and/or analytic hemisphere. Suppose for a moment that they succeeded in becoming right-handed, as they were supposed to, though the language-analytic hemisphere continued to be their right. As a result, a conflict might have been generated between global and analytic function, and one consequence was difficulty in learning to speak. Sometimes the child became a stutterer. The fascinating thing about these circumstances is that the stutterer could frequently alleviate his speech impediment by singing his utterances. According to our speculation, this works because the stutterer is able to get his global hemisphere, presumably his left, to utter the words along with the melody.

Another function of the right, or global, hemisphere is to mediate the experience and expression of emotion. Perhaps this is why musical perception and expression are so closely tied to the global right hemisphere and more distant from the reasoning left hemisphere.

A caveat. Up to now, we have treated the subject of hemispheric specialization in a relatively strict and uncompromising way: speech mechanisms are located in the left hemisphere of right-handers and music in the right hemisphere. The prevailing view that the neural substrate for speech is fixed and unvarying has lately received some critical reevaluation. Though the ability to process language signals seems to be a biological given, it is clear that training can modify the inherited asymmetry of the brain. To judge from the evidence of neural plasticity, there may well be superimposed a process of acquisition of hemispheric specialization for language (see Chapter 6 in Orbach, 1998). And if hemispheric specialization for language is not as fixed and unvarying as hitherto was thought, there seems to be little point in carrying this conception over into the domain of music, for this domain is at least as multi-dimensional as the domain of language. Although singing in pitch depends on the integrity of the left hemisphere, as we have already seen, we have good reason to believe that the execution of rhythm is independent of either hemisphere. Rhythm is a more primitive musical dimension, belonging properly with biological drives rather than with higher mental functions, and thus depends upon the function of the limbic system, the brain stem, and other more primitive parts of the brain.

Chapter 20

MUSIC THERAPY

Those who play music as therapy assume that music has palliative and even curative powers. Some therapists recommend music for the treatment of mental disorders, and that is why music has been introduced in a systematic way into the modern psychiatric setting. Remarkable effects of music have been claimed even for those suffering organic or bodily diseases. It has even been alleged that music can prevent individual crimes and mob riots. The obverse, that music can incite the individual and the crowd, as martial music has been known to raise hostile feelings and aggressive tendencies, seems also to be true.

As a species, we have made music since our beginnings. Songs attend us from the cradle to the grave, lulling us to sleep, accompanying us when we celebrate, consoling us when we grieve, entertaining us when we choose to be amused, and sending us to eternal repose with the knell and the hymn. The sounds of nature must have served as models. Nature is full of sounds that evoke human emotions: the song of the bird, the gurgle of running water, the roar of the lion, the rush of the ocean, and the crash of thunder. The human infant has a repertoire of sounds, such as crying and cooing, some of which are emitted without prior learning. Psychologists believe that very young infants cry in order to signal their state, and that a number of their cries can be differentiated and identified. Many mothers of young babies allege that they can identify the hunger cry, the cry of anger, the cry of pain and the attention-getting cry. Soothing techniques include music, especially the singing of lullabies in the high pitched voice of the mother. To express our innermost emotions and supplement the voice, we have constructed sound-makers of all manner of objects: for blowing, such as pipes; for plucking and bowing, such as strings; and for pounding and shaking, such as drums and bells.

The healers of antiquity must have resorted to song when advising and treating others. Group ceremonies must have been conducted with the participation of healers, family members, and neighbors who might sing, blow a pipe, shake a rattle, beat a drum, and dance. These sounds must have lent a bizarre quality to the event, permeated as the event must have been with supernatural thinking, with dreams and visions and altered states of consciousness.

The medical practices of contemporary Chippewas Indians are revealing. Among these Indians, the medicine man is a musician as well as doctor, lawyer, priest, philosopher, and botanist. Their religion teaches that men must be good in order to live long, and the chief aim of their society is to bring health to its followers. Music is as important in the healing of the sick as is medicine. The healing song must be the right song for the occasion, and it counts as much as the herbs that must be carried in a bag by the sick person. The medicine-man might also be called to provide a love-charm for which there is a love song, or an evil charm for which there is a cursing song.

THE ANCIENT THEORY OF EXCESSES AND IMBALANCE

The belief that music has extraordinary power is one of the ancient legends of music: the power to suspend the laws of nature and overcome the realms of heaven and hell. A sense of wonder or fear accompanies most accounts of music's power. As the legends suggest, music and healing have always been related. Both the ancient Thracian Orpheus and the god Apollo were linked with the curing of disease, oracular prophesy and purifying ritual – three different ways of focusing the healing forces of nature upon the body and the mind. Today, we might refer to the first one as regulation, the restoring of mind and body to a state of equilibrium, arousing or soothing as needed, to temper excess or deficient emotion; to the second as the creation of the sensation of pleasure through movement; and to the third as the induction of an ecstatic experience which purges the mind of emotional conflict.

The healing powers of music were recognized by the ancient Chinese, Hindus, Greeks, Egyptians and Hebrews. Orpheus, was celebrated as a healer and musician who made enchanting music with the aid of a golden lyre. He could tame wild beasts (the passions), move rocks (the unfeeling hearts), and even revive the dead. The conception of a cosmic and bodily harmony was held by Orpheus and, later, by Pythagoras and his disciples, and by Hippocrates. The harmonies were derived from the cooperation between the quaternaries: the primordial elements of earth, air, fire, and water, and the corresponding body fluids, black bile, yellow bile, blood and phlegm. An imbalance or excess of any of these humors produces illness.

Phlegm collects in the nose and throat during a head cold. When the skin is broken, blood flows. Bile is secreted in the body after an internal wound. This theory of disease influenced diagnosis and treatment into the twentieth century. Bloodletting to vent excessive, or bad blood was practiced by those who kept leeches and proclaimed their services by means of a red-and-white striped pole outside their shop - the barbers.

Galen (175 A.D.) described four temperaments based on the Hippocratic theory of humors. In the person of stable temperament, the four humors are in balance. But in excess, the humors lead to an overflow of emotion and even to disorders of temperament:

- Too much black bile, and the person is ill-tempered, peevish and melancholic.
- Too much yellow bile, and the person is irascible, easily angered and choleric.
- Too much blood, and the person is overly cheerful, optimistic and sanguine.
- Too much phlegm, and the person is apathetic, dull, sluggish and phlegmatic.

Galen's domination of medicine ended with the Renaissance but his vocabulary is used to this very day: "Why are you in such a vile humor today?" "Because I'm melancholic."

Fig. 20.1. David playing the harp before King Saul. An engraving by Lucas van Leyden (c.1530). 'Saul...raged in his house, and David... played the harp...while Saul was holding his spear' (1 Samuel, 18, 10). David is drawing the demons from Saul's soul by playing on a Renaissance harp [sic] before the distraught king. Van Leyden's engraving is a study in human emotions. It is full of contrasts, showing the interplay of good and evil: the youthful upright David before the seated, tortured, and bent Saul; the soothing harp on one side and the menacing spear on the other. Print in the collection of the New York Public Library, New York.

We still recognize the ancient Greek adage: nothing in excess, everything in moderation. Yet there are rhythms of both matter and psyche that move things into the range of excesses. There are cataclysms, calamities and suffering that cannot be reconciled with the universal harmonies. These are the dissonances, or disharmonies, of the cosmos and of man. They are memorialized in music and in dance. The rhythms of dance, especially, were given an important role in the curative ceremonies of early humans.

However, the excesses are unnatural abnormalities and require treatment and rectification. How better than with the harmonies of music? Orpheus employed music and poetry to restore the harmonies: the harmony between cosmos and human, the harmony between *psyche* and *soma* and the balance of the humors. In the teachings of Plato and Aristotle, music was assigned an important role in education, interpersonal relations, art, religious ceremony and public life. In short, music was considered indispensable for the preservation of mental and bodily health, and in the treatment of disease.

During the Renaissance, music was described as communicating from performer to listener directly. It penetrates the body in the form of air, pressure, meaning and movement and its effects are felt by the body and the mind. The view that musical sounds seize and possess the listener has sexual connotations. This view remains with us in popular attitudes toward the virtuoso performer: when he is described as 'playing' upon his audience; it seems clear that we equate musical communication and sexual experience. Music has frequently been discussed in frankly erotic language. Consider Benedick's exclamation in Shakespeare's *Much Ado About Nothing:*

"Now, divine air! Now is his soul ravished! Is it not strange that sheeps' guts should hale (haul) souls out of men's bodies?"

Act 2, Scene 3

And in *The Merchant of Venice* consider Lorenzo's remark:

"Come ho! And wake Diana with a hymn. With sweetest touches pierce your mistress' ear and draw her home with music."

Act 5, Scene 1

Fig. 20.2. Concert for banishing a nobleman's melancholia. A miniature of the fifteenth century. From the manuscript of Boccaccio's Filostrato. With the aid of psaltery and harp, ladies and maidens try to divert the melancholy lord. Bibliotèque Nationale, Paris.

Like the coupling of music and sex, the coupling of music and death is described in Renaissance literature as an ecstatic loss of consciousness and as timeless. Death by music is no dreadful, painful death but a state of rapture symbolized in the *liebestod* (love-death) of Wagner's Isolde and by the madrigal of the silver swan. Here is a version of the XVIth century anonymous song with a musical setting by Orlando Gibbons:

> The silver swan, who living had no note,
> When death approached, unlocked her silent throat;
> Leaning her breast against the reedy shore,
> Thus sung her first and last and sung no more:
> Fairwell all joys; O death come close mine eyes;
> More geese than swans now live, more fools than wise.

Finally, Dryden had this question in his *A Song for St. Cecelia's Day*, 1687:

> What passion cannot music raise and quell?
>   When Jubal struck the corded shell,
> His listening brethren stood around,
> And, wondering, on their faces fell
> To worship that celestial sound:
> Less than a God they thought there could not dwell
>   Within the hollow shell
>   That spoke so sweetly and so well
> What passion cannot music raise and quell?

In his ringing *Grand Chorus*, Dryden calls for the final dissolution of the universe in response to the trumpet call:

> As from the power of sacred lays
>   The spheres began to move,
> And sung the great creator's praise
>   To all the Blest above;
> So when the last and dreadful hour
> This crumbling pageant shall devour,
> The trumpet shall be heard on high,
> The dead shall live, the living die,
> And Music shall untune the sky!

In conclusion, the legends on behalf of music claim a penetrating intensity that is not subject to natural law. Music cannot be understood by means of reason, but it is a life- and health-giving agent that can be applied throughout the whole range of human experience. To possess this power is to be godlike.

Modern Conceptions of Music Therapy

Numerous references to the healing powers of music are found in the musical and medical literature of the sixteenth and seventeenth centuries. In 1807, a book by P. Lichtenthal appeared under the title, *Der Musicalische Artz (The Musical Physician)*. Since that time, the body of scientific research on the psychophysiological effects of music has expanded enormously. Interest in music therapy developed during World War II, particularly in military hospitals. In 1946, a book by Van de Wall was published by the Russell Sage Foundation under the title, *Music in Institutions*. In 1950, the *National Association of Music Therapy* was established to foster programs of research, to distribute helpful information, and to set standards for therapists. A number of institutions of higher learning now offer academic and clinical training leading to a degree in music therapy.

Today. music is being used in hospitals and in mental health clinics as part of a comprehensive therapeutic program, together with traditional psychotherapy, persuasion and training, occupational therapy and other forms of art therapy. Music is also found to be valuable in rehabilitation programs. Just as you and I can benefit from the introduction of music in our lives, so do a wide range of clinical patients. Imagine then how valuable a scheduled program of musical activities might be to patients who are handicapped in some way. Patients who have benefited from such a program include:

- Mentally retarded children and adults.
- Physically disabled children and adults, including the sensory impaired, even the hard-of-hearing, crippled and speech impaired.
- Cerebral palsied children and adults, including those suffering the effects of early brain damage.
- Those with muscle diseases such as muscular dystrophy, and those having extrapyramidal motor disorders such as parkinsonism.
- Autistic children and those otherwise mute.
- Schizophrenic children and adults as well as those suffering bipolar disorders and other forms of psychoses.
- Behavior-disordered and emotionally disturbed children and adults.
- The aged.

It has been found that music can be used in non-clinical settings to help in altering unwanted behavior, or to initiate desirable behavior: to calm, to excite, to make contact and to communicate, to revitalize, to socialize, and to just plain entertain. These settings include schools, residences, day-care centers, music and dance studios, and industrial settings.

Many musical activities have been tried with beneficial results:

- Group singing.
- Singing accompanied by 'signing' or miming.
- Musical games such as musical bingo, musical crosswords, and 'name that tune.'
- Exercise accompanied by music.
- Dance accompanied by music.
- Music appreciation.
- Playing musical instruments in groups, such as a rhythm band. No special musical skill is required.
- Composing and improvising music.
- Drawing and painting accompanied by music.
- Drama accompanied by music (psychodrama is a special case).
- Eurhythmics of Delcroze where the whole body is used as an instrument.
- The Orff instruments and Orff's rhythmic exercises.
- Music writing, reading, and manual 'signing' as recommended by Kodaly.

Unfortunately, the science of music therapy is still in a very primitive state. Modern prescriptions for the use of music as a therapy in the psychiatric and neurological clinics are frequently based on little more than good common sense, sometimes on little less than superstition, and rarely on solid experimental evidence. On the use of background music in psychiatric wards, for example, it has been suggested that excessively loud music should be avoided so as to foster a background of calm during working, eating, reading, and talking or that entertainment should be arranged at least once per week, preferably on Sunday afternoons, so that relatives and friends might participate. These prescriptions are simply good common sense.

In contrast, consider the following prescription that was offered quite seriously:

> Musical compositions should be chosen to correspond to the prevailing mood of the patient (following the principle of homeopathy). For depressed states, they should have a tone quality of melancholy. In hypomanic patients, the music should be joyous, though not frenzied. In states of tension, do not use wind instruments as they may intensify

uneasiness; tension is more likely to be reduced by a trio of piano, violin and cello. In states of psychosis, it is best to start with rhythmic stimuli, then melody and lastly harmony. Only then is music used to stimulate imagination.

This may all be true in some cases, but does it not matter what particular composition is selected, in what setting, with whom as companions, at what time of day, etc.? Without answers to questions like these, the prescription is simply ludicrous.

This is not the place to review in any detail the prescriptions of music therapists. Suffice it to note the following:

Singing in a chorus and playing in an ensemble have been tried in some clinical settings with encouraging results. These activities strengthen self-confidence and the feeling of social worth. Embedded in the group, the patient is protected against the stresses of solo performance. Words of songs that inspire enjoyment of life, love, admiration of nature, and warm feelings toward humanity are preferred.

In children, rhythmic movements have been found helpful in rehabilitation after brain damage. These movements include clapping, stamping, beating the drum, playing triangle and xylophone. The Orff instruments are useful. Some of the pyramidal and extrapyramidal disorders can be treated in the same way.

Finally, some talented patients have been encouraged to write their own music. It has been found that a cathartic experience sometimes accompanies musical composition. Less musically talented patients are encouraged to find for themselves the music that best evokes images and feelings in them. They are also encouraged to improvise by singing and moving.

Despite these encouraging prescriptions, music therapy should not be raised to the level of a unique method of treatment, or even to the level of a most important treatment. It belongs in the category of art or humanist therapy: theatre, opera, painting, sculpture, prose and poetry reading and writing, all intended to entertain, give pleasure, and elicit emotions and movements that can improve the state of the individual. Art in any form provides opportunities for combating the deleterious effects of hospitalization. Music has the one advantage, that it can envelop the individual and elicit a wide variety of emotions.

Some mental patients prove to be inaccessible to the verbal influences of the therapist. What should not be neglected is body language, the handshake, the smile, the friendly look, and the warm attitude. Music, too, can exert a profound influence on the personality and emotional life of the patient, and on his accessibility in the therapeutic situation.

Many patients tend to talk incessantly about their complaints and those of others. Music provides a respite. It forces a silence, which sometimes has a healing power. Thus, traditional oral psychotherapy can be aided by non-oral means. The skillful combination of bodily influences, occupational therapy, physical exercises, dancing, drug therapy and music provides a road toward recovery and rehabilitation.

The use of music as therapy is burgeoning. There is so much to try and to discover in psychiatric and neurological settings. It would not be surprising to learn that music can be used to get mute autistic children to speak, to overcome stuttering, to relax the spastic patient or just to get people to be in touch with their emotions. Recently, it has been suggested that musical instruction in children facilitates their learning to be more competent in learning academic subjects like mathematics. Such transfer of training has been suspected by psychologists in the past but has never been shown systematically.

Research is badly needed in this field. What are the conditions under which music therapy can be effective? This is a clinical field that merits serious attention.

Epilogue

MUSIC CRITICISM - WHO SETS THE STANDARDS?

What authority can the critic claim for his or her opinions? This question is frequently asked by those composers, performers, record producers and recording engineers who feel, rightly or wrongly, that they were misinterpreted or misunderstood by the reviewer. The listener too may ask the same question when he finds that his or her musical experiences are contradicted by the reviewer's opinion.

Most musicologists concede that the musical evaluations of authorities are, for the most part, personal and reflect the past experiences of the critic (personal relativity) and the fashions of the day (cultural relativity). This is the point of view of the aesthetic relativist. However, there are those who maintain that absolute standards of beauty exist, as well as taste and criticism (Platonic ideals or absolutes) and expect the public to defer to the authority of the standard-bearers. In this essay, I focus on aesthetic relativity, though I will have something to say about aesthetic absolutes at the end.

The writer of music criticism is actually one of a triumvirate of writers consisting of reviewer, teacher and critic proper. These three need not be separate persons. For example, a music critic may assume the role of reviewer and/or teacher. But the purposes of each should be distinguished.

For most of us, the 'music critic' conjures up the image of the 'reviewer' whose columns sometimes appear regularly in the press. In fact, many reviewers write as though they practice the high art of music criticism. But their *genre* is narrowly delimited to the review of specific performances. Consider the parallel in the world of letters. The book reviewer rarely poses as the literary critic. As a matter of fact, some fine literary critics will not confine themselves to a single book. Indeed, some review no books at all.

The reviewer writes primarily for the consuming public. His readers defer to the reviewer's opinion: what concerts to attend, what records to listen to, what audio equipment to select, and what to think about what he hears. Though the reviewer's hearing apparatus is fundamentally like that of his reader's, the reviewer's is expected to be sharper, more focused and more educated. His review of a concert is expected to be descriptive: how the music sounded, how it was received, if it was new or old, how well it was performed, etc. Reviewing new audio equipment and recordings, he is likely to review technical developments and compare the new with the more familiar. The reviewer's descriptions should prompt the reader to say,

> "Yes, that is what I heard" or "That is what I should have heard had I been more attentive and/or more knowledgeable" or "That is what I would have heard had I been there."

But the reviewer is expected to go beyond mere description. He is expected to make judgments about matters of interest to the reader and to answer questions like,

> "Is it worth hearing? Worth attending? Worth talking about? Worth buying? Will I like it?" or "Should I like it?"

The process works best if the reviewer's taste is seen as trustworthy which means, ironically, that the reviewer's taste resonates with the reader's own. Only then will he be admired for his erudition and read as an authority. The reviewer's position of authority lies in his ability to evoke empathic responses in his readers. He may even regard himself as a critic, but only properly so if his descriptions are expanded into interpretations that apply more broadly, and when summary judgments give way to reasoned evaluation.

Compare the music reviewer who writes as a professional with the teacher who acts as a professional educator. His readers (or his auditors) are likely to be studying some aspect of the musical enterprise as a performer, composer, audio engineer, etc. His students are not so much consumers as they are makers of music. His judgment is not pronounced for its own sake but rather to help students improve or perfect their music-making. His judgment has a practical purpose: to help each student reach his musical goals. But more than that: it is the teacher's responsibility to question the student's methods and to evaluate the results in the context of his goals. Indeed, the effective teacher tries to help the student define and reshape his goals as he continues his studies. The effective teacher is also a skilled pedagogue. Constantly evaluating and reevaluating, the teacher becomes a music critic. In short, the teacher's authority is his competence: the precision of his technical knowledge, the breadth of his musical experiences, and his ability to apply both knowledge and experience to the solution of musical problems.

What then is our music critic? Just as the reviewer is a layperson writing for other laypersons, and the teacher is a musician training other music practitioners, so the music critic is an educated and informed music lover writing for other music lovers. It has been suggested that "criticism is the formal discourse of an amateur" (one who has enough love and knowledge of that represented in the discourse). Unfortunately, the contemporary meaning of 'amateur' carries with it the connotation of 'amateurish' or inexperienced dabbling, thus losing its original meaning of 'lover.'

To pose as an authority, the true critic must possess at least three levels of understanding. First, there is the musicological level, the facts that form the background of the piece of work. These facts include ethnic, social, political, historical and biographical items that are relevant to the discourse. Second, there is the technical level, which deals with the syntax of the musical language. The music critic must possess the ability to analyze and to explain the nature of that syntax. Third, there is the experiential or personal level: the insights that come from personal contact with a wide range of music, a familiarity with numerous styles, not only with the style embodied in the work at hand, and of course careful study of that work in all its aspects.

We have seen that the consumer wants to know what and how to buy and the reviewer provides relevant information. We have also seen that the musician wants to know how to perform and the teacher helps him discover how. What does the music lover want to know from the music critic? He wants to know how to listen. The music critic is the teacher of appreciation in the broadest sense. It is the critic's job to articulate his insights in order to make them available to his music lover readers. These insights include his interpretation of the work and his evaluation of it in relation to other works, so as to understand its meaning and significance.

Music lovers do not constitute a well-demarcated class. A music lover may be a layperson or a professional, a performer or a composer. Hence, a critic can be any or all of these. He may write reviews in order to make a living. He may be a first-rate musician or historian. When he points out what is right and what is wrong in a composition or a performance, he is a teacher. But the critic is most closely allied to the performer, for every good performer is necessarily a kind of critic, and every critic is a kind of performer.

What are the standards by which a composition is evaluated by the music critic? The critic starts with the score, which represents the composer's explicit instructions. But the score is lacking in detail, in nuance, and in feeling. What interests us as music lovers is the piece of music that we actually perceive. The score is the ultimate source of our experience, to be sure, but it is the perceived composition that is the object of critical thought. The facts of our past experiences, not just the facts embodied in the score are relevant to our perceptions. As perceivers of music, we contribute to our perception of it. And if the critic's historical data are correct, and his analysis is textually demonstrable, they too become part of our perceptions, which in turn are the source of our conceptions of the composition.

While the score remains the authoritative measure of the validity of a work's conception, the music can never be so completely notated as to permit only one uniquely correct performance. We should speak, then, not of *the* correct performance, but of *a* correct performance. It is true that a correct performance is one that accurately interprets the work's notational code. But there is more than one valid interpretation, and we ordinarily have the choice between alternate interpretations. In short, we are not satisfied with just correct performances and valid critiques. The authoritative performance is more than just correct, and the authoritative critique is more than just valid. The authoritative performance and critique must each include a certain intensity and conviction. It is the intensity of the performer's involvement coupled with his knowledge and craft that result in conviction or a convincing performance. Similarly, it is the coupling of the critic's intensity with his knowledge and writing craft that produces the convincing literary critique. We recognize the intensity of appreciation when we hear a brilliant performance that illuminates a great composition, or when we read a convincing critique that makes us long to hear the work in question.

Musical experience and insight lead to the conviction conveyed by both performer and critic. They must have an accurate sense of how the work sounds from hearing it played and from hearing it in the mind's ear. They must grasp not only its formal structure but also its dramatic rhetoric. They must empathize with whatever expression of mood or emotion they believe it to convey, with due consideration to its textual or other verbal associations. They must grasp its spirit, that mysterious quality that reflects the outlook of the composer and his social milieu, and understand the age that produced it. These are not just awarenesses, they are feelings. Deeply felt experiences become the source of conviction of the value of a composition and the validity of one's conception of its performance. The performance embodies that conception in sound, and the critic tries to communicate it by verbal suggestion.

The criticism of a performance starts with description, but it must move on to judgment. The only way a critic can interpret a performance is to relate it to his own view of the composition. That means comparing two perceptions of the composition, the performer's and the critic's, and hence two conceptions of its proper performance.

Another dimension of criticism of the performer is the evaluation of the performance itself. Reviewers frequently concentrate on this aspect to the exclusion of others, forgetting that performance is never pure execution. There is, after all, a score or a composition, if you like, that is executed. Hence the praise sometimes bestowed on sheer virtuosity, with the disclaimer, 'The composition made no sense to me, but it was well played.'

Should the composer be regarded as the final arbiter of his work? After all, he wrote it; is he not then the ultimate authority? In the field of drama, for example, the author is frequently denied the position of ultimate authority because there is no single recognized interpretation of his text. Drama critics might argue that the author may not have been aware of his underlying intentions. In the field of music, it is certainly true that a performer can bring out aspects of a composition that were unknown to, or at best vaguely felt by, its composer. After all, the performer has to learn the piece, every note, every nuance. The composer, in retrospect, may have forgotten them as well as his conscious intentions. Sometimes composers report that, like performers, they become intimate with their compositions only when they are forced to perform them.

In short, a reference to the score need not reveal the authenticity of the performance. Today, more than ever, performers and public demand 'authentic' performances of accurately reconstructed scores, played on instruments of the period, renaissance, baroque, etc. Musician and critics pore over treatises to discover just what the old notation meant. They revive old methods of articulation and phrasing, eschewing modern style involving vibrato. Their aim is to present the work exactly as the composer conceived it, or as consonant as possible with the composer's conception as far as it can be ascertained -- and if that is not possible, to present the work exactly as the contemporary audience heard it. These efforts may seem pointless to those who deny the composer ultimate authority; such performances, they argue, possess only historical significance. But, even if it were possible to reconstruct the performance as it must have been played centuries ago, we are still left with our modern ears and brains to hear with. Our brains have been conditioned not only by the graceful murmurings of Mozart, but also by the crashing sounds of Mahler and Stravinsky. There is no going back to an earlier era of virgin listening. Though we remain earthlings and members of the same species, *Homo sapiens*, our modern brains can never hear as did the unspoiled XVIIth and XVIIIth century listeners. How then can we, in the XXth century, evaluate the performance of early music? What are the standards, and who is the authority?

To return to my earlier contention, most of us can know a piece of music only through its performance. So, when the discussion turns to judgmental criticism, a critic's praise or blame of a composition can only be based on his judgment of a performance of that composition. Is it possible to distinguish the composer's work from the interpreter's? In Plato's world, the composer's work is permanent (ideal) and the performer's is fresh (shadows). Platonic thinkers have to contend with esthetic absolutes. In such a world, judicious criticism must depend on a faith concerning the conception of a composition, for neither technical competence nor ultimate significance of the composition can be determined without reference to it. The critic must be able to demonstrate the kind of musical insight that arouses confidence in his evaluations of compositional technique: his sensitivity to sheer sound, his response to rhythm, his powers of harmonic discrimination, his sense of line and form, his analytical ingenuity. All these enable the critic to discuss the music in more or less objective terms, to make statements about it that can be checked against the score and the reader's own experiences of the score. But such judgments can be meaningless or misleading without reference to a properly defined conception.

In any non-representational form of art, the conception and execution are indistinguishable aspects of a single process. This is certainly true of music. Arbitrary separation of the two is purely academic. Traditional composers don't think of writing a work in sonata form first and then dream of the themes to fill it out. Nor does the serialist decide on an abstract plan and then arrange the notes in accordance with that plan. For the composer, conception and execution are inextricably bound together in the sense that conception can be defined only in terms of execution. The critic, then, must be wary of trying to define the conception abstractly. For he may be forced into the position of condemning Brahms' second piano concerto because it failed to display the soloist as a concerto should. But Brahms was not writing a concerto; he was writing that concerto. What he produced was not a bad example of the traditional concerto and at the same time he produced the prototype of a new conception of the concerto.

In the end, the critic must be willing to stand judged. Ultimately all of us are revealed by our taste. Every great work of art eventually reveals the inadequacy of even the best critic. Art fakes inevitably give themselves away. They succeed for a time only by capitalizing on the prevailing view of the artist they imitate. But when some years pass and aspects of the artist, not apparent before, are brought to light, the result is a new point of view and the fake, produced under earlier conditions, is unmasked.

We constantly need new criticism of great works. The greater the work, the more interpretations are conceivable and the view of one age is inevitably superceded by the next. We should not feel dispirited by this aesthetic relativity. To call an old recorded performance, or a critique of it, 'dated' is not to disparage it. What the performer brought out, what the critic explained, was important news to the music lovers of that day, even though to later generations the interpretations may seem exaggerated or bland or misconceived. Yesterday's misconceptions contribute to today's insights and may, in the future, prove not to have been misconceptions after all. The critic succeeds, not by uncovering eternal truths about a work, but by helping the reader make close and affectionate contact with it. Ultimately, the music stands in judgment over the critic, not the critic over the music.

REFERENCES

Attneave, F. & Olson, R. K. Pitch as a medium: a new approach to psychological scaling. *American Journal of Psychology*, 1971, 84, 147-166.
Bachem, A. Note on Neu's review of the literature on absolute pitch. *Psychological Bulletin*, 1946, 45, 161-162.
Bauer, M. & Peyser, E. *How Music Grew*. G. P. Putnam's Sons, 1925.
Beck, S. & Roth, E. E. *Music in Prints*. New York Public Library, 1965.
Békèsy, G. von *Experiments in Hearing*. McGraw-Hill, 1960.
Belzano, G. J. Absolute pitch and pure tone identification. *Journal of the Acoustical Society of America*. 1984, 75, 623-625.
Benton, Arthur L. The Amusias. In Critchley, MacDonald, & Henson, R. A. (eds.) *Music and the Brain*. William Heinemann Medical Books Limited, 1977.
Bernstein, L *The Unanswered Question: Six Talks at Harvard*. Harvard University Press, 1976.
Bever, T. G. & Chiarello, R. J. Cerebral dominance in musicians and non-musicians. *Science*, 1974, 185, 537-539.
Blackwell, H. R. & Schlossberg, H. Octave generalization, pitch discrimination and loudness threshold in the white rat. *Journal of Experimental Psychology*, 1943, 33, 407-419.
Bogen, J. E. & Gordon, H. W. Musical tests for functional lateralization with intracarotid amobarbitol. *Nature*, 1971, 230, 524-527.
Boiles, C. L. Tepehau thought-song. *Ethnomusicology*, 1967,11, 267-292.
Borchgrevink, H. M. Prosody and musical rhythm are controlled by the speech hemisphere. In Clynes, M. (ed.) *Music, Mind, and Brain*. Plenum Press, 1982.
Boring, E. G. *Sensation and Perception in the History of Experimental Psychology*. Appleton-Century-Crofts, 1942.
Chailley, J. *40,000 Years of Music*. Da Capo Press, 1975.
Cleaver, D. G. & Eddins, J. M. *Art and Music*. Harcourt Brace Jovanovich, 1977.

Clynes, Manfred (ed.) *Music, Mind, and Brain*. Plenum Press, 1982.
Colwell, R. The development of the Musical Achievement Test series, *Council for Research in Music Education, Bulletin number* 22, 1970, 57-73
Critchley, MacDonald & Henson, R. A. (eds.) *Music and the Brain*. William Heinemann Medical Books Limited, 1977.
Davies, J. B. New tests of musical aptitude. *British Journal of Psychology*, 1971, 62, 557-565.
Davies, J. B. *The Psychology of Music*. Stanford University press, 1978.
Deutsch, Diana (ed.) *The Psychology of Music*. Academic Press, 1982.
Deutsch, Diana Auditory illusions, handedness, and the spatial environment, *J. Audio Engineering Soc.*, 1983, 31, 607-617 (with recording).
Dorgeuille, C. *Introduction a l'Etude des Amusies*. These, 1966.
Dowling, W .J. & Harwood, D. L. *Music Cognition*. Academic Press, 1986.
Drake, R. M. Factorial analysis of music tests by the Spearman-Tetrad-Difference technique. *Journal of Musicology*, 1939, 1, 6-16.
Farnsworth, P. R. *The Social Psychology of Music* (2nd edition). Iowa State University Press, 1969.
Fletcher, H. Loudness, pitch and the timbre of musical tones and their relation to the intensity, the frequency, and the overtone structure. *Journal of the Acoustical Society of America*, 1934, 6, 59-69.
Galamian, I. *Principles of Violin Playing and Teaching*. Prentice-Hall, 1985.
Gaston, E. T. (ed.) *Music in Therapy*. MacMillan and Co., 1986.
Gedalge, Andre, *L'Enseignement de la Musique*. Archambault, 1924.
Gordon, E. *Musical Aptitude Profile*. Houghton Mifflin, 1965.
Gordon, E. *Primary Measures of Music Audiation*. Chicago: G. I. A., 1977.
Gordon, H. W. Hemispheric asymmetries in the perception of musical chords. *Cortex*, 1970, 6, 387-398.
Gordon, H. W. & Bogen, J. E. Hemispheric lateralization of singing after intracarotid sodium amylobarbitone. *Journal of Neurology, Neurosurgery and Psychiatry*, 1974, 37, 727-738.
Grey, J. M. Scaling the musical timbre, *Journal of the Acoustical Society of America*, 1977, 61, 1270-1277.
Hebb, D. O. *The Organization of Behavior*. Wiley, 1949.
Helmholtz, H. von *On the Sensations of Tone as a Physiological Basis for the Theory of Music*. Edited by A. J. Ellis. Dover, 1954.
Igaga, J. M. A Comparative Developmental Study of the Rhythmic Sensitivity of Ugandan and English Schoolchildren. Ph.D. thesis, *University of London*, 1974.
Kalmus, H. Tone deafness and its inheritance. *Proceedings of the International Congress on Genetics*, 1949, 605.
Kendall, A. *The World of Musical Instruments*. Hamlyn, 1972.
Kimura, Doreen Left-right differences in the perception of melodies. *Quarterly Journal of Experimental Psychology*, 1964, 16, 355-358.
King, F. L. & Kimura, D. Left ear superiority in dichotic perception of vocal nonverbal sounds. *Canadian Journal of Psychology*, 1972, 26, 111-116.
Komma, K. M. *Musikgeschichte in Bildern*. Alfred Kroner Verlag, 1961.
Kubovy, M. & Pomerantz, J. R. *Perceptual Organization*. Erlbaum, 1981.
Kwalwasser, J. & Dykema, P. W. *Kwalwasser-Dykema Music Tests*. Fischer, 1930.
Landis, B. & Carder, P. The Eclectic Curriculum in American Musical Education. *Music Editors National Conference*, 1972.

Lang, P. H. & Bettmann, A. *A Pictorial History of Music*. W. W. Norton, 1960.
Lashley, K. S. The problem of serial order in behavior. In Jeffress, L. A. (ed.) *Cerebral Mechanisms in Behavior*. Wiley, 1951.
Lesure, F. *Music and Art in Society*. Pennsylvania State University Press, 1968.
Libin, L .*Keyboard Instruments*. The Metropolitan Museum of Art Bulletin, 1989.
Licklider, J. C. R. "Periodicity" pitch and "place" pitch. *Journal of the Acoustical Society of America*, 1954, 26, 945.
Licklider, J. C. R. Three auditory theories. In Koch, S. (ed.) *Psychology: a study of a science*, vol. 1. McGraw-Hill, 1959.
Lockhead, G. R. & Byrd, R. Practically perfect pitch. *Journal of the Acoustical Society of America*, 1981, 70, 387-389.
Longuet-Higgins, H. H. The perception of music. *Interdisc. Si. Rev.* 1978, 3, 148.
Luria, A. R., Tsvetkova, L. S. & Futer, D. S. Aphasia in a composer. *Journal of Neurological Science*, 1965, 2, 288-292.
Maconie, R. *The science of music*. Clarendon Press, Oxford, 1997.
Mechner, F. *The Science of Practicing*. Unpublished, 1985.
Menuhin, Y. *Theme and Variations*. William Heinemann, 1972.
Meyer, L. B. *Music, the Arts and Ideas*. University of Chicago Press, 1967.
Mills, E. & Murphy, T. C. (eds.) *The Suzuki Concept*. Diabolo, 1973.
Milner, B. Laterality effect in audition. In Mountcastle, V.B. (ed.) *Interhemispheric Relations and Cerebral Dominance*. Johns Hopkins Press, 1962.
Morton, D. Vocal tones in traditional Thai music. *Selected Reports in Ethnomusicology*. Vol. 2. UCLA, Institute for Ethnomusicology, 1974, 88-99.
Neu, D. M. A critical review of the literature on absolute pitch. *Psychological Bulletin*, 1947, 44, 249-266.
Neu, D. M. Absolute pitch - a reply to Bachem. *Psychological Bulletin*, 1948, 45, 534-535.
Orbach, J. (ed.) *Neuropsychology After Lashley*. Erlbaum, 1982.
Orbach, J. *The Neuropsychological Theories of Lashley and Hebb*. University Press of America, 1998.
Pahlen, K. *Music of the World*. Crown Publishers, 1949.
Pallucchini. R. & Rossi, P. Tintoretto. Gruppa Editoriale Electa, 1982
Pederson, P. The perception of octave equivalence in twelve-tone rows. *Psychology of Music*, 1975, 3, 3-8.
Penrose, L. S. & Penrose, R. Impossible objects: a special type of visual Illusion. *Brit. J. Psychol.*, 1958, 49, 31-33.
Pierce, J. R. Attaining consonance in arbitrary scales. *Journal of the Acoustical Society of America*, 1966, 40, 249.
Pierce, J. R. *The Science of Musical Sound*. Scientific American Library, 1983.
Plomp, R. *Aspects of Tone Sensation*. Academic Press, 1976.
Plomp, R. *Experiments on Tone Perception*. Institute of Perception RVO-TNO, 1966.
Plomp, R. & Levelt, W. J. M. Tonal consonance and critical bandwidth. *Journal of the Acoustical Society of America*, 1965, 38, 548-560.
Pribram, K. H. Brain mechanism in music: prolegomena for a theory of the meaning of meaning. In Clynes, M. *Music, Mind, and Brain*. Plenum Press, 1982.
Ratner, L. G. *The Musical Experience*. Freeman, 1983.

Rigden, J. S. *Physics and the Sound of Music.* 2nd Ed. Wiley, 1985.
Rosenstiel, L. *Nadia Boulanger.* W. W. Norton, 1982.
Rowell, L. Thinking about Music. University of Massachusetts Press, 1983.
Seashore, C. E. *Psychology of Music.* McGraw-Hill, 1938.
Sergeant, D. The incidence and characteristics of absolute pitch amongst musicians. Paper given at *Third Conference in Research on Music Education*, University of Reading, 1967.
Shankweiler, D. P. Effects of temporal lobe damage on the perception of dichotically presented melodies. *Journal of Comparative and Physiological Psychology,* 1966, 62, 115-120.
Shepard, R. N. Circularity in judgments of relative pitch. *Journal of the Acoustical Society of America,* 1964, 36, 2346-2353.
Shepard, R. N. Structural representations of musical pitch. In Deutsch, D. (ed.) *The Psychology of Music.* Academic Press, 1982.
Shower, E. G. & Biddulph, R. Differential pitch sensitivity of the ear. *Journal of the Acoustical Society of America,* 1931, 3, 275-287.
Skinner, B. F. *Walden Two.* Macmillan, 1948.
Sloboda, J. A. *The Musical Mind.* Oxford University Press, 1985.
Stevens, S. S. The relation of pitch to intensity. *Journal of the Acoustical Society of America,* 1935, 6, 150-154.
Stevens. S. S. A scale for the measurement of a psychological magnitude: loudness. *Psychological Review,* 1936, 43, 405-416.
Stevens, S. S. & Davis, H. *Hearing: its Psychology and Physiology.* Wiley and Sons, 1938.
Stevens, S. S., Morgan, C. T. & Volkman, J. Theory of the neural quantum in the discrimination of loudness and pitch. *American Journal of Psychology,* 1941, 54, 315-335.
Stevens, S. S. & Volkman, J. The relation of pitch to frequency: a revised scale. *American Journal of Psychology,* 1940, 53, 329-353.
Sundberg, Johann The acoustics of the singing voice. *Scientific American,* 1977, 236, 82-91.
Tonnedorf, J. Shearing motion in scala media of cochlear models. *Journal of the Acoustical Society of America,* 1960, 32, 238-244.
Van den Wall, W. *Music in Institutions.* Russell Sage Foundation, 1946.
Ward, W. D. Absolute pitch. *Sound,* 1963, 2, 14-21; 33-41.
Ward, W. D. Musical perception. In Tobias, J. V. (ed.) *Foundations of Modern Auditory Theory,* volume 1. Academic Press, 1970.
Wegel, R. L. & Lane C. E. The auditory masking of one pure tone by another and its probable relation to the dynamics of the inner ear. *Physical Review,* 1924, 23, 266-285.
Werner, E. The Jewish contribution to music. In Finkelstein, L. (ed.) *The Jews: Their Role in Civilization.* Schocken Books, 1971.
Winternitz, E. *Musical Instruments and their Symbolism in Western Art.* Yale University Press, 1979.
Wing, H. D. A revision of the Wing Musical Aptitude Test. *Journal of Research in Musical Education,* 1962, 10, 39-46.
Zenatti, A. Melodic memory tests: a comparison of normal children and mental defectives. *Journal of Research in Music Education,* 1975, 23, 41-52.

NAME INDEX

Attneave, F., 118, *399*
Bachem, A., 121, *399, 401*
Bauer, M., *403*
Beck, S., *399*
Békésy, G. von, 137
Belzano, G. J., 123, *399*
Benton, A. L., 369, *399*
Bernstein, L, 283, 351, *399*
Bettmann, A., *400*
Bever, T. G., *399*
Biddulph, R., 128, *402*
Blackwell, H. R., *399*
Bogen, J. E., 375, *399, 400*
Boiles, C. L., 226, *399*
Borchgrevink, H. M., 375, *399*
Boring, E. G., *399*
Byrd, R., 123, *401*
Carder, P., *399*
Chailley, J., *399*
Chiarello, R. J., *399*
Cleaver, D. G., *399*
Clynes, M., *399, 401*
Colwell, R., 341, *399*
Critchley, M., *399, 400*
Davies, J. B., xviii, xxi, 336, 338, 339, 340, *400*
Davis, H., *402*
Deutsch, D., xviii, 118, 119, 278, *400, 402*
Dorgeuille, C., 370, *400*

Dowling, W. J., *400*
Drake, R. M., 341, *400*
Dryden, J., 32, 66, 385
Dykema, P. W., 342, *400*
Farnsworth, P. R., 362, *400*
Fletcher, H., xvi, 110, 125, 126, *400*
Futer, D. S., *401*
Galamian, I., 322, *400*
Gaston, E. T., *400*
Gedalge, A., 309, 315, *400*
Gordon, E., 336, 338, 342, 343, *399, 400*
Gordon, H. W., 374, 375, *400*
Grey, J. M..182, 183, *400*
Harwood, D. L., *400*
Henson, R. A., *399, 400*
Hebb, D. O., *400, 401*
Helmholtz, H. von, 97, 137, 144, 146, 148, 149, 152, 156, 157, 158, 165, 168, 179, 244, 246, 247, *400*
Igaga, J. M., 343, *400*
Kalmus, H., *400*
Kendall, A., *400*
Kimura, D., 374, *400*
King, F. L., 374, *400*
Komma, K, M., *400*
Kubovy, M., *400*
Kwalwasser, J., 342, *400*
Landis, B., *400*
Lane, C. E., xvii, 269, 270, *402*

Lang, P. H., *400*
Lashley, K. S., 326, 327, *401*
Lesure, F., *401*
Levelt, W. J. M., xvi, 159, *401*
Licklider, J. C. R., 109, *401*
Lockhead, G. R., 123, *401*
Luria, A. R., 371, 373, 376, *401*
Maconie, R., 217, *401*
Mechner, F., 323, 327, 328, *401*
Menuhin, Y., 362, *401*
Meyer, L. B., *401*
Mills, E., *401*
Milner, B., 374, *401*
Morgan, C. T., 137, *402*
Morton, D., 225, *401*
Murphy, T. C., *401*
Neu, P. M., 121, *399, 401*
Olson, R. K., 118, *399*
Orbach, J., *401*
Pahlen, K., *401*
Pederson, P., *401*
Peyser, E., *399*
Pierce, J. R., 161, 162, *401*
Plomp, R., 119, 145, 157, 158, 159, *401*
Pomerantz, J. R., *400*
Pribram. K. H., 351, *401*
Ratner, L. G., *401*
Rigden, J. S., *401*

Rosenstiel, L., *402*
Roth, E. E., *399*
Schlossberg, H., *399*
Seashore, C. E., xxi, 336, 337, 338, 374, *402*
Sergeant, D., 121, *402*
Shakespeare, W., 383
Shankweiler, D, P., 374, *402*
Shepard, R. N., xv, xvi, 112, 113, 114, 115, 116, 123, 226, 352, *402*
Skinner, B. F., 323, *402*
Shower, E. G., 128, *402*
Sloboda, J. A., 222, 229, 280, *402*
Stevens, S. S., xx, 135, 136, 137, 255, *402*
Stumpf, C., 149, 151, 254, 350
Sundberg, J., 271, *402*
Tonnedorf, J., xvii, 252, *402*
Tsvetkova, L. S., *401*
Van Den Wall, W., *402*
Volkman, J., 137, *402*
Ward, W. D., 121, *402*
Wegel, R. L., xvii, 269, 270, *402*
Werner, E., 119, *402*
Wever, E. G., 249, 250
Winternitz, E., *402*
Wing, H.D., 336, 337, 338, 343, *402*
Zenatti, A., 342, *402*

SUBJECT INDEX

Absolute pitch, 40, 105, 106, 107, 117, 118, 122, 123, 318
  and relative pitch, xxi, 33, 43, 106, 120, 121, 122, 124, 309
  and the piano, 123
  octave errors, 123
Acoustic medium, 84, 101
Aesthetics, 351
  meaning in music, 57, 98, 164, 267, 276, 313, 347, 352, 354, 355, 357, 358, 372
Amusia, 3, 70, 107, 369, 370, 371, 373, 375
Aphasia, 6, 17, 21, 30
Attention, xix, 74, 144, 148, 167, 267, 268, 273, 274, 275, 276, 306, 308, 309, 350, 355, 364, 380
Audiation, 316, 342
Auditory pathways, xvii, 251, 260
Audiogram, xvii, 126, 134, 258, 259, 260
Bach, xviii, 39, 42, 71, 212, 217, 232, 334, 349, 353, 354
Baroque, 14, 57, 59-66, 69, 71, 283, 294, 299, 337
Basilar membrane, xvii, 129, 148, 242, 243, 244, 245, 246, 247, 248, 249, 250, 253, 272, 273
Beats, xvi, xx, 152, 153,154, 155, 156, 157, 158, 163, 168, 180, 183, 196, 198, 200, 204, 207-212, 217, 219, 269, 270, 271, 279, 349
Beethoven, 4, 71, 78, 100, 121, 140, 150, 151, 163, 217, 234, 263, 280, 348, 350, 354, 358, 361
Berlioz, 71, 140, 361
Biblical Hebrews
  King David, FP, 10, 11, 34, 38, 77, 358, 382
  Jubal, xiv, 8, 28, 385
  Levites, 11, 34
  Moses, 8, 37
Boulez, 162, 234, 298
Brahms, 71, 164, 234, 348, 354, 397
Bowed instruments, 295
Chopin, 71, 191
Chords, 60, 118, 119, 159, 162, 163, 165, 217, 227, 228, 230, 333, 337, 341, 363, 374
Circle of fifths, xvii, xx, 112-114, 221, 224, 225, 307
Classicism and romanticism, 71, 72
Clefs, xviii, 301, 302, 303, 310
Cochlea, xvii, 81, 124, 129, 137, 148, 149, 156, 239-247, 249-253, 257, 259, 260, 261, 262, 266, 272, 273
Combination tones, 166, 167, 168, 187
Computer music, 181, 234
Consonance, xvi, xx, 3, 89, 111, 141, 151, 152, 156, 159-164, 171, 194, 202, 204, 212, 217, 219, 349, 350
Critical bandwidth, xvi, 153, 157-162,

163, 177, 269, 271, 272
Deafness, 243, 251, 257
  cochlear implant, 261
  conduction, xxi, 258, 259, 260, 261
  effects of noise, 257
  fenestration, 262
  inner ear damage, 260, 261
  nerve, xxi, 258, 261
  otosclerosis, 262
  retrocochlear damage, 260, 261
  stimulation, 257
  tone (tune) deafness, 107, 263
Dissonance, xx, 141, 150-152, 156, 157, 158, 160-164, 177, 194, 349, 383
  inharmonic partials, 171, 172
Dryden's ode, 32, 66, 385
Duration, xx, 99, 105, 106, 139, 171, 181, 185, 234, 250, 251, 252, 254, 279-282, 286, 294, 295, 296, 297, 298, 299, 337, 341
Emotion, 3, 4, 7, 21, 22, 60, 64, 65, 66, 71, 75, 78, 180, 181, 240, 267, 305, 334, 335, 350, 354, 358, 365-369, 372, 376, 377, 379-382, 386, 388, 389, 394
  and reason, 3, 4, 5, 11, 15, 18, 29, 33, 41, 52, 69, 71, 73, 353
Equivalence
  in performance, 326, 327
  in transposition, 119
  of intervals, 117, 118
  of octaves, 118
Evolution, xviii, 73, 75, 78, 239, 318, 366
  Darwin's theory, 75, 76
Feedback, 123, 306, 308, 309, 324, 325, 342, 344
Formants, 32, 168, 169, 170, 172
Fourier analysis, xvi, xx, 108, 144, 146-148, 172
Frequency, *see* Pitch
Frère Jacques, xvii, 119, 218, 227, 300
Fusion, 144, 148, 149, 151, 153, 165, 172, 349, 350
Gestalt psychology, 276
  laws of perceptual organization, xx, 276, 278, 286, 356, 374
    good continuation, 277
    proximity, 356
    similarity, 356
Glissando, 123, 191
Golden calf, xiii, 9

Greek myths
  Apollo, xiii, 11, 12, 13, 14, 15, 16, 17, 379
  Argonauts, 19
  Athena, 11, 13
  Hermes, 11
  Marsyas, 11, 13, 14
  Orpheus, xiii, 17, 18, 19, 34, 63, 380, 381, 393
  Pan, xiii, 15
  Satyrs, 11, 13, 14, 15
  sirens, 16, 19, 20
Gregorian chant, xiv, 38, 39, 45, 48, 50, 51, 195
Grouping, 278, 279, 281, 282, 283, 357, 363
  scale illusion, xviii, 278
Guido of Arezzo, xiv, 39, 42, 43, 44, 45, 46, 150, 296
Harmonic series, xvii, 148, 170, 187, 196, 198-201, 204, 215, 337, 350
Harmonics, 92, 93, 94, 95, 96, 97, 89, 108, 109, 124, 141, 143-149, 152, 153, 156, 157, 159, 168-177, 179, 182, 183, 185, 187, 188, 196, 197, 198, 199, 200
Handel, 39, 66, 71
Hasidism, 41
  Baal Shem Tov, 41
Hebrew singing, 32, 34, 35, 38, 39, 40, 41
  Hallelujah, 36, 39, 40, 66
  Jubilus, 40,
  Psalmody, 35, 45
  Song of Songs 11, 38
Helix of pitch, xv, 112, 114
Helmholtz, 97, 137, 144, 146, 148, 149, 152, 156, 157, 158, 165, 168, 179, 244, 246, 2497
Illusions, 168, 181, 275
  Auditory, xx, xxiv
  Deutch's scale illusion, xviii, 278, 279
  Endless rise in chroma, 115, 116
  Necker cube, 277
Improvization, 293, 295, 311, 312, 313, 319
Instruments
  of the ancient world
    aulos, xiii, 11, 12, 23, 24
    lute, xiv, 48, 49, 52, 53, 62, 63, 320
    pipe, 8, 11, 22, 28, 78, 380

range, 188
shofar, xiv, 10, 37
of the Renaissance
haut and bas, Frontispiece
Intervals of pitch, 3, 88, 106, 110, 117, 118, 123, 124, 150, 151, 159, 160, 163, 167, 193, 194, 195, 197, 199, 200, 202, 203, 209, 211, 216, 226, 310
critical band width, *see* critical bandwidth
fifth, 29, 51, 88, 89, 99, 107, 110, 160, 167, 193, 230, 340
memory for, 290, 333, 337, 339, 341, 343, 362, 373, 374
octave, 99, 111, 117, 152, 160, 205, 297
semitone, 24, 25, 118, 190, 191, 212, 213, 214, 216, 226
sol fa, *see* solfège
sruti, 219, 225
tone, 190
transposition, *see* transposition
of time
judgments, 279
spontaneous tapping, 279
Lassus, x, 58
Lateralization,, xxi, 253, 367, 371, 372, 377
Liberal arts, xv, 70
Ligeti, 141
Loudness, xvi, xx, 65, 86, 88, 97, 98, 99, 105, 110, 125, 126, 129, 131, 135, 136, 137, 139, 140, 148, 153, 155, 157, 167, 170, 180, 185, 186, 253, 256, 268, 286, 294-298, 307, 337
intensity, 86, 92, 97, 98, 106, 108, 110, 115, 116, 124-127, 131-136
sone scale, 135, 297
Lully, xv, 65, 66
Madonna and child, xiv, 53
Madrigal, x, 56, 57, 58, 384
Mahler, 72, 119, 140, 396
Masking, xx, 109, 133, 158, 256, 268-273
Melancholia, xviii, 384
Melisms, 40 42
Melody, 7, 19, 21, 22, 32, 33, 36, 39, 40, 41, 44, 48, 50, 51. 65, 66, 70, 78, 99, 105, 106, 110, 117, 119, 140, 141, 162, 165, 188, 190, 192, 208, 210, 218, 227, 228, 231, 262, 263, 273, 274, 275, 289, 297, 300, 310, 312, 337-343, 356, 361, 369, 370, 374, 376, 377,
and tonality, *see* tonality
contour, 290, 291, 339, 374
memory for, *see* Memory
scale illusion, see Illusions
transposition, *see* Transposition
Memory
for pitch, 262, 290
long term, 104, 257
short term, 262, 341
Methods of instruction
Dalcroze, 310, 311-314
Kodaly, 314-318
Orff, 310, 314, 318-320, 323, 387, 388
principles of learning, 323
Mechner, 323, 327, 328
Suzuki, 292, 310, 320-323
teaching machines, 328
Meter, 32, 283, 284, 286, 297, 299, 338, 340, 341, 343, 373
Mozart, 4, 71, 100, 164, 166, 191, 217, 350, 354, 361, 362, 363, 396
Multidimensional scaling, 112, 183
Music appreciation, *see* Aesthetics
Music reading,
disabilities of, *see* Amusia
Music theory, xx, 112, 224, 307, 309, 311, 312, 349
Musical ability,
and intelligence, xxi, 16, 336, 337
aptitude and achievement, 331-345
notation, 39, 42, 43, 100, 136, 150, 185, 198, 289-294, 296-303
therapy, *see* Therapy
training, xix, xxi, xxii, 22, 45, 106, 121, 122, 163, 292, 305-330
Musique concrète, 233
My Country 'tis of Thee, xviii, 36, 105, 227, 299, 300
Octave
Errors, *see* Intervals
Illusion, *see* Illusions
Ohm, 148
Opera and oratorio, 63, 64, 65, 66, 67, 69, 165, 271, 347
Organ pipes, xv, 82, 85, 94, 95, 96, 97, 144, 186, 187, 188, 269
Ossicles of the middle ear, xvii, 241, 242
Paleolithic man, xiii, 56

Palestrina, xiv, 56, 58, 59, 60
Perceptual organization, xx, 276-278
Performance, 289-303
Phase, xvi, xx, 146, 147, 152, 154, 155, 168, 173, 174, 175, 176, 177, 178, 189, 180, 234, 254, 255, 260
Pindar, 16, 22
Pitch,
  absolute, see Absolute pitch
  analogy with vision, 97, 98, 107, 192, 280
  and critical bandwidth, 153, 158, 159, 160, 161, 162, 163, 177, 269, 271, 272
  chroma and height, xv, 111, 112, 113, 114, 115, 116, 123, 124
  circle of fifths, see Circle of fifths
  combination tones, see Combination tones
  discrimination
    helix of pitch, 112, 113, 114
    of complex tones, see Timbre
  frequency, 106, 107, 110, 116, 124
  missing fundamental, xv, xx, 108, 109, 124, 187
Plato, 21, 24, 383, 391, 396
Polyphony, 50-52, 55, 58, 150, 208
Polyrhythm, 57
Pythagoras, xiv, 25, 26, 27, 28, 29, 195, 200, 201, 205, 226, 381
  ratio of small numbers, 3, 70, 107, 111, 152, 193, 194, 204
Resonance, 64, 102, 137, 141, 143, 147, 148, 156, 168, 169, 179, 171, 187, 244, 246
Reverberation, 100, 254
Rhythm, 32, 55, 66, 74, 76, 77, 78, 98, 99, 100, 141, 256, 279, 280, 281, 282, 283, 284, 285, 287, 289, 290, 292, 296, 307, 309-315, 318, 319, 327, 328, 334-338, 340, 341, 343, 351, 352, 356, 357, 360, 361, 369, 370, 373, 375, 377, 383, 387
  subjective rhythmization, 281, 286
  testing of rhthmic ability, 334, 335, 336, 337, 338, 340, 341, 343
Risset, 116, 182, 234
Roman deities
  the days of the week, 30
Scales
  are scales necessary? 234
  chromatic, 112, 113, 115, 161. 191, 192, 199, 202, 206, 212-215, 219, 221, 222, 223, 226-228, 230, 232, 234, 300, 307, 309, 316
  diatonic, xx, 43, 118, 165, 192-195, 196, 199, 219, 222, 223, 225, 227, 230, 300, 315, 319, 320
  ecclesiastical, xi, 24, 40, 45, 197, 208-211, 358
  equal tempered, 149, 204, 212, 214, 216, 219, 223, 225, 226, 349
  Indian SA-grama, xiii, 199, 219, 225, 226
  jazz, 209, 211, 289, 348
  just temperament, 128, 203, 213, 217
  mean-tone, 200, 204, 208, 211, 212, 215, 216, 217
  pentatonic, 24, 196, 199, 232, 319
  Pythagorean, see Pythagoras
Schoenberg, 72, 232, 354
Schubert, 71, 348
  An Die Music, Dedication
Sensation quality, 237, 238
Seven
  liberal arts and sciences, xv, 70
  muses, xiii, 12, 13, 16, 17
Shakespeare, 383
Sibelius, 72, 180
Sightreading, 291, 293, 310, 370
Silver swan, 384, 385
Singing
  formant, 32, 168, 169, 170, 172, 172
  masking by orchestra, xvii, 271, 272
  register, 186, 187
  solfège, see Solfège
  vibrato, see Vibrato
Siren, 90, 91, 107, 139
Solfège, xxii, xxiii, 45, 106, 189, 292, 307, 309-312, 323, 328
Songs without words, 40, 41, 349
Sound localization, 255
  Stereo, xxiv, 100, 101, 240, 253, 254, 256, 257, 278, 279, 326, 352
St. Cecelia, 31, 32, 163, 164, 353, 386
Stockhausen, 234
Stravinski, 163, 164
Strauss, R. 72, 350, 353, 358
Synthesized music,
  square waves, xvi, 173-175, 177, 179
  sawtooth waves, xvi, 173-181, 182
  triangular, xvi, 173, 176, 177, 178
  role of phase, xvi, 4, 146, 147, 154, 155, 168, 172-179, 183, 234, 254

envelope, xvii, 98, 181, 182, 185, 233, 248, 295, 298
Talent, xix, xxi xxii, 263, 294, 308, 314, 321, 331, 332, 334, 335, 336, 337, 341-344, 374, 388
Tchaikovsky, 71, 358
Tempo, 55, 135, 136, 280, 282, 284, 297, 299, 312, 313, 324, 338, 343, 358
   Preferred, 181
Testing, 258, 260, 343, 344, 369
Tetrachord, 25, 30, 31, 33, 193, 194, 195, 204, 205
Texture, 48, 57, 139, 256, 269, 274, 275, 276, 341
Therapy, xviii, xxi, 358, 379-389
Timbre
   complexity, xx, 97, 98, 139
   inharmonic partials, 144, 164, 171, 172
   onset of tone, 166, 170, 171-173, 183, 185, 233, 252, 254, 255
   offset of tone, 98, 146, 173, 181, 183, 185, 233, 235, 254, 295, 296,
   synthesis, 149, 172, 174-177, 179, 181, 182, 233
   timbral space, 184, 185
Tonal expectations, 5, 166, 180, 231, 279, 283, 284, 350, 352, 354, 355, 357, 367
Tonality, 72, 166, 226, 227, 228, 230, 231, 319, 342, 375
Torah (Five Books of Moses), 8, 43
Transcription, 289, 290, 326
Transposition, 110, 118, 119, 121, 204, 308, 212, 221, 326
Travelling waves, xvii, 247, 248
Troubador, xiv, 47, 48, 51, 52
Tuning fork, xv, 62, 82, 86, 87, 88, 91, 92, 141, 145, 149
Velocity of sound, 85, 103, 254
Vibrations
   of organ pipes, 85, 94, 95, 96, 97, 144, 186, 187, 269
   of strings, 27, 62, 63, 107, 109, 142, 143, 153, 184, 187, 192-196, 244, 246, 273, 329
Vibrato, 98, 148, 149, 180, 181, 185, 295
Viola da gamba, 31, 62, 320
Violin, xv, 62-64, 82, 88, 90, 91, 92, 102, 108, 109, 139, 140, 142, 143, 153, 167, 171, 180, 182, 183, 187, 191, 203, 233, 256, 273, 274, 292, 294, 295, 301, 302, 308, 310, 319-323, 329, 330, 362, 369, 389
Volley theory, 104, 250
Webern, 348